METASTATICS AND MACROECONOMICS

WILLIAM S. VICKREY
COLUMBIA UNIVERSITY

Metastatics and Macroeconomics

HARCOURT, BRACE & WORLD, INC.
New York · Burlingame

TO 'CILE

Library of Congress Catalog Card Number: 64-11636

PRINTED IN THE UNITED STATES OF AMERICA

CONTENTS

PART II *Equilibrium and Macroeconomics*

PART III *The Dynamics of Changing Expectations*

PREFACE

THIS *is the second of two volumes on theoretical economics. The other, entitled* Microstatics, *covers the usual neoclassical theory of consumption, exchange, production, competitive equilibrium, monopoly, and imperfect competition, with considerable emphasis on the use of indifference curves as a technique and on welfare economics as a motivation. There is also a brief introduction to game theory as an illustration of the difficulties encountered in pushing very far with a priori theoretical analysis into the area of imperfect competition.*

The present volume covers the salient points in the areas loosely termed "dynamics" and "macroeconomics." In order to familiarize the student thoroughly with the element of change through time and its implications in as simple a form as possible, we have first dealt with a somewhat artificial category termed "metastatics," in which the element of uncertainty is excluded. Under this heading are discussed the notion of general intertemporal equilibrium in a hypothetical "futures" economy, the general analytical framework for capital formation, growth, and progress, including some tentative remarks concerning population problems, the application of the theory to anticipated fluctuations, and the Bernouillian theory of risk. The basic elements of monetary theory are presented as a prerequisite to the formulation of complete macroeconomic models, in a manner that attempts to steer between "hypothetical history" on the one hand and an undue preoccupation with the accidental features of contemporary monetary institutions on the other. As a second prerequisite, the basic concepts of national income accounting are presented, a special attempt being made to relate the aggregates encountered in practice to underlying analytical concepts.

The greatest attention in this volume has been focused on the problem of presenting the Keynesian and the classical modes of general equilibrium analysis in a manner that will permit the student to arrive at a synthesis in which the salient elements of each approach are given their due share of emphasis. Indeed, this part has been considered sufficiently important to warrant the presentation of two complete alternative forms of the analysis.

Following all this groundwork, there is room for only a brief introductory treatment of macrodynamics proper. There would indeed hardly be room for a complete treatment of the complicated subject in an introductory two-semester course in economic theory, nor could such a treatment be carried very far without recourse to more elaborate mathematical tools than have otherwise been used here. It is hoped at any rate that what is presented here will whet the appetite of some and give others a glimmering of what is involved in the development of a really adequate dynamic theory.

While the present volume has been written as a sequel to Microstatics, *it stands as a fairly discrete entity, which may be used with profit in dealing with macroeconomics. Although there may be little here that can claim to be entirely new, some of the presentation, including the methods of representing graphically the integration of classical and Keynesian analysis, may be sufficiently novel to merit the attention of many of whom the basic ideas have long since been familiar.*

Again it is highly in order for me to express my indebtedness to successive classes of students who with great patience have borne with the early stages of this book, the colleagues who have helped with their suggestions, and the pioneers over whose shoulders I have clambered.

WILLIAM S. VICKREY

Columbia University
October 1963

PART I

Metastatics and Risk

CHAPTER ONE

Intertemporal Exchange

STATIC economics, strictly speaking, is the study of economic systems where there is no change, or where at most, as in comparative statics, a single, once-for-all change is superimposed and the equilibrium that the system approaches after the change is compared with the equilibrium that existed before the change. The analysis of such systems is kept relatively simple, in part by the absence of change, but even more by the absence of uncertainty. Thus in entering upon the study of dynamics, we are faced with two complicating factors: change and uncertainty. If both of these complicating factors are introduced at once, analysis becomes formidably difficult. Moreover, there is considerable interest *per se* in determining which of the possibilities that emerge in a dynamic situation are traceable to the introduction of uncertainty, and which can adequately be developed in terms of change through time without uncertainty.

Accordingly, rather than jump boldly into the middle of an analysis of a "dynamic" model in which change both through time and uncertainty exist, it seems better to tackle dynamics by easy stages, and examine first the implications of change without uncertainty by means of a somewhat artificial model in which the participants make no mistakes in forecasting the price at any future date of any commodity or service in which they may be interested. Such a model will admittedly be somewhat artificial, and may at first seem even more remote from the realities of everyday economic experience than the model of perfect competition. The study of such a model, however, will bring us much closer to the ultimate dynamic model we are looking for without greatly increasing the difficulty of the analysis, so that when we come to take the jump to a model involving both change and uncertainty there will be less to tackle all at once. This is indeed the method of "successive approximations" that has been used with such success in the natural sciences. Moreover, it is only by comparing such a model with one where uncertainty is present on the one hand and the static model on the other that we can distinguish clearly the implications of time difference and change from the implications of uncertainty.

This simplified model, in which we have change through time, but in which all such change is correctly anticipated, can be termed the "metastatic" model in that it represents in effect merely a minor generalization of static analysis.

The applications of the methods of static analysis in this new dimension do produce some new results, but in general no new methods are needed, and the results are quite analogous to those of static analysis proper.

The Nature and Role of the Metastatic Model

HAVING pursued the elusive solutions to the problems involving imperfect competition for as long as seems profitable (or longer), we return to the basic assumption of perfect competition, namely, that each economic unit acts on the assumption that prices are determined by forces not subject to substantial influence by any actions it might take by itself. Instead, we now drop the static assumption that there is no change in the situation from one period to the next, and for the first time we introduce specifically the notion of the passage of time and change through time, so that events in our economic system must be dated relative to each other.

In order to have a concrete image of a metastatic model, it is desirable to first specify a little further the process by which the model is supposed to arrive at equilibrium. To suppose that information is so complete that each participant can determine for himself what set of present and future prices will lead to equilibrium is unsatisfactory, not only because it is unrealistic, but because such a degree of knowledge is almost certain to involve knowledge about the reactions of others; as we have just seen, if the reactions of others are taken directly into consideration, the results may be indeterminate. A more satisfactory structure for our model can be obtained by extending and generalizing the "futures" markets that we actually observe in operation in some basic commodity exchanges. If each participant makes provision for all his future needs on the basis of advance contracts to purchase or sell at specified prices in such futures markets, he can plan with certainty on the basis of the prices quoted in these markets, and he does not have to make any estimates as to what "spot" prices will actually be some time in the future.

Accordingly, in the "futures economy" we assume the existence of a perfect futures market in all commodities and services, in which one can buy or sell contracts for the delivery of all types of goods and services at all future dates (without incurring any extra costs by reason of the sale or purchase itself). We then further assume that each individual as a consumer can choose systematically and consistently between alternative consumption plans beginning with the present and stretching to the time of his death, which is also supposed to be known with certainty. How to represent the economic activity of generations yet unborn in such a model is a conundrum we will allow to remain unsolved since our objective in setting up this model is to clarify concepts rather than to achieve realism. If need be, we would assume that the decisions of the unborn generations are made by some kind of representatives:

for example, by their parents; or that we are dealing with a fixed population of immortals; or that the population has become sterile.

Such consumption plans stretching over a period can be made analytically analogous to static consumption patterns by considering time to be divided into a number of short intervals, each of which can be treated as a unit; what we are doing in setting up the metastatic model is then merely multiplying the number of commodities among which the individual chooses in the static case by the number of time intervals. That is, we treat meat for consumption in period 1 and meat for consumption in period 2 as two different commodities. The formal analysis follows exactly the same course, whether the difference between the two commodities is one of quality or one of time, since the delivery, and not the transaction, is what is deferred in the case of meat bought for consumption in the second period.

In the same fashion, we assume that each entrepreneur knows his production function, where now each output or input for each period is considered a factor or product distinct from a similar output or input for any other period, and the production function tells the entrepreneur—given all the inputs for all periods, given all but one of the outputs for all periods, and given the remaining output for all periods but one—what is the maximum possible output of this commodity for the remaining period. Or, conversely, the production function indicates the minimum quantity of a particular given input for a particular given period that will be needed, in addition to any specified quantities of other inputs in all periods and of this particular input in other periods, to obtain any specified patterns of outputs. Again, in effect we can consider this case as resulting merely from the multiplication of the number of factors and products for the pure static case by the number of time periods.

Given this knowledge of preferences as to consumption patterns and of the possibilities of converting factors into products over time, we then assume that entrepreneurs, and consumers and suppliers of the original factors of production, meet in a market where they contract in advance for the delivery in the future of all the factors, commodities, and services that they plan to provide, to use, or to consume, for the various future periods. For brevity we may call the right to demand a unit of a particular commodity or service from some particular supplier in some particular future time period a "delivery." While in each case a contract will call for the delivery of the commodity by a particular supplier, we assume that the value of the delivery will be independent of the identity of the supplier.

Metastatic Equilibrium

WE ASSUME that the ratio of exchange between any two deliveries, involving in general two different commodities at two different times, will be the same as the ratio of their prices expressed in terms of some particular delivery taken as a numéraire. This result will be brought about presumably by arbitrage, since if this condition does not prevail there will be a clear profit to be gained merely by performing the proper circular chain of transactions, and in the absence of costs of trading or uncertainty, such transactions would tend to be performed until the potential profit is eliminated by the consequent adjustment of the prices. Accordingly, if we determine all prices in terms of such a numéraire, we will have determined all exchange ratios. It is ordinarily convenient to take some "spot" commodity, i.e., a contract for the immediate delivery of the commodity, as a numéraire; for example, the classical numéraire was "spot gold."

An equilibrium will result in such a market when, at the prevailing prices, each consumer or entrepreneur has arranged for all the exchanges of deliveries that he desires to make; i.e., when no person can derive any further profit or advantage from any further exchange of deliveries. As with the static case, this equilibrium requires that the marginal utilities of the various deliveries to any given individual are proportional to their prices in terms of the numéraire, that prices of all factors be equal to their respective marginal products, and, conversely, that prices of all products be equal to their respective marginal costs.

But to specify our model completely we need, in addition to characterizing the equilibrium position, to outline some mechanism by which it could be brought about. In the static case, we could perhaps imagine that buyers or sellers who on any one occasion leave the market unsatisfied at the prevailing price would take action having the effect of raising or lowering the price that will obtain on a subsequent occasion, until by a series of such moves an equilibrium is reached, after which economic activity will continue in a steady state. In the metastatic case, however, everything is to be decided once and for all, and there can be no such trial-and-error process. However, we can approximate this process by another quite similar one, which might be termed "cut and try." We may suppose that initially some set of prices for all deliveries, present and future, is announced, either chosen at random or determined by some rough estimating process. Each consumer, factor supplier, and entrepreneur then determines what his supply or demand for the various deliveries would be if he took these prices as definite and acted to maximize his utility or profit subject to the constraints imposed by the limitations of his budget, i.e., that he remain able to fulfill all of the contracts for future deliveries that he sells. These supplies and demands are reported to a central agency and are added up, and wherever there is a discrepancy between supply and demand, prices are adjusted in the indicated direction and a new set of prices is announced. Again, individuals indefatigably report what they would buy or sell if these new prices prevail, demands and supplies are again added, and the various prices again adjusted in the direction indicated by the discrepancy, and in an amount indicated by the size of the discrepancy divided by the responsiveness of excess demand observed at the previous price change. If this new set of prices fails to produce equilibrium, the process is repeated until a set of prices is found for which all demands and supplies for each delivery are equal, at which point the process is concluded and the contracts closed. Such a process is sometimes referred to as "recontract"; Léon Walras used the term "tâtonnements" for a somewhat analogous process.

Of course, it should be noted that it has not been demonstrated that an equilibrium position would eventually be approached by such a method, or even that such an equilibrium would exist in all cases. Indeed, it is possible, even in the static case, to construct models where no equilibrium exists, and this is all the more true here. However, it seems plausible that in most normal cases such an equilibrium would exist, and also that one would be able to arrange the price-adjusting process so that it would lead to this equilibrium rather than oscillate around it. Since in any case the metastatic model is but an artificial intermediate construct bearing only limited resemblance to reality, it seems not worthwhile to attempt to determine in any strict sense the conditions under which such a process would lead to equilibrium, particularly since in most of the more realistic models to be examined later on other possible reasons for failure to reach equilibrium will be found that seem more relevant to real problems.

Once such an equilibrium is reached and the contracts confirmed, the economic problem is solved for the entire future: a consistent set of plans will have been arrived at, and nothing remains but to execute these plans. Since we assumed that each consumer and entrepreneur was able to forecast accurately his wants and the results of his productive processes, and since the amounts of the various deliveries needed and to be supplied are in agreement, there is nothing to prevent the carrying out of these plans. Indeed, life in such a futures economy might be extremely flat and uninteresting once the planning process had been carried through, since what would remain to be done would then have been completely predetermined. Indeed, to keep such elements as the desire for flexibility and liquidity from complicating the analysis at this point (they will be reintroduced later), it is necessary in this model not to allow anyone to change his mind and thereby fail to supply or take the planned amount of any given delivery when the time comes.

It might be thought at first that if prices of a commodity for future deliveries could be determined in advance with certainty, there could be no difference between the price for delivery at one time and that for delivery at another. To be sure, if it were known with certainty that the price of a certain durable commodity is going to rise sharply ten days from now, purchasers will buy now rather than later, and speculators will enter the market by purchasing now, holding the commodity in storage, and selling later at a profit; this will take place to whatever extent necessary to drive the present price up and the future price down until they are more nearly in agreement and there is no longer a profit to be secured by such arbitrage. Thus certain types of variation in the prices of a specific commodity according to date of delivery are impossible in a futures economy. In particular, sharp rises in the price of a storable commodity are ruled out. Gradual changes, however, are still possible, and in some circumstances fairly sharp changes may occur. For instance, fairly rapid declines in the prices of newly developed commodities are likely to occur; any gradual increase in price that does not exceed the cost of storing a commodity, allowing for deterioration (where the price is expressed in terms of a numéraire of fixed date), is quite possible. In the case of perishables, and especially services, extremely rapid fluctuations in price are possible.

Interest Rates

DIFFERENCES in the price of a single commodity for different delivery dates can be expressed in the form of a rate of interest. A "money" rate of interest is of course a way of expressing a rate of exchange between present money and future money. Similarly, a "wheat" rate of interest would be the rate of exchange between present, or spot, wheat and future wheat. For example, if prices are such that 100 bushels of spot wheat exchange for 121 bushels of wheat for delivery two years hence, this relationship can be expressed by saying that the "wheat rate of interest" is 10 per cent per annum over this period ($121 = [1 + .10]^2 100$). In exactly the same way, a commodity rate of interest can be defined for any commodity capable of precise definition. Indeed, since in the futures economy all commodities must be precisely definable in order that future contracts have a precise meaning, there are in principle as many rates of interest for a given time interval as there are commodities (and services!) that have deliveries at both ends of the interval.

Interest rates will of course not only vary with the commodity in which they are expressed, but also according to the length of the time period covered and the dating of that time period. If 100 bushels of wheat on hand will exchange for 105 bushels one year hence, alternatively to purchasing 121 bushels two years hence, then the one-year wheat rate of interest for the first year is 5 per cent, contrasted with the two-year rate of 10 per cent per year, and the one-year rate for the second year of approximately 15 per cent. In general, in a futures economy any long-term interest rate will always be a kind of average or compounding of the short-term rates for the short periods that make up the long period, since any exchange spanning a long period can be broken down into an equivalent sequence of exchanges each spanning a short period. More precisely, if i_{ab} is the interest rate for the period from time a to time b (considering, for simplicity, interest to be paid or compounded annually), then we have

$$(1 + i_{ac})^{c-a} = (1 + i_{ab})^{b-a}(1 + i_{bc})^{c-b}$$

Any long-term interest rate can be computed then in terms of the various one-year interest rates as follows:

$$(1 + i_{an})^n = (1 + i_{01})(1 + i_{12})(1 + i_{23}) \ldots (1 + i_{n-2,n-1})(1 + i_{n-1,n})$$

These relations will hold for interest rates expressed in terms of any given commodity.

However, to minimize the confusion that would result from such a multiplicity of interest rates, we can confine our attention to the rates of interest expressed in terms of some one particular commodity selected as the numéraire. To do this we depart somewhat from the concept of making the standard way to express prices as in terms of some particular delivery as a numéraire. Instead, we select some commodity to act as a numéraire through time, and express the prices of deliveries of commodities other than the numéraire in terms of deliveries of the numéraire commodity for the same time period. The only direct standard-price quotation involving different time periods is for exchange of delivery of numéraire at one date for delivery of numéraire at another date. In general, under this scheme of price quotation, rates of exchange between deliveries of different dates will then involve three of the standard-price quotations: the price of each delivery in terms of the numéraire of the same date, and the price of the numéraire of the one date in terms of the numéraire of the other. In this way the intertemporal features of the rates of exchange are consolidated in the intertemporal exchange of the numéraire and the new elements brought in by the intertemporal nature of the transaction will be easier to follow. Indeed, this scheme of price quotation comes closer to the way actual contracts for future delivery are customarily framed: payment is ordinarily made at the time of delivery, or soon after; relatively seldom does a contract for future delivery of goods involve immediate payment, other than possibly a moderate deposit or margin as evidence of responsibility.

If this method of price quotation is followed, the rate of interest upon which attention will be focused will be the "numéraire" rate of interest; the level of this interest rate and its behavior through time will then depend upon the particular commodity selected as numéraire. The results of the analysis will appear more immediately significant if we are careful to select as our numéraire a commodity such that variations in the prices of other commodities in terms of this numéraire will vary about equally in both directions through time. That is, in terms of such a numéraire, some prices will rise through time while others fall, so that the average price in some sense is fairly constant. Indeed, there is considerable advantage in considering as a somewhat artificial numéraire some combination or basket of goods representing an appropriate sample of goods that are traded. If this is done, then the "general price level" in terms of this numéraire will remain fairly constant, and the "numéraire rate of interest," which we may take for present purposes as "the" rate of interest, will also represent the "real" rate of interest, i.e., the rate of exchange between "general purchasing power" as of different dates.

Saving and Dissaving

IF WE CONSIDER in this way that all intertemporal transfers are channeled through the selected numéraire, we can then talk of "borrowing," "lending," "saving," and "dissaving," all of which terms will be strictly meaningful only with reference to a specified numéraire.

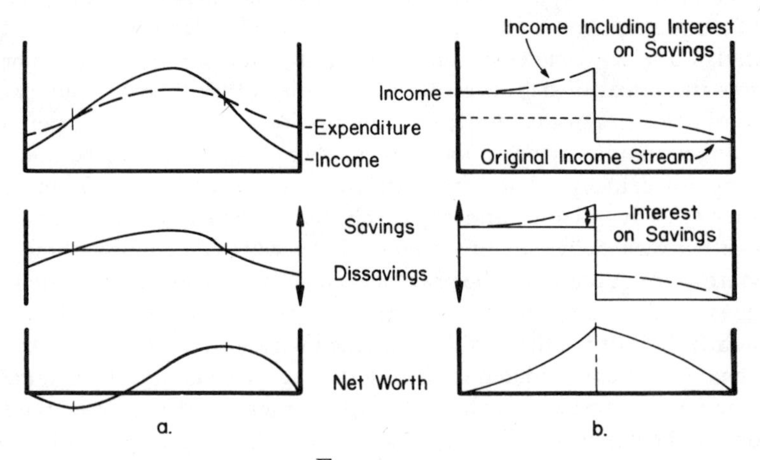

FIGURE 1

To begin with, let us take as given some stream of earnings that an individual is counting on receiving over the remainder of his life from the supply of his labor and possibly also from the rental of property which he owns or from the profits of a business which he operates. This income stream may in principle have almost any pattern at all, but if we look, for example, at an individual who plans his economic life at the age of 20, he may plan to go to work almost immediately, at relatively low wages at first, but at gradually rising wages until a maximum rate is reached at the age of 40 or 50, then remaining steady until retirement, as illustrated in FIGURE 1. Such an individual could if he wanted to, spend his entire income as he receives it on personal consumption, thus needing to have no recourse to intertemporal exchange at all. However, he will usually wish to arrange the time pattern of his expenditures somewhat differently from the time pattern of his income, and if he has access to the capital market where intertemporal exchanges take place, he may make use of such exchange to arrange his expenditures over time in a manner more satisfactory to himself as illustrated in FIGURE 1. During the earlier years he may borrow (i.e., buy current numéraire in return for his promise to deliver numéraire at future dates) in order to maintain his early consumption at a level closer to the average level that he expects to maintain throughout his life; in middle age when his earning power has increased he may pay off these earlier loans and save (i.e., sell current numéraire in return for promises for the delivery of numéraire at future dates) planning to liquidate these savings in maintaining the level of consumption after retirement when earnings will have fallen off.

At this point some confusion is possible as to the exact meanings to be attached to "income," "savings," and "dissaving" or "borrowing." One can use income to continue to mean the original flow of receipts before it was altered by the borrowing and saving process. In this case, the total amounts saved and dissaved or borrowed will not cancel out over the life of the individual: there will be a residual representing interest. A somewhat more useful set of concepts arises, however, if we use "income" to mean the original income stream plus or minus the interest accruing on the accumulated savings or dissavings of the individual. In this usage, the original income stream will itself be modified to a new income stream as a result of the intertemporal exchanges. But now the stream of savings and of dissavings, defined as the difference between the income stream and the stream of consumption expenditures, will cancel out over the life of the individual, if we assume that he starts with no possessions and plans to have nothing left at his death. Or, more generally, we can define the "net worth" of the individual as being the excess of his assets over his liabilities, valued at a given point of time in terms of the current numéraire. The change in the net worth of an individual between two points of time will then, on this definition, be equal to the excess of savings over dissavings during this time interval. The variations of net worth over time can then have a pattern such as is shown in FIGURE I. If we think of the supply of investment funds as being provided in this way by a series of similar individuals whose life spans cover different and overlapping periods of time, we can think of the average level of the net worth of the individual as being a measure of his over-all contribution to the supply of capital funds.

The Supply of Savings

THE TIME pattern of the saving and dissaving of such an individual will in general depend on the exchange ratios prevailing between the numéraires of different periods, as will the corresponding time pattern of net worth. But it is not safe to assume, as many classical economists did, that the higher the interest rate (i.e., the lower the price of future funds in terms of current funds) the greater would be the demand for future funds (i.e., the greater the amount of saving), for just as in the supply of commodities, there is an income effect to be reckoned with. Indeed, it is not even safe to assume that for generally

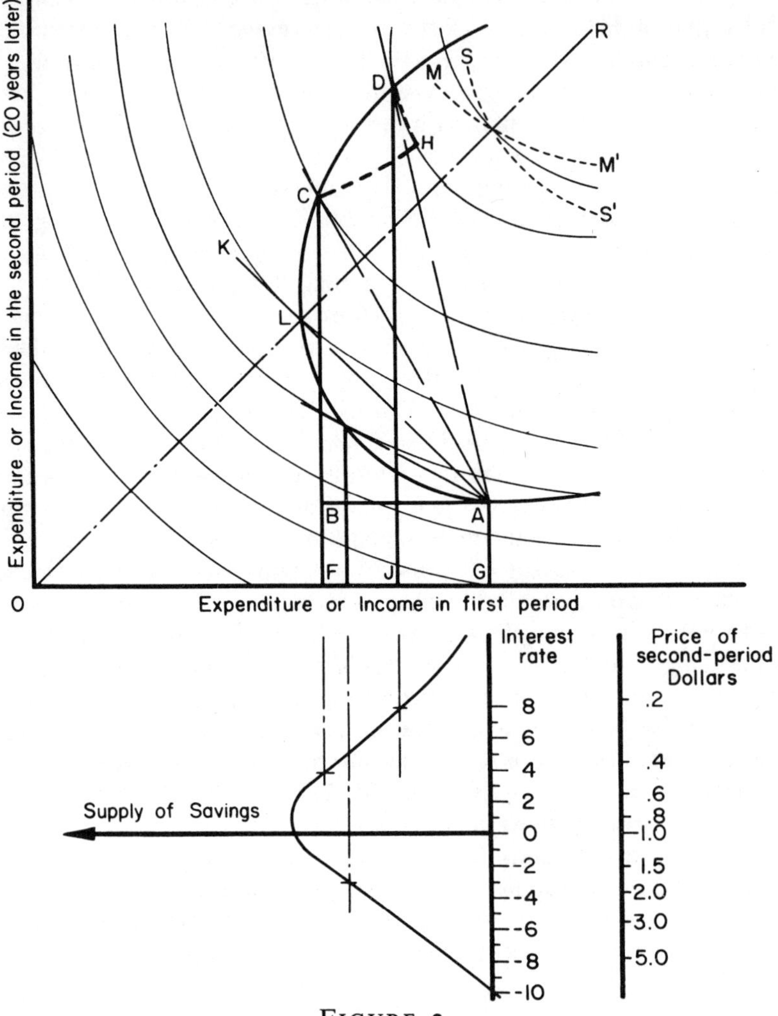

FIGURE 2

higher rates of interest the average level of net worth maintained by an individual over his lifetime would be higher. But to permit detailed analysis of the relationship between interest rates and the volume of saving, it is necessary to simplify the picture and consider initially exchanges involving only two time periods, so that each period can be represented by a dimension on a plane diagram.

Accordingly, in FIGURE 2 we can measure in the direction of the x axis the income or expenditure in the first of two periods, in terms of the numéraire of that period, and similarly on the y axis the income or expenditure of the second period, in terms of the numéraire of the second period. We will assume prices of all commodities to remain fixed in terms of the current numéraire, so as to make these measurements meaningful, though the price of a given commodity need not be the same in the two periods. Thus any combination of levels of expenditure for the two periods can be represented by a point on the diagram. Exactly as for two commodities, the preferences of the individual between alternative patterns of consumption over the two periods can be indicated on the diagram by indifference curves. These curves may be drawn, for example, on the assumption that consumption for periods other than the two under consideration is fixed. Or we may divide the entire life span of the individual into two "periods," as suggested in FIGURE 1b.

To avoid the complications that might arise from the possibility of significant shifts within a time period, however, while at the same time allowing scope for fairly substantial changes in the exchange ratio between the numéraires of the two periods without undue violence to realism, it is perhaps most useful at this point to consider two relatively short periods of, say, one year each, separated by perhaps 20 years, and to consider only shifts between these two years, leaving the other years unaffected. The analysis can then be generalized to apply as between any pair of years and thus a picture of an equilibrium between several years can be built up. For example, FIGURE 2 can represent various combinations of expenditure levels for the year 1960 with expenditure levels for the year 1980. It would indicate, for example, that if offered a choice between a plan calling for an annual expenditure of o*G* in 1960 and *GA* in 1980, represented by the point *A*, and a second plan calling for expenditures of o*F* and *FC*, respectively (expenditures for other years being the same in both plans), the latter would be preferred, as is indicated by the fact that *C* is on a higher indifference curve.

A point can also represent an income pattern, and movement from such a point to another would represent an exchange of part of one's income in one period for more funds to spend in the other period. For example, the line *AC* represents the opportunity path that is obtained if the price of funds for the second period in terms of funds for the first period is 0.5; i.e., if saving $100 now will produce $200 for the second period. If the two periods are considered to be 20 years apart, this would represent a compounded interest rate of about 3.75 per cent per annum.

If an individual with this indifference pattern has the income stream indicated by *A*, and is able to exchange present for future funds at the ratio indicated by the line *AC*, he will choose to exchange *AB* of 1960 funds for *BC* of 1980 funds, thus providing for the expenditure pattern *C*. *C* is the best pattern open to him among those represented on the diagram, since the opportunity path *AC* is tangent to an indifference curve at this point. Thus out of the 1960 income o*G*, an amount represented by *FG* will be saved.

Now if the interest rate rises further, so that the opportunity path moves from *AC* to *AD*, the amount saved will be diminished, from *FG* to *JG*.This is because of the income effect of the increase in interest rates, which improved this individual's situation in such a way that he wishes to take part of this improvement in the form of current expenditures, in spite of the substitution effect of the higher interest rate. That is, the income effect *CH* outweighs the substitution effect *HD*. The income effect will in general oppose the substitution effect whenever the individual is a saver rather than a dissaver; i.e., whenever the income pattern is on the average earlier than the desired expenditure pattern. But where the two patterns are fairly close to each other, so that the volume of savings is small, the income effect will be correspondingly small, and it is likely that the substitution effect will then outweigh the income effect. And if the income stream is later than the desired expenditure stream so that the individual is on balance a borrower rather than a lender, then as long as expenditure for each period remains a normal good (and it is hard to see how it could well be otherwise), the income effect and the substitution effect will reinforce each other and the savings of such an individual will rise (or rather, his dissavings will decrease) with an increase in interest rates.

But before leaving the supply of savings, it is perhaps worthwhile to note that these relationships between the volume of savings and the interest rate are derived on the basis of defining and measuring savings in terms of the numéraire of the earlier of the two periods. If we were to measure savings not in terms of the amount of current numéraire paid for future numéraire, but in terms of the amount of future numéraire bought, the relationships would be different: savings would always be positively related to changes in the rate of interest as long as savings are positive, and perverse relationships would be possible only for individuals who are primarily borrowers rather than lenders. Of course, savings are often accumulated without the saver having in mind any definite future time at which they will be spent, so that in the real world as distinguished from the futures economy it may not always be possible, even if desirable, to state savings in terms of the future funds bought. Yet something akin to this does actually occur in the purchase of life insurance: the amount of insurance purchased is commonly referred to in terms of the face amount, i.e., in terms of the magnitude of the future benefits purchased, rather than in terms of the current premium payable. A rise in the rate of interest, bringing with it a reduction in premium rates, would be expected to increase the face amount of insurance purchased, but might very well lead to a reduction in the total amount of current premiums payable. That is, an increase in interest rates increases savings measured in terms of future numéraire, but decreases savings measured in terms of current numéraire. It does appear, however, that for many problems in dynamics proper, to be considered later, it is the current-numéraire concept of savings that is the more appropriate one to consider.

Intrinsic and Marginal Time Preference

IN FIGURE 2 it should be noted that the indifference curves were made symmetrical about the 45-degree line o*R*, and that hence a given expenditure pattern lies on the same indifference curve as the pattern that results if the same amounts are spent in reverse order. In other words, if we make the assumption that the numéraire is so chosen as to make the general price level the same in the two periods, the individual represented by this indifference map has no *intrinsic* time preference; a given rate of expenditure produces just as much satisfaction if it occurs later as it does if it occurs immediately. This lack of intrinsic time preference is to be distinguished from the positive "*marginal* time preference" that exists at any point on the map above the line o*E*. For example, the marginal time preference at *C* is equal to the slope of the tangent line *AC*, or 3.75 per cent per annum. At *C*, to produce the same overall increase in satisfaction as would be produced by a given small increment in the expenditures for the first period, an increase in the second period would have to be twice as great. That is, the marginal time preference arises in this case not because of any intrinsic impatience, but because the individual, in response to the opportunity to save and earn interest, deliberately adopts an expenditure pattern in which later expenditures are at a higher level than the earlier expenditures, so that the marginal utility of additional expenditure in the later period is reduced relatively to the marginal utility of additional expenditures in the earlier period, and thus a marginal time preference is created which matches the rate of interest, in exactly the same way that consumption of two commodities is adjusted until their marginal rate of substitution matches the ratio of their market prices, whatever may have been the original or intrinsic preference of the individual for the two commodities.

Only if the interest rate were zero, as would be represented, for example, by the line *AK*, would this individual have no marginal time preference, and in this case the point of equilibrium would be at *L* along the line o*E*, indicating that he will arrange to spend equal amounts in both time periods.

Of course, indifference maps between present and future consumption can be constructed to show either an intrinsic time preference or the reverse. Thus if the indifference curves are tilted in the direction indicated by the line *SS′*, we have the map of a person with "spendthrift" propensities, and the combinations having zero marginal time preference occur below the line o*R*, so that with a zero rate of interest such persons would select a consumption pattern having the early-period consumption greater than the later-period consumption. Conversely, for a person with "miserly" propensities, the indifference map would be tilted in the direction indicated by the line *MM′*, and consumption would be higher in the later period, even in the absence of interest.

We do not pretend of course that intrinsic time preference is necessarily infrequent. It is, however, important to show that marginal time preference does not necessarily require or imply the existence of any intrinsic time preference, and that the willingness of individuals to borrow or lend at varying rates of interest does not necessarily mean that they have an improvident disregard for the more remote future. "Impatience" is thus not a necessary condition for the existence of a positive rate of interest, though it may be a factor tending to make that rate higher than it otherwise might be.

Capital and Production

OVER AGAINST the consumer side of the capital market, where consumers convert the time pattern of their income stream into an expenditure stream with a time pattern more to their liking, there is the production side of the capital market, where entrepreneurs make exchanges that permit the time pattern of their inputs to differ from the time pattern of their outputs, thus opening a wider range of possibilities and uncovering more profitable modes of operation. In general, production requires time, and inputs must usually be acquired considerably in advance of the time at which the outputs can be delivered. Corresponding to this time lag between input and output will be a lag between income and expenditure on the part of individuals. Corresponding to the net worth of individuals will be a quantum of capital invested in the production process.

The amount of capital invested in the production process at any given point of time can be measured in three ways: currently, by valuing the assets involved in terms of direct exchange value; retrospectively, by valuing the excess of past inputs over past outputs; and prospectively, by valuing the excess of future outputs over future inputs. In a perfectly competitive futures economy, all three of these procedures, where they are applicable, should give the same results, since any discrepancy would indicate a possibility for profit that is not being availed of, or a loss that could be avoided.

The simplest method of valuation, the current exchange method, can be used, strictly speaking, only with production processes that are fully "liquid," i.e., where the assets in the production process are at all times capable of immediate conversion into final output without loss. Perhaps no process completely satisfies this criterion, but the raising of cattle seems to come fairly close to it, particularly if one is willing to take a year as a unit and ignore seasonal fluctuations in liquidity. In this simplified case the capital tied up in the enterprise (ignoring land and other items that may be thought of as being rented) is simply the market value of the herd.

Most production processes are not fully liquid in this sense; however, we can extend somewhat the current-value measure of capital by thinking of the nonliquid assets of an enterprise as being rented. Thus land and machinery may be owned by others than the entrepreneur using them, and rented for each period for which they are to be used in the particular process. We need then to investigate the relationships between such rentals and the value of the asset. Every asset indeed can be thought of as merely a bundle of future "uses," the value of each of these uses being the rental which would be paid. The value of the asset itself as of any given time t_k, in terms of t_k funds, can be found by taking the future rental for each period, say t_x, in terms of t_x funds, and multiplying each such rental by the price of time t_x funds in terms of t_k funds. Or the same result can be obtained somewhat more indirectly by multiplying each future rental in current funds by the price of such funds in terms of the spot numéraire on the planning date, say t_o, and then dividing the sum of all such amounts by the price of t_k funds in terms of the spot t_o numéraire.

Depreciation

THE VALUE of an asset so determined will of course vary with time. If we compute a value one year later, say at time t_{k+1}, we will in general get a different value for the asset as it exists at time t_{k+1}, expressed in t_{k+1} funds. This value will in the usual case be somewhat lower than the value at time t_k in t_k funds. This reduction in value during the year can be termed "depreciation," and is the result of several factors, the exact influence of which will depend in general on the numéraire chosen. The value would generally be constant if the uses to be obtained from it continued indefinitely into the future, if these uses all commanded the same price in terms of the contemporary numéraire, and if rates of interest in terms of this numéraire remained constant from year to year. These conditions of course will seldom if ever be completely met, but are approached in some cases for land. Depreciation, accordingly, can be ascribed to the approach of the end of the useful life of the asset, to the falling off in the value of the uses through time, or to increases in rates of interest.

If we happen to have a "one-horse-shay" asset where the values of the uses remain constant to the end, and there is no change in interest rates, then the depreciation follows the "sinking-fund" pattern, where the constant use value is divided into an interest charge that declines with the decline in the value of the asset, and the depreciation charge that increases through time so as to make up a constant total. In most cases, however, the values of the successive uses will form a decreasing sequence through time, either through growing competition from other similar or newer assets, from the deterioration in the quality of the service rendered by the asset, or from changes in demand patterns resulting from general progress. Depreciation resulting from competition from newer machines or from demand changes is often segregated as "obsolescence," and the term "depreciation" itself is sometimes used to refer merely to the "wear and tear" element in the loss of value, although when this usage is adhered to there is left no common term for the more inclusive concept, and to repeat "depreciation and obsolescence" on every occasion is a bit tedious.

Depreciation resulting from changes in interest rates is seldom, in practice, given specific consideration in physical assets, although it is a factor affecting the change in value through time. It is to be noted that depreciation is often crucially dependent on the character of the use made of the asset and on the care and resources expended in its maintenance. Indeed, maintenance expenditures blend gradually into "improvements" that may be carried to the point of causing the value to increase rather than decrease through time. Such improvements, however, are normally considered as additional investment.

In some cases the value of an asset, aside from the effect of "improvements," may also increase from one period to the next. This can be termed "appreciation" and is thought of chiefly in connection with land, although it may occur also with other assets. In general, this occurs where the current use of the asset is of relatively little value compared to uses that will be obtained later on, though it may also occur as a result of decreases in the rates of interest from year to year. Land may increase in value as towns and cities grow in size; railway embankments and grades settle gradually to a more stable condition requiring less annual maintenance of the track; a new machine or piece of equipment may gradually get the bugs worked out of it, or improve as a result of the gradual elimination of initially defective pieces. In any case, in an economy of certainty the rate of appreciation in value, other than that due to "super-maintenance" (or possibly to the beneficial effects of "working" the asset) can never exceed the rate of interest, since this would mean that the "own" rate of interest of such an asset would be so negative as to permit a profit to be made from speculative holding of the asset, even though no rent were received.

Indeed, in an economy of certainty the current rental will turn out to be in every case equal to the sum of the interest on the value of the asset at the beginning of the period and the depreciation for the period (or to the interest less the appreciation) plus allowance for any maintenance expenses to be borne by the owner. If this were not so, there would be a profit to be made by buying or selling the asset at the beginning of the period, renting it, and selling or buying it at the end, borrowing or investing at the going rate of interest so as to keep other transactions undisturbed. Entrepreneurs would offer to do this until prices and rentals are driven to the point where the discrepancy vanishes.

It is important to have clearly in mind, however, that both depreciation and interest can be computed only relative to a specified numéraire. The capital value of two different assets will remain in the same ratio whatever numéraire is used to describe the situation; and the ratio of their rentals for a given brief period will also be independent of the choice of numéraire; however, the way in which this rental is broken down between interest and depreciation is dependent on the arbitrary choice of the numéraire. In terms of one numéraire, say copper, having a tendency to become relatively scarcer as time goes on, the rental may be found to consist largely of "depreciation," whereas if a numéraire is selected that is becoming relatively more plentiful, say aluminum, the rental will be found to consist largely of interest, interest rates being relatively high and the value of the asset expressed in terms of aluminum tending to fall relatively little.

The Capitalization of the Firm

JUST AS a single asset can be valued in terms of discounting the value of future uses of rentals, a firm as a whole can be valued in terms of discounting the future stream of net receipts that are to flow to the proprietors of the firm. This flow of net receipts is in turn the difference between the flow of receipts from the sale of products and the flow of outlays for the factors to be used. The value of the firm at any given time will thus be a function of the future plan laid out or envisioned for the operations of the firm. The aim of the entrepreneur may be described as the devising or selecting of a plan of operation that will make this present value a maximum. In pursuit of this aim, we can describe the behavior of the entrepreneur in terms analogous to those of the static analysis by saying that any given set of amounts of inputs at various times will be so used as to maximize the present value (or the value in terms of the planning-date numéraire) of the products to be derived, while the amount of each input to be used at each time will be determined by using each input up to the point where the discounted value of the marginal product resulting from employing an additional unit of such input will equal the discounted cost of the input.

If we assume a state of perfect competition in which all entrepreneurs are equally able, the value of the firm derived from one entrepreneur's program for the firm will be the same as that for another, and the value of the firm as a whole will thus agree with the value derived from such an optimum program. Indeed, under perfect competition, this value will be driven down to a level corresponding to the net current value of the past stream of net investments by the proprietors, i.e., to the value of all past inputs with compound interest added up to the current date, less the value of past outputs, with interest added similarly. If competition is less than perfect in that some entrepreneurs are more skillful than others with respect to a particular firm, then such superior skill would be revealed, for example, in the fact that the past activity of such an entrepreneur has brought the firm to the point where even outside potential entrepreneurs recognize that its future earning power is greater than would be derived merely from the capitalization of past net inputs. Or the current value of the firm may not exceed the value of past inputs, but the skillful entrepreneur may have a plan which he is confident will return more than merely the interest on this current value. Indeed, the innovating entrepreneur will frequently carry his firm through a period in which its value, in terms of what others will consider his firm worth, drops below the level set by the capitalization of inputs, i.e., a period in which sale of the firm to a new set of owners would result in a loss (at least as compared with normal rates of return obtainable on other investments), in that the assets of the firm are put in such shape that only the particular entrepreneur can handle them effectively.

To bring out the intertemporal impact of the activities of the firm, we want to describe them in terms of the related concepts of capital, investment, and disinvestment. The capital employed by a firm at time t can be taken, under competitive conditions, to be the value of the firm as a whole at time t, and with perfect competition it makes no difference whether this value is a market value for the firm as a whole, a value derived from discounting future earnings, or a value derived from capitalizing past inputs. Imperfect competition at this point gives rise to considerable conceptual difficulties and these different measures must then be distinguished. It will be noted that the measurement of capital at a given point of time does not depend on the choice of the numéraire, in the sense that the ratio between the amounts of capital used by different firms at the same time will be the same regardless of the numéraire chosen. This, however, does not apply to comparisons involving different points of time.

Investment and disinvestment in the firm are usually taken to mean the increase and decrease, respectively, over a given time interval, in the capital employed by the firm. The increase in the capital of the firm is, in turn, the sum of the interest on the capital value of the firm at the beginning of the period, plus the net excess of inputs added to the firm's resources over the proceeds withdrawn from the firm during the period. Where withdrawals exceed inputs plus the interest, there is disinvestment. It should be noted that the definition of investment and disinvestment, like savings and dissavings, depends on the selection of the numéraire: a firm that in terms of one numéraire was deemed to be maintaining its capital intact and thus to be neither investing nor disinvesting, would, with a numéraire that is becoming relatively plentiful and cheap, be considered to be investing and increasing its capital, though the real picture would be unchanged.

The amount of capital that an entrepreneur will want to employ in a given firm will in general vary according to the rates of interest prevailing in the capital market. A higher rate of interest means that future outlays and receipts are more heavily discounted relative to the present, so that it will become more important to secure early receipts rather than later receipts, and to make outlays later rather than earlier in the production process. Shifts of the production plan in either of these directions will have the effect of reducing the capital employed by the firm. Accordingly, it appears clear that the demand for capital by firms decreases with increases in the rate of interest. Similarly, reductions in the rate of interest tend to increase the demand of firms for capital.

This reaction of firms to changes in interest rates can be expressed in another way by saying that entrepreneurs adjust the amount of capital they use at each point of time until the marginal productivity of capital is equal to the rate of interest. The marginal productivity of capital is the ratio of the increment of output made possible over a unit time interval by the employment of an increment of capital, to the increment of capital. For example, we may suppose an increment of input to be introduced into a production process at one point of time, and then find the maximum resulting increment of output that can be withdrawn from the production process at a given later time without disturbing outputs and inputs at other times. If the increment of input at time t_k is f_k, and if the increment of output n time units later is q_{k+n}, then the marginal productivity of capital $r_{k,n+k}$ per time unit, over the period from time k to time $n + k$ is given by

$$f_k(1 + r_{k,n+k})^n = q_{k+n}$$

If the time interval is one year, this reduces to simply: $f_k(1 + r_{k,k+1}) = q_{k+1}$ or $r_{k,k+1} = (q_{k+1} - f_k)/f_k$. The inputs and outputs f and q are of course valued in terms of their respective contemporary numéraires. For simplicity, it can be assumed that the production function is smooth in all directions, so that for sufficiently small increments in input, assuming the state under consideration to be an equilibrium one, it will make no difference which particular pair of outputs or inputs are chosen, and the marginal productivities obtained for different time intervals will be related to each other according to relationships analogous to those presented on page 9. If these relationships do not hold, and the production function is smooth, the original production plan will then be inefficient, in that it will be possible to rearrange production so as to obtain more of some output with no change in any of the other outputs or inputs. Accordingly, we can focus our attention on the marginal productivity of capital as found for short intervals, say for a single year or "period," and regard all longer term marginal productivities as being the result of compounding the component short-term values.

The postulate that an equilibrium would be reached by a series of adjustments through recontracting, or "tâtonnements," implies that for each time period there will emerge an equilibrium rate of interest such that at this rate of interest no consumer will want to make further alterations in his time pattern of consumption, and such that no entrepreneur will want to make further adjustments in the time pattern of his inputs and outputs. That is, as between each pair of time periods, the marginal time preference of each individual, the marginal productivity of capital for each entrepreneur, and the market rate of interest will all be equal. Moreover, in the absence of illusory assets, such as government bonds, which represent no real capital, the capital demanded and used by entrepreneurs will correspond and be equal to the net worth of individuals. We can thus consider the interest rate as the price that brings the demand and supply of capital into balance. This analogy between the capital market and the market for particular commodities must be used with caution, however. As long as equilibrium is assumed, the analogy bears up fairly well, but as soon as we begin to consider what happens when there is a disequilibrium in the capital market, consequences arise that are quite different from what happens in most commodity markets. This, however, must be set aside for consideration as part of general equilibrium theory.

The numerical value obtained for the marginal productivity of capital, like the marginal time preference and the rate of interest, will vary according to the choice of a numéraire. But the nature of the equilibrium itself will not depend on the choice of numéraire: the "real" aspects of the equilibrium will remain the same whatever numéraire is used to describe them; a change in numéraire will change marginal time preference, marginal productivity, and interest rates all by the same amount. Thus if we take a fairly representative commodity as a numéraire, or better, a representative basket of commodities, we may find the interest rate, marginal time preference, and marginal productivity of capital all equal at equilibrium at a level of 6 per cent per annum; but if some new commodity in which rapid reductions in cost of production were being made—as was the case with aluminum, for example—is taken as the numéraire, the interest rate might appear as 10 per cent or even 20 per cent per annum, and likewise for the marginal productivity of capital. On the other hand, if a perishable and increasingly scarce commodity is taken as the numéraire, such as beaver pelts, a figure lower than 6 per cent, and perhaps even a negative figure, could be obtained for the marginal productivity of capital and the related interest rate and marginal time preference.

We may attempt to get away from this difficulty by referring marginal time preference and marginal productivity of capital to a hypothetical numéraire specified so as to maintain a level trend in some general price index. Indeed, this is often done in speaking of a "real" rate of interest. But in this case these concepts turn out to be inherently subject to the same difficulties and inaccuracies as any general price index.

But in spite of these defects and of the inescapable lack of precision, the concepts of "real" interest, marginal productivity of capital, and marginal time preference are sufficiently definite for practical purposes and are very useful concepts in economic analysis. Indeed, the marginal productivity of capital and the marginal time preference are after all merely ways of expressing marginal rates of substitution between present and future goods in production and consumption, respectively, and any single measure that attempts to reflect a quantitative comparison between two groups of goods is dependent upon the accuracy with which the magnitudes of the two groups of goods can be described by a single measurement. The accuracy of such measurement is itself subject to index-number difficulties.

The marginal productivity of capital can be thought of for many purposes as a rate of growth of capital. Indeed it is not entirely misleading, for many purposes, to think of capital as a mass that tends to grow through time at this marginal-productivity rate. Additions to this mass of growing capital can be made in the form of savings from other sources, and pieces of this capital mass can be lopped off and consumed or devoted to other purposes. The part consumed can constitute part or all of the interest, or can consist in part of dissavings of the corpus, when the amount consumed exceeds the interest. This image comes fairly close to realization in such "liquid" production processes as the raising of cattle, where capital and product are substantially the same commodity. A herd of cattle may have a gross increase of, say, 25 per cent per year, and if the owner of the herd sells off as many head as he needs to pay the cowhands and perhaps rent for the land (or even pays these factors of production directly "in kine"), he may have left a net increase of, say, 10 per cent per annum. If we take cattle for the numéraire, then this is directly the marginal productivity of capital in this case. The herd may of course actually increase at a greater or lower rate than this, through adding to the herd by purchase from outside, or through selling off part of the increase for consumption. Or sales may exceed the net increase, thus constituting in part "disinvestment."

Optimum Properties of the Competitive Capital-Market Equilibrium

THE PERFECTLY competitive futures economy, producing as it does an equality between marginal time preference and the marginal productivity of capital, preserves and extends into a new dimension the optimum properties of the perfectly competitive static economy: in particular, the property that no readjustment from the equilibrium position is possible that benefits some and harms none. Provided that in appraising the allocation of resources between provision for the present and provision for the future we look no further than the desires of individuals as expressed by their decisions as to the time patterns of their consumption, and feel collectively no greater concern for future generations than is shown by individuals for their own heirs, we can say that the volume of savings that results from such free competition is an optimum. Additional savings resulting from curtailing current consumption would, to be sure, still make possible an addition to consumption in the future greater than the current curtailment, but individuals would have indicated their preference for the smaller addition to their currently lower rate of expenditure over the alternative larger addition to future expenditures, possibly in part because they plan in any case to have a higher standard of living in the future than they have currently.

This conclusion is of course valid only provided the very unrealistic assumptions of the futures economy are met, and the qualifications that must be made in translating this proposition to terms applicable to the real world are even greater than for the static model. Most of these qualifications are fairly obvious, but one or two of the less obvious are worth emphasizing here. For one thing, we have assumed that in the futures economy the only motive for saving is future consumption, either by the saver himself or by his heirs. In the real world, however, much saving may be made for the purpose of acquiring economic power. Admitting acquisition of economic power as a motive for saving may still not impair the validity of the theorem, however, if the kind of power satisfactions sought are the kind that are actually added to by increasing the aggregate capital of society, i.e., the kind of satisfactions that might be obtained from managing or operating larger amounts of capital equipment. However, much of the economic power that is sought is power over other individuals, or at least power that infringes on the like power of others. Thus we may have a sort of external diseconomy in the production of economic power, and to the extent that savings are undertaken in a competitive striving for a larger share in a limited aggregate of economic power, savings will tend to exceed the optimum level. However, the political implications of such considerations appear to overshadow the economic, and we may pass over this consideration with a brief mention.

Another implicit feature of the futures economy is that each individual can borrow any amount that he is in fact able to repay. For ordinary entrepreneurs this presents no difficulty, for with certainty assumed, the assets purchased or produced by the entrepreneur with the aid of the loan would presumably be adequate to secure repayment of the loan. The exception to this would be the case where the entrepreneur is possessed of a unique skill such that much of the value of the assets into which he proposes to convert the loan would become irrecoverable without his cooperation. For such entrepreneurs, and for individual consumers, we assume that borrowing may be carried even to the point where repayment can only come out of the personal earnings of the borrower. The borrower is thus assumed to be able to put himself in a position where he will be under compulsion to work to pay off a debt. In effect, he is supposed to have the right to sell himself into a modified form of partial or total slavery. Thus the futures economy, to be consistent, must admit a type of contract that cannot, under the laws that prohibit slavery, be enforced directly by recourse to law (though there may be some degree of enforcement in certain types of exclusive contracts and in informal private pressures within a given field of work).

The nature of the optimum adjustment provided by the futures economy may perhaps be brought out more clearly by considering the way this adjustment is affected by certain types of taxes. A long and respectable line of economists, beginning with John Stuart Mill, has maintained that from a theoretical point of view the preferred base for a progressive tax is expenditure on personal consumption, rather than income, and that income that is saved should be exempted from such taxation until it is dissaved and spent (or possibly until it is transferred to heirs). Indeed, it does appear that such a spendings tax preserves the equality between the marginal rate of time preference and the marginal productivity of capital, while an income tax disturbs this equality. For example, if the market rate of interest is 5 per cent, then in the absence of any tax an individual with $100 has a choice of either spending $100 now or investing the $100 at 5 per cent and spending the proceeds of $105 next year. Under a spendings tax of 25 per cent, an individual with $125 this year may still either spend $100 now and pay the $25 tax on these spendings, or invest the $125, obtaining $131.25 the following year, out of which he can spend $105 and still have enough left to pay the $26.25 spendings tax, assumed still to be at the rate of 25 per cent. On the other hand, with an income tax of 20 per cent, the individual with $125 will have in any case an immediate tax of $25 to pay, and then can either spend the $100 now or invest it and have $105 in proceeds next year; but of these proceeds $5 is considered further interest income on which a further tax of $1 will be due, leaving only $104 for consumption. Thus the income tax disturbs the natural exchange ratio between present and future consumption, in a manner analogous to the way an excise tax on oranges would disturb the natural price ratio of oranges to apples, thus impairing the adaptation of consumption patterns to consumer preferences and production potentialities. It is possible to construct simplified models that will show the reduction in welfare resulting from this distortion of savings and consumption patterns by an income tax.[1] Another possible reason for regarding a spendings tax as theoretically sounder is that the impact of the spendings tax will in general be independent of the choice of the numéraire, whereas the impact of an income tax will depend on the numéraire used in defining income. A numéraire producing a high rate of interest would increase the tax relatively on large savers, while the use of a numéraire that gave a zero rate of interest would produce a tax having an impact no different from that of a spendings tax, the difference being entirely one of time of payment, not of total burden.

The Period of Production

MUCH OF the older theory of capital productivity was based on the concepts of "roundaboutness" and the "period of production." The ability of the entrepreneur to pay interest was ascribed to the inherent superiority of

1. One such model is produced in Appendix VII of William Vickrey, *Agenda for Progressive Taxation* (New York: Ronald, 1947).

"roundabout methods of production" and the degree of roundaboutness was taken in some cases to be measured by the "period of production." While there is a modicum of significance in these concepts, they need interpretation. Not all roundabout methods are superior merely for being roundabout, nor are processes having a long period of production more productive than those having a short period. Rather, bringing the indirect methods into consideration multiplies the alternatives open to the entrepreneur, and it may happen that in a significant proportion of cases the most productive method of production, by some relevant standard, will be found among the indirect ones. In other cases there is no advantage to be gained by the use of an indirect method and the direct method is retained.

The concept of the period of production as a measure of the degree of roundaboutness or of the degree of "capital intensity" of a production process is a fairly appealing one, and for certain limited purposes it may be useful. If we have a simple one-shot production process in which we can identify specific inputs as being responsible for the production of a given output, then the production period can be defined roughly as the difference in time between the average date of the inputs and the date of the outputs. This is satisfactory as long as the inputs in question are in some sense "original factors of production," such as labor and the services of land. But where one firm uses as inputs the outputs of another, then difficulties arise, for a period of production computed for each of the two firms separately will be shorter for either of them than for an integrated operation; on the other hand, the amalgamation of two competing or parallel firms would lead to no change in the production period. To get around this difficulty, it is necessary, conceptually at least, to trace each production process back to original factors, a procedure at best difficult. Moreover, such an attempt will generally involve us in continuing production processes stretching far into the past and indefinitely into the future, where because it will not be possible to identify the factors of production responsible for a given output, the method fails. If one attempts to take outputs as a whole in comparison with inputs as a whole, it will in general be necessary to employ some scheme of weighting, which will depend on the rate of interest. If the rate of interest is itself one of the variables to be examined, the process becomes extremely difficult. Other anomalies are likely to arise where recycling occurs: if one farmer sells his entire crop and purchases his seed while another saves his seed from his own crop, it may be difficult to avoid getting spurious differences in the production period.

A fairly universally applicable measure of the time dimension of a production process can be obtained by merely taking the ratio of the capital tied up in the process at a point of time to the rate of input of labor, both being valued in the same numéraire. If one could ignore land as an original factor of production, the measure so obtained, which will have the dimension "time," would correspond fairly well with the period of production for a one-shot production process, and if the process being considered can be constructed by combining a sequence of one-shot production processes at a uniform level of output, the two concepts are approximately the same. Where production is not in a steady state, some kind of averaging of this measure over time seems called for, but it is not clear in detail how this should be done, nor how one should deal with differences caused by the use of intermediate factors of production of varying degrees of prefabrication. The whole problem of measuring the capital intensity of production seems to be in a somewhat loose and unsatisfactory state.

EXERCISES

1. Many writers—for example, Keynes and Marx—have used a quantum of standard labor as a numéraire ("wage unit"). Consider an economy in which technological progress through research and innovation (as distinguished from mere capital accumulation) is rapid, while population is stationary or declining, so that the marginal productivity of labor is increasing rapidly. Could the interest rate, expressed in such a numéraire, become negative? Compare the distribution of income between unearned and earned that would be reported if a wage-unit numéraire were used with that which would be reported if a commodity-bundle numéraire were used. Would "land" depreciate?

2. Draw a "supply-demand curve" for savings from the starting point *A* in FIGURE 2 in which the amount of savings is measured in terms of second-period purchasing power. What would be required in order that such a curve should have a perverse slope?

3. Show how the total supply-demand curve of savings for a given individual over a given (short) time interval can be obtained as the sum of curves derived in the manner of FIGURE 2 for appropriately selected pairs of periods. What complementarity and substitution assumptions are needed in order to make this procedure an accurate one? What is required of the various rates of interest?

4. What is the essential difference between the nature of the consumer's relation to the capital market and the entrepreneur's relation to that market that makes it plausible to admit of perversely sloping supply curves in the one case but not to admit perversely sloping demand curves in the other?

CHAPTER TWO

Capital Accumulation and Progress

Individualistic Modes of Capital Accumulation

THE FUTURES economy provides us with a completely deterministic model of economic change, in which plans are made at an initial instant for the entire future, and in which these plans are so adjusted as to be mutually consistent. Such a model can be constructed to represent either gradual expansion or gradual contraction through time in the total output. To parallel the history of recent Western economic development, as well as the prospects for the immediate future, one is inclined to pay more attention to versions of the model in which both the total output of the economy and the standard of living of consumers increase through time as the result of saving, capital accumulation, and technological improvements. On the other hand, it is also possible to imagine a model in which, whether because of a rapid increase in the population or the gradual exhaustion of an essential, nonreproducible and possibly nonstorable natural resource, perhaps accompanied by a general inherent time preference on the part of consumers, the metastatic economy might exhibit a gradual consumption of capital and diminution of the standard of living.

The two major elements in economic progress—technological improvement and capital accumulation—interact in various ways, but in principle they can be separated, and either could result in economic progress without the other. It is useful to distinguish clearly at this point the state of technological knowledge at a given point in time, in the sense of the sum total of possible production processes that are generally known to interested entrepreneurs on the one hand, and the technology actually in use on the other. With a given technological knowledge and a given steady quantum of capital available, some progress through time would be possible as the given volume of capital is gradually reworked into forms more adapted to the given technology, and the technology in use gradually shifts in response to shifts in relative prices, generally in favor of more advanced technologies within the set that is known. It must be noted of course that the meaning of keeping the total quantity of capital constant in a context of changing relative prices may not be very precise, since it would depend on the choice of numéraire. But if we agree to choose a numéraire, for example, such as to keep the cost of living approximately constant, the range of error here is reasonably small. In any event, if capital and technological knowledge are both kept constant, the possible scope for economic progress is probably quite limited, and one may suppose that under these circumstances the economy would more or less gradually approach a static limit.

Continued and possibly unlimited economic progress may become possible if we admit of technological improvement, even though the quantity of capital is still kept constant in some sense. There is then no limit to the degree to which the fixed quantum of capital can be reshaped to higher and higher technological efficiency. Indeed, recent technological innovations have to a considerable extent been capital-saving in that they have permitted a given quantum of end-products to be obtained with the aid of smaller and smaller quantities of capital of a more and more effective kind, thus releasing capital for new processes. Of course, in this case the concrete meaning of keeping capital constant may be quite different than it was in the absence of technological advance, since the value of specific capital assets will now be affected by obsolescence that in turn is a function of the rate of innovation. But even if capital is kept constant in a sense that makes no allowance for obsolescence, there would presumably always be some opportunity for the replacing of worn-out equipment with equipment of more advanced design or adapted to a more advanced process. Thus while there has been a tendency with many writers to treat capital accumulation as a *sine qua non* of economic progress, there is at least the abstract possibility of substantial progress with capital at a constant level, or even perhaps moderately declining. Technological knowledge and the forces leading to its increase are, however, so diverse and so little amenable to treatment with the tools of economic analysis, that we leave it at this point and turn our attention primarily to the accumulation of capital.

The accumulation of capital in a community is often assumed to depend primarily on the institution of inheritance, and indeed in some types of society inheritance has been the most conspicuous means by which accumulated capital is transferred from one generation to the next. However, the transmission and accumulation of capital can take place in many other ways as well, even in completely atomistic societies where each individual is assumed to be a completely self-contained economic unit with no direct concern for the welfare of future generations. And current trends have tended rather strongly in the direction of limiting the role of individual inheritance and toward greater reliance on other methods in the transmission of capital from generation to generation.

Even in a completely atomistic society, and even where there are no direct economic interrelations between generations, some capital would be passed on from one generation to a succeeding one as a result of the mere fact that some of the capital instruments developed by one generation cannot be physically liquidated and consumed by them. Roads, canals, terracing, implements, metalware, and the like will be left for future generations to enjoy because there is nothing to be gained from their destruction and no way of using them up, if for no other reason, though they might be left in a somewhat dilapidated state. One generation, building on the detritus of the last, may thus achieve a higher standard of living and in turn itself accumulate a larger stock of capital of which a part must willy-nilly be passed on in turn. Thus capital may be transmitted, and even be increased in amount from generation to generation, though each generation were to be thought of as completing its economic life cycle in a separate period distinct and isolated from those of previous and subsequent generations.

There is, however, an overlapping of generations. Thus even though capital were liquid and completely consumable (as is the case, for example, where capital consists primarily of herds of cattle), the older generation will in general have an opportunity to make a mutually advantageous bargain with members of the younger generation, whereby the younger generation performs services in exchange for part of the capital accumulated by the older generation. The seniors may obtain in this fashion services that they prefer to any satisfactions they might be able to get from the direct liquidation of their capital, while the juniors will be able to obtain in this way a larger amount of capital than they could create directly by their own efforts. A generation that can obtain capital in this way is thus better off than one that had to start from scratch, and therefore will in turn be able to accumulate a larger amount of capital during its life, so that each successive generation will be able to secure its initial capital on relatively better terms, leading to a progressively larger stock of capital for the community.

Further, though, strictly speaking, this is outside the rubric of certainty, capital may be accumulated and kept as a protection against various calamities; in particular, the uncertainty of individual life spans may make it impossible to plan to exhaust exactly the capital of the individual during his life, and to the extent that a margin for error is kept, there will be additional transmission of capital to future generations. Under modern conditions, to be sure, the development of various kinds of insurance, and particularly of life insurance and annuities, would in principle abate this motive for maintaining capital; there remain, however, a sufficient number of risks against which insurance is not feasible, or is obtainable only at relatively high cost, for this motive to have some importance even yet.

Capital may also become the means of exercising economic dominance, as was pointed out on page 24, and where this becomes a strong motive for the maintenance of capital at a high level, individuals may maintain their capital in order to exercise the power that its possession brings beyond the time when a complete consumption of their capital in the remaining short period of their life would satiate their consumption wants, thus leaving something over to pass on. And in certain cultural environments, maintenance and preservation of capital come to be considered a duty of the individual, more or less effectively enforced by social pressure, wholly aside from any rational considerations of self-interest that might motivate the individual. And finally of course there is the deliberate accumulation of capital for transmission to one's heirs, motivated either by concern for their welfare as such, or perhaps by a desire for posthumous ostentation or prestige.

Government Action and Capital Accumulation

NOT ALL accumulation of capital depends on the action of individuals. Governments and semi-public agencies not only influence the actions of individuals, but accumulate and dissipate capital on their own account in large and increasing volumes. The activities of governments and the way they are financed can have large effects on the rate of capital accumulation in an economy.

If each government were to carefully divide its outlays into capital expenditures and expenditures on current account, if suitable depreciation were charged on investments made by the government in the past, and if taxes were made equal to current account expenditures, including interest and depreciation charges on past investments, leaving the net addition to government capital to be financed by borrowing, then we could in effect consider a government as merely a type of business, analogous to a firm that borrows its capital and sells its current services. In effect, investment in government buildings and other public improvements would be represented by government bonds, which in turn would represent the savings of individuals, so that the total capital of the community would still correspond to the net worth of the individuals in it. The essential difference between a democratic government and an ordinary competitive business would then be merely that the government is able to collect indirectly through compulsory taxation for the services it renders to individuals on the basis of the collective consent of the voters, instead of having to collect directly and individually through voluntary purchase of the service with the direct consent of each individual purchaser.

But few governments make any very serious attempt to segregate their expenses between current outlays and capital investment, and probably none make any pretense of maintaining their total indebtedness outstanding at a level representing the depreciated value of past capital outlays. Indeed, even in principle, it is difficult to decide, for example, just what proportion of the expenses involved in the passing of current legislation should be treated as a current expense and what proportion should be considered as producing future as well as current benefits, and if so over what time period. Nevertheless, it is clear that if a government reduces its outlays on public band concerts and increases them correspondingly on the development of parks, the capital resources of the community are increased thereby.

It is perhaps not so immediately apparent that if a government changes its methods of financing a given budget of expenditures—for example, by increasing taxes and reducing the amount of borrowing—a considerable increase in the total capital of the community will take place. This is because individuals by and large consider government bonds as assets regardless of whether or not there is any real capital that they could be said to represent.

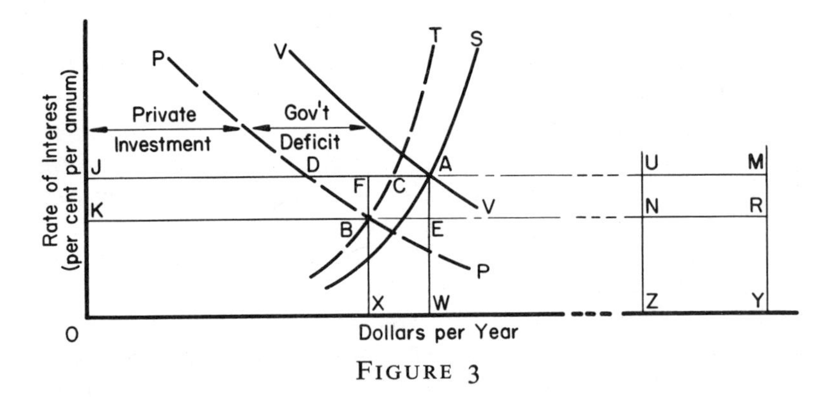

FIGURE 3

The effect of changes in government finance on the capital formation of the community may be followed by reference to FIGURE 3. Initially, the total demand for investment funds at various interest rates is given by the curve *AV*, which consists of the (horizontal) sum of the private demand for investment funds, given by the curve *PDB*, plus a constant amount *DA* equal to the amount of government borrowing. The supply of individual savings at various interest rates is given by the curve *AS*. The equilibrium is therefore at *A*, with a rate of interest o*J*, private investment of *JD*, additional savings of *DA* being absorbed in the purchase of new government-bond issues.

If now the government, without changing the character of its expenditure, ceases to borrow the amount *DA* and instead increases taxes by this amount, this increase in taxes will reduce the disposable income of individuals. Individuals will therefore have to apportion this reduction in disposable income in some way between a decrease in consumption expenditure and a decrease in savings; ordinarily, most of this decrease will come in consumption, and the reduction in the supply of savings will therefore be much less than *DA*. We can represent the new supply schedule of savings by the curve *BCT*, which must lie to the right of point *D* and will normally be much closer to *A* than to *D*. The total demand for investment funds, after the elimination of the government as a borrower, will now be *DBP*, so that the equilibrium is now indicated by the intersection of demand and supply at *B*, with an interest rate reduced to o*K*. Private investment has increased, in response to the reduction in interest rate, from *JD* to *KB*, or an increase equal to *DF*. Individual savings have been reduced by *AF*, of which *AC* was due to the reduction in disposable income and *CF* to the reduction in interest rates. Since disposable income was reduced by *AD* and savings were reduced by *AF*, consumption must have been reduced by the difference, *DF*. That is, consumption has been reduced by the same amount as that by which investment has been increased, while government outlays, it was assumed, have been kept unchanged. The net result in the change in the fiscal policy of the government has thus been to transfer an amount of resources *DF* from current consumption to capital formation.

The above analysis assumes, of course, that the demand for capital is sufficiently elastic to produce an intersection at *B* within the range of workable rates of interest, and also that there is an effective mechanism for maintaining total output at a full employment level. Further consideration of these assumptions, however, must be postponed until later.

To be sure, if we stick strictly to the metastatic concept in which the entire future is definitely planned for, a decision of the government to tax now rather than to borrow may be considered to involve a corresponding reduction in taxes for some future time when as a result of not borrowing now there will be fewer bonds to be paid off and less need for funds. If individuals were to take full account of the change in the prospects for taxes later on, they would be able to consider the increase in taxes payable now as merely a prepayment of the taxes they would otherwise have to pay later on, so that they would not consider themselves any the less well off and thus might make no change in their consumption. If this were the case, then the change in fiscal policy would have no effect on the rate of investment of the community. In practice, however, any repayment of government borrowing is likely to be so far in the future, and the means by which repayment is effected is capable of being varied in so many different ways, that it is ordinarily safe to assume that few, if any, individuals pay much attention to the magnitude of the national debt in determining how much to spend and how much to save out of their disposable income. The above analysis thus may be considered a fairly good reflection of what is actually likely to take place, although at the same time it must be admitted that this analysis does not fall strictly within the metastatic framework.

The Classification of Innovations

WHILE a large part of the analysis of technological advance lies outside the ambit of economic theory, certain aspects are susceptible of treatment with the tools of economics. Technological knowledge indeed can be produced to a considerable extent by the application of resources to research, experimentation, and engineering and development. Nevertheless, technological knowledge differs from other forms of "capital" in that the use of a given technology or technique by one producer in no way lessens its availability to others, whereas one producer's use of a given piece of land or item of equipment does, in general, preclude others from using it. Technology can thus be considered to be "inexhaustible" capital as distinguished from "exhaustible" capital consisting of the tangible assets of various kinds. With the occasional exception of lost arts, such inexhaustible capital is perforce handed on from one generation to the next, inasmuch as there is no way of "consuming" it. The process of transmission may involve restriction on the free use of the technology, as with trade secrets and patents, and in the form of trade secrets and patents technological information may become assimilated in the market to other forms of capital and form a part of the values underlying the value ascribed to a firm or to its securities. Nevertheless, the economics of knowledge and research differs fundamentally from the economics of physical capital and investment, and is very difficult indeed to fit into a precise analytical model. The problem of how the application of resources to the acquisition of knowledge should or might be determined is difficult to treat in any precise manner. It can be said in general that even under the most complete secrecy or the most rigid patent restrictions research is an activity that nearly always has substantial unappropriable benefits, so that the volume of research that could be motivated by private gain will nearly always fall short of the volume that would be justified in terms of the marginal social benefits to be derived from the application of further resources to research. Research carried on under government auspices, or by private nonprofit institutions, or by individuals spurred by intellectual curiosity of course helps cover the deficiency, but it may well be doubted whether it comes close to bringing the total volume of research to the optimum level. Inappropriable benefits occur internationally, of course, as well as between firms. And of course the problem of estimating, ex ante, the probable marginal product of resources applied to a given proposed line of research is inherently refractory to exact analysis, and can only be treated by intuition, hunch, or insight.

Accordingly, economics ordinarily leaves the problem of the determination of the level of research activity and of its results to one side, and assumes, for the purposes of the remaining analysis, that improvements in technology occur in a more or less exogenously determined manner, independently of whatever variations in economic activity are being considered at the moment. But if we are unable to develop a satisfactorily exact theory of the development of innovations, we can at least examine in somewhat greater detail the impact of given innovations on the remainder of the economy.

Analytically, a technological improvement can be represented by a change in one or more production functions. An innovation will ordinarily increase aggregate output for each combination of inputs, or at most leave it the same, since nobody is compelled to use the new technique and recourse to the old is normally always possible if it should prove more productive at any point. Exceptions to this rule may be noted in the case of certain relatively rare "irreversible" innovations, such as, for example, the introduction of rabbits into Australia. But while an innovation will normally increase the aggregate output for each combination of inputs, it need not increase the marginal productivity of the factors, so that the effect of an innovation on owners of particular factors of production may even in the moderately long run be unfavorable.

However, rather than consider particular processes and specialized factors in detail, it is of general interest to consider the effect of innovations on the relative productivity of broadly defined factors of production such as land, labor, and capital. For this purpose we may consider the economy as a whole as having a production function, varying from time to time as innovations are made, which gives the aggregate output possible as a function of inputs of land, labor, and capital, all of these quantities being measured in terms of some appropriate index number. For this purpose we can treat all types of nonreproducible resources as varieties of land, aggregated into a "land" index, all other forms of tangible investment as capital, aggregated into an index of "capital," and all forms of human effort as "labor," aggregated into a suitable index. A marginal productivity for land, labor, and capital, respectively, can then be computed by determining the effect of small increments of each of these, separately, on the total volume of production which the production function indicates is attainable. If the economy is perfectly competitive, each of these three factors will receive a return at a rate equal to its marginal productivity. If the production function is homogeneous, as it must be if perfect competition is to prevail, the resulting imputation of the total product to land, labor, and capital, in the form of rents, wages, and interest, will just exhaust the product.[1]

If this is done, then innovations can be classified according to their effects upon the marginal productivities of the various factors. For example, if an innovation increases production by the same proportion at all combinations

1. Indeed, statistical investigations have been made that tend to indicate, so far as they can be trusted, that for most national economies as a whole the production function may well be approximately homogeneous. Values have been found for marginal productivities of capitol and labor (treating land as a form of capital) that are in reasonably close agreement with their respective shares in the national income (see Paul Douglas, "Are There Laws of Production?" *American Economic Review*, 38, March 1948, 1). However, it should be noted that these results cannot be considered highly reliable, in that the indexes correlated to obtain them all have highly important trends through time so that it is difficult to distinguish improvement in the underlying production function from the growth through time of the factors.

of the factors in a given neighborhood, then the marginal productivity of each factor will be increased in like proportion, and if the inputs of the factors remain the same, the proportionate shares of the factors in the increased total product will remain the same as before. Such an innovation may be termed a "neutral" innovation, for this particular combination of factors.

There is, of course, no reason to expect that innovations will be exactly neutral. An innovation may increase the marginal productivity of some factors by a smaller proportion than the increase in the total product. If this is the case, however, the marginal productivity of one or more of the other factors must increase by a larger proportion than the total product if the production function is to remain homogeneous. If, for example, an innovation, or a series of them, increases total product (for a given set of inputs) by 10 per cent, but increases the marginal productivity of labor by only 5 per cent, we may term this a "labor-saving" innovation. Most of the striking innovations of the industrial revolution, and particularly those in the field of textiles, appear to have been of the labor-saving variety, according to this definition.

The relevance of the term "labor-saving" in this connection may not be immediately apparent, although the above definition is probably the simplest and clearest way of defining the idea in precise terms. An equivalent definition that may more closely suggest the term, but which is somewhat more cumbersome, is as follows: If after an innovation one were to produce the same output as before, using that combination of factors that would minimize their aggregate cost at the factor prices previously prevailing, then if the amount of labor used diminishes by a larger fraction than does the total cost, the innovation may be termed "labor-saving." The equivalence of the two definitions may be seen by noting that if the innovation is neutral according to the above definition, the homogeneity of the production function will show that all marginal productivities remain proportional to their former values if all factors are reduced in amount by the same percentage, and such a combination will thus be a minimum-cost combination at the old prices. If instead we have a labor-saving innovation, by the first definition, reducing all factors proportionately would insure that the marginal productivity of labor would be relatively lower than that of the other factors, so that minimizing the total cost would require shifting in the direction of using relatively less labor.

Naturally enough, there can also be "capital-saving" and "land-saving" innovations, since the three factors are analytically symmetrical. Some highly important innovations consisting of the introduction of higher-yielding and hardier strains and varieties of various crops have probably been primarily "land-saving" in their specific effect. To be sure, land rentals have risen, even in real terms, but this has been in considerable part the result of the increase in population and capital; had population and capital thus increased without the benefit of the land-saving innovations, rentals would have absorbed a considerably larger share of the national product, even though in absolute terms real rents might have been lower.

Capital-saving innovations seem to have been on the whole somewhat less striking than labor-saving and land-saving innovations, either because they are actually less frequent than the others or because they are less appealing to the imagination and so get less attention. Economizing in the need for capital may at first seem somewhat less urgent than economizing in the use of land or labor, yet it is the capital-saving and land-saving innovations that do most in the direction of immediately increasing the share of labor in the national product. Indeed, it is difficult to point out, offhand, any very large number of clear-cut examples of capital-saving innovations. One may, however, mention the development of railway signaling systems and other means of speeding up railway operations so as to permit a given number of freight cars and locomotives to perform a greater amount of service in a given time, or to permit the reducing of the number of running tracks required. Multiplex and carrier-wave telephony and telegraphy may be another instance, with the more recent counterpart of micro-wave radio for toll telephone circuits. There have indeed been intimations that recent emphasis has been on capital-saving innovations to a much greater extent than was the case a century ago, but there appears to have been no thorough investigation of the matter. If such a tendency should exist, it will be of considerable importance in indicating that the downward pressure on interest rates resulting from the gradual increase in the total stock of capital might not be so strongly offset, in the future, by upward pressures resulting from innovations of a predominantly labor-saving type.

But not only may an innovation increase marginal productivity in different proportions for different factors; an innovation may actually result in a decrease in the marginal productivity of one or more factors, even though the total product be increased and even though the production function remain homogeneous. This means that an innovation, even though it increases the total product, may actually diminish the absolute as well as the relative share of the national product imputable to such factors under competitive conditions. Indeed, it is quite usual for an innovation to impair the marginal productivity of at least a small number of specialized factors. When these factors are items of capital equipment, the effect is included in "obsolescence"; when this occurs with specialized parcels of land, the effect is sometimes referred to as "blight"; it can also occur, causing great personal hardship, to workers who have mastered a highly specialized craft. This is generally recognized in particular cases. But by the same token it is also possible, though perhaps less probable, for an innovation or series of innovations to diminish the marginal productivity even of very generalized factors, and even for a fairly long period of time.

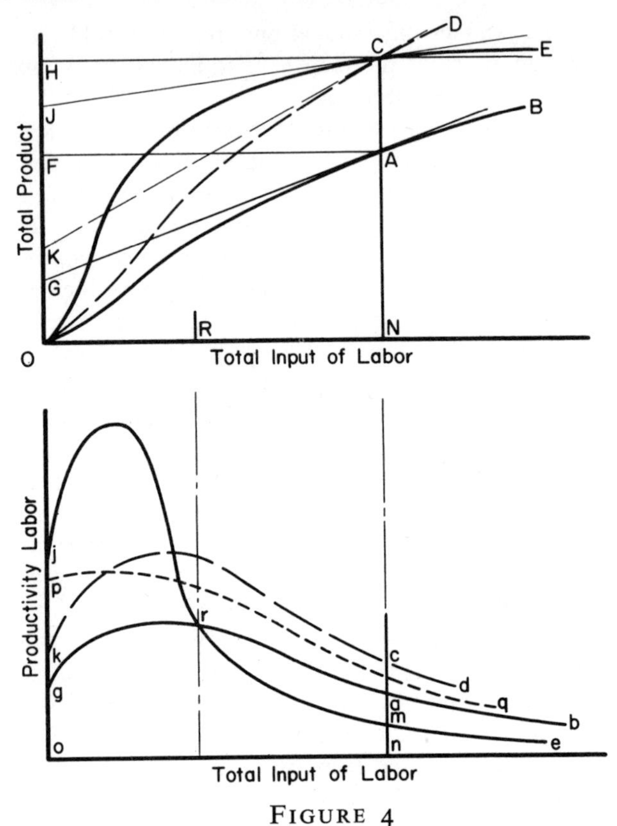

FIGURE 4

To distinguish this case, we may designate as "very-labor-saving," or perhaps more briefly as "labor-spurning," an innovation that has the effect of decreasing the marginal productivity of labor generally, and even after appropriate adjustments in training have taken place. Similarly, we may define "capital-spurning" and "land-spurning" innovations.

The possibility of labor-spurning innovations is illustrated in FIGURE 4, where for simplicity we have assumed that the stock of capital and land is completely fixed, so that the diagram can be drawn in terms of labor and total product. The curve o*AB* is the total product that can be obtained from various inputs of labor combined with the fixed quantity of land and capital before the innovation; the corresponding marginal-product curve is shown as *gab*. With an input of labor equal to o*N*, the output is *NA* = o*F*; this is divided between labor's share *FG* obtained by multiplying the input of labor o*N* be the marginal productivity of labor at *A*, which is given by the slope of the line *GA*, tangent to o*AB* at *A*. The balance of the product, o*G*, represents the share of land and capital in the distribution of the total product.

From this as a base, a neutral innovation is shown by the curves o*CD* and *kcd*, respectively; this innovation increases the total product by 50 per cent for each input of labor; the marginal productivity is also increased by 50 per cent at each point. The total product from an input of o*N* is *CN* = o*H*; of this labor obtains *HK* and land and capital obtain o*K*, which is a 50 per cent increase in the amount distributable to each set of factors, the proportionate shares in the total product are the same as before.

A labor-spurning innovation is shown by the total-product curve o*CE* and the corresponding marginal-product curve *jme*. Here the slope of the total-product curve is flatter at *C* than at *A*, and the share of labor in the total product, computed as before on the basis of the marginal productivity as indicated by the slope of the tangent line *JC*, is now only *HJ*, which is less than *FG*, the share of labor before the innovation. The share of capital and land has increased from o*G* to o*J*, i.e., by more than the total increase in product *AC*. The marginal product of the first units of labor has been increased by the labor-spurning innovation from *og* to *oj*, i.e., even more than in the neutral innovation, for which the marginal productivity increases only to *ok*. Indeed, this is necessary, for if the total increase in product to *NC* is to be the same for the neutral and for the labor-spurning innovation, area *ojmn* must equal *okcn*, since both represent the total product *NC*. To be sure, the analysis would be a little different here if the total-product curves did not start at the origin as we have tacitly assumed. However, it seems reasonable to suppose that no product is obtained without at least some labor, and that some product can be obtained for any labor input.

The classification of an innovation as labor-saving, neutral, or otherwise, depends on the combination of inputs for which the evaluation is being made, as can be seen from FIGURE 4. While the innovation o*CD* is neutral throughout, the innovation o*CE* is labor-spurning only for inputs of labor larger than o*R*, which is determined by the intersection at *r* of the before-and-after marginal-productivity curves. For outputs slightly smaller than o*R*, this innovation is merely labor-saving, while for very small inputs, near *j*, it happens to be capital-saving. Indeed, it is impossible for an innovation to be labor-spurning (or indeed spurning of any factor) for all levels of output, unless some output can be produced without any of the factor, since this would mean that the new marginal-product curve is entirely below the old and the new total product would be less than the old, which of course is a contradiction (except for possible "irreversible" innovations). It is possible for an innovation to be labor-saving throughout, however, as is indicated by the marginal-product curve *pq*.

Thus we see that it is not possible to exorcise, at least on general theoretical grounds alone, the fears of labor that technological innovation may impair its position, even when a long run is taken in which labor can be retrained and redeployed. There may be innovations that labor should rightly fear, if not on the grounds that they produce technological unemployment, at least on the grounds that they reduce real wages. To be sure, if a strongly organized labor movement curtails the supply of labor sufficiently by enforcing shorter hours or by other methods, there will always be a point where the innovation will enable it to secure a higher wage rate than otherwise, i.e., in the region where the innovation is not labor-spurning. But this higher wage rate may not produce a higher total wage, nor even a higher level of satisfaction, than the original competitive wage. It is indeed possible to construct an example where labor would have either to secure a major alteration of the competitive system or to obstruct the technological improvement, if it is not to suffer a reduction in its standard of living as a result of the "progress."

It remains to be seen, however, how prevalent labor-spurning innovations are, if indeed any important examples can be found. It might be felt that the "dark, satanic mills" of the industrial revolution may well have been the result of the prevalence of "labor-spurning" innovations during that period. For the present, it appears rather that the trend is in the other direction, and that on the average, at least, innovations are now much less labor-saving than they were then, even if an occasional labor-spurning innovation can be found. And in any case it is difficult to know how, with the information at hand, a labor movement could determine which were the labor-spurning innovations, considering labor as a whole rather than merely types of specialized labor.

In any case, it is important to distinguish between effects of innovations on the distribution of the national product among factors of production and the distribution of the total product among individuals. Of course, it frequently is true, especially in societies in which there is a sharp demarcation between the propertied classes and the proletariat, that large numbers of individuals are dependent entirely on wages as a source of income. In such cases, individuals who are primarily labor suppliers usually obtain only a much lower standard of living than do those who are primarily or in addition suppliers of capital. If under these conditions we rule out the use of outside redistributive devices such as progressive taxation or the distribution of a "social dividend," then it is possible that a labor-spurning innovation might be considered on the whole undesirable, in that the resulting increased inequality in the distribution of income among individuals would more than offset the benefits that might arise from the increased total product.

Increasingly, however, individuals are becoming suppliers of both labor and capital simultaneously, rather than exclusively proletarians or capitalists. As small investors, as owners of life insurance, as beneficiaries of pension plans, and as users of services supplied by endowed benevolent institutions, suppliers of labor are in a position to benefit from an increase in the marginal productivity of capital. Thus even an innovation that might reduce the return to labor, *qua* labor, might still not impair the total return to any individual in all of his factor-supplying capacities. In particular, if ownership of capital is distributed equally among individuals, then no reversible innovation, no matter how damaging it might be to the marginal productivity of either labor or capital, could be anything but beneficial on balance to each individual. For example, if in FIGURE 5 we draw in a set of indifference curves for such an average individual, and the original per capita total-product curve is o*A*, the competitive equilibrium will be found where this curve is tangent to an indifference curve at *A*; the slope of the line *EA* will represent the market

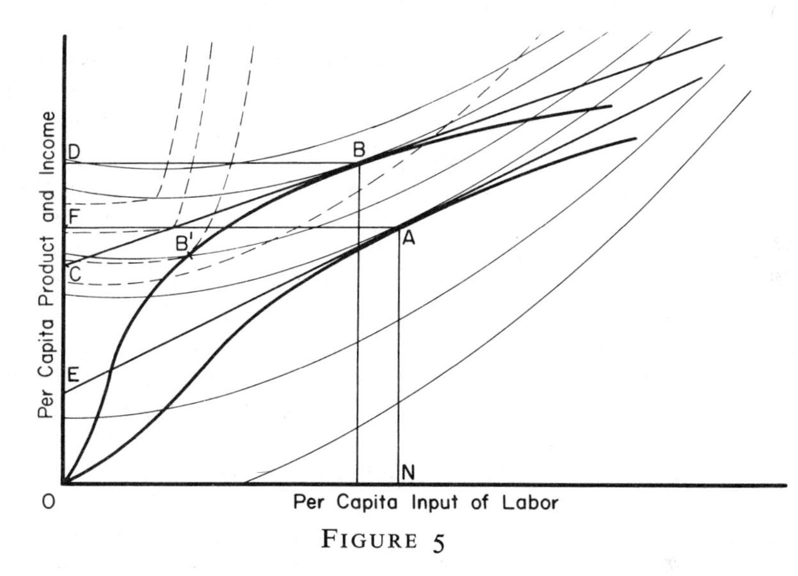

FIGURE 5

wage rate, *E*o representing the return on the amount of capital owned by each individual. The opportunity path for each individual, able to sell his labor at this rate will be *EA*, and each individual will be in equilibrium at *A*. If an innovation changes the per capita total-product curve to the curve o*B*, the new equilibrium will be found where this curve is tangent to an indifference curve at *B*, with the new wage rate represented by the slope of *CD*, which may be greater or less than the slope of *EA*. The total amount of wages *CD* may be less than *EF*, and the total money income may even be smaller than before, as would be the case for the dotted indifference curves, where the point *B′* is lower than *A*; nevertheless, the point *B* or *B′* is necessarily on a higher indifference curve than *A*, and the individual has improved his condition as a result of the innovation.

Even if capital is not distributed equally among individuals, if the labor-supplying classes own substantial amounts of capital, moderately labor-spurning innovations may affect adversely only a small number of individuals. And if redistributive institutions are available, such as progressive taxation, the introduction of even very labor-spurning innovations may be accompanied by a simultaneous strengthening of the redistributive operations, such that the combined change will be beneficial to nearly all individuals.

Population

THE OTHER major factor in long-term economic development is population. In spite of much study, the fundamental factors that affect the growth or decline of populations are not well understood, and of those that do appear significant, few appear to be such as to be readily embodied in a precise theoretical framework. Indeed, for most analytical purposes it appears to be necessary to leave population outside the framework and treat it as an exogenous variable, determined by factors outside the scope of the analysis.

The best-known analysis in this field is of course the classical analysis, which is expressed most dramatically in the writings of Thomas Malthus. Malthus based his analysis on two propositions that he considered to be adequately verified by observation. The first was that the application to agriculture of the law of diminishing returns in static terms, together with an implicitly assumed moderate rate of technological innovation, would place relatively severe limits on the rate at which the production of foodstuffs could be increased through time. The second was that the population tended to increase, in the absence of restraints, at a relatively rapid rate. This was expressed somewhat arbitrarily by saying that the productivity of land tended to increase arithmetically, while the population, in the absence of restraints, tended to increase geometrically. This implies that in the absence of restraints the increase in population must sooner or later overtake the increase in productivity, resulting in a decline thereafter in the average standard of living. This decline would then continue until some restraint on population was encountered. The "disastrous" restraints on population growth included war, disease, and famine: if the growth was not restrained sooner, the standard of living would eventually reach the level at which the restraints of famine and possibly disease would become effective.

This tendency of the standard of living of the mass of the population to sink to a level that restrains population growth is expressed in the "iron law of wages," which states that wages can never for any long period rise above the level at which the fertility of the working population is kept in check by poverty. The enunciation of this principle properly earned for classical economics the designation of the "dismal science," but it did to some extent serve to explain why the great technological advances of the industrial revolution failed to produce a commensurate improvement in the lot of the proletariat.

However, the concept of the iron law of wages was somewhat relaoed to allow for a certain amelioration of the lot of the working classes to the extent that these classes raised their own standards of what would be an acceptable level of existence at which to rear a family. Indeed, Malthus himself held that the only hope for the improvement of the lot of the proletariat lay in encouraging "moral restraint," i.e., late marriage, celibacy, and the eschewing of unsanctioned intercourse.

Since the time of Malthus, actual developments have been so dramatically different from those that he predicted, at least in western Europe and America, as to lead many to consider that his premises must have been faulty, or at least that his analysis no longer applies. It is difficult to ascribe the failure of the Malthusian prognosis to any one factor, as several important elements combined to raise the standard of living above the subsistence level pictured by his school. One factor was the unexpected and unprecedented rapidity with which the industrial revolution took hold—the improvements in agriculture especially: the opening of new areas to cultivation and improved methods of transporting and preserving food increased the total amount of agricultural products available to the population around the North Atlantic. Another was the development of methods of contraception acceptable to the mores of the bulk of the population, and the dissemination of information concerning them. A third was the development of free education with the consequent elevation of the standards of the population. A fourth may have been the change in the economic relations between children and their parents, brought about by the decline in the relative importance of the agricultural population, the restrictions on child labor, and compulsory education, all of which tended to make children less of an immediate economic asset to their parents.

As a result of this favorable concatenation of circumstances, it appears possible that the countries of western Europe and North America may have permanently escaped from the Malthusian circle. Had the same absolute increase in productivity taken place over a longer period, the result might have been merely to bring the population to a point where it would increase more rapidly and eventually again overtake production, with little permanent improvement in the standard of living. But the increase took place so rapidly that before the population had time to catch up, the standard of living had been raised beyond the point of maximum population increase and to a level where reproduction tends to be held effectively in check by factors other than those associated with misery. It is still uncertain what factors of this type are actually important, but higher standards of rearing, the availability of diversions, and the emancipation of women are some of the elements that appear to have contributed to the result. Other more dubious factors that have been suggested are the development of patterns leading to later marriage, the possible physiological effects of a less strenuous life, the sociological influences of urbanization, absence of fertility-promoting elements from a more luxurious diet, or biological degeneracy resulting from the withdrawal of the selective influence of a high mortality rate. But here the evidence is quite inconclusive and the effects, if any, of these factors has probably been quite small.

The leaping of the Malthusian hump by Western civilization has been salutary in terms of the standard of living, but unfortunately it leaves theoretical economics without any effective theory of population to replace that of Malthus. The wide margins of error that have already been observed in demographic predictions made during the 1930's are evidence of the low state of theory at this point. The theorist indeed tends in the end to dump the whole problem in the lap of the sociologists, demographers, and possibly to some extent the institutional economists, and to consider population for his own purposes as an exogenously determined variable in his system.

But the Malthusian specter has not been completely exorcised from the earth. There remain vast areas on the globe where severe overpopulation exists and where the potential fertility of the population appears ample to swamp in very short order any but the most drastic increases in production. Moreover, it no longer suffices merely to apply the techniques of modern industry to create the spurt in output needed to pull these areas over the Malthusian hump. It is not possible for the Chinese and Indians to colonize vast new agricultural areas, nor can they, by industrialization, reap the larger rewards that accrued to those who were first in the field and were able to obtain favorable terms of trade for the products of their new techniques. Industrial products from underdeveloped areas must compete with those from established industrial areas, and to these inherent difficulties are added the recent proliferation of encumbrances to international trade.

More important, the character of the initial impact of the introduction of modern technology on population trends has changed drastically in the last fifty years. Modern technology now brings with it not only increases in productivity, but highly effective and relatively inxepensive medical and public-health measures. Formerly, industrialization made its impact felt on birth and death rates primarily as a result of the improved standard of living that it made possible, though there are some indications that part of the effect on birth rates was through its effect in dislocating pre-existing social structures. The modern medical measures that are likely to accompany any large-scale industrialization of an area are capable of producing a substantial decline in death rates even before a substantial improvement in the standard of living in other respects has made itself felt. The stimulating effects on the growth of population of introducing modern techniques are thus likely to be much more immediate than they were during the industrial revolution, and thus the time margin within which the increase in productivity must pull the standard of living over the hump before the population begins to catch up is very much shorter.

On the other hand, the greater availability of contraceptives may have moved the hump, i.e., the standard of living at which the rate of population increase no longer exceeds the feasible rate of increase in national income, a little nearer the subsistence level, so that the amount by which living standards must be increased to get past this hump may be smaller than formerly. Also in many fields technological improvements are available that can be applied with a relatively small amount of capital, so that substantial improvements in productivity can be achieved with a relatively small application of outside resources. Nevertheless, there are many underdeveloped countries for which it is doubtful whether they can break out of the Malthusian circle merely by a program of generalized industrialization.

But if the resources at the disposal of a given country, whether derived from within or contributed from without, are insufficient to raise the entire population over the Malthusian hump at once, it may be possible to concentrate resources on one area or group so as to raise their standard of living sufficiently rapidly to a point where their fertility will remain within bounds so that during the transition there will not have been time for any serious increase in their numbers to have taken place, and having done this with one group, to carry out a similar process with further groups in succession. What may not be possible for a nation as a whole, or for the underdeveloped areas of the world all at once, may be possible if tackled bit by bit. This of course involves a program of deliberate arbitrary discrimination that runs counter to many deep-seated sentiments of equity and egalitarianism. But it may be the only way out of a serious dilemma.

Indeed, it is possible to consider that the rapid increase in the standard of living of western Europe and North America was possible only because other areas of the world were exploited, and that without this exploitation western Europe would not have surmounted the hump, but would have fallen back to a dissipation of the increase in productivity in a fecund subsistence for a larger mass of population. One might even attempt to justify the great inequalities in the distribution of wealth during the early stages of the industrial revolution and the immediately preceding period on the grounds that this inequality permitted a suppression of the population increase through the poverty of the masses, simultaneously with a sufficient accumulation of capital for the later surge over the hump. But such arguments come dangerously close to a casuistic pragmatism.

The whole concept of surmounting the Malthusian hump by a rapid dash from subsistence levels at which "disastrous" restraints on population operate to higher levels at which nondisastrous restraints operate rests on the basic premise that there is a simple relation between standard of living and population growth, such that any moderate increase in living standards above the subsistence level will result in fairly rapid population growth, but that there is a higher standard of living such that if it is attained, population growth will subside to a moderate level or even turn into a decline. In the light of more recent investigations, however, this basic concept has been more and more questioned. Communities have been observed in which population has been stable or even declining over long periods, without this result being accompanied by any of the restraints postulated by the Malthusian doctrine or its modern variants. Neither acute poverty, nor specific moral interdictions, nor effete luxury, nor considerations of property inheritance seem entirely adequate to explain such situations. In Western countries also, variations in the birth rate have been observed that do not seem explicable in terms of economic factors. The postwar surge of the birth rate in the United States tends specifically to refute the easy assumption that a sufficiently high standard of living will automatically result in a low rate of population growth. Increasingly, it appears that population growth is affected by the entire sociological environment as well as by economic factors, and particularly by the fluidity or rigidity of the status structure within the community. Indeed, the population growth that accompanied the industrial revolution may have been not so much an economic phenomenon resulting from increased productivity as a sociological phenomenon resulting from the breaking down of the status structures that had previously been changing relatively gradually since the Middle Ages.

The fundamental fact remains, however, that the population problem has not been solved. The Malthusian specter continues to haunt much of the world, even though its outlines have become more indistinct and its operations more mysterious. And it is particularly important that Westerners who do not directly feel or observe the effects of population pressure should keep this fundamental determinant of economic progress in mind.

EXERCISES

1. The Prime Minister of Indigenia has been haunted by the ghost of Malthus who has told him that though he can expect to increase his national income by 5 per cent of its current value each year, in linear fashion, his population is fated to increase at the rate of 3 per cent per year, geometrically. If this prediction is fulfilled, how many years hence will the per capita income reach its maximum? When will it have fallen back to its current level?

2. Is the classification of an innovation as capital-saving or labor-saving independent of the choice of numéraire?

3. Consider an economy with a stationary population and stationary technology; children are maintained and educated up to the age of 21 in a standard manner by an agency to which each individual must later repay, with interest at the going rates, the cost of this upbringing. Bequest of property is neither desired nor permitted. Indicate the nature of the developments through time if the economy starts from a very low level of capital accumulation. What would be the results if the economy started off with an extremely large endowment of capital?

CHAPTER THREE

Anticipated Fluctuations

Seasonal Fluctuations with Storage

EVEN IN the futures economy, it is not necessary to assume that everything proceeds smoothly. Some types of more or less sudden or irregular fluctuations cannot be avoided even if there is perfect foresight.

One form of fluctuation which is often anticipated with fair accuracy in the real world is the seasonal fluctuation. We have already discussed the case of seasonal demand for services, where there was no possibility of storage and the time sequence of the various stages of demand made no essential difference in the analysis. Where storage is possible, price fluctuations will in general be less severe, and will tend to conform to a fairly uniform general pattern conditioned by the costs of storage. FIGURE 6 shows the more extreme case where supply and demand have seasonal fluctuations in opposite directions, although the analysis will apply whenever the seasonal patterns of supply and demand differ from each other. Two yearly cycles are shown on the diagram, in order to bring out more clearly the continuity from one year to the next.

The year may be divided into a productive season, in which production exceeds consumption, the excess being added to stocks, a consumption season, in which production falls below demand and stocks are drawn on for the difference, and possibly also an "equilibrium season," in which production and consumption are in balance. If anticipations have been correct, stocks will have been exhausted at the end of the consumption season, and their replenishment during the following productive season will start from zero. The price pattern that results is that during the entire portion of the year when stocks are being held, the price rises just enough to pay the cost of storage, plus interest at the going rate on the investment in the stocks. Any price rise smaller than this would make it unprofitable to hold stocks over the period, and if holders of stocks could anticipate this inadequate price rise they would tend to sell their stocks at the beginning of the period of too slow price rise, and restore their stock position at the end of this period by purchase, depressing the price at the beginning of the period and raising the price at its end, thus tending to restore the normal gradient. Similarly, if the price trend is steeper than necessary to yield a normal return on the operation of storage, speculators will find it profitable to buy additional stocks at the beginning of the steep-price trend and hold them to the end of it, thus again tending to

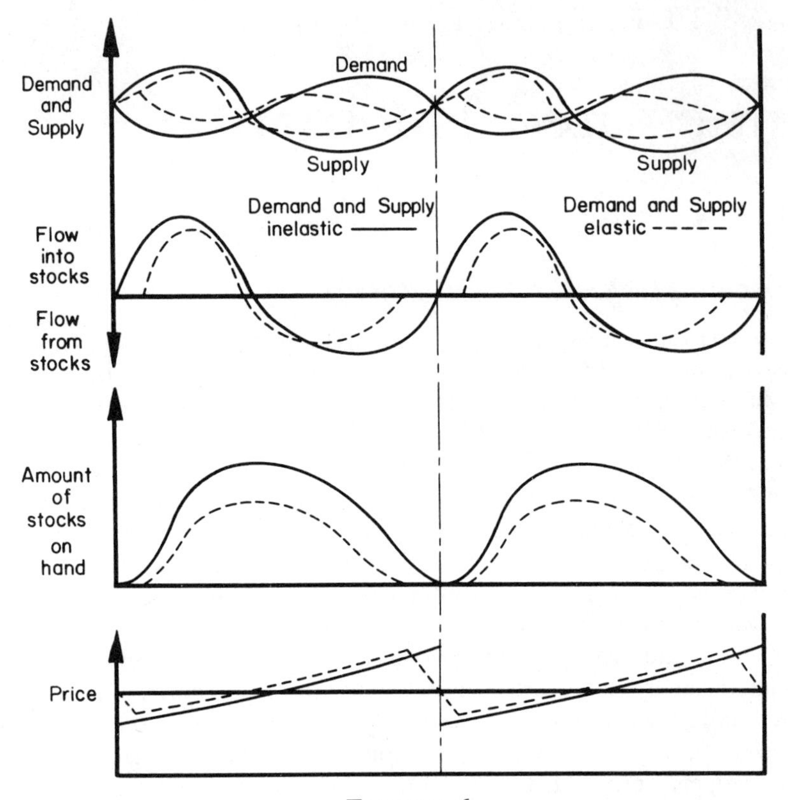

FIGURE 6

restore the normal trend. At the end of the consumption period, when stocks are exhausted, the price will in general fall below this trend, though it may still rise at a lower rate; usually it will fall off fairly sharply. In the absence of uncertainty, no one will hold marketable stocks during the period of falling prices, for to do so would be to incur a loss.

If demand and supply are completely inelastic, the price drop will be completely sudden, and the seasonal patterns will be as indicated by the solid lines in FIGURE 6. But if either supply or demand is elastic, there will be a period during which the falling price is able to keep the effective demand and effective supply in balance, so that during this period stocks remain constant at zero, as shown by the dotted lines in FIGURE 6. After the price has reached a minimum, supply will again begin to exceed demand and stocks will begin to accumulate as the price begins to rise at the rate that represents a normal profit to the holders of stocks. The price decline need not be smooth or regular, but will in general follow whatever pattern is necessary to balance supply and demand; it may even rise over part of the equilibrium season, but must never rise more rapidly than would cover storage cost and interest. There may of course be more than one cycle of stock accumulation and stock depletion during a year, and each such cycle may or may not be followed by an equilibrium period. However complicated the seasonal pattern, the rule is that whenever stocks are being held, the price must be rising at the appropriate rate, and that whenever price fails to rise at this rate, stocks must be zero.

In practice, of course, things do not work out so neatly, since there is always some uncertainty over whether the stocks on hand will last out the season. If toward the end of the consumption season stocks should appear to be short, price will rise above the normal trend (quite sharply so, if demand is inelastic) and holders of stocks will reap a windfall profit. If stocks should prove excessive, so that with the usual seasonal price pattern there would be a "carry-over," the price will begin to fall earlier than usual, while there are still stocks on hand, and holders of stocks will suffer a loss. In either case, the rapidity with which the price departs from the normal trend will depend upon the rate at which the surplus or deficiency becomes apparent to speculators: at any given instant the price will tend to move to a point such that if the price follows the normal trend starting from the current price, stocks will just have been exhausted by the time the seasonal increase in production overtakes consumption. If production or consumption is elastic, this moment will itself be later the lower the current price, so that lowering the price not only raises the rate at which stocks are worked off, but extends the period for doing so. If the excess stocks turn out to be large, the current price may even be pushed below the normal trend for the following season, in which case the trend for the entire season will be depressed, and stocks will not drop all the way to zero, but will have an actual rather than merely a potential carry-over.

The above analysis is strictly applicable only to "marketable" stocks, and the requirement that stocks be zero whenever price fails to advance at the proper rate does not of course imply the elimination of working stocks, such as goods in transit, work in process, or the working inventory needed to service customers. Strictly speaking, of course, goods in transit or in process are different commodities. And of course minor deviations from the normal trend may be too small to cover the cost of the indicated arbitrage transactions. To some extent there may be a deliberate carry-over from one season to the next where a possibility exists of a serious crop failure: this would involve loss in the normal years but might return sufficient profit in years of serious shortage to make up for the more frequent moderate losses. However, the making of profits on the occasion of a public calamity is likely to lead to public condemnation and obloquy, if not to expropriation or price control or excess-profits taxation; as a result, speculation of this nature is probably not carried to the socially optimum point by private operations, and stockpiling for emergencies thus becomes a function appropriate to government or public agencies.

The Acceleration Principle

ANOTHER interesting pattern that may arise in the futures economy is that which arises when changes occur in the output of an industry for which the production function is such that a fairly rigid ratio of capital to output is required to secure economical operation. In such cases, relatively minor changes over time in the demand for the product can produce substantial and abrupt changes in the demand for capital equipment by the firms producing the product. If the capital equipment is itself specialized and produced in a specialized plant with a fairly fixed ratio of required capital to rate of output, the relative effect may become very sharp indeed, though usually in terms of a smaller over-all magnitude. This effect is termed the "acceleration effect."

For example, if a plan emerging from the futures market requires that at some future time there should be an increase in the rate at which the volume of bus travel is increasing, this may produce a rather sudden jump in the demand for buses. If the rate of expansion of bus travel later subsides to its former level, then even though there may never be a diminution in the volume of bus travel, there may be an absolute drop in the demand for buses. And at a later date, as the buses purchased during the spurt of expansion are replaced, there may be an "echo effect" in that the spurt in the demand for buses is reproduced when these buses begin to wear out, although random variation in the useful life of individual buses will tend to blur this effect considerably and spread the surge in replacement demand over a longer period than that during which the original spurt in expansion took place.

Thus in FIGURE 7 the demand for bus service represented by the curve *ABCD* is seen to grow at an accelerated rate from time *F* to time *H*, reverting to the former rate of growth at time *H*. The total demand for buses, D_t, is made up of the demand for replacement, D_r, plus the demand for expansion, D_e. The demand for expansion is proportional to the slope, or rate of growth, of the demand for bus service. The demand for replacement, in the simple case where all buses have exactly the same life span, is equal to the total demand for buses at a time one bus-life earlier; i.e., if all buses wear out after exactly ten years, D_r would be obtained by shifting D_t ten years to the right. If buses wear out after varying periods rather than always after exactly ten years, D_r is obtained by smoothing D_t somewhat as well as by shifting it to the right, with the results shown by the dotted lines. (Variations in the lifetimes of buses need not be a violation of our assumption of certainty, since these variations may arise from differences in intensity of use as well as from accidental causes.)

If in their turn the bus manufacturers require machine tools more or less in proportion to their rate of output, the expansion of their output at *F* will require a sharp increase in their purchases of machine tools, which in turn would create a substantial disturbance in the machine-tool industry. However, bus manufacturers will in general not find it profitable to expand their output instantaneously, for to do so would ordinarily involve installing capacity in advance and holding it idle until the time for the increase in output. Rather, given advance notice of the demand, they would begin their expansion of production at time *E* somewhat in advance of the time the demand is to

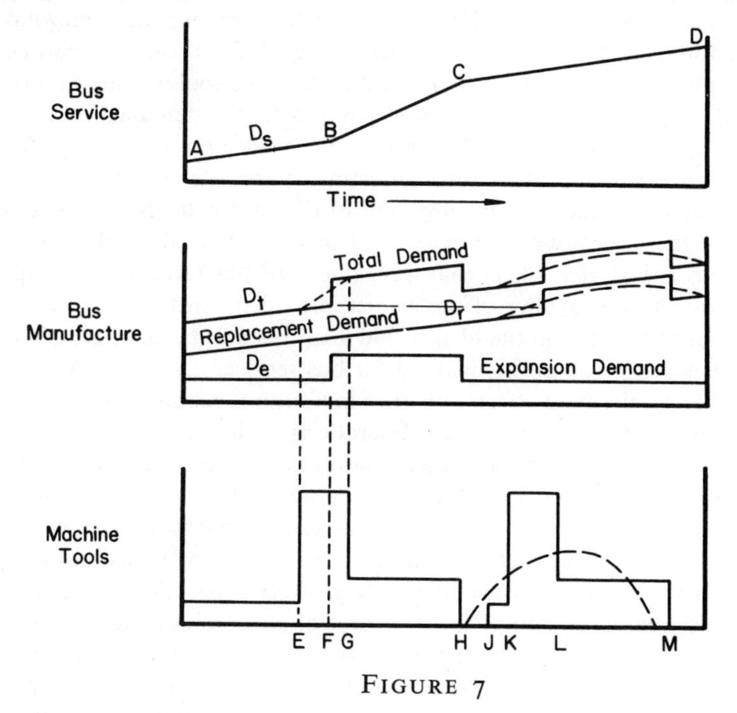

FIGURE 7

increase, stockpiling the excess output and then drawing on this stock during the period from *F* to *G* when output is not yet abreast of demand. Or instead of stockpiling the buses, operating companies might be induced to take delivery in advance of their actual need by suitable price concessions. In either case this will require a sharp increase in purchases of machine tools lasting for only the relatively brief period from *E* to *G*. Then having once supplied the tools needed for the spurt in output of buses, the sales of machine tools to the bus manufacturers would then return approximately to the former level from time *G* to time *H*, with perhaps some increase over previous levels for minor items of short life. But after the accelerated expansion of the bus operators is over, bus manufacturers will cut back their output, and will need no further machine tools for expansion. Indeed, even their replacement demand may dwindle almost to zero, since they can probably bring unused equipment back into service when the equipment in use wears out, and may even cannibalize their machines for replacement parts. From *H* to, say, *J*, then, demand of bus manufacturers for machine tools may go down to practically zero, and this period may last until the echo effect is felt, or even longer.

The over-all experience of the machine-tool industry is of course not likely to involve such wide fluctuations as would be indicated from the fluctuations in the demand of the bus manufacturers, since acceleration effects converging from different sources on a particular industry are likely to overlap somewhat as to time. Moreover, in a futures economy where effects of this sort can be foreseen and adjusted for, it would be likely that machine-tool manufacturers, if threatened with such severe peaks and troughs in the demand for their output, would raise prices for deliveries near the peak and lower them for deliveries near the trough; if these price adjustments are reflected in the prices charged ultimate consumers, a readjustment of demand is likely that would greatly reduce the intensity of the peaks and troughs. Indeed, in the above example of bus travel, it is likely that adjustment of bus fares and perhaps some fluctuation in the quality of the service provided, through occasional crowding or longer waits and the like, would absorb a substantial part of the impact of the acceleration in the demand for bus service.

Indeed, while acceleration effects can arise in a futures economy, this is not where they are of greatest interest. If accelerations in different industries are reasonably well scattered through time, acceleration effects are likely to be localized in their impact and thus not effect the over-all picture very greatly. Only if accelerations in many industries arise synchronously, as may occur, for example, as a result of a major catastrophe, a war, or a revolutionary innovation of wide scope, are acceleration effects likely to become a prominent feature of the economic system. A major source of concomitant accelerations in different industries is of course the business cycle, and it is in this context that the acceleration effects are of greatest interest. It must be noted, however, that the operation of the acceleration principle in a business-cycle context may differ considerably from the operation described above. We have in effect been discussing an "ex ante," or "anticipatory," acceleration effect, in which the response of entrepreneurs has been a response to correctly anticipated future shifts in demand. In the context of the business cycle, while anticipations concerning future changes in demand exist, they are as a rule not held with any great degree of certainty, and thus do not serve as determinants of behavior to the extent assumed in the futures economy. Rather, much of the effect of accelerations is an "ex post" reaction to current experience and the experience of the immediate past, especially to the experience of having more or less equipment, or more or less inventory, relative to the current rate of output, than the entrepreneur would like to have in order to minimize total cost. Needless to say, the economic phenomena arising in such circumstances differ substantially from the patterns that have been developed here. Nevertheless it is felt that a clear understanding of the ex ante acceleration phenomena, which are relatively simple and amenable to analysis, is essential to a study of the more general acceleration phenomena, which will usually contain both ex ante and ex post elements, as entrepreneurs react both to their experience and to their expectations.

CHAPTER FOUR

Risk

Risk and Cardinal Utility

THUS FAR, with minor exceptions, we have been carrying the analysis along on the basis of the important simplifying assumption of certainty. Each economic unit, in determining its course of action, is supposed to have a definite and unique idea of the results that will be obtained from each possible course of action. In choosing a course of action, accordingly, each unit is in effect choosing the corresponding result, and in the theory of choice we need not distinguish between the action and the results of the action.

This does not necessarily mean that the expected result will always occur: indeed, we have seen examples under imperfect competition where sellers selected their action on the basis of one expected result, while the actual result turned out to be different. However, in perfect competition, at least, the results, in the state of equilibrium, are assumed always to agree with expectations, while in a futures economy it really does not matter, in terms of determining the equilibrium achieved on any given planning date, whether the plans made are actually carried out or not, provided only that they be required to be consistent and that no participant has any doubts that they will be carried out. If it turns out that errors have been made in the plans, or if a catastrophe supervenes, a new equilibrium based on a new set of plans can be arrived at on precisely the same principles, provided that nobody learns from experience that the best laid plans gang aft a-gley, or at least provided that nobody attempts to allow for such contingencies. Thus the essential difference between an economy of certainty and one allowing for risk or uncertainty is not in the actual reliability of plans, but rather in the certainty with which individuals feel they can predict the results of their actions.

When the choice between different courses of action must be made in contemplation of numerous different possible outcomes for each course of action, a new and far-reaching complexity is introduced into the system, as compared with the case where the choice between courses of action is merely the reflection of the choice between the unique outcomes that are thought of as sure to result from each choice. In attempting to handle this new element, a distinction is often made between "risk" and "uncertainty." In a situation involving "risk," the participant is supposed to know, for each course of action open to him, the probability associated with each of the possible outcomes of the action. For example, in a case of pure gambling, if a person bets $10 on the toss of a coin, he is assumed to know that the probability is one-half that he will win $10, and one-half that he will lose $10. If he decides not to bet, he knows of course that he will neither win nor lose. Or if an individual owns a house valued at $20,000, he may consider that there is one chance in 1,000 of the house burning down during the next ten years, and 999 chances in 1,000 that it will not; he may have the choice between bearing this risk himself and buying insurance for, say, $40 for the ten years. Even when the probability distribution is less objective than this, in the sense that there is no observed frequency that can be appealed to as evidence of the probability, an individual may be thought to have a certain subjective idea of the relative likelihood of various outcomes and to base his choices on this notion. It is even possible that two individuals in the same situation would appraise the probabilities differently and react differently, even though their basic tastes might be the same: the same theory could explain both of the divergent courses of action by reference to this difference of opinion.

On the other hand, there are cases where it is difficult to discern or even to impute any such notion of probabilities to the individual. Such cases are distinguished by terming them cases of "uncertainty." We may perhaps include in this category cases in which the possible outcomes are so numerous as to make any evaluation too tedious, or where such singular events as the outbreak of war or the discovery of penicillin are concerned. The chief difficulty is that once having ruled out appeal to a probability distribution, objective or subjective, it is difficult to devise any meaningful theory of choice that will fit into a general economic model. Indeed, it is difficult even to specify the expectations of an individual in any precise terms without reference, at least implicitly, to notions of probability.

Even in cases where an individual does not bother to concern himself with the probabilities of particular specific outcomes, he may yet have some sort of a probability distribution of the net or aggregate effect of the possible outcomes. For example, a grocer may have some idea of the probability he would assign to various levels of sales for a prospective period, without even attempting to specify in detail what the composition of this aggregate of sales might be. Or an individual may have an idea of the probabilities of various possible amounts or percentages of profits or losses, without attempting to assign separate probabilities to the various events that might contribute to the realization of any given level of profits. It is quite possible to make significant over-all decisions, such as the size of store to be built or whether to invest in an enterprise, without a complete breakdown of the probabilities of all of the specific future states. Indeed, such a breakdown will often be quite irrelevant to the over-all decision to be made, and an individual would thus be irrational to devote time and effort to appraising such separate probabilities, unless and until still other important decisions depend upon them.

If we can assume that underlying the choices that individuals make in situations involving risk there is a definite probability distribution over the outcomes in the mind of the individual making the decision, then it is possible to construct definite theories covering such cases. Unfortunately, such theories are almost always extremely difficult to test by reference to observation, since situations in which the underlying subjective probability distributions are available are quite rare, outside of gambling situations where the behavior of individuals is also influenced by recreational elements and even in many cases by irrational obsessions. And since in principle it is possible to develop any number of theories of risky choice, it may be extremely difficult to choose among them on empirical grounds.

However, one particular theory of choice that has great aesthetic appeal as being outstandingly simple and tractable is that which can be summarized by stating that individuals act in such a way as to maximize the mathematical expectation of their utility. That is, an individual is supposed to ascribe a certain utility, expressible as a numerical value, to each possible outcome of the various courses of action open to him. If for each possible course of action he multiplies the utility of each possible outcome of that action by the probability that that outcome will occur if he chooses the particular action, and adds these products together with respect to each action separately, the result will be the expectation of utility corresponding to each course of action. The course of action is then chosen for which this expectation of utility is the greatest.

For example, if, as in FIGURE 8, we consider that for a given individual an income of $5,000 a year (or perhaps better, rate of expenditure of that amount) can be assigned a utility level of, say, 1,000 units of utility (or "utils") and, similarly, an income of $6,000 a year is assigned a level of 1,200 utils, while on the scale so established an income of $10,000 is found to have a utility level of 1,400 utils, we can draw a curve giving the relation between the levels of income and the respective levels of utility associated with them. Now if such an individual has a course of action, *A*, open to him that will, he considers, have a 50 per cent chance of producing an income of $10,000 per year and a 50 per cent chance of producing an income of only $5,000 a year, then the expectation of utility associated with this course of action will be $.50(1{,}000) + .50(1{,}400) = 1{,}200$ utils. If there is another course of action, *B*, which will certainly result in an income of $6,000 per year, the expected utility in this case would be 1,200 utils; an individual, if presented with a choice between action *A* and action *B*, would be on the margin of indifference: any improvement in the prospects of either action *A* or action *B* would tilt the balance in its favor.

The essential difference between the simple theory of choice between certain alternatives and the expected utility theory of choice in risky situations is that for the latter it is not only necessary to know the rank of the various alternatives in the preference scale of an individual, but also to be able to assign numbers on a scale of utility to these various alternatives. Thus it is in connection with risk that the hypothesis of the declining marginal utility of money has meaning. According to this hypothesis, we should expect that any utility curve such as that in FIGURE 8 should be concave downward.

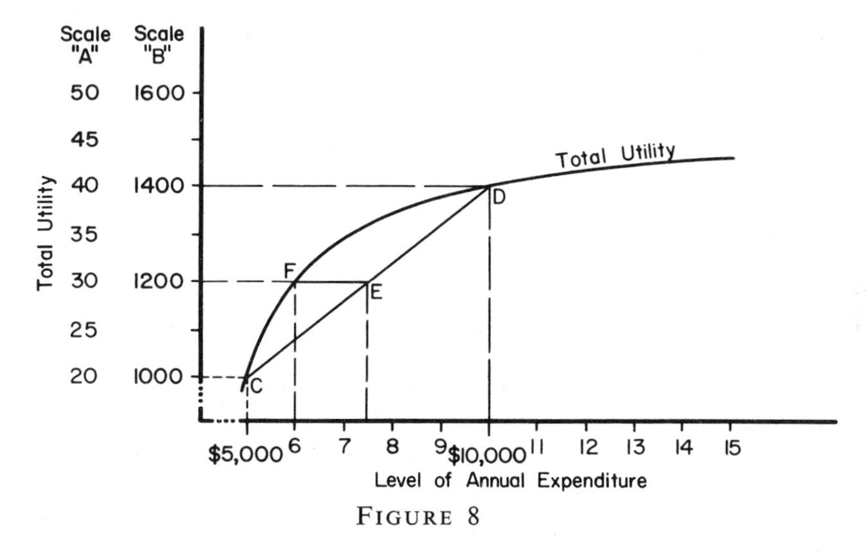

FIGURE 8

The degree to which this curve is concave downward is an indication of the difference between behavior that would maximize the expectation of income and behavior that would maximize the expectation of utility. In the case of action *A*, in the example discussed above, the expectation of income was .50($10,000) + .50($5,000) = $7,500, whereas the expected income in action *B* is of course only $6,000, so that were the individual maximizing expected income he would definitely choose *A*, and it would take a sure income of $7,500 to have the same income expectation as action *A*. In terms of utility, an expected income of $6,000 with no dispersion of possible outcomes is in this case the equivalent of an expectation of income of $7,500 if the outcomes have the dispersion found in action *A*. This difference of $1,500 between the expectation of income in the risky situation and the equivalent certain income can be termed the "net risk premium" or simply "risk premium"; it represents the additional amount that must be offered the individual in terms of expected income in order to compensate him for the risk that his actual income may be lower.

"Net risk premium" as so defined has a somewhat different meaning from that sometimes assigned to the term "risk premium" in somewhat analogous situations where attention is focused on a maximum return expected with a high degree of probability rather than on the average expectation. For example, if a ten-year gilt-edged bond can be sold to yield 3 per cent, while a ten-year bond on which there is a risk of default can be sold only if the promised yield is 4 per cent, the extra 1 per cent is sometimes referred to as "risk premium." We can distinguish this concept by terming it "gross risk premium." But if the chance of default can be represented by saying that there is one chance in ten of complete loss of principal, with nine chances in ten that payment will be made in full, this extra 1 per cent interest for ten years would bring the average expected return (for example, on an assortment of bonds of the same degree of riskiness) to approximately the level of the return on investment in the safe bond, and there would be no "net risk premium" in the more restricted sense in which the term is used here. Only if the market required, say, 4.5 per cent for such a risky bond would there be a "net risk premium" since the average expected return in this case would be 3.5 per cent on the risky bonds, and the difference between this and the 3 per cent on the safe bond would be a net risk premium of 0.5 percentage points, as compared with the gross risk premium of 1.5 percentage points in this case.

This gross risk premium indeed is a concept that can be defined only in those rather special cases in which there is an upper limit to the outcome of a given choice that has a fairly high probability of being attained: the gross risk premium is then the difference between the maximum return that must be promised where there is a risk that it will not be obtained, and the return that would be sufficient to compete if no risk were present. Outside of bonds, mortgages, and money loans, however, there is seldom any well-defined upper limit to the possible return, so that the concept of gross risk premium has no applicability, and only the net risk premium can be given a precise value. Even this, however, is likely to be somewhat difficult to measure, since it depends on the probability distribution of outcome involved, concerning which there may be no general agreement. Gross risk premium, on the other hand, if it can be defined at all, can ordinarily be estimated on the basis of market phenomena much more readily.

Given that a utility scale is to be constructed by reference to choices involving risk, there is still some latitude in the choice of the scale on which utility is to be measured. There is nothing in the observable data that will indicate where the "zero" of the utility scale should be set, or how large the unit of measurement should be: the choice of the zero point and the unit of measurement are completely arbitrary. We may thus take two situations, or two indifference curves, and assign to them any numerical values for utility that we find convenient (much as on a centigrade thermometer the freezing and boiling points of water are assigned the values 0° and 100°, while on the Fahrenheit thermometer an equally arbitrary selection is 32° and 212°). Once we have made these selections, the utilities that must be assigned to all of the other indifference curves are determined. For example, we might have called the utility of an income of $5,000, 20 utils, and that of $10,000 40 utils, in which case the fact that action *A* and action *B* are indifferent would require us to set the utility of an income of $6,000 at 30 utils. The only difference would be that the scale on the utility axis of FIGURE 8 would be changed: the $6,000 income will still be just midway on the utility axis between the $5,000 income and the $10,000 income.

To look at it the other way, if our theory of risky choice is valid, and we have thus arbitrarily assigned utility values to two situations, we would then be able to determine by experiment the value for the utility of any other situation. For example, if we wish to know what utility to assign to an income of $8,000, after we have arbitrarily assigned 1,000 utils to an income of $5,000 and 1,400 to an income of $10,000, we can proceed as follows: Offer the individual under consideration a choice between the certainty of $8,000 and a situation in which he will have a .40 chance of an income of $5,000 and a .60 chance of $10,000; then, if he prefers the certainty of $8,000, repeat the question with a higher probability for the $10,000 alternative, adjusting in this way until a probability is found that makes the individual indifferent as between the two prospects. If these probabilities turn out to be .86 and .14, respectively, for example, then the utility assigned to an income of $8,000 will be $.86(1{,}400) + .14(1{,}000) = 1{,}344$ utils. The same procedure can be followed for each level of income between $5,000 and $10,000. For incomes above $10,000 a certain income of $10,000 can be compared with various probability combinations of $5,000 and the income in question, and conversely for incomes below $5,000. In this way, a table such as the following may be constructed, which corresponds to the utility curve shown in FIGURE 8:

INCOME (OR EXPENDITURE RATE) (dollars per year)	TOTAL UTILITY ("utils")	MARGINAL UTILITY (utils per dollar)
$ 5,000	1,000	.32
6,000	1,200	.125
7,000	1,291	.067
8,000	1,344	.041
9,000	1,377	.028
9,900	1,398	.021
10,000	1,400	.020
14,000	1,450	.0078
20,000	1,480	.0032
30,000	1,500	.0012

The "marginal utility of money" is simply the slope of the total utility curve, i.e., the increment of utility corresponding to a small increment of income.

(The particular utility function chosen is not intended to have any particular verisimilitude: it was selected with a fairly sharply declining marginal utility in order to illustrate the various points somewhat more clearly.)

Having thus constructed such a table or curve for any given individual, we are in a position to make a prediction as to how this individual will behave (if he conforms to the theory) in *any* situation where he is confronted with choices for each of which there is a probability distribution of the possible resulting incomes. This possibility of predicting behavior in situations that differ from the situations from which the table was constructed is what makes the hypothesis of maximizing expected utility meaningful and tractable.

One can, for example, predict from such a table the maximum premium that an individual would be willing to pay for insurance of a given risk, given sufficient information about the circumstances. For example, suppose an individual has a total income of $10,000, of which $4,000 is derived from property worth, say, $100,000. Suppose further that this property is subject to a risk of total loss that is estimated to have one chance in 100 of occurring, and that if it does occur, the income of the individual will be reduced to $6,000. The expected utility of this individual is thus $.99(1{,}400) + .01(1{,}200) = 1{,}398$. If he were to pay a $2,500 premium for insurance against this loss, his income would then be reduced by the interest on this amount, which at 4 per cent would be $100; he would then have a certain income of $9,900, which has a utility of 1,398 utils, or the same as without the insurance. $2,500 is thus the maximum premium that he would be willing to pay for such insurance. But an insurance company would need to collect only .01($100,000) or $1,000 to provide a fund for the payment of losses on such risks, plus perhaps another $1,000 for expenses and commissions, making the gross premium $2,000. If the insurance is thus available at $2,000, the individual will take it, and obtain a consumer's surplus of $500; his income will be $9,920, rather than the $9,900 which is the certain income that would provide the same utility as the risky situation.

It should be noted that the consideration of this insurance is not a mere repetition in other language of the same experiment by which the utility of an income of $9,900 was determined: in the determination outlined above the possible incomes for the risky alternative were $10,000 and $5,000, while here they are $10,000 and $6,000. The difference is not great, but it is significant, and of course other illustrations of the use of a utility table could be considered in which the difference between the construction of the table and its application would be much greater.

Actually, of course, most risks against which insurance is taken out are not one-time risks but are steadily recurring, such as those of fire, accident, sickness, and the like; moreover, various degrees of casualty may occur, which means merely that a larger number of possible outcomes must be considered with their respective probabilities. The recurrence factor may perhaps be dealt with by first assuming that if the disaster does not occur the first year, insurance will in any case be taken out beginning with the second year, thus turning the question into one of a choice concerning the risk during the first year. With this question answered, the same procedure can be followed for the second year.

Unfortunately, actual verification of this theory of risky choice is extremely difficult. Few consumers, in purchasing insurance, are conscious of the actuarial probabilities of the various risks, or indeed have any specific probability in mind; their decisions are greatly affected by custom, the persuasion of agents, and other influences. Moreover, in a typical case it is not always clear over how long a period a given loss should be considered to affect income: for example, if a house valued at $20,000 burns down, it is not easy to tell whether the individual concerned views this as equivalent to reducing his income by $5,000 for four years, or by $1,000 in perpetuity for himself and his heirs, or by $2,000 for the rest of his own life.

Another difficulty with this explanation of consumer behavior is that individuals are often observed to court risk rather than avoid it, as in gambling. In some cases we even find the same individuals insuring against some risks while paying a premium for the privilege of incurring others by buying lottery tickets. It is possible, though only by rather strained assumptions, to bring even such behavior within the framework of maximizing utility expectations if it be admitted that the marginal utility of money may be increasing over part of the income range for some individuals. For example, in FIGURE 9 the total-utility curve is concave downward over the lower range of incomes, indicating a declining marginal utility of money, but is concave upward in the higher range of incomes, indicating an increasing marginal utility of money. (The proportions have been made somewhat extreme to permit the diagram to be drawn clearly to scale.) We may suppose that the individual whose utility this curve represents starts at *A* with an income of $3,000, giving him 250 utils, subject to a hazard with a probability of one-tenth that would cut this income to $1,000, yielding 50 utils, as shown at *B*. The expected income and expected utility can then be represented by the coordinates of the point *C* on the straight line *AB*, *C* being one-tenth of the distance from *A* toward *B*, i.e., at the expected income of $2,800 and expected utility of 230 utils. If such an individual is able to purchase insurance against the hazard for a premium of $300 a year, of which $200, or *DC* represents the actuarial value of the risk (one-tenth of $2,000), and $100, or *CE*, represents overhead, he will have an assured income of $2,700, giving a utility of 240 utils, as indicated at *F*. This is an improvement of 10 utils over his original position at *C*.

But now if this individual's utility function is concave upward in the upper ranges, indicating an increasing marginal utility of income (rather than the normally assumed continuation of a downward concavity, indicated by the dotted curve *AL*), he may now spend another $500 on lottery tickets that give him one chance in eight of obtaining a prize of $3,200, or a total income of $5,400, as at *H*, with of course seven chances in eight of reducing his income to $2,200, as at *G*. The actuarial value of the ticket will be only $3,200/8, or $400, as compared with the purchase price of $500, so that the expected income will be further reduced by $100 from $2,700 to $2,600; but if the slope of the line *GH* exceeds the marginal utility of money at *G* (indicated by

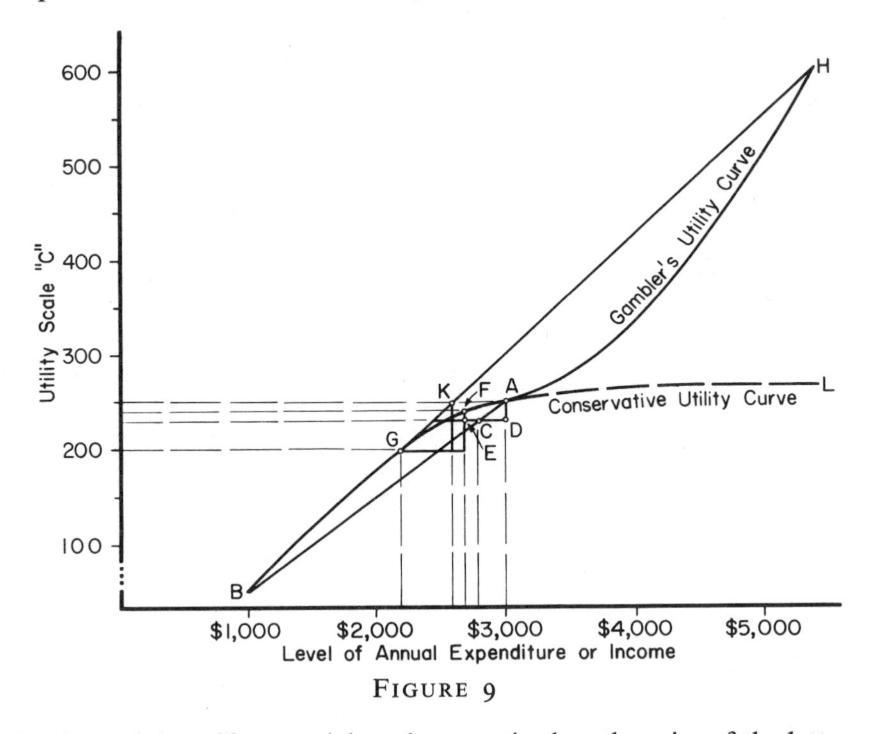

FIGURE 9

the slope of the utility curve) by a larger ratio than the price of the lottery ticket exceeds its actuarial value (i.e., by more than one-fourth), the result will be to increase the expectation of utility to 260 utils, as at *K*. Indeed, if more tickets are available, the purchase of lottery tickets will be continued until the ratio between the two slopes at *G* corresponds to the rate of overhead on the tickets, since this will put the resulting point *K* as high as possible on the utility scale.

This interpretation of gambling, however, is more useful as an exercise in the manipulation of the concepts of utility and risk than as a realistic model. While it may be possible to explain some instances of gambling in this way, not all can be so explained, and in any case other explanations are available that seem to many to be more satisfactory than one that involves postulating an increasing marginal utility of money. Thus some gambling is motivated by the presence of an eleemosynary element, as at church bazaars; a good deal can be ascribed to the presence of utilities associated with the process, rather than with the end result, as in playing poker or bridge. Some reflects the persistence of the egoistic delusion that one's own skill, judgment, or "luck" is better than that of other participants. Even the purchase of lottery tickets, where these other elements may be considered at a minimum, can perhaps best be considered as the purchase of the right to hope, however forlornly, in a situation otherwise intolerably barren of this psychological need: the very real pleasure derived from daydreaming may be considerably enhanced if there exists some tangible possibility, however small its probability, that the dream might be realized.

Even in the somewhat more coldly rational atmosphere surrounding the purchase of insurance, maximizing expected utility is far from the whole story. Insurance may be taken out because it is the "sound" thing to do, or because creditors require it, without much regard to cost. Or insurance may be purchased to avoid the responsibility for precautions against the risk, or to avoid worry over its possible occurrence. This seems particularly true of insurance of jewelry and similar items against theft: indeed, it seems unlikely that the change in income brought about by such a loss would be relatively large enough for the curvature of the utility function over the range involved to leave any substantial margin to cover the costs of the insurance company except in cases where the jewelry is so valuable in relation to income as to be a disproportionate extravagance. And there are even policies that provide a specific indemnity in case of a flat tire.

Thus maximization of expected utility is far from a complete or satisfactory explanation of actual behavior in risky situations. The "first approximation" which it might be considered to furnish is much rougher than is the case with most other hypotheses of economic theory. But it remains the only definite and tractable theory in the field, so that however bad an approximation it appears to be, we seem to be stuck with it. Actually, the case for using this theory is even stronger than this: it can be shown that this theory or one equivalent to it is the only one that will be consistent with certain very appealing axioms of rational behavior. One set of such axioms is as follows:

1. *Completeness.* For any two prospects *A* and *B*, an individual can say either that he is indifferent as between them, or that he prefers one to the other.

2. *Transitivity.* *A* preferred to *B* and *B* preferred to *C* implies *A* preferred to *C*, and similarly for indifference.

3. *Independence.* If *B* is preferred to *A*, then any uncertain prospect having *A* and *B* as the only possible outcome is preferred to the certainty of *A*, however small the probability of *B* may be, as long as it is not zero. In other words, any probability of improvement, however small, is preferred to the certainty of no improvement.

4. *Continuity.* If B is preferred to A, and C is any other outcome, however desirable, then there exists some prospect having A and C as possible outcomes such that B is preferred to the uncertain prospect. In other words, however desirable an outcome may be, its influence on decisions may be made smaller than any given difference by making its probability sufficiently small, though still positive.

5. *Compounding of probabilities.* It makes no difference to the attractiveness of a prospect whether the probabilities attached to the various possible outcomes arise from a single event or arise from the compounding of probabilities in a sequence of events. Thus it makes no difference whether a man has a lottery ticket with one chance in 10,000 of winning a prize of $5,000, or a ticket that has one chance in 1,000 of winning a prize consisting of a ticket in a second lottery with one chance in ten of winning the $5,000. That is, the A, B, and C in the previous axioms can themselves be taken to refer to probability distributions over outcomes.

It has been shown that if these axioms are accepted, then it must be possible to assign numbers to the various outcomes in such a way that individual behavior can be predicted in terms of maximizing the expected value of such numbers; these numbers will in effect be the utility of the preceding theory. Thus to reject the maximization of expected utility one must necessarily reject one or more of the above axioms. Indeed, the first two axioms are generally accepted as the basis for indifference-curve analysis, so that it is really only the last three that are in question.

Alternative Theories of Risky Choice

BUT IN SPITE of the logical difficulties that thus await anyone who attempts to develop a different theory, there has been no dearth of attempts. G. L. S. Shackle, for example, has developed a theory around the concept of "surprise." With each conceivable outcome there is associated in the mind of the individual making a decision a degree of "potential surprise" that would be experienced if this outcome should occur. The impact of a possible outcome on the consciousness of the chooser is supposed to vary inversely with this "potential surprise," and of course directly with the amount of gain or loss associated with the outcome. Among the favorable outcomes there will thus be one that stands out as having the greatest impact on the consciousness of the chooser, and similarly there will be an unfavorable outcome that has an impact greater than all other unfavorable outcomes: these are termed the "focus gain" and "focus loss." Choice among uncertain alternatives is explained as being made primarily in terms of these focus gains and focus losses for the alternative courses of action.

But appealing as this theory is as a way of bringing the theory of risky choice into closer agreement with the limitations and frailties of the human mind, especially in dealing with an almost infinite and in any case bewildering variety of possible outcomes for each possible action, it seems to be on the one hand oversimplified and on the other hand almost empty. It seems unlikely, for example, that the purchase of a ticket in a lottery in which there are many prizes is motivated by the selection of one particular prize or outcome as a "focus outcome" in such a manner that given the amount and potential surprise associated with this particular prize, the choice would be unaffected by, for example, the elimination of all other prizes. To be sure, the theory may claim to be applicable only to cases involving uncertainty and not to cases involving mere risk, but it would appear that cases of uncertainty with similar characteristics could be constructed. On the other hand, unless it proves practicable to identify these focal outcomes directly, as by questionnaire, there may be considerable difficulty in discovering or producing data of a type that could conceivably disprove the hypothesis. Thus while this theory has come in for a considerable amount of discussion, it has not as yet become an integrated part of any comprehensive theoretical structure.

Another approach to the problem of uncertainty and risk has been through the use of some kind of minimax principle. In one form of the minimax theory, the chooser is imagined to be playing a two-person zero-sum game against "nature," but in this case nature is not merely a dummy, but is rather an active participant doing his best to minimize the gain of the chooser. The chooser is supposed to select his course of action so that the poorest possible outcome of that action will be as favorable to him as possible. This has been called the "strategy of expecting the worst" and perhaps could be thought to describe the behavior of an obsessively pessimistic individual. But despite the notorious "perversity of inanimate objects," "nature" is usually somewhat less consistent in making the chooser's gain as small as possible than even a relatively poor human "player" would be, so that a chooser who was somewhat less than fully pessimistic would be likely to deviate considerably from this minimax principle.

Or the minimax principle can be applied to "regret," regret being the difference between the actual outcome and the outcome of what, ex post, will be considered the most advantageous choice that could have been made. This implies, of course, that one can, retrospectively, determine what would have been the actual outcome of alternative courses of action, which is only rarely the case. "Minimaxing regret" means choosing a course of action such that the maximum possible regret that could be experienced as a result of that action is made as small as possible. This theory, however, seems even more difficult to apply in economic situations than any of the others, however much it may appeal as a psychological insight. It must be admitted, however, that in certain experimental game situations results have been obtained that are more nearly in line with what this theory would call for than what is required by the expected utility formulation.

Utility and Norms of Income Redistribution

THE "expected utility-maximizing" theory of risky choice does have still another attraction over many of the alternative theories in that it gives us for the first time a means of measuring utility "cardinally" so that we can add and subtract utilities rather than merely ranking utilities "ordinally" as was the case where we dealt only with alternatives that were certain. But this measurement, and the adding and subtracting that it permits, is still, strictly speaking, limited to utilities of a single individual: we have as yet no way of making interpersonal comparisons on any solid basis. That is, we may set up units of utility for one person, and an arbitrary zero for his scale, entirely independently of the unit and zero point for any other person. Even if we decide to use the same two income levels as a basis for the measurements in the case of two or more individuals, any relationship between the scales for different individuals would still be purely arbitrary, and indeed different relationships might be obtained by choosing different pairs of income levels for the calibration of the scales. In strict theory, thus, there is still no basis for adding or subtracting or otherwise combining the utilities of two different individuals.

Still, it may be felt necessary for some purposes to attempt such comparisons, however tenuous their foundation. For lack of anything better, it may be necessary to assume that the utility curves of various individuals in terms of money income are roughly the same. This must be considered a very forced assumption, however. If tastes differ, as they assuredly do, then even if the relationships between utility and income for each of a group of persons were found to be identical when income is given the concrete significance implied by some one particular set of prices, the income-utility scales would in general differ under another set of prices. And such experimental data as we do have seems to show that utility-income relationships differ fairly markedly and systematically between individuals coming from different backgrounds and situations. In any case, some differences would presumably arise in relation to age and perhaps sex and state of health.

Cavalierly setting aside all these doubts and difficulties, we may wish to assume for some purposes that there is a determinable uniform function representing the utility of income for all individuals, and seek to apply the traditional theories of progressive taxation, for example. Of the three traditional formulations—namely, equal sacrifice, equi-proportional sacrifice, and minimum aggregate sacrifice—only the latter appears to be directly related to the utility as determined on the basis of risky choices. Equi-proportional sacrifices, meaning the depriving of each individual of a given proportion of his total utility, can be eliminated by observing that the application of this principle requires that we have some zero point determined, and as we have seen, the theory of risky choice gives us no basis for determining any such zero point, although some writers have attempted to specify such a zero point in terms of a minimum income required for biological subsistence. The principle of equal sacrifice may or may not result in progressive taxation, even with a steadily declining marginal utility of money. Whether or not progression results would depend on the relative rapidity of the decline, and there are no a priori grounds for assuming that the decline would in fact be sufficiently rapid to produce progression. In any case, there seems to be no close or obvious reason why a utility scale determined from considerations of risky choice should be the same as the utility scale with reference to which the principle of equal sacrifice should be applied.

With a declining marginal utility of money, the minimum aggregate-sacrifice principle would require that any given fixed aggregate income be distributed equally among individuals. If such a goal were pursued by taxation, however, this would mean a 100 per cent tax on all incomes above a given level, with consequent elimination of incentives and detriment to the aggregate to be distributed. Because of this obviously inacceptable result for this oversimplified case, the minimum-sacrifice principle has often been rejected out of hand. However, if we apply the principle in a broader fashion, and consider the effect of the redistribution process on the size of the aggregate income to be distributed, we can speak of obtaining a maximum of aggregate utility, or a minimum of aggregate sacrifice, by a suitable compromise between a complete equality and inequality sufficient to provide the maximum aggregate income. Determining the progressivity of tax schedules that would bring about such an optimum compromise so as to yield maximum aggregate utility would be a difficult problem but in principle a soluble one, given the assumptions concerning measurability and comparability of utilities.

Indeed, such a maximizing of total utility could be brought into a fairly close conceptual relationship with the theory of risky choice. If we think of the different economies that would result from the adoption of different tax schedules (or for that matter from any variation in policy affecting the distribution of income), we may imagine an individual being asked to choose one of them, on the understanding that once he has indicated his choice of an economy, his particular role in that economy, or perhaps his rank on the income scale, will be determined by lot in such a manner that he has an equal chance of being given the role of any particular individual in it. His choice among the different economies will then be such as to maximize his expected utility, which in turn will be the same thing, if we assume population to be held constant, as maximizing the aggregate utility of all individuals, or, in other words, of minimizing sacrifice. Needless to say, we are a long way from being able to make any such calculation, even if the many hurdles to the acceptance of the resulting prescription could be leaped. Thus far, economic theory can say little that is of immediate quantitative applicability to the problem of the proper graduation of income-tax rates. Moreover, policies of progressive taxation, and other redistributive policies, may also have effects on the total population as well as on the aggregate income and its distribution: since this is the case one can well ask whether average utility should be maximized regardless of the numbers involved, or whether perhaps an economy with a slightly larger total population might not be preferable even if the average per capita utility level is lower, and even perhaps at a slight sacrifice of aggregate utility. On a formal level, this requires the assignment of a zero point on the utility scale; more broadly, it becomes an ethical or even a theological question as much or perhaps even more than an economic one.

Risk and Liquidity

BUT CONSIDERATION of risk and uncertainty involves more than merely the addition of a new factor in the making of static choices: in a dynamic world it adds a new importance to the time at which decisions are made. Where outcomes are certain we can without too great difficulty assume that all decisions are arrived at on some base date. Where risk or uncertainty is present, however, and where estimates of the dispersion of the results of a choice are themselves expected to change through time (but in an uncertain manner), there will often be a substantial advantage to postponing the making of final choices for as long as possible. For example, if an excursion is decided upon two weeks in advance, one will have to take his chances on the weather. But if the decision can be postponed until the morning of the excursion, there may be considerably less uncertainty about the state of the weather. If preparations are made a long time in advance, resources will become committed in a way that will involve some considerable loss if the plan is not carried through; those resources lose some of their "intrinsic liquidity," which may be defined as the ability of resources to serve a multiplicity of alternative purposes with relatively little loss in value when put to the alternative uses. Thus a loaf of bread has a certain amount of liquidity, which it loses if it is made up into sandwiches. Similarly, a stock of coal or a steel ingot has a relatively large amount of "intrinsic liquidity," steel rails have somewhat less, and dies and castings valued as such rather than as scrap have very little. On the other hand, liquidity is not inevitably lower the more advanced the product: a die for making auto fenders is useless except as scrap unless it is used in conjunction with a relatively large volume of other resources to produce a given model of car; a finished car has a fairly wide range of possible uses.

If there were no uncertainty, liquidity would be of little importance, since plans are made in advance and no changes are necessary. Where uncertainty is present, however, preservation of liquidity increases the power of the individual to postpone the making of decisions until more information is available, and the choice can be made with greater certainty as to the outcome.

An asset has liquidity to the extent that it confers on its possessor the power to postpone decision and thus preserve a wide range of freedom of action.

From the standpoint of the community as a whole, the liquidity that matters is "intrinsic liquidity," i.e., the direct convertibility of commodities to different uses. A community with a relatively large part of its assets in the form of lumber, coal, steel, and the like, will be on the whole better able to meet an emergency, or to take advantage of a revolutionary innovation, than an economy where the assets are in the form of dies, speacilized tools, and furniture parts.

From the standpoint of the individual, however, needs for liquidity are satisfied if he can divert his resources to other uses by exchanging them for different kinds of resources. It is on the whole less important to the individual that the particular asset be directly convertible to a new use than that it be exchangeable on reasonable terms for other assets that suit his revised plans. In a market where most exchange takes place through the medium of money, such exchange ordinarily requires as an initial step the sale of a given asset for money. For the individual, therefore, liquidity comes to mean primarily the case with which an asset can be converted into money without undue sacrifice in terms of price. Moreover, the fact that debts are incurred very largely in terms of money means that many contingencies may arise where an individual in revising his plans finds his need for money greater than anticipated, and liquidity may then be needed solely as a means of securing money to meet these obligations, even more than for the purposes of making purchases with the money so secured. This aspect of liquidity is so important in the economics of the individual or firm that the term "liquidity" has come to be used almost entirely in relation to its monetary and exchange aspects, and, accordingly, further discussion of liquidity is here deferred to the section on monetary theory.

The Certainty-Equivalent Fallacy

IT SHOULD be noted however, that the fact that decisions can often be postponed means that it very often is not possible, as is often attempted, to convert an analysis of risky situations back to terms of certainty by the use of some kind of "certainty equivalent," conceived of as a sort of weighted average of the possible outcomes of a given situation. In a very few restricted cases it is possible to construct some certainty equivalent of the probability distribution of outcomes from a given course of action, such that the action of the individual in the risky situation would be correctly predicted if we considered what he would do if the certainty equivalents were substituted for the range of outcomes corresponding to each of his choices of action. Thus in the case discussed on page 56 a prospect *A* consisting of probabilities of .5 each of incomes of $5,000 and $10,000 has a "certainty equivalent" of

$6,000 in terms of expected utility. For some purposes only, the choice between this prospect and other prospects, for which analogous certainty equivalents are specified, could be predicted on the basis of the comparison of these certainty equivalents.

But many actions, and in particular those relating to the preservation of liquidity, will be undertaken in the presence of uncertainty that would never be undertaken in the face of any possible set of certain alternatives. If it is certain whether or not a given house will burn down, the writing of insurance is impossible. A manufacturer who is uncertain of the demand for his products in the future will tend to install machinery designed for flexibility of a type that he might never consider if he knew in advance just what the volume and character of his sales would be. Margins for error, factors of safety, and reserve capacities have no place in an economy of certainty. The certainty equivalent is a useful device in a narrowly circumscribed area, but in using it care must be exercised to avoid slurring over some of the essential characteristics of risky situations.

EXERCISES

1. In connection with automobile collision and liability insurance, insurance companies often offer, for a small additional premium, to indemnify the owner for costs incurred in connection with flat tires and other similar breakdowns. Discuss the rationality of such insurance in terms of the expected utility analysis.

2. Insurance policies are often issued on a "deductible" basis, in which the insured bears the entire burden of the first $100 or $500 of any loss, the insurance policy covering only the excess over this deductible amount. Discuss the rationality of this procedure from the point of view of expected utility theory.

3. Lotteries often offer a wide variety of prizes, from a few very large prizes to a comparatively large number of small prizes, in some cases amounting to no more than a refund of the purchase price of the ticket. On the basis of the Friedman-Savage theory, compare the relative attractiveness of such a lottery with a lottery in which all of the prizes are for an equal sum.

PART II

Equilibrium Macroeconomics

CHAPTER FIVE

Money

THUS FAR we have succeeded in carrying our analysis along without assigning any essentially unique role to money. To the extent to which we have used money, it has been a mere convenience in having a common denominator in which to quote prices, state values, and measure flows. For this purpose any commodity that can be strictly defined could be used, and while prices and even interest rates might change according to the numéraire used, a change of numéraire was considered to have no influence on the underlying real economic phenomena. Money has thus been a convenient measuring stick, but has not been a factor in determining the behavior of the real variables in the economic system.

The Basis for the Real Impact of Money

THIS TREATMENT of money purely as a numéraire was sufficient as long as we held to either of two implicit assumptions: costless exchange or certainty. As long as exchange is costless, it makes no difference whether an individual effects a given exchange in a single step, as in direct barter, in two steps, using some intermediary commodity as a medium of exchange, or in several steps, as in some forms of arbitrage. As long as exchange is costless and, perhaps we should add explicitly, requires no lapse of time, no commodity has any advantage as a medium of exchange over any other.

But if there are costs associated with exchange, individuals will try to keep these costs as low as possible. If, as is usually the case, the direct exchange of something produced for something wanted is not possible, or involves very high costs of exchange, individuals will strive to make two or three exchanges do by the use of a suitable intermediary commodity. Such an intermediary commodity will usually be selected on the basis of its having a widespread demand and of its having become acceptable to a large number of individuals, among whom there would be a greater chance of finding one with a supply of the commodity sought. To keep the costs of exchange low, such an intermediary commodity will be sought among commodities that can be transferred with a minimum of expense and readily appraised as to quality and quantity, and that are either completely fungible or are available in units of convenient size. Indeed, any initial tendency for certain commodities to be preferred in this way as media of exchange tends to reinforce itself, since a good part of the acceptability of such a commodity as an intermediate in an exchange process will depend not only on the possibility that the recipient can use it himself but on the likelihood that the recipient can readily and without excessive cost trade it for what he himself wants. One can therefore expect that in any organized market there will emerge some few commodities (or types of transferable property rights) that serve as intermediaries in the exchange process almost to the complete exclusion of others.

In the end result this acceptability may become simply an institutional fact, divorced from the properties of the commodity as such that may have given it the initial edge over others as a medium of exchange. Widespread direct use of the intermediary commodity may become relatively unimportant in qualifying it for such use, as compared with ease of transfer, fungibility, and ease of identification.

Where ease of identification is the chief difficulty, exchange may be facilitated by some form of certification as to quantity and quality. The minting of full-valued coins is essentially such an operation. With such coinage, however, there is still the trouble involved in carrying any large amount of coin, the tedium of counting out large sums, the loss from abrasion, and a certain inevitable residual possibility of loss from false coinage.

The ease of transfer criterion can often be met, if a commodity does not otherwise satisfy this criterion, by substituting warehouse receipts for the commodity itself. Such receipts are less burdensome to carry, do not suffer loss in value from wear and tear, and may be even more difficult to falsify than coin. Warehouse receipts can be issued in convenient units, even if the underlying commodity is not itself either fungible or available in convenient units. Moreover, where the magnitude of the unit warrants it, warehouse receipts can be made transferable only by endorsement, minimizing the risk of loss or theft. Such a receipt would be similar to a traveler's check. In some circumstances, also, warehouse receipts can be made out for preassigned odd sums (as cashier's checks), thus avoiding the tedium of counting. Thus even when a commodity itself might not be suitable as a medium of exchange, either by reason of bulk, fragility, or difficulty of identification, a warehouse receipt for such a commodity might still become a satisfactory medium of exchange. Indeed, it has been suggested that warehouse receipts for common building brick would have made an excellent form of money.

Nevertheless, as long as the warehouse receipts used in exchange are required to represent actual stocks of physical commodities kept for delivery on demand, there will be a certain amount of productive capital tied up in these stocks, usually in an unproductive manner, at least insofar as their direct usefulness to a production process is concerned. In some exceptional cases, commodities can serve productive purposes without suffering impairment and still be deliverable on demand without too much expense. For example, during the war monetary silver was loaned to power stations and the like for use as bus bars in place of scarce copper. Cattle on the hoof may be considered deliverable on demand (warehouse certificates in this case might be in terms of pounds of live weight) while still serving a productive function. Seasonal stocks of commodities might in some cases serve a monetary purpose without requiring extra unproductive sequestration of resources. But these are limited and exceptional cases, and a commodity money has almost always required holding idle stocks out of productive use and thus reducing the aggregate real output of the economy.

Accordingly, if a medium of exchange can be created that does not require a corresponding stock of real commodities to be kept in idle storage, then in a very real sense the productive capital of the community will be increased and with it the aggregate output. Such a medium of exchange can be created in a number of ways. One of these is for the holder of a stock of a money commodity to issue promises to deliver the commodity on demand, in amounts in excess of the stock actually held, relying on the superior convenience of the notes as a medium of exchange to prevent any large proportion of them being turned in for redemption at any one time. This may be done either by private banks or by the state: in the one case we have bank notes, in the other a convertible paper currency with a partial reserve. Another method is for the state simply to issue a suitable number of certificates for use as a medium of exchange without any reference to any possibility of redemption in any given commodity at any fixed price. Still another is for agencies such as banks to accept deposits, the right to which may be transferred in any designated amount to third parties (i.e., by check). If the banks perform services in connection with such accounts, that makes their transfer an acceptable means of payment, and, more important, makes the transferees by and large willing to use these deposits in the same manner without drawing them out in currency, then only a small amount of currency need be kept to honor such occasional demands as do occur, and another increase in the effective means of payment arises.

The Predominance of Money Debt

GIVEN some commodity that has become the predominant medium of exchange, either directly or through instruments based on such a commodity, or even merely given some *ad hoc* instrument created to serve as a medium of exchange, any of which we can now call "money," a further likely development in any economic system, though perhaps not an absolutely necessary one, is that intertemporal exchange should in the bulk of cases take the form of money loans.

To a considerable extent this would be true only as a consequence of the presence of uncertainty in the system. In an economy of certainty it is difficult to indicate specific motivations that would bring this about: in the futures economy a right to the delivery of money at any one date should be as acceptable for any given purpose as a right to the delivery of money at any other date, and one would expect to find just as many contracts calling for the exchange of early money for a late commodity as for the exchange of an early delivery of a commodity for a later delivery of money. Indeed, if it were physically possible, one might even conceive of a tendency to make all purchases and sales of commodities for future delivery in terms of delivery of money at or near the planning date; the fact that any medium of exchange cannot circulate at more than a certain limited rate would tend to induce a spreading of money transfers more or less evenly through time, but this would still not account for a predominance of money loans as the means of intertemporal exchange.

What would happen in an economy of complete certainty is of course largely idle speculation. With uncertainty added to the existence of a cost of exchange in our economic model, we create a situation in which the borrower may not know precisely which commodity he will be able to supply in payment on the due date of the loan, and in which the lender may not be in a position to know what commodities he will be wanting to acquire on the due date, so that if anything other than money is specified as the means of repayment of a loan, extra and more expensive exchanges may be required either to provide the borrower with the means of meeting his obligation or the lender with the commodity he desires. Accordingly, except for special circumstances, money becomes the preferred commodity in which loans are expressed.

Once such a preference is established, it also tends to be auto-catalytic. Lenders may themselves have obligations coming due payable in money, so that their desire to have their loans paid in money rather than in anything else will be reinforced, since they will wish not only to avoid needless extra exchanges, but also to minimize the risk of a change in prices if the payment were to be made in kind. Or even if the lender definitely intends to use whatever he receives from the repayment of the loan in purchasing commodities rather than in turn repaying money obligations, the loan tends to be made in terms of money by reason of the risk to the borrower involved in the use of any other basis. For example, it has often been suggested that in order to provide real security to life insurance policy-holders, policy proceeds should be payable in terms of some given amount of purchasing power as indicated by an appropriate cost-of-living index, otherwise the policy-holder is subject to risk of loss through inflation. But insurance companies find it difficult to invest in ways that would provide a sure means of meeting such an obligation, so that money remains the predominant medium even here.

Actually, not all obligations to pay money in the future arise from loans in money. Many transactions are exchanges of present commodities for future money, as when goods are bought on the installment plan, or on credit.

Charge account or open-account purchases also involve a time element, though in most cases this is for convenience in payment rather than for the sake of the intertemporal transfer as such. Indeed, any purchase, even for cash, may be regarded as the setting up of a debt plus its immediate settlement. But the important fact is that intertemporal exchanges are predominantly of present goods or money for future money, and relatively rarely of present goods or money for future goods. Only in somewhat special cases are goods paid for in advance of delivery, as where the supplier is short of working capital, or where the supplier must commit himself in a way that would be costly if the purchaser were to cancel his order. Even here, the advance may be only a minor fraction of the full price.

This tendency to express debt in terms of money is reinforced by the ease with which such obligations may be specified in a clear and unequivocal way and the ease with which it can be determined whether the obligation has been met. With many commodities, the execution of a contract for future delivery or performance involves questions of quality and even of quantity that may be difficult or even impossible to specify completely; even with a satisfactory specification, the verification that the specifications have been met may be costly and may involve dispute between the parties. Thus one of the practical prerequisites for the establishment of a futures market in any given commodity is the establishment of standard grades and grading procedures, and also often of standard price differentials or allowances for variations in quality from the standard. With a money obligation there is usually little difficulty in determining to just what extent the stipulations of the contract have been met.

Liquidity in Terms of Money

HOWEVER arrived at, the prevalence in the economy of a predominantly large volume of obligations to pay money at various times in the future is a fact of far-reaching significance. The need of individuals for money to meet these obligations provides a new focus for liquidity, and a new pressure for the maintenance of liquidity. Liquidity comes to mean not merely the ability to change plans, or to adapt in a general way to unforeseen changes, but specifically the ability to provide money on short notice. Lack of liquidity in terms of money may mean not merely the missing of opportunities for adaptation to new circumstances, or for expansion in new directions, but the possibility of substantial loss in case difficulty is encountered in finding money to meet obligations, with the danger of bankruptcy through insolvency.

Another result of the predominance of money obligations is the crucial importance of the exchange ratios between money and other commodities, and of changes in the general price level. In a futures economy, gradual changes in the price level in terms of any given numéraire would, within limits, make no difference, provided only that the money rate of interest is substantially positive. The difference between one price trend and another would in effect be the same as the difference between the use of two different numéraires, and as long as the hoarding of money involves an adequate sacrifice in terms of interest yield forgone, the real trend of the economy should be substantially the same, the money rate of interest differing in the two situations sufficiently to offset the difference in the price trends. There is, to be sure, one minor difference between two such economies: where the money rate of interest is high, individuals will try harder to avoid the loss of interest from the keeping of unnecessarily high cash balances on hand, and relatively more real resources will be used in maintaining the velocity of circulation at a high level. But for the present we may ignore this minor difference.

In an economy with uncertainty, however, changes in the price level may occur that are unanticipated and even fairly sudden. In such a case the real burden represented by an obligation to pay a given sum of money may turn out to be considerably different from that anticipated at the time the obligation was entered into. Moreover, this may turn out to be the case on a large scale, and not merely because of some circumstance peculiar to a given individual or industry; the effects of such surprises may thus become fairly general. Accordingly, it behooves us to examine more particularly the factors that affect the value of money, or its reciprocal, the general price level.

The Value of a Commodity Money

THE VALUE of a strict commodity money (such as, for example, gold, whether used directly as specie or through warehouse receipts) might be expected to be fixed by the relation between the supply and the demand for consumptive use. Indeed, if the money were simply a numéraire and not also a medium of exchange, this would be the case. The use of a commodity as a medium of exchange, however, nearly always requires the keeping out of production and consumption channels a certain stock of the commodity to serve as the necessary cash balances held by individuals and firms, and thus the value of the money commodity tends to be somewhat higher (and the general price level, in terms of this numéraire, somewhat lower) than if the commodity is merely a numéraire. However, if the monetary use is a small part of the total, and particularly if the demand for consumption and the supply from production are fairly elastic, the price of the money commodity may remain fairly close to the level that would have obtained in the absence of its use as money. Moreover, if the demand (or supply) is fairly elastic, fluctuations in supply (or demand) or in the monetary use will result in relatively small changes in general price levels.

However, if the monetary demand becomes relatively large, and the consumption demand and the supply from production are fairly inelastic, then substantial fluctuations in the price of the money commodity (in terms of other commodities in general) are likely, with far-reaching consequences. Indeed, if the monetary demand for the commodity is large relative to the consumption and production flows, the tail begins to wag the dog and production and consumption of the monetary commodity may be more affected by the way it is used for monetary purposes than vice versa. Thus the concentration on gold as the monetary commodity in the latter part of the nineteenth century, for example, gradually led to a position where the nonmonetary supply and demand for gold no longer had any marked stabilizing effect on the general price level. On the other hand, in earlier periods the general concentration on gold and silver as money commodities made the economic structure rather vulnerable to shocks from the introduction of supplies from newly discovered sources, especially America.

Proposals have been made from time to time to establish a commodity basis for money in a manner that would diminish the susceptibility of the price level to erratic fluctuations such as were experienced under the gold standard. The movement for "bimetallism," or the free coinage of silver, can thus be considered in part a reasonable program for "broadening the base of the currency" although at the time it was primarily thought of as one of the few methods then respectable for bringing about an increase in the price level. In any case, an effective broadening of the base would require that the ratio legally adopted be agreed to internationally, and that it be not too far from the natural equilibrium ratio of exchange between the two metals, otherwise Gresham's law would operate to drive one or the other of the metals from effective use as money, leaving the effective base perhaps no broader than originally. Had bimetallism been adopted at any of the ratios popularly advocated, the ultimate result might well have been a shift to a silver standard as supplies of silver increased relative to gold, which shift might or might not have resulted in a complete displacement of gold. In any case, the cost of photography would have gone up. A proposal that would have had a better chance to promote stability was that of "symmetallism," in which the monetary standard would have been a combination of gold and silver in stated proportions, not necessarily minted, but held as a monetary reserve. Such a standard would have insured that the monetary stocks would have been a smaller proportion of the total than would be the case for either a gold or a silver standard.

Of the single commodities that might be used as a base for a representative currency, it has been suggested that common building bricks would be one of the best, by reason of the wide distribution of the necessary raw materials and the very elastic supply. One difficulty with such a base would be that the moderately high cost of transporting the commodity would mean that regional differences might arise that would cause some awkwardness. Suggestions have also been made, somewhat more seriously, that the currency should be based on some composite basket of goods representing as wide a variety and as substantial a proportion of the total volume of goods traded as possible. If such a "commodity dollar" could be adopted with full backing of each dollar with corresponding stocks of commodities, it is likely that a reasonably stable price level would result. Anyone presenting the treasury with warehouse receipts corresponding to the stipulated basket of goods would be entitled to a fixed number of dollars in exchange, and anyone presenting, say, $10,000 to the treasury would be entitled to obtain in exchange a package of orders on various warehouses for the delivery of the various commodities making up the basket, which could then be sold by him separately. The relative prices of the various commodities within the package might fluctuate, but their average would be held constant, since any substantial deviation would permit a profit to be made by making up a package and getting dollars for it at the treasury, or buying a package from the treasury and disposing of it in the various markets. To the extent that the commodities in the package have close substitutes, their prices will in turn be kept fairly steady, and thus the stabilizing influence of the monetary basket might permeate the economy.

Of course, the carrying out of such a program on the basis of 100 per cent backing for the currency in circulation would require the holding of a corresponding amount of the basket commodities in stocks, which of course would involve a cost of storage. The commodities in the basket will therefore have to be chosen in such a way as to keep the cost of storage and handling down to reasonable levels, to minimize the dangers of deterioration or obsolescence, and obviate difficulties arising from variations in quality. These requirements might interfere with getting as representative a bunch of commodities as might be desired. And in any case there will be the loss represented by the tying up of this amount of real capital in essentially unproductive stocks.

Some of this loss may be avoided by maintaining only a partial reserve, in which case the system would be automatic only up to a point, and supplementary means might be needed to keep the system operating. That is, something other than the automatic "coinage" of commodities or "redemption" of the currency on demand is needed to ensure that demands for redemption do not exceed the reserves, and the manner in which this other means is operated would become increasingly crucial as the ratio of reserve stocks to currency in circulation is diminished. This will become clearer as we examine the extreme case where there are no reserves at all and the currency in circulation owes its value to something other than a convertibility into commodities at a legally established rate.

Fiat Money

ONCE WE depart from a full-bodied commodity money, either in the form of specie or in the form of "representative money," i.e., warehouse receipts with 100 per cent backing, the simplest case to consider is the other extreme of a pure fiat paper currency. A convertible paper currency with partial reserves represents an intermediate stage with elements of both extremes.

Fiat money owes its value, in the last analysis, to its acceptability in trade. This acceptability may in turn be due to any of a number of factors. In some cases, fiat money is made legal tender: creditors are required by law to accept it at face value in payment of debts or other obligations. At the time of original transition to a fiat currency, outstanding obligations may have been entered into on the basis of a commodity currency, or at least of a convertible currency: making the fiat currency legal tender is in effect a modification of the terms of such contracts. In terms of the United States Constitution, however, the Supreme Court in deciding the gold clause cases in 1935 in effect ruled that the power of Congress to regulate the value of the currency was paramount over the clause prohibiting legislation impairing the obligations of contracts.

Making a fiat currency legal tender may serve to establish a certain continuity between the value for certain purposes of the fiat currency and the value of the currency that preceded it. Over a longer run, and in the absence of specific price controls, there is nothing to compel new contracts to be entered into on terms that would reflect any particular value attached to the fiat currency. Willingness to accept such currency in current sales of goods, and especially to enter into more or less long-term loan contracts in terms of such a fiat currency must rest to some extent on confidence that its value will be maintained, although for many individuals not able to invest directly in physical goods or equities, even a substantial prospect of a reduction in the value of the currency may be insufficient to deter from the making of loans. Moreover, to the extent that there is a general expectation that the value of the currency will decline, this may be offset by increase in the rate of interest.

Another means sometimes adopted to secure acceptability is to provide for the acceptance of fiat money in the payment of taxes and other public dues. This, however, is neither necessary nor sufficient: a fiat money can circulate even when the issuing government is so inconsistent as to require duties and other payments to be made in some other form, while an excessive issue of fiat currency can result in hyper-inflation and a flight from the currency even when the fiat currency is accepted in payment by the government.

Actually, the acceptability of a fiat currency is likely to be fairly independent of the legal attributes of the currency, and to depend much more immediately upon the degree of risk and inconvenience involved in its use as compared with other media that are available. Indeed, acceptability, once established, seems very likely to perpetuate itself, at least for current and short-term transactions, as long as the fiat money is available in reasonable quantities and denominations, does not depreciate too rapidly in value, and is not subject to too active competition from other currencies. A mere casual patriotism, or familiarity, or force of habit may be sufficient to prevent a shift to other currencies, even in the absence of legal sanctions, provided that the immediate incentive for such a shift is not too great.

The Quantity Theory

BUT IF we have a currency divorced from any real commodity, in the long run, what can be said to determine its value or, inversely, the price level? The classical answer to this is the quantity theory of money, which in its conventional form is expressed by the relationship: $MV = PT$. In this equation, M represents the quantity of money issued or in circulation, V is the average number of times money changes hands during a given period, P is the price level, and T is the real volume of commodities traded during the given period. In measuring V, it is tacitly agreed that mere change-making is to be left out of account.

As it stands, this equation is a mere tautology, as can be seen better, perhaps, if we write it in the form $V = PT/M$. The three quantities on the right-hand side of this equation can be observed, while V cannot be. That is, we can go out and construct a price index, and either construct a "volume-of-trade" index or estimate the total money transactions PT directly; likewise the amount of money in circulation can be estimated. But the velocity of circulation cannot itself be observed or estimated directly, but must be computed by dividing PT by M. In effect, then, the equation $MV = PT$ is merely a definition of V.

But there is a substance to the quantity theory of money, and that is the implicit postulate that the velocity of circulation so defined is relatively constant. That is, V is supposed to depend entirely on the institutional arrangements, the habits of individuals, and the organization of production, and not on the price level, the volume of trade, or other parameters of the economic system that might undergo relatively rapid change from one period to the next. Accordingly, any change in the quantity of money tends to result in a similar change in the total volume of money transactions PT. If the quantity of money increases, and resources are fully employed so that no further increase can take place in T (at least not without creating additional stages of production or adding to the eddies of financial transactions outside the main flow of production), then the price level must rise. On the other hand, if the quantity of money decreases, then either prices must fall or the physical volume of trade must decrease. If the volume of trade decreases without a corresponding shift in the structure of production some resources will be left idle, which will usually involve unemployment of labor. In a competitive market the presence of idle resources would tend to drive their prices down, which with a constant money supply and velocity of circulation would produce an increase in the physical volume of production, and this process would continue until resources were fully employed. In the long run, then, the quantity theory of money implies that the price level tends to vary directly with the quantity of money, and that if the quantity of money is kept reasonably stable, full employment will result through a reduction of the price level. The persistence of unemployment has been ascribed by adherents of the quantity theory to the perverse behavior of the monetary and banking system in generally contracting the supply of money at times of business recession, thus preventing the decline in prices from having the desired effect.

Later theories of the determination of the value of money have arisen from dissatisfaction with the proposition that the velocity of money can be considered a constant. Possibilities for variation in the velocity of circulation have appeared too important, particularly in short-run considerations, to be left out of account. Of the many factors that of course influence the velocity of circulation to a greater or lesser extent, two—namely, the interest rate and the level of income—have generally been selected as significant within the framework of the theory. Most of the others are felt to be either insignificant in effect or to be determined by forces outside of the economic equilibrium process so that the changes they produce can be considered as shocks to the system rather than as elements in the equilibrating process. The importance of income as a factor affecting the velocity of circulation is immediately apparent when we consider that an increase in income requires a greater use of money to provide for its flow around the circuit; the loss of interest can be regarded as the price or opportunity cost of holding wealth in the form of cash rather than in the form of interest-earning assets.

While the quantity theory of money in its original formulation dealt with a "transactions velocity" of money—i.e., the number of times money changes hands, on the average, in a given period—for most purposes it has proven convenient to use instead the "income velocity," which is the number of times money is used in the payment of income during a given period. With a given structure of industry and a given proportion of "eddy" payments such as are involved in the trading of one capital asset for another, the average number of transactions in going the circuit from wage earner to retailer to wholesaler to manufactuer to wage earner (and other similar shorter or longer circuits) will be fairly constant so that the variations in income or circuit velocity will parallel fairly closely the variations in transactions velocity. Thus in a given state of organization of production, the transactions velocity might be fairly uniformly, say, five times the income velocity, so that if the transactions velocity averages, say, 20 transactions per year, the income velocity may average four payments of income per year. If we represent by Y the national income (which for the present we may define simply as the aggregate of the incomes of individuals, leaving a more precise definition for later), and by M the stock of money (assumed for the present to consist entirely of currency), than the circuit velocity of money F (for *F*requency) will be defined simply as the ratio $F = Y/M$. If, for example, the national income is $200 billion per year, and the stock of money is $50 billion, then the circuit velocity is four times per year. For some purposes, however, it is convenient to look at the reciprocal of the circuit velocity, or the circuit period $k = 1/F = M/Y$. Thus if the circuit velocity is four times a year, the circuit period will be 13 weeks, which means, in effect, that the stocks of money held by individuals and by firms with whom they do business, directly or indirectly, amount to 13 weeks' income, on the average.

The Demand for Cash Balances

IF WE CONSIDER now the effect of the interest rate i and the level of income Y on the amount of money that individuals and firms wish to keep on hand, we can write in general that $M = f(Y, i)$; i.e., that there is some relationship such that given Y and i, the desired quantity of money (i.e., the demand for cash balances) can be determined. This does not mean that the total quantity of money in the system is determined by these variables: the supply of money, we shall assume for the present, is determined absolutely by the decision of the government as to how much currency will be printed and issued. Actual money holdings, then, will always have to conform to this total supply. However, if this aggregate supply does not equal the demand for cash balances, some individuals or firms will find themselves with more or less money on hand than they would wish to hold in view of the rate of interest they can obtain from investments and the current income or volume of business. If their balances are too high, they will attempt to adjust them, possibly by increasing their rate of consumption or purchases of raw materials, but more likely by buying interest-bearing securities or perhaps by investing in earning assets directly. Similarly, if balances are too low, they may attempt to replenish their supply of cash by curtailing purchases, by delaying payments, or by selling assets.

However, while any one individual may thus increase or reduce his cash balances, he can do this only by reducing or increasing someone else's cash balances, as long as the total supply of money remains fixed. If such operations are to restore equilibrium, therefore, it will not be restored by changing the money supply, but rather by changing the demand for money by influencing Y or i or both. And indeed attempts to reduce cash balances operate either to increase security prices, thus lowering interest rates, or to increase the rate of flow of income payments, in either case bringing about an increase in the demand for cash balances, and if this process is continued until the demand has risen sufficiently to absorb the entire fixed supply, equilibrium will be achieved. Conversely, attempts to increase cash balances tend to check the flow of income payments or to drive interest rates up, thus reducing the demand for cash balances until the demand can be satisfied with the existing stock of money.

Variations in income and interest rates thus play a crucial role in bringing the demand and supply of cash balances into equilibrium. If we examine more closely the roles of income and interest in determining the demand for cash balances, we can immediately make an important simplification if we assume that the demand for money will be directly proportional to income. This assumption seems justified in particular if the increase in Y represents merely an increase in the price level with no change in real income: if a correspondingly larger amount of money is available, the same transactions, measured in real terms, can take place as before, and the real value of cash balances is the same. For a change in real income, the case is not quite so clear, but in general it seems likely that this assumption will not be too far from reality. Doubling the volume of transactions will double the minimum amount of money needed to perform them without running into an absolute shortage of cash, and an increase in income will be likely to produce a roughly corresponding increase in the amount of money held to meet contingencies. To some extent, if we regard the holding of larger-than-necessary cash balances as a luxury, perhaps an increase in real income would produce a larger-than-proportional increase in the demand for money; however, since a large proportion of cash balances is held by firms where this luxury aspect of the matter would be of less importance, the proportionality assumption still seems warranted, at least as a rough first approximation. Thus instead of the general form $M = f(Y, i)$, we write $M = Y \cdot L(i)$, where now $L(i)$ is some function of the interest rate alone. $L(i)$ is often termed the "liquidity-preference" function.

The Structure of Interest Rates

BEFORE examining the relation between interest and the demand for cash balances as reflected in the liquidity-preference function, it is necessary to examine more particularly the structure of interest rates in order to be able to specify more clearly which of the many interest rates will be the most appropriate one to consider as the independent variable in the liquidity-preference function. Rates of interest will, of course, differ as between borrowers by reason of their credit standing and the amount of risk involved in the loan, and according to the amount of the loan and the costs of servicing it. But these factors are not the important ones here: we will consider primarily loans on gilt-edged security, made under favorable cost conditions in substantial amounts. The important aspect of interest rates for monetary theory is the variation in the rate according to the duration of the loan.

Long-term bonds and many other credit instruments customarily provide for periodic payments of interest plus the repayment of a lump sum at the end of the term, or in some instances they may provide for the repayment by a series of constant periodic payments made up in varying amounts of interest and amortization. However, it will considerably simplify the argument if we talk solely in terms of contracts providing for only a single payment at the end of varying periods of time, such as, for example, the Series *E* ten-year savings bonds. Interest-bearing bonds may then be thought of as merely a bundle of such single-payment contracts, one for the principal, and one for each of the series of interest payments.

In an economy of certainty, we were able to show, on page 9, that long-term interest rates could always be thought of as merely a compounding of the short-term interest rates for the successive periods within the long term. Indeed, one could think of the short-term rate as being *the* rate of interest in effect at a given time, longer-term rates being a sort of average of the short-term rates. However, as we shall see, this turns out to be rather an oversimplification when the certainty assumptions are abandoned. In an economy of uncertainty, the price of a given bond at a future date short of its maturity is uncertain even though there may be no doubt whatever about its payment at maturity. This is because future short-term interest rates are not known in advance, and the discount to be applied in computing the present value of such a bond may turn out to be somewhat different than that which is anticipated at the time the bond is originally bought. Thus even though there is no risk of default and the bondholder knows exactly what he will get if he holds the bond to maturity, nevertheless, if he finds himself in need of funds at some time short of maturity, there is a possibility that he will be able to sell his bond only at a sacrifice, as compared to what he might have gotten from a shorter-term bond, if the rates at which his bond is then discounted prove to be higher than originally anticipated.

Thus suppose an individual in 1960 plans to need an additional $1,000 in cash in 1980, and suppose further that 1980 bonds are priced at 50 per cent of maturity value, 1970 bonds are priced at 70 per cent, and that he expects that in 1970, 1980 bonds will be priced at 75 per cent. If he is certain not to need funds before 1980, or if he is confident that the price of 1980 bonds in 1970 will not fall much below 75 per cent, he will naturally purchase 1980 bonds with a maturity value of $1,000, paying $500, rather than purchasing $750 maturity value of 1970 bonds for $525, which is what he would have to do if he wanted to be in a position to buy $1,000 of 1980 bonds in 1970 at the expected price of 75 per cent.

But if such an individual is not certain of the price of 1980 bonds in 1970, and considers that he may find himself in need of cash in 1970, then he may, for the sake of liquidity, choose to buy the 1970 bonds, even though this means that his $1,000 in 1980 will cost him $25 more in 1960. If he does this, then no matter what happens to interest rates, he is sure of having available $750 in cash in 1970 if he should need it, and he will be able to secure not less than $750 for 1980, even if the interest rate were to fall to zero for the period 1970–1980; there will be a corresponding possibility that he could secure substantially more than $1,000 for 1980 if it turns out that interest rates for this second decade are higher than anticipated, so that he may be able in 1970 to buy 1980 bonds for 40, 50, or 60 per cent, instead of the 75 per cent that he anticipates in 1960.

If, on the other hand, he buys the 1980 bond, then he is certain of $1,000, no more and no less, for 1980, but if he finds himself in need of funds in 1970, he may be in trouble. The best that can happen is that interest rates drop to zero for the 1970–1980 decade and that therefore his bond will sell for $1,000 in 1970. But this is the extreme limit, and the amount of gain over his expectation of $750 is not likely to be anywhere near this large. If the interest rate drops from the 2.9 per cent per year (corresponding to the price of 75 per cent of maturity value) to 2.0 per cent, which is about the maximum drop that is likely to be considered as having a material probability, the price will rise to only 82 per cent. But if the interest rates for the second decade were to rise to 6 per cent, which might not be at all out of the question, the price would fall to 56; even more drastic drops in value are possible, wholly aside from risk of default, if longer-term bonds or higher rates of interest are considered.

Accordingly, an individual may consider that the security against loss in case assets must be liquidated before maturity is worth the extra $25 that he estimates will be needed to provide for the same $1,000 in 1980 through purchasing ten-year bonds in succession as compared with purchasing a 20-year bond. Because of this tendency on the part of investors, the interest rate on long-term bonds will generally be higher than the average of the expected short-term rates over the same period, and it is not a matter of indifference what interest rate we select as the relevant one for the analysis of liquidity preference.

In effect, the range of possible values for a long-term bond in the period immediately after purchase is much wider than for a short-term bond, so that as an asset a long-term bond is less liquid, i.e., is less secure as a source of cash, than a short-term bond. In general, as a result of this, long-term interest rates tend to be higher than short-term interest rates, the differential being a price paid for the advantages of superior liquidity of the short-term bond. Of course, it is still possible for the short-term interest rate at a given time to be higher than the interest rate for a long period beginning at that time: this will ordinarily reflect an expectation that short-term interest rates for later periods will be lower than the current short-term rate. While in such cases the long-term rate is lower than the current short-term rate, it will still be higher than the average of the current short-term rate and the short-term rates that are currently expected to prevail in the later of the periods covered by the long-term loan. Thus a person investing in a long-term bond normally expects to get a higher return over the entire period than if he were to invest in successive short-term issues. To be sure, he may, in the actual event, secure a larger return by investing in successive short-term issues, but this would be only if the later short-term rates turned out to be higher than originally anticipated.

However, it is important to note that this differential between long-term interest rates and expected short-term rates does not in all cases reflect a liquidity preference in the pure sense of a desire to retain the ability to change plans, but may reflect merely "risk aversion." For example, we may consider an individual or firm that is sure of needing liquid funds five years hence, but is fairly certain of not needing them any sooner. Such a firm might consider purchasing a five-year bond that would give a yield of 3 per cent, or alternatively a 20-year bond that could be sold after five years, the yield depending upon the price for which it is sold, which in turn might vary according to the then prevailing rates of interest. The firm might decide in favor of the five-year bond, even though it could expect that on the average or in some modal sense the 20-year bond could be expected to yield 4 per cent; the possibility exists that the price for this bond would turn out to be higher or lower than expected, resulting in a larger or smaller return than 4 per cent or even perhaps in a net loss. "Risk aversion," or perhaps better "certainty preference," may well be sufficient to overcome the 1 per cent differential in expected yield. This motivation can be distinguished from that of "liquidity preference" in the more restricted sense of the term, in that liquidity preference proper would involve the desire to allow for possible changes of plan as to the time of conversion into money. Indeed, if risk aversion were generally absent, firms of this type would bid up short-term interest rates relative to long until the expected differential vanished. Other firms could then satisfy their desire for liquidity, i.e., flexibility of action, at no cost. The differential between long- and short-term interest rates thus requires both liquidity preference and risk aversion to sustain it.

The reverse case, where a firm certain not to need money for a long time nevertheless considers buying short-term securities rather than long, would not normally arise, for the return on the short-term securities being less and the yield for the full-term less certain than if a long-term bond is bought, there would seem to be no reason in any case for buying short-term securities, unless indeed the individual has a propensity to gamble, or "risk preference" so that he is willing to take a lower expected yield for the privilege of being uncertain.

If because of the liquidity preference of lenders, short-term interest rates thus tend to be generally lower than long-term rates, one may inquire why it is that borrowers do not do all of their borrowing on a short-term basis so as to take advantage of these lower interest rates. To some extent, indeed, they do. But there are many deterrent factors. To some extent the costs incurred in the constant renewal of short-term loans may cancel the advantages of the lower interest rates, especially where the loans are relatively small in amount, though sometimes arrangements may be made to have the renewal take place more or less automatically in the absence of positive action by one party or the other to a loan: this is in effect what happens with "call" loans. But more fundamentally the short-term debt that represents improved liquidity to the lender represents a corresponding drain on the liquidity of the borrower. Unless the borrower's credit is extremely strong, there is always the danger that the due date of a short-term loan may find him without the cash with which to meet the obligation and without credit resources adequate to renew the obligation on favorable terms. Indeed in most instances there will from the beginning be a limit to the amounts that a given individual or firm can borrow at favorable rates on a short-term basis, by reason of his general credit standing and the nature of the assets that the borrower possesses or proposes to acquire with the proceeds of the loan. There are thus limiting imperfections in the loan market that keep the demand for borrowed funds—i.e., the supply of securities—from being shifted entirely into short-term forms or from shifting in that direction sufficiently to equalize short- and long-term interest rates. The one borrower that could thus saturate the short-term loan market—namely, the government—has in most cases refrained from doing so. This behavior is usually rationalized on somewhat vaguely conceived grounds of public policy, but it can also be regarded as a consequence of monopsonistic discrimination in that the government is normally a much larger part of the short-run market than of the long-term market.

With uncertainty giving occasion for liquidity preference and risk aversion to operate, we thus produce a complex of interest rates in which the long-term rate differs from the current short-term rate not only by reason of possible expected trends in future short-term rates but also because of liquidity preference. If we consider a stable situation where the complex of interest rates is not expected to change much through time, so that the current short-term rate can be taken as representative of future short-term rates, then we can expect a simplified structure of interest rates to obtain in which there will be a more or less smooth graduation from low short-term rates to higher long-term rates. The shortest rate is clearly the rate on demand or "call" loans. On the other hand, there is in principle no specific limit to the length of a loan, so that there is no one type of loan that can be selected on principle as representing either an extreme or a representative long-term rate. To be sure, loans have been issued in the form of perpetual annuities, with no provision for repayment of principal, as was the case with the English "consols," but even this is not the longest term possible, since it would still be possible to have a security calling for a repayment in the form of a deferred perpetual annuity, with payments to begin only after an interval of ten, 20, or any given number of years. However, rates of interest on safe securities do not seem to show much further increase for terms longer than 20 years (with interest payable annually, in this case). It will not be too drastic a simplification, therefore, if we take the rate on 20-year securities, or thereabouts, or perhaps the rate on consols, if such securities exist in substantial amounts, as representing *the* long-term interest rate. The rate on call loans could perhaps be taken as representing, in principle, the shortest term possible, but in using the call-loan rate as the representative short-term rate, care should be taken to allow for the institutional restrictions that from time to time have surrounded this rate. Indeed, at some times the call-loan rate has been of so little importance in terms of the number of transactions based on it that for many purposes it may be better to take rates on 60- or 90-day loans as representing short-term rates.

The Relevance of Various Interest Rates

IN PRINCIPLE, if we are to study the effect of interest rates on the demand for cash balances, we should examine each element in the whole complex of interest rates. However, if the analysis is to be kept simple, we will want to stick to a single parameter and select some particular type of interest rate, or perhaps some composite or average of interest rates as representative of the effects of the entire complex. We must take care in making such a simplification, lest we lose track of important elements of the situation.

If we could assume that all holders of cash balances had ready access to all parts of the capital market, we would probably want to consider a short-term rate (either the call-loan rate or the 60- or 90-day rate) as the most relevant one. Short-term securities or notes are in effect the closest substitute for cash, in that a shift from cash to such securities involves a minimum of change in the economic position of the individual or firm, beyond the essential change that we are concerned with in the stock of means of payment kept on hand. Use of the short-term rate also recommends itself on grounds of convenience and definiteness, since a long-term rate as quoted at any particular time is a yield to maturity, and need not represent what the expected return is where such a security is to be held for a year or so and then sold. The long-term rate of itself thus fails to reflect at any particular time the strength of the considerations that might induce a person to shift for a short while from cash to long-term securities.

However, many holders of cash balances do not have access to the short-term money market in a way that would make such rates of interest effective in influencing their demand for cash. For small borrowers, the costs of borrowing may well be such as to raise the effective interest rate for them to levels close to or even above long-term interest rates, and such persons in deciding upon the appropriate level of cash balances that they would like to maintain may be more likely to think in terms of cash vs. long-term bonds, expansion of plant, increase in inventory, savings-bank rates, rates for insurance-policy loans, and rates on mortgages, especially where the mortgages may have provision for accelerated repayment. For such individuals, long-term interest rates may come closer to representing the rates that are actually effective in influencing cash holdings. Another reason for possibly considering the long-term rate of interest as the independent variable in the liquidity function is that in setting up a general equilibrium model, it will be to a considerable extent long-term rates of interest that are most important in influencing savings and investment, and a simpler model will result if we can manage to use one rather than two or more rates of interest.

However, if we consider that the relation between the long- and the short-term rates tends to be determined by the preferences of borrowers and lenders for the two types of loans, and that these preferences are likely to remain relatively stable, it is possible to assume without too much danger of going far wrong that there is a fairly stable functional relationship between short-term rates of interest and the expected yields from investment in long-term securities over corresponding periods. If this can be justified, then we can expect to get reasonably good results regardless of which particular interest rate we choose as having the dominant effect on the demand for cash balances.

The Shape of the Liquidity-Preference Function

THE LIQUIDITY-PREFERENCE function is nothing more than a relation between the income period k and the interest rate, since we can put $L(i) = M/Y = k$. This function is supposed to have the general shape shown in FIGURE 10. This diagram shows the demand for cash balances in a manner somewhat similar to the demand for any other capital asset in terms of its rental: here the interest rate serves as the rental paid for the privilege of holding cash balances. For moderately high rates of interest, possibly from 6 per cent to 20 per cent, the cost of holding cash balances is sufficiently high so that these balances are on the whole kept fairly close to the minimum level necessary to carry on business. At very high rates of interest, it is possible that some moderately costly steps might be taken to economize on cash balances, such as special arrangements for the timing of payments, use of more expeditious methods of communication and of transfer of funds, and the like, but on the whole these are not likely to be very effective, and over this range it is generally thought that the demand for cash balances is inelastic.

At somewhat lower rates of interest, the demand for cash balances is thought to expand somewhat and have a substantial elasticity as shown in the diagram for rates of interest between, say, 2 per cent and 6 per cent. But for very low rates of interest, ordinarily thought to be in the neighborhood of 2 per cent for long-term rates and 0.5 per cent for short-term rates, the demand for cash balances becomes extremely elastic; in effect, it is thought that no expansion of the supply of money can in itself drive the long-term interest rate much below 2 per cent, or the short-term rate much below 0.5 per cent. This assumption concerning the liquidity-preference curve is sometimes expressed by saying that for these low rates of interest "liquidity preference becomes absolute."

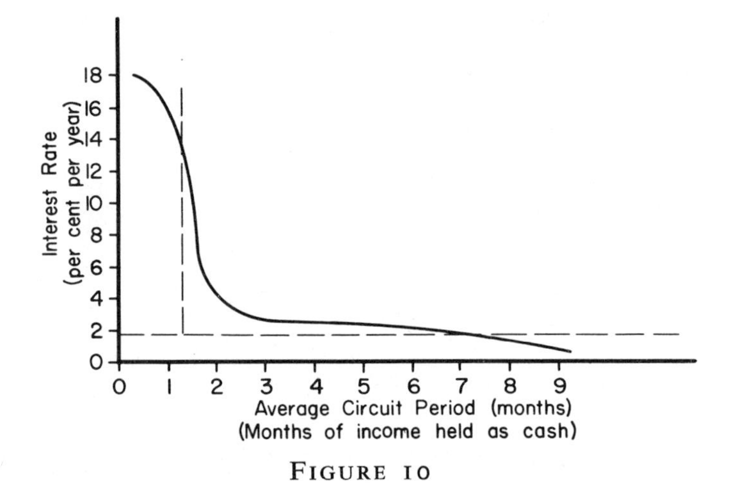

FIGURE 10

While there is little but speculation to go on, and perhaps the extreme situations involved cannot properly be represented on a diagram such as this, it seems possible that for extremely high rates of interest there may be a tendency to abandon the given type of money as a medium of exchange. Instead of a non-interest-bearing medium, interest-bearing securities may be used as a medium of exchange, the interest rate being high enough to make it worthwhile to compute the accrued interest up to the time of each transaction, at least in approximate fashion and for the larger denominations of such an interest-bearing currency. Indeed, there appear to have been periods when bills of exchange and acceptances circulated in payment of obligations to a considerable extent, reducing the need for money by a corresponding amount. Or if the high rate of interest is due to a general upward trend of the price level in terms of the given type of money, some other commodity may be used as a means of exchange in terms of which prices are not rising so rapidly. Or foreign currency of more stable value may come to usurp the native currency, unless its use is prohibited in some way. However, this is of importance only in analyzing very unusual situations, and for present purposes this upper section of the liquidity-preference curve will be ignored.

The Inventory Theory of Cash Balances

SOME ANALYTIC basis for the liquidity-preference curve may be obtained by examining a model in which cash balances are treated as an inventory to be managed so as to minimize over-all costs. These costs may be considered to be made up of the loss of interest on the cash balances held, plus the cost of whatever transactions are engaged in for the purpose of keeping these balances at a low level.

For the sake of simplicity, let us suppose that each firm or individual has an "entrepreneurial program" of sales and purchases, which is determined by productivity and utility considerations, and that this program is only slightly, if at all, affected by changes in the rate of interest. The net resultant of these activities can be represented by an entrepreneurial balance, which will vary over time, and represents the cash balance that he would have (which may be negative) if he made no other transactions. Because his actual cash balance can never be negative, and in order to keep it from becoming too large in the positive direction, "financial transactions" outside of the entrepreneurial program will be undertaken, consisting of exchanges of cash for interest-bearing assets. If financial transactions were costless, and interest were paid on loans for no matter how short a period, it would pay to keep the entire entrepreneurial balance invested at all times (or never to borrow more than the exact amount of any negative entrepreneurial balance), thus keeping cash balances at zero.

Financial transactions, of course, do involve some expense of time and effort, if nothing else, and this expense has some minimum value no matter how small the size of the transaction. If for simplicity we assume the cost per transaction to be independent of the size of the transaction, and that the time pattern of entrepreneurial balances consists of fairly extended periods of more or less steady growth alternating with periods of decline, then the average cash balance that results from the attempt to minimize total costs will be inversely proportional to the square root of the rate of interest.

This can be shown as follows: Assume that the entrepreneurial balance grows or declines over some moderately long period at a steady rate A; let q be the interval between financial transactions, each such transaction being such as to bring the cash balance to zero just before or just after the transaction. The size of each transaction will then be Aq, and the average cash balance will be $Aq/2$. The loss of interest will be $iAq/2$, and the number of transactions per period will be $1/q$, and their cost C/q, C being the cost per transaction. The total cost will be $T = iAq/2 + C/q$, and if we determine q

in such a way as to minimize T, we have $dT/dq = iA/2 - C/q^2 = 0$, and solving for the average cash balance, $Aq/2 = (CA/2i)^{1/2}$. The computation is identical to that sometimes used in computing the optimum management of inventories, and this analysis can, accordingly, be termed the "inventory theory of liquidity preference."

Equilibrating Mechanisms

BUT WHATEVER the precise shape attributed to the liquidity-preference curve, we have in effect here a demand curve for cash balances, for any given level of income, as a function of the cost of holding these cash balances, which is the money rate of interest. If we compare this demand curve with the supply of money, which we can for the time being consider to be absolutely fixed by government fiat, we can determine the interest rate that will bring demand and supply into agreement, thus producing equilibrium. In addition, we can describe a process by which this equilibrium, if disturbed, will be restored. For if individuals find themselves with smaller cash balances than they wish to hold at current interest rates, they will attempt to increase these balances. The easiest way of doing this is to sell securities, keeping total assets constant; a general pressure toward selling securities or other assets will drive their prices down and push interest rates up, thus reducing the effective demand for cash balances until it is equal to the money supply. Similarly, possession of excess cash balances will lead to a desire to purchase securities to restore the balance, which will drive security prices up and interest rates down, until at the lower interest rates individuals find they are willing to hold amounts of money that in the aggregate equal the amount of money that actually exists. Demand and supply for cash balances thus determine the rate of interest paid on loans, in exactly the same way that the demand and supply for housing determines rents.

We thus have two conflicting views concerning the way in which the impact of a change in the supply of money will affect the functioning of the economy. The quantity theory of money in its more rigid form maintains that with a constant velocity of circulation, changes in the money supply will change the money volume of transactions and money income flows; changes in money flows may initially take the form either of changes in prices or changes in real output and employment, but in the long run prices will tend to fall as long as any factors of production are unemployed until a price level is reached at which the given money income represents sufficiently large real income to imply the full employment of productive factors. Of course, this process may take a long time to work itself out, and in the meantime changes may take place in the volume of money or in other underlying conditions such as to produce new disturbances.

According to the liquidity-preference theory, on the other hand, the initial impact of a change in the quantity of money is on the rate of interest. While there may be some effect on the flow of income, through individuals attempting to adjust their cash balances by changing outlays on commodities, either for consumption or for use as productive assets, such adjustments are generally considered to be less prompt and less prominent than the adjustment through financial transactions, and it is generally considered that the interest-rate structure will change more rapidly in response to monetary changes than will the national income, unless the interest-rate structure is held rigid by some institutional restraints. One point at which such institutional restraints may be considered to arise is where the supply of money is already so large as to have driven interest rates down to the point where liquidity preference is "absolute" and the demand for money has become perfectly elastic. Here changes in the money supply affect neither interest rates nor the national income, but merely cause corresponding inverse variations in the velocity of circulation.

The liquidity-preference theory thus pretends to be a theory of the determination of interest rates, at least in the short run, and as such runs into possible conflict with the classical theory of interest rates in which interest rates are determined by the interaction of the supply schedule of savings and the demand schedule for investment, which are in turn explained in terms of the marginal productivity of capital and marginal time preference. One way out of this dilemma, which is often taken by adherents of the liquidity-preference theory in its more rigid forms, is to assert that savings or investment or both do not respond readily to changes in interest rates and that therefore the supply of savings and demand for investment cannot effectively determine the rate of interest. More generally, as we shall see in the discussion of general equilibrium, disequilibrium between savings and investment that is planned for at a given level of interest rates may create changes in income such as to bring them into agreement. And, finally, if this income level does not happen to involve a full-employment level of real output, existence of unemployed factors will tend to cause prices to decline, which in turn will mean that the given quantity of money will come to represent a higher amount of real purchasing power, which in turn will set into motion forces tending to increase the flow of income so as to bring about full employment.

Thus in the long run, if the equilibrating forces are permitted to work themselves out without the intrusion of new disturbances, and especially without the development of dynamic effects such as the expectation of further declines in prices as a result of an initial decline in prices, the ultimate equilibrium will be the same whether reached by the processes assumed by the quantity theory or by the liquidity-preference theory. The liquidity-preference theory could perhaps be considered merely a spelling out of the quantity theory in that the steps in the propagation of the effects of an increase in the quantity of money (or a decrease) are traced out in greater detail and with more flexibility. But the difference is important, since the path to final equilibrium is in either case a long one, and since differences in the route to final equilibrium may well set up, through the operation of expectations, differences in the responses of individuals and firms that do affect the results achieved. Even if the long run is not so long that we are all dead, it is likely to be long enough for the experiences to have given rise to new forces affecting the final result.

It might be thought that the two theories of the determination of the rate of interest might be reconciled by distinguishing between the short-term money rate of interest that is the motivating factor in the demand for cash balances, and the long-run real rate of interest that is the motivating factor in savings and investment decisions. If we examine in detail the sources of the differences between the various interest rates, however, it is difficult to fit them to such a division of influence. The difference between long- and short-term rates of interest is, as we saw above, fairly closely determined by a modified sort of liquidity preference, while the difference between real and money rates of interest depends on anticipations concerning the trend of the price level. It would be purely coincidental if a combination of liquidity preference and expected price-trend considerations were to result in a long-term real rate that reflected an equilibrium between savings and investment schedules. There appears to be no equilibrating mechanism associated with either monetary equilibrium or savings-investment disequilibrium that would operate on either liquidity preference or price expectations in such a way as to bring about equilibrium through adjusting the relationship between the various rates of interest. The dual equilibrium between savings and investment and between the demand and supply of money must be sought in the adjustment of both of the two factors that occur in the more general form of these various demand and supply schedules: namely, the rate of interest and the flow of income. Consideration of these matters, however, must be deferred until we consider general equilibrium theory.

The Supply of Money: Banking and Credit

FOR ANALYTICAL purposes, it is convenient to assume that the supply of money consists solely of fiat money, the amount of which is controlled directly and exclusively by some responsible agency, with no direct influence being exerted on the supply of money by other economic variables. Actually, it may be difficult to secure this degree of control over the money supply. With a commodity money, of course, stocks of the commodity may shift from monetary use to consumptive use, and from production to money stocks, in accordance with conditions existing from time to time; with some forms of commodity currency, as we have seen, this flow into and out of monetary stocks is part of the equilibrating mechanism. But, more important, various instruments that have served as a medium of exchange have been created at various times by private agencies who have found it possible to make a profit through this operation, and who have in general not been motivated by any overriding direct concern for the general welfare. Moreover, it may prove difficult to design institutional arrangements that will be altogether proof against this practice, so that assumptions of a constant or rigidly controlled quantity of money may be unrealistic not only historically but in a planning sense.

Historically, the amounts of money created privately have fluctuated from time to time in accordance with the opportunities existing for the making of profits from the operations and in accordance with changing institutional arrangements, spontaneous or legally imposed, with serious effects on the economy. Where institutional arrangements prevail that permit the private creation of money instruments, it is necessary to study the manner in which the supply of money may fluctuate in response to changes in other economic variables of the system.

If we are to discuss with any precision the variations in the quantity of money, it is necessary first to distinguish clearly between those things that are money and those things that are not. Unfortunately, this line is not always easy to draw, and has in fact been drawn in a number of different ways. Many objects, rights, or instruments may from time to time serve as a medium of exchange in the sense that a creditor may consent to accept them in payment of part or all of an obligation, and to this extent they serve as money. However, we wish to define money to include only those instruments that are held in substantial degree because of their ability to serve directly as media of exchange. Thus we distinguish money proper from certain items sometimes referred to as "near money" or "money substitutes" such as savings deposits, short-term notes, and the like, in that these latter are not ordinarily used directly in payment of obligations, but are almost always first converted into money proper.

Fortunately, in the current situation little use is made of instruments other than currency and non-interest-bearing checking accounts for the payment of obligations, so that the line between money and money substitutes (things that serve as media of exchange more or less infrequently) is fairly easily drawn in practice. There have been times, however, when because of a higher interest rate and slower communications, a substantial amount of payment was made through interest-bearing instruments; there have also been times when interest was paid on checking-account balances, and there is no fundamental reason why such situations might not recur. Contrariwise, suggestions have been made for creating a currency that would bear a negative rate of interest, so that the instrument would gradually lose value over time in terms of the money of account. For the present, however, the generalization holds fairly well that instruments used as money bear no interest, at least explicitly.

The volume of checking-account balances, also termed "deposits" or "bank credit" (although this latter term may also be used to refer to the excess of deposits over the currency or reserves held by the banks) will vary from time to time, and on some occasions may vary in sharp independence of the action of the government or legal monetary authority, or of the amount of currency in circulation. Traditionally, the expansion or contraction of bank credit has been associated with the making or paying off of loans, made by the banks to firms in connection with the circulation of goods in the course of their processing, transportation, or trade. Indeed, under the "real-bills" doctrine, loans on the basis of such goods in the channels of trade were considered to be the prime legitimate occasion for the extension of bank credit, and other types of loans or investments by commercial banks were considered to be more or less improper, as they appeared to make banks less liquid than might be considered to be necessary to be sure of being able to meet possible demands of depositors for cash. In effect, banks were supposed to be certifying to a certain minimum value of the goods underlying the loan, and converting the "real" liquidity of these goods into negotiable form. This tradition was never very widely observed in the United States, and has now virtually disappeared even in England.

The notion does persist, however, that expansion of bank credit is necessarily associated with the making of loans by banks to business firms. This is indeed the manner in which the expansion of bank credit very often takes place, but it is by no means the only or even a necessary method. In the simpler type of case, the firm executes, say, an 90-day interest-bearing note in favor of the bank in exchange for which the bank sets up a corresponding deposit on its books in favor of the firm, which is in effect a non-interest-demand obligation in favor of the firm. There is thus in effect an exchange of promises to pay. The firm is willing to pay interest, since it can draw upon its deposit at any time, so that it will thus obtain additional real capital, or at least additional real liquidity in the form of the ability to make payments at any time. If, for the moment, we consider the banking system as a single unit, and if we assume that the firms in whose favor the borrowing firm draws checks on its account will in turn leave the amounts so transferred on deposit with the bank and use them only by drawing further checks, then the bank will find that its holdings of currency are unaffected. In effect, the money in the hands of business firms generally has increased without any corresponding dimunition in the currency in the hands of the bank.

But deposits can be increased without necessarily making any business loans of this character at all. The banks (still considered as a unit) can purchase notes, bonds, mortgages, or other securities in the open market and pay for them by issuing cashier's checks. As long as the persons from whom the assets are purchased are willing to keep their proceeds in the form of deposits at banks, and likewise the persons to whom they in turn transfer these balances in the course of whatever spending they do, additional money will have been placed in the hands of the public without the banks collectively losing any of their cash.

The Limits to Bank-Credit Expansion

THERE ARE, however, limits to this process, even if we consider the banking system as a monolithic unit. Not all persons who receive checks will wish to keep the money in the form of a deposit. Some will wish to have currency, either as pocket money, till money, for hoarding in the mattress, or for the china pig on the mantel. Indeed, just as individuals and firms will in general decide for themselves to what extent they wish to hold assets in the form of money and to what extent in the form of interest-bearing securities, they may also decide on how much of their money they wish to hold in the form of currency and how much in the form of deposits. Each form has its own uses, its advantages and disadvantages. A streetcar fare cannot conveniently be paid by check, but on the other hand to pay for a locomotive or a carload of cotton with currency would be tedious and a bit risky. While there is a large area of overlap where either method of payment is fairly convenient, it seems that given the institutions of the community and the habits of the public as to methods of payment, there may be a fairly steady relationship between the quantity of currency and the quantity of deposits that the public will wish to keep.

Accordingly, we might for simplicity assume that the public always tends to hold one-fifth of its money in the form of currency and four-fifths in the form of deposits. Suppose that the total amount of currency issued by the government is $20 billion; then if the banking system buys sufficient assets, either in the form of marketable securities or in the form of loans to customers, to raise deposits to a level of $40 billion, then corresponding to this $40 billion in deposits the public will want to have $10 billion in currency, leaving $10 billion in currency in the banks. (We might think of the $20 billion in currency as originally in the hands of the public, before the establishment of banking facilities. The establishment of checking account facilities would induce the public to deposit $16 billion of this to be used as checking accounts, leaving $4 billion to be used as hand-to-hand currency. To build up deposits to the $40 billion, the banks would buy $30 billion of assets, but of the $30 billion thus paid out, only one-fifth would be withdrawn in currency, the remaining $24 billion remaining on deposit.) If the banking system now buys another $25 billion of assets, initially setting up another $25 billion in deposits, the public will withdraw one-fifth of this in currency in order to keep the assumed ratio of currency to total money, leaving the banks with $5 billion in currency. If the banks were to purchase another $25 billion of assets, expanding deposits to $80 billion, the corresponding public holding of currency would be $20 billion, leaving the banks stripped of currency. Any further attempt to purchase additional assets would lead to a demand for currency that the banks could not supply, causing the immediate insolvency of the banking system. Thus the ultimate limit on the expansion of bank deposits depends upon the supply of currency and the proportion of deposits to currency desired by the public.

Actually, of course, this limit can never be reached, for the banks must retain some currency in order to stay in business. Not only are there day-to-day and seasonal variations in the demand for currency that the banks must be prepared to meet (unless the government is prepared to bail the banks out by varying the total supply), but a sufficient margin must be maintained to convince the depositor that he will be able to secure currency whenever he wants it. Indeed, any doubts of this sort are likely to prove self-realizing in the form of a run on the bank that will rapidly produce the feared shortage of currency. An attempt of a bank to meet an unexpected demand for currency by a sudden and rapid sale of some of its assets is likely to depress the price obtainable for these assets, with at best a loss to the stockholders of the bank, and at worst the conversion of mere insolvency (i.e., inability to pay obligations promptly due to inadequate liquidity) into a bankruptcy (i.e., inability to meet obligations in full on any terms due to an excess of liabilities over the liquidation value of assets). Accordingly, a bank will try to preserve a fairly substantial reserve against its deposits, either in the form of specie, bullion, legal-tender notes, or perhaps simply the right, in the form of a deposit at a central bank, to demand currency from the responsible monetary authority in case of need, the monetary authority being in effect under obligation to create additional currency if necessary. Traditionally, this reserve has been in the neighborhood of 10 per cent of demand deposits; in the United States, however, legal requirements have been established as to reserve ratios, which have been varied from time to time, and now stand at 12 per cent and 16.5 per cent for different types of banks.

Thus in the above example, if reserves were required to be one-sixth of demand deposits, the maximum level of deposits would be $48 billion, corresponding to which there would be $12 billion of currency kept by the public for hand-to-hand use, with $8 billion in the form of reserves, either kept at the bank or deposited by the bank with the monetary authority. The total amount of money in the hands of the public, currency and deposits combined, would be $60 billion as compared with the $20 billion in currency that would have been the only money in the hands of the public in the absence of banking. The difference of $40 billion is sometimes referred to as "bank credit," though this term has an unfortunate connotation of credit extended by banks, whereas as we have seen bank credit can expand merely by purchase of securities by banks, as a result of the public's "propensity to deposit" the proceeds of such sales. "Bank credit" so defined is equal to the excess of the volume of deposits over the amount of currency and reserves held by banks. In general, if we put d for the "propensity to deposit" (in the above example, equal to 0.8) and r for the reserve ratio (for example, one-sixth), then the total effective money supply can approach the limit

$$M = C_p + D = \frac{1}{1 - d - rd} C$$

where C is the total supply of currency, including reserves, C_p is the currency in the hands of the public, and D is the volume of deposits. The coefficient $1/(1 - d - rd)$ can be termed the "credit multiplier," as it is the ratio by which the existence of bank credit multiplies the effective quantity of money.

Of course, to treat bank credit as merely a multiplication of the effective quantity of money by some ratio is an oversimplification, inasmuch as the liquidity-preference function may be considered to be somewhat different where the money in question is available in the form of deposits as well as in the form of currency, as compared with what the liquidity-preference function would be if the only money available were currency. Indeed, Irving Fisher in his formulation of the quantity theory attempted to express this qualification by considering the two parts of the money supply explicitly and attaching to each of them an appropriate velocity: $PT = MV = M'V' + M''V''$, where M' represents currency (the C_p of the above formulation), and M'' represents deposits (D, above), with V' and V'' the respective velocities of circulation. It is doubtful, however, that this separation really helps the analysis: the velocity of circulation of currency, V', is almost certainly different where checking services are available than it would be if all payments had to make direct use of currency. As a first approximation, it is probably reasonably satisfactory to assume that the composite velocity, V, does not vary very much solely by reason of the variations in the ratio of M' to M''. Indeed, this ratio is itself determined by the propensity to deposit, which in turn is more likely to vary with the character of banking services offered to depositors than with general economic conditions.

Actually, of course, bank-credit expansion may fall considerably short of the limit set by the above formula, particularly if r represents a fairly stringently enforced legal-reserve ratio. Of course, if r is defined as the ratio of currency and reserves to deposits that actually exists, then the formula is a tautology, being a consequence of the various definitions. If r is a target figure more or less steadily aimed at by the banks, then the formula indicates the degree of bank-credit expansion that will tend to be approached, though it may not be achieved at any particular instant. On the other hand, if r is the legal-reserve ratio, and if banks falling short of this ratio are required to take prompt, drastic, or costly steps to remedy the situation, then in fact banks will aim at an over-all ratio somewhat higher than this, particularly if till money is not counted as part of the legal reserves. Moreover, banks may feel that in order to preserve an adequate degree of confidence it is necessary to carry reserves higher than those required by law or considered as a minimum level by custom.

Another factor that may operate to limit the expansion of bank credit may be a limited supply of securities or other assets of a type that are deemed acceptable for banks in general to hold. In effect, the liability side of the balance sheet of a bank consists predominantly of demand deposits, whereas the interest-earning assets in which the bank invests are of varying maturities. In expanding its deposits, in effect, a bank is providing liquidity for others by impairing its own relative liquidity, hoping that because of the checking facilities it offers to depositors it will not be called upon to make good at any one time on any large amount of its promises to pay cash on demand. Accordingly, a bank is likely to feel constrained to invest in assets of high liquidity: i.e., assets that are not only safe from serious risk of default, but are also of short term and thus safe from loss of current value due to changes in interest rates. This normal preference of conservative bankers is likely to be reinforced by government regulation in the form of legal limitations on the types of assets in which banks are permitted to invest. If then in a given state of affairs the supply of such satisfactory securities forthcoming is limited and their interest yield falls to a low level, banks may find it not worth their while to expand their deposits to the extent that otherwise would be permitted by the state of their reserves.

Behavior of Individual Banks

THE FACT that a banking system ordinarily comprises several banks rather than a single bank complicates the picture by introducing inter-bank transfers, and modifies the motivations for the actions of individual banks as compared with what the motivation of a single monopoly bank would be, but does not change the over-all quantitative relationships. The chief difference is that now no one bank can by its own action expand or contract deposits very far (even in proportion to its resources); substantial expansion of bank credit requires action in the same general direction by banks generally, though not necessarily by prearrangement, since this can happen when all banks react similarly to a common stimulus.

For example, let us suppose that there are altogether ten banks with depositors distributed at random so that the accounts of persons with whom a given depositor has dealings are randomly distributed among all ten banks. If one of the banks makes a loan of $1,000 to a customer, a deposit is first set up to his credit on the books of the bank. But as he checks it out, making payments to others, only one-tenth of the $1,000 will be transferred to depositors of the lending bank, the remaining $900 going to depositors of other banks. As the other banks present the checks for payment through the clearing house, the original bank will lose currency (or balances with the central bank) to other banks, and so its ability to make loans or expand its earning assets will rapidly dry up, while the other banks will find their cash or reserves increasing relative to deposits. Only if other banks simultaneously expand their loans or earning assets so that the clearings balance out can an individual bank expand its assets without losing currency or reserves.

The same thing happens, only more rapidly, when a bank purchases notes or securities in the open market. The main difference is that when a loan is made, the borrower is usually a depositor, so that the drain occurs only after the borrower begins to make payments. But when a security is purchased, the seller is likely not to be a depositor of the bank buying it, and thus the drain on the reserves of the buying bank begins immediately. The lag between the making of a loan and the resulting drain on reserves, plus the fact that the making of commercial loans in some cases tends to attract deposits, accounts in part for the preference for this type of loan over the purchase of securities in the open market as a means of investing bank funds, and for the attention given to this type of transaction in the analysis of the expansion of bank credit.

Thus bank credit can be substantially expanded or contracted only so long as the entire banking system keeps fairly well in step. No one bank can do it alone. Whenever any one bank attempts to expand its holdings of interest-earning assets at a more rapid rate than the banking system as a whole, it will lose cash and thus be held back, unless at the same time it manages to expand its share of total deposits. Since the allocation of deposits among the various banks is controlled by the public and not by the banks, each individual bank thus feels controlled by competitive forces and is hardly likely to consider that it has any direct responsibility for maintaining the aggregate volume of deposits and money at a proper level. Moreover, the operation of these automatic checks on individual banks creates the illusion that banks in general are subject to the same type of automatic checks and balances that are supposed to keep other types of economic activity co-ordinated and in balance, whereas in reality the banks as a whole, acting individually in accordance with a competitive search for profit, are likely to take action in similar directions that in its collective effect will have profoundly disturbing influences on the economy.

Indeed, there is a tendency for the expansion and contraction of demand deposits to be perverse in that during an upswing conditions are favorable for the expansion of the volume of deposits, and conversely for a downswing. During an upswing there may be a tendency for the propensity to deposit to increase, i.e., for the public to hold a larger proportion of its money in the form of deposits. There is a plentiful supply of what appear to be suitably liquid assets, and good credit conditions obtain for the extension of loans to business. The effective money supply is thus increased by the expansion of bank deposits, adding to the boom. During the downswing, the volume of bank credit tends to contract even more rapidly than the expansion: an initial contraction may initiate a frantic pursuit of liquidity resulting in a drastic collapse of credit.

Control of Bank Credit

REALIZATION of the fact that banks if left to themselves may take action tending to promote rather than abate cyclical swings has led to the establishment in most countries of central banks or other agencies, one of the functions of which has been to attempt to control the expansion and contraction of the aggregate supply of money, including the demand deposits with banks, with a view to mitigating or controlling business booms and depressions. Many devices have been developed for exercising this control, but so far most of them seem to have been only loosely effective, with the result that the degree of stability obtained by their use has been halting and uncertain.

The most venerable of these methods of control has been the change in the rediscount rate. One of the basic ideas in the setting up of central banks was that they would serve as "bankers' banks," making loans as needed to banks on suitable collateral. Such loans can be made by rediscounting commercial paper or other assets of suitable grade that the borrowing bank has acquired in the course of its business. The central bank usually has the power of issuing currency where demanded, in paying for the rediscounted paper, but often it is more convenient to make payment in the form of a credit at the central bank, which credit can then be used as a reserve or to pay off accounts owing to other banks, and such a credit will thus be as good as cash to the discounting bank. From the point of view of the commercial banks, the quotation of a firm rediscount rate by the central bank amounts to an undertaking by the central bank to create as much currency as the banks wish to demand at that rate of interest.

If the commercial banks operated as a monopoly unit, the opportunity to obtain additional reserves at any time by in effect paying interest on them at the quoted rediscount rate would be an invitation to a very substantial expansion of loans. Indeed, for every $1,000 of rediscounts at, say, 3 per cent, costing $30 per year, the bank could expand its deposits by $2,400, if we assume that the demand of the public for currency would increase by one-fourth of the increase in deposits (i.e., by one-fifth of the total increase in the money held by the public), or $600, and that reserves required are one-sixth of deposits or $400. Of the $1,000 obtained from rediscounting, the bank would leave $600 on deposit with the central bank as a reserve, and take out $400 in currency to pay out to the one-fifth of the sellers of the

$3,000 of securities that the bank might buy who would want their proceeds in currency rather than deposits. If the bank is able to earn 1 per cent on this $3,000 worth of additional assets, it would break even, aside from expenses. A rediscount rate of 3 per cent would, accordingly, result in a rate of interest on appropriate discountable assets of something exceeding 1 per cent by a sufficient margin to cover the costs of operation of the bank, including the cost of performing clearing services in connection with the additional $2,400 of deposits.

With many independent banks in the system, however, the situation is substantially different. Any one bank, in rediscounting, obtains additional reserves, but can expand its earning assets in the first instance only by a corresponding amount, at least if the business done by that bank is a negligible fraction of the total. Checks drawn in paying for assets, or by the firm that borrows from the bank, will rapidly distribute the additional reserves created by the rediscount more or less evenly among all banks. Thus if a particular bank does 1 per cent of the total business, then if it obtains $1,000 by rediscounting, it will, after equilibrium is reached, have been able to expand its earning assets by only $1,030; its action will have increased the asset potential of the other banks in the system by $1,970, but this will be of no profit to the discounting bank.

In effect, then, as long as no one bank has more than a small fraction of the total deposits, it can profitably rediscount only so long as the rate of interest on the assets that it could purchase in consequence is higher than the central bank's rediscount rate, by a sufficient margin to cover the expenses involved. Actually, general reluctance to make use of the rediscounting mechanism except in emergencies or to take care of transitory demands for currency is likely to mean that the relation between the rediscount rate and the rate on commercial paper is rather looser than a strict profit-and-loss analysis would indicate.

However, situations exist where the number of independent commercial banks is so small that they may be conceived to take account of their interactions on each other. In such a case it might be possible to arrive at some sort of gentleman's agreement among banks to rediscount to a greater extent than would be profitable for any one of them considered individually, in consideration of the fact that it would be very much worthwhile for these commercial banks considered as a group. And even in the absence of collusive action, the expenses of the commercial-banking system are interrelated in such a way that it might well be possible for the costs of rediscounting to be indirectly shared among the banks through the way, for example, in which costs of clearing operations are allocated, so as to lead to a greater expansion of credit than would otherwise occur. However, banks have in general been reluctant, for reasons of tradition or prestige, to use the rediscounting mechanism except in emergencies, and this reluctance has so far appeared sufficient to prevent any such collusive abuse as this. Indeed, this reluctance has tended to make the variation of the rediscount rate a somewhat ineffective instrument of control.

Even to the extent that it does operate to control the operations of the banking system, variation of the rediscount rate is a form of control that tends to have very bad "hunting" characteristics. The effects of the rediscount rate are primarily felt through an approximate fixing of the interest rate on certain types of loans, and, through the substitution in the market, of the rates on loans generally. If the rediscount rate is set so as to push market rates of interest slightly below the equilibrium level, for example, expansion will be encouraged, followed by an increase in the expected level of future demand or future prices or both, which in turn would tend to raise the money rate of interest corresponding to the real marginal productivity of capital and the real marginal time preference, even assuming these latter two to remain fixed. To restore equilibrium, the rediscount rate must now be raised, not merely to the equilibrium level that existed originally, but to the new higher equilibrium level that has been created by the rising price expectations. And if an attempt is to be made to bring about a halt to the inflationary trend, the rate may have to be raised even higher than this. On the downward side, the situation is even more difficult: a rediscount rate initially set too high, if it is effective in establishing interest rates generally, will tend to bring about a contraction and to lower price expectations, which in turn may so lower the money equilibrium rate of interest that it may be difficult or impossible to lower effectively the rediscount rate or the market rates that it influences so as to get below the equilibrium rate and stimulate expansion. The practice of rediscounting at a fixed rate does serve to avert financial squeezes due to temporary shortages or maldistributions of currency, but for medium-term control it does appear a somewhat difficult mechanism to manipulate properly.

Another method of control has been through open-market purchases and sales of securities by the central bank itself. Here the central bank increases or decreases the total amount of currency plus central-bank deposits by buying or selling securities in the open market. The effect of buying in the open market is substantially the same as when a bank rediscounts its paper at the central bank, but here the volume of the transaction and the quantity of currency or reserves created is directly under the control of the central bank. In the one case, in effect, the interest rate is fixed and the demand for money determines the amount of currency and reserves supplied; in the other, the central bank determines the amount of currency plus reserves, and lets the interest rate be determined by the reactions of the market.

Either method can in principle achieve substantially the same results, but of late open-market operations have been in greater favor because of the closer control that is possible with them and the lesser tendency they have to produce "hunting" effects. However, in some cases the open-market policy has been pursued in a fashion that has the same characteristics as the determination of a rediscount rate: the central bank may establish a "support price" for certain types of securities and undertake to purchase all that are offered at this price, or to sell if prices of such securities rise. In effect, the establishment of the support price or "peg" fixes the interest rate on the specified type of security, and this by substitution effects tends to set the level of interest rates generally.

In some periods these controls, and particularly control through the fixing of rediscount rates, have made their influence felt less through their mechanical-incentive effect on the operations of the banks or through their effect on the rate of interest than through their psychological effect on general anticipations as to levels of demand and of prices. For a long period changes in the Bank of England rediscount rate were regarded as a signal for a general expansion or contraction, and banks and firms adjusted their actions more on the basis of a vague belief that something was being done that would affect the general prospects of the situation than on the basis of any direct impact of the change in rate upon their transactions. Announcements of changes in support prices for securities have had somewhat the same effect, although of course one of the features of the open-market policy that distinguishes it from the rediscount policy is that it can be changed at any moment without there being necessarily any public announcement. More recently, confidence in the effectiveness of minor monetary operations of this kind has diminished, and at the same time the relative importance of fiscal operations has increased and distracted attention from these monetary matters; as a result, the psychological effect of changes in the policy of the monetary authority has greatly diminished, and possibly the degree of change in policy now required to produce a given result is greater than it was in the past.

A third method of control has been direct change in the legally required reserve percentages. This of course is effective only where legal requirements exist, and is a very powerful method. However, it is, in extreme cases, almost too drastic, since it may operate with substantially different effects on banks that happen to be in different states of liquidity. As a result, this method has on the whole been used sparingly, and in most cases where reserve requirements have been raised it has been done at a time when banks generally had substantial amounts of excess reserves on hand so that the change in requirements did not compel many individual banks to take any very strong action.

A fourth method of control has been the qualitative control of the type of assets in which banks are permitted to invest their funds, and particularly in the control of the nature of the loans to be made by banks. For example, limitations have been imposed from time to time on the amount that could be loaned on securities as collateral (i.e., the margin requirements); similarly, minimum down payments have been required for the extension of consumer credit. In some cases this form of control has been exercised by agencies other than the monetary agency, as when controls of this character are exercised in conjunction with rationing or price control.

Taken together, these methods of control appear to be more adequate for producing a contraction in the total amount of money in the hands of the public than for expanding it. The increasing of rediscount rates alone can of course go no further than to inhibit rediscounting completely, and in a situation where banks are reluctant to engage in rediscounting in any case, such increases may have very little effect, no matter how far they are pushed. But open-market operations can cut into currency reserves to any extent desired, and raising reserve requirements can also cause a severe contraction of deposits if used with vigor, though the effects may perhaps be somewhat unevenly distributed. Of course, if anything substantial is to be accomplished, policy must be consistent: raising the reserve requirements while keeping rediscount rates low may merely drive banks to borrow more reserves, maintaining the same volume of deposits, the chief effect being on the profits of the banks rather than on the money supply. But a consistent policy carried far enough can curtail the total money supply to any extent desired.

On the expansion side, however, the central monetary authority can pay out on the leash, but banks may very well fail to use the additional slack. Particularly when interest rates are low, banks have relatively little incentive to make loans or purchase short-term liquid assets: in some cases the interest may not pay the costs associated with the transaction. Or where business conditions are unsettled, banks may purchase all the assets that they consider to have a suitable degree of safety and liquidity without using up their asset potential. Under these conditions, lowered rediscount rates may fail to induce more rediscounting, and lowered reserve requirements or open-market purchases may merely increase the excess reserves of banks without inducing any increase in deposits. Monetary control of a banking system is thus a fairly effective ceiling on the supply of money, but a rather weak floor.

Interest on Cash Balances

THUS FAR we have proceeded on the assumption that neither currency nor checking-account balances bore interest in any direct form. But this is not a necessary condition, and indeed is not fully correct even at present. Currency, to be sure, by its very nature is unlikely to bear interest: the difficulties of allowing for interest in exchanges of small coins or bills would make this incompatible with their free use as a medium of exchange. Indeed, advocates of the introduction of a "depreciating currency" or "demurrage money" have continually had to contend with the objection that if coin or bills were to vary in value from day to day or month to month in terms of the unit of account, much of their convenience in use would vanish.

But while banks have for some time been prohibited from paying explicit interest on demand deposits, there have been times when such interest has been paid, and even at present there is a sense in which imputed interest is paid on deposits. For banks perform certain costly services for depositors, which these depositors would be willing to pay for, if necessary. Indeed, depositors do pay for these services when banks consider their balances to be too small, in relation to the services performed, for the bank to be able to make a reasonable profit on the account by reason of the interest earned on the corresponding assets. Thus if a bank is willing to allow a depositor three checks a month for every $100 of balance, and if a charge of five cents per check is made for additional checks above this free allowance, then if a depositor with an active account increases his balance by $100, this will reduce the service charges by 15 cents a month, or by $1.80 a year, which is equivalent to paying interest on the balance at the rate of 1.8 per cent.

Other services may be performed for depositors that are less uniform and more difficult to evaluate, and the connection between the amount of service and the size of the balance may be less direct. They have ranged from making up payrolls through giving financial advice to minding Junior while Mrs. Depositor goes shopping. In general, it is possible to suppose that in the absence of legal or other restrictions, if interest rates on good security were moderately high, and if mechanization reduces the operating expenses of banks, competition of banks for deposits might well result in the payment of interest on checking-account balances at a rate differing from the market rate or that offered on savings accounts by just enough to cover the expenses connected with the checking accounts. Under such circumstances the interest rate relevant to a demand curve for checking-account balances would not be the market rate of interest, but rather the differential between this rate and the rate paid on checking-account balances. Monetary theory might require considerable modification to make it applicable to such a situation.

Indeed, it would in principle be possible for banks to charge explicitly for all checking-account, accounting, and other services performed, independently of balances held, and to pay interest on all deposits at a rate that would then reflect merely the cost of functioning as an investment trust. In effect, the distinction between savings and checking accounts would disappear, except as banks might wish to preserve such a distinction for the sake of applying different methods of handling to the more active and to the less active accounts. If in addition one imagines a situation where nearly all transactions are carried out by checks on such accounts, with only a negligible and incidental use of hand-to-hand currency, the applicability of current types of monetary theory would indeed be doubtful.

To be sure, these possibilities have little to do with the analysis of the current situation. But these and other possible arrangements for facilitating the exchange of goods should be kept in mind, lest it be assumed too readily that money necessarily earns no interest, or that interest rates can always be regarded as reflecting the price paid for the sacrifice of liquidity. Our present monetary theory, indeed, is restricted in its applicability to a fairly narrow range of possible institutional arrangements. The theory discussed in preceding chapters could to a large extent be considered to be based on underlying and more or less immutable technological and psychological understructure, and while the economic superstructure could take varying institutional forms, the basic economic principles could be applied in only slightly modified form to all of the varying institutional arrangements. When we come to monetary theory, however, we find that the theory no longer retains any substantial invariant framework but depends almost entirely upon the institutional superstructure. Perhaps in time a more comprehensive theory of the mechanisms of exchange will be developed, of which monetary theory will be only a variant, that will remain in some sense applicable under all or at least a wide range of institutional arrangements. But pending such a development, it behooves us to keep in mind the provincial and particular nature of much if not all that comes under the heading of monetary theory.

EXERCISES

1. What is the relation among the "numéraire," the "currency," the "denominator-of-loans," and the "liquidity" functions of money as discussed above, and the traditional formulations of the functions of money as "measure of value," "store of value," and "means of payment"?

2. Discuss the relative merits of the following as (a) physical currency, (b) a basis for a representative currency, (c) a basis for a fiduciary currency, (d) a numéraire, (e) a denominator for loans:

Gold
Silver
A combination of gold and silver (some ancient coins were made of electrum)
Cowrie
Tobacco (cf. the early American colonies)
Cigarettes (cf. Second World War prisoner-of-war camps and early occupation periods)
Beaver pelts (cf. Hudson's Bay Company trading posts)
United States ten-year bonds
United States Treasury 90-day bills
Shares of American Telephone and Telegraph Company stock
Shares of Studebaker-Packard Corporation Stock
Shares of the Blue Wildcat Mining Company Stock
Cattle

Millstones (cf. the stone "money" of Yap)
Pig iron
Common brick
Miles of railroad travel (the French railways have issued bonds redeemable, at the option of the purchaser, in certificates good for a given number of miles of railway travel)
Haircuts
A specified basket or bundle of basic commodities (cotton, sugar, etc.)
A specified combination or bundle of personal services

3. Suppose some alchemist or his modern equivalent had been as successful in discovering a cheap process for producing gold as Hall was for aluminum. What might have been the consequences if this had occurred at various dates in the past? At present?

4. Suppose a propensity to deposit such that non-bank transactors tend to hold 80 per cent of their money in the form of demand deposits, 20 per cent in currency. Suppose that banks require till money of 3 per cent of their deposits, and in addition are required to maintain a reserve in the form of a deposit at the central bank equal to 15 per cent of deposits. The central bank follows a policy of maintaining total currency outstanding plus the amount of deposits to the credit of the commercial banks at the central bank at a figure of $100 million (i.e., total currency of $100 million is issued, and the central bank holds of this total an amount equal to its deposits as a reserve). What is the total amount of non-bank deposits and of currency outside banks that can be maintained under this system? What happens to this total if the propensity to deposit rises to 90? If deposits turn over 40 times a year, and currency in the hands of the public turns over 25 times a year, what is the total annual volume of transactions?

5. If the banking system is composed of a large number of banks, no one of which does more than, say, 1 per cent of the total business, and the central bank offers to rediscount suitable securities at 3 per cent (either issuing more currency to stand as a reserve against the additional deposits thus created in favor of the banks, or allowing its own reserve ratio to drop below the 100 per cent of the previous case), at what interest yield does it become profitable for the banks acting individually to rediscount in order to make additional loans? In order to purchase additional securities on the market? What expense is it worthwhile for the bank to incur in the form of banking services or otherwise in order to secure an additional $10,000 in deposits?

6. Suppose on the other hand the banking system to consist of one large bank which attracts 40 per cent of all deposits, and a large number of smaller banks, no one doing more than 1 per cent of the business. If the central bank posts a rediscount rate of 5 per cent, at what yield can the large bank afford to make loans or purchase securities? What can it afford to pay in costs to secure deposits? What are the consequences for the smaller banks?

7. Several U.S. banks have recently inaugurated a "ready-credit" scheme for credit-worthy individuals, under which upon the filing of appropriate information a "line of credit" is made available permitting checks to be drawn on the bank up to a given sum. No deposit is required and no charge is made until checks are drawn, the resulting loan being subject to an interest charge of 12 per cent per year. If such a scheme becomes generalized, what becomes of the concept of "money" as the total of "means of payment"? What if the rate of interest charged were 5 or 6 per cent instead of 12 per cent? (Actually, one bank which initially imposed no service charges other than interest on outstanding daily balances was compelled to institute a 20 cents per check service charge to prevent the scheme being used as a cheap medium for numerous small current payments.)

CHAPTER SIX

Macroeconomic Variables and Concepts

Circular Feedbacks and the Need for Aggregation

THUS FAR we have been engaging primarily in what is known as partial equilibrium analysis in which we take a given element in the economic system, such as a firm, an industry, a household, or a market, and determine what the equilibrium conditions will be provided all the influences outside this element are determined independently of what happens within the unit under study. To the extent that there has been an interaction between the element and its environment, as in the analysis of the firm in relation to an industry, this interaction has been of a direct, reciprocal type that could be represented by supply and demand curves, or, as in the analysis of the more sophisticated oligopoly and theory-of-games situations, has been of a conjectural or hypothetical type. Such partial analysis is a fairly instructive type of procedure as long as we are primarily interested in gaining an appreciation of the behavior of these economic elements as elements. But when we try to follow this approach through to the analysis of a model of a complete economic system, we encounter, if we are to be reasonably realistic, a new element: the indirect feedback.

The fundamental difference between partial-equilibrium analysis and analysis of complete economic systems is that indirect "feedback" effects that may be negligible as long as we are looking at the behavior of a single small element of the economic system will often build up, when we consider the system as a whole, to a crucial importance. A change in the wages paid in a shoe factory or even in the shoemaking industry as a whole may have negligible effects on the demand for shoes if we are looking at this part of the economy in isolation; this is slightly less true of, say, the automobile industry, but it is not true at all for industry as a whole. When we turn to look at the economy as a whole, the aggregate effect on the demand for shoes, or for most products, of a change in wages in industry as a whole is likely to be too large to ignore. And even if we are not interested in the economy as a whole but are merely analyzing an element that is either large enough or is so placed in the complete scheme that it produces substantial indirect feedback effects upon itself, as, for example, would often be the case with an analysis of savings, it may be necessary to extend the analysis to include these feedbacks if reasonable realism is to be achieved.

But if we attempt to analyze these feedbacks in a model built up of large numbers of small units, the analysis immediately becomes so intricate that it is difficult to follow the over-all working of the model. It is nevertheless vital to resist the temptation to take a short cut by making inadequately supported generalizations from the results of partial analysis. One way of simplifying the complete model to the point where it is reasonably tractable is to combine the economic units in various ways and continue the analysis in terms of a smaller number of aggregated variables. In fact, most general equilibrium analysis that attempts to deal with this indirect feedback element in economics is couched in terms of a fairly small number of variables representing aggregates for the economy as a whole, or at least for fairly large segments of the economy. This approach constitutes what is known as "macroeconomics." Where the number of sectors is large and must be dealt with through fairly massive arrays of interrelationships the subject becomes "input-output analysis." In this chapter we consider the nature of some of the aggregate variables and concepts that have been used in the more highly aggregated forms of macroeconomic analysis; we will then be in a position to proceed with our analysis in terms of these variables with less risk of overlooking entirely the many important factors and relationships that are necessarily more or less concealed or glossed over in the process of combining the similar but not quite identical elements to make up the various aggregates, and with a fuller appreciation of the inevitable differences between the conceptual variables and the aggregates actually assembled in the available statistics.

The Nature of Aggregate Variables

AGGREGATION is essentially a process whereby simplicity is gained at the expense of precision and detail. Detail and simplicity are to a degree directly antithetical, but the degree to which precision must be given up for the sake of simplicity will depend on the circumstances, and may be greatly reduced if the aggregation process is carried out with proper care. Loss of precision can indeed be avoided entirely in special cases where some fairly restrictive arbitrary assumptions are satisfied; in general, however, some loss of precision will be inevitable, though for most purposes a sufficiently close approximation can be maintained so that the results remain useful.

For example, in the most elementary form of aggregation where we are simply adding together the demand curves of different individuals for the same closely defined commodity to obtain an aggregate-demand curve in the corresponding market, there is virtually no loss of precision through the aggregation process per se. But if we turn to considering the effect on demand of a change in income, an "aggregate Engel curve" showing the relation between the aggregate income of a group and their aggregate purchases of a given commodity at a given price cannot be defined precisely unless some assumption is made about the way in which different aggregate incomes will be distributed among the individuals. In this case, ordinarily, aggregative analysis ignores differences in total demand that may arise from differences in the distribution of a given aggregate income, and thereby loses some of its precision. If necessary, some of this precision may be recovered by dividing the consumers into suitable groups according to the way they may be expected to respond to changes in their income, or according to the way their income may be expected to vary in relation to the aggregate income, but as such a procedure is often quite difficult, it is rarely carried out, though it is frequently discussed as a theoretical possibility.

A similar and more serious impairment of precision occurs when outlays or proceeds from buying or selling numbers of different commodities included in a broad category are aggregated. Unless there is a fixed relation maintained within the category as to the prices or quantities of the various items, a given aggregate may mean different underlying phenomena in different circumstances. Even when such a fixed relation is known to exist, its exact form may be unknown, or the form may be such that the computation of the corresponding aggregate is unduly difficult, or such as not to lend itself readily to incorporation in the model under consideration, so that even though the theoretical possibility exists of avoiding loss of precision, this possibility is not realized.

Dimensions of Aggregate Variables

WHEN ITEMS that differ qualitatively are aggregated, the aggregate, almost of necessity, is expressed in the first instance in terms of money as a common denominator, even though subsequently an attempt may be made to factor this money aggregate into a price element and a quantity element through some kind of a price-index construction. Usually the procedure is to compile a price index from observations on prices, and then deflate the money aggregate by this price index to obtain a figure indicative of quantity, though the reverse procedure is also conceivable: namely, to construct a quantity index from observations, and then divide the money figure by this quantity index to obtain a figure representing price. It is even possible to derive both the quantity and the price indexes from relevant observations, without the direct use of a money aggregate, but in this case it is generally considered desirable to do this in such a way that the product of the price and quantity indexes will agree as closely as possible with the money aggregate. In any case, most macroeconomic analysis deals predominantly with money aggregates, and many macroeconomic models are expressed exclusively in terms of money aggregates.

These money aggregates are in general of two kinds: flows, such as income, wages, expenditures or profits, and stocks, such as cash on hand, assets, debts, inventory, and the like. Stocks have the dimension "dollars"; flows have the dimension "dollars per year" or per some other unit of time. It is also in principle possible to have aggregates of "acceleration" that have the dimension "dollars per year per year," indicating, for example, a rate of growth of income, a change in wage payments, or a rate of increase in the capacity of a plant. But such aggregates are of importance only in relatively specialized types of analysis.

By far the largest part of aggregative analysis concerns itself with flows and stocks, and even stocks tend to be accorded relatively little attention in themselves, being chiefly considered as factors influencing flows, leaving flows to hold the center of the stage. But while attention is concentrated on flows, in many instances it is not possible to define flows accurately without reference to stocks. Indeed, in many cases a net flow is measured as the rate of change of a stock or, less instantaneously, as the change in a stock over a given period of time. Thus saving, for example, may be defined as the increase in net worth over a period of time. To know precisely what we mean by the various flow concepts, it is necessary to investigate first the nature of the stock-type aggregates.

Net Worth

THE MOST comprehensive of the stock aggregates is wealth, or, more precisely, net worth. The net worth of an individual consists of the value of his assets less the value of his liabilities. For example, if an individual's only possession is a house worth $20,000, and if he owes $5,000, his net worth is $15,000. But even such a relatively simple concept as this causes difficulty as soon as any attempt is made to apply it on a wide scale. Two questions arise: What items should be included in the assets and liabilities, and how should they be valued?

Whatever the theoretical difficulties may be in drawing the line as to the inclusion or exclusion of items going to make up the aggregate of assets and liabilities, in practice there are relatively few items over which there will be any serious disagreement in an actual case. While good health, a college education, or the possession of some special skill or talent are indeed assets in a general sense, no attempt is ordinarily made to include them in an evaluation of the net worth of individuals for purposes of the usual type of macroeconomic analysis. In a community in which slavery is outlawed and in which contracts for the future rendering of personal services are severely limited in scope and enforceability, such assets cannot be marketed directly, nor are there any very closely comparable marketable assets. On the other hand, an obligation to support an invalid relative is ordinarily not allowed for as a liability, particularly if the obligation is not legally enforceable. While in principle, perhaps, all such items should be evaluated and included in the aggregate, the difficulties of evaluation, plus the relative remoteness of such elements from direct impact on economic activity and their relatively slow change, at least in their aggregate sum, have led most economists to leave them out of account. Net worth is ordinarily calculated by taking into account only these liabilities that are legally enforceable and impose a fairly definite and measurable drain on the resources of the economic unit being considered, and only assets that can be more or less readily sold, or are closely comparable to such saleable assets.

Valuation of Assets and Liabilities

BUT GIVEN the items to be included, their evaluation in money terms is still a problem. For some items, such as securities with a fairly wide market, a market value can be assigned within fairly close limits, and while even here in principle we have the question of whether the value should be inclusive of brokerage and other expenses (i.e., the cost of acquisition) or net of such expenses (i.e., amount realizable on sale), the difference is relatively unimportant. When there are substantial frictions in the market, however, the matter becomes of greater, and sometimes crucial, importance. If an individual owns a home, for example, there may be a very substantial difference between the amount it would be necessary to pay to induce him to sell it, with the consequent necessity of purchasing another and moving into it, and the amount that he could realize if he were suddenly required to move. Moreover, this differential may vary considerably from time to time according to the plans and prospects of the owner. Corresponding differentials may be even more marked in the case of a small business or of closely held stock: individuals owning the business, or shares in it, may have good and sufficient reason for believing the value in terms of prospective future profits to be greater than anything they could get for it within any reasonably short period, and even if buyers could eventually be found who were willing to accept an equally sanguine view of the prospects, the cost of finding and educating such prospects would have to be allowed for in a "liquidation value." Moreover, the finding of such buyers is a matter into which a considerable element of chance enters, so that liquidation value must allow also for the element of risk.

To make a rational choice within this range of possible values as *the* measure of wealth, it is necessary to consider more precisely just what use we intend to make of the figure we come out with. In relation to individual owners, the chief use for a net-worth figure seems to be either to provide a parameter indicative of the economic welfare of the individual or household concerned or, alternatively, to provide a parameter that will help explain or predict the behavior of such an individual. While liquidation value has some influence on the behavior of individuals, and would provide an indication of the level of security provided by the assets, more importance, both as an influence on behavior and as a component of welfare, would attach to a value giving proper weight to the degree to which the assets are particularly adapted to the needs of the individual or household. Accordingly, a value nearer to the price that would be needed to induce the surrender of the asset seems called for. This is particularly apparent if we consider such assets as clothing or specialized items that have very little resale value. In relation to corporations and business firms, the aim is more nearly a figure related to the contribution of the asset to the future profitability of the firm; somewhat similar considerations apply.

When it comes to the practical matter of a procedure by which value can actually be determined, however, additional difficulties are encountered. It is obviously impractical to ask in every case what the minimum price is that would induce a given individual or firm to part with a given asset. What such an asset would fetch if dumped on the market may be roughly estimated by observing the price at which similar assets are currently changing hands, taking due account of the status of the seller in the market (i.e., whether he is a normal source of supply for the item, how large a factor he would be in the market, etc.). Such a liquidation value furnishes a rough lower limit to the value of the asset to an individual: he will not ordinarily take less for it or value it at less than he can obtain for it in the market, unless perhaps he is ignorant of the market possibilities.

An upper bound to value may be estimated by determining the cost of replacing the asset, or in some cases of providing an asset capable of producing equivalent services or returns. But this is only an upper bound, since in many cases an asset, if somehow destroyed, would not be worth replacing, or would be replaced with something substantially different, as when improved types of equipment become available, styles change, or needs shift. If replacement with a new rather than a worn asset is the most economical form of replacement, allowance in valuing the old asset must be made for the services of any which the new asset is expected to continue to render after the time at which the old asset would have been worn out, in addition to any difference in the quality of the service rendered by the two assets prior to the time the old one would be worn out. This allowance ordinarily appears in the accounts as depreciation or obsolescence, but often is computed on a quite arbitrary basis, in part for the sake of preserving objectivity in the accounting procedure, which means that the depreciated value reflected in the books of business firms often bears only a very rough relation to market value or value to the owner.

On occasion, of course, the value to the individual may even exceed this "replacement cost" if replacement would take time and the item is of critical immediate importance. But such "emergency" valuations can be accepted only with great care, if at all; it would obviously not be proper, for example, to compute a net worth for an individual (or firm) by adding together the sums that would be required to induce him to part separately with each of a number of highly complementary items (the classic example is that of the three legs of a three-legged stool). In short-run terms, sensible results will be obtained only when assets are valued in assemblies that are reasonably non-complementary or at least capable of effective use with a reasonably wide range of interchangeable complements.

Thus value to the user will not only vary according to circumstances, but the methods of estimating value will vary widely according to the nature of the asset. Where an active market exists, market value furnishes a measure of value to within a fairly narrow range; where assets are somewhat differentiated but are traded in fairly actively as a class—such as real estate—value may be indicated by the price at which comparable assets are currently being sold. Here, however, an addition to this market value may be appropriate in consideration of the fact that for the average owner there remains a period of expected occupancy or possession during which he still expects some return on whatever expense over and above the market price he has been put to (or would be put to if he were to shift his ownership) in acquiring the property, moving in, becoming familiar with it, and adapting it to his particular needs. For current supplies and inventory, the cost, adjusted for changes in the prices of the component parts, materials, and labor, may ordinarily be taken to be a fair measure, though even here there will be occasions arising from blunders or unforeseen developments that require inventory items to be written down to a clearance sale or even to a scrap value. The more highly specialized and processed an element of inventory is, the more uncertain is likely to be its value. For durable and semi-durable consumers' equipment, such as clothing, refrigerators, furniture, or automobiles, original cost adjusted for price changes and for depreciation may furnish a guide, although with the exception of items for which a fairly active secondhand market exists, as for automobiles, the amount of the depreciation will involve a substantial subjective element.

Indeed, in practice it is generally observed that the value ascribed to a given asset depends on the purpose of the valuation as well as on the circumstances. Thus we have valuation for tax assessment, for determination of corporate solvency, for corporate reorganizations, for public-utility rate regulation, for condemnation of property for public purposes, for settlement of insurance or damage claims, and, finally, for econometric analysis. In strict theory it might be possible to hold that at a given time and in given circumstances value for all of these purposes should be identical. But valuation is a costly process, and where an actual valuation is required, as distinct from the mere definition of a hypothetical value by the theorist, and especially where the process of valuation is repeated more or less continuously, expense is saved by making occasional valuations do for a more or less extended period, or by being satisfied with a rough value where the issues at stake are relatively minor, or by adopting a conscious bias in the valuation procedure where this may be acceptable. Thus values for property-tax purposes tend to move fairly sluggishly; values ascertained for the protection of creditors may be determined at intervals on a basis sufficiently conservative to allow for some degree of fluctuation between occasions, as is the practical effect of many of the valuation conventions adopted by accountants, such as "cost or market, whichever is lower." Values for property-tax assessment may be ascertained with somewhat less care than for rate regulation, and this in turn perhaps less meticulously than for condemnation or sale of a piece of property. By and large it is these valuations made for practical purposes that furnish the data which the economist must use, and in using them the economist must be aware of the gap between the actual figure and the concept it is taken to represent.

Private and Social Wealth

IF WE CAN for the moment set aside the difficulties posed by valuation methods and can assume for the time being that every asset and every liability can be assigned a definite value, so that we can obtain the net worth of each individual, it would then be possible to simply sum these individual net-worth figures to get an aggregate net-worth figure. In a simplified model in which all economic goods are assets of some ascertainable individual (or partnership or corporation), and all assets not consisting of such goods correspond to liabilities of other individuals, then such an aggregate of individual net worth would be a measure of the net wealth of the community as a whole. In practice, however, such a figure would be seriously deficient as a measure of the capital resources of the community as a whole. Many assets are so controlled that their value is not reflected in the net worth of any individual or set of individuals, while on the other hand many assets that are of value to individuals and add to their net worth neither reflect any real capital nor represent any liability on the part of any other individuals. There are many types of divergence between private and social wealth, and indeed many forms of social wealth are difficult to evaluate in purely economic terms without inconsistency. While it is impossible to take all such divergences into account, it is essential to allow for those items of nonprivate social wealth and nonsocial private wealth that impinge most directly on the market economy and that are most directly substitutable in one way or another for items that are both social and private wealth.

One very large category of assets that are social wealth but not private wealth consists of those assets owned by governments, such as government buildings, public works, roads, dams, monuments, and the like. It would obviously be absurd to say that the wealth of a community had decreased merely because the government had taken over a power plant or a building previously in private hands (and was paying the owner with funds obtained by increasing taxes). However, not all government property can properly be simply evaluated and added to net private wealth without the danger of a considerable amount of double counting. The primary benefits derived from certain types of publicly owned assets often accrue chiefly if not exclusively to owners of specific items of private property, and since in effect the beneficial enjoyment of the publicly owned property is transferred along with the transfer of the benefited private property, the value of the publicly owned property is substantially included in the market value of the benefited property, and to count both would be double counting. For example, a house on a paved street may be expected to sell for more than a similar one on an unpaved street by an amount roughly corresponding to the cost of the paving (otherwise the paving would not have been worthwhile), assuming that the owner of the house on the paved street will not be facing special assessments or higher taxes to pay for the paving. Or consider two residential streets of identical appearance, differing only in that the property lines are set back further from the center of the street in one case than in the other, making the publicly owned area larger in one case than in the other, the actual width of the pavement being the same. One would expect houses and lots to sell for about the same price along one street as along the other (except possibly where there is a prospect of the street having to be widened, with payment of compensation to owners in one case but not in the other). To value the street as a public asset differently because of the difference in the area of the nominally public property would be to create a difference where no real difference exists. Accordingly, one would expect the value of local streets, some local public parks, and to a lesser extent schools and other community facilities to be reflected in the market prices of property in the neighborhood, so that part or all of the cost of such items must be eliminated as a duplication in obtaining an aggregate figure for social wealth.

Besides governments, there are a number of private agencies and organizations that have assets in which no ownership can be imputed to specific individuals or households. Endowed educational, philanthropic, and religious institutions ordinarily spread their benefits so widely that no individual may be said to have a transferable proprietary interest in them; since the assets of these institutions presumably do render service, they must be included in aggregating the capital resources of the community. Moreover, in many cases even organizations that are ordinarily looked upon as business ventures have assets in which no effective individual proprietorship interest can be traced. The surplus of a cooperative accumulated out of patronage savings in strict theory belongs to the customers whose purchases gave rise to the savings, but in practice the customer receives only such part of this sum as the management sees fit to declare as a dividend, and he has no enforceable or transferable claim on the remainder, unlike the stockholder in a regular corporation who by selling his stock transfers his interest in the undistributed surplus and is thereby able to obtain for his shares a price that in some degree reflects this surplus.

Surpluses of cooperatives can thus constitute a kind of "no man's property" the beneficiaries of which, if any, are likely to be an undetermined set of future patrons of the cooperative. Or, to look at the matter more through the eyes of enthusiasts of the cooperative movement, the beneficiaries are the future generations at large that benefit from the pervasive influence of the spread of the cooperative idea through the application of this surplus directly and indirectly to the promotion and expansion of the cooperative form of enterprise. On the other hand, a more cynical viewer would consider that the chief beneficiaries are the officers and employers of the cooperative, to whom the existence of the surplus provides assurance of continuity of employment and tenure (though it would not be impossible to provide this assurance with a fund to which the original patrons retained a reversionary claim). The amounts involved are not trivial: in 1960, the admittedly unassigned reserves of mutual life insurance companies amounted to six billion dollars, in addition to which the policy reserves are usually computed with a very liberal margin. In this case, it would be relatively simple to maintain the cooperative principle strictly by distributing an appropriate share of the unassigned surplus as a termination dividend upon the termination of the policy, but this is seldom done.

Even the undistributed surplus of profit-making corporations, though in principle belonging in equity to the stockholders, may in practice fail to contribute dollar for dollar to the wealth of the stockholders, as can be seen from the behavior of market quotations. Corporate policy is often directed more toward providing continuity of the organization and security for management and employees, or expansion of the corporate empire, than toward maximizing the ultimate return to the shareholders, and in a company with widely held shares, amounts added to surplus may add very fractionally to the value of the shareholders' expectations, witness occasions on which corporate shares have sold for substantially less than the excess over liabilities of the liquidation value of the readily saleable assets of the corporation.

On the other side of the ledger, certain items of private wealth bear no direct relation to any corresponding social wealth. Government bonds, in general, reflect the future taxing power of the government rather than any productivity of physical assets. To individuals owning them they represent specific and effective wealth no less than private obligations secured by real property, and are invariably counted as an individual asset. The converse obligation on the part of taxpayers generally to pay taxes to provide for interest and the repayment of the principal of the bonds is vague both as to time and as to the individual who will have to bear the burden. Few if any individuals make any specific adjustment in their actions or attitudes for what they might consider to be their share of the liability represented by a government debt. Where a specific allowance is made in balance sheets for future taxes, these are usually either taxes already incurred but not yet paid, or are taxes calculated at rates currently in effect, without specific allowance for the effect of the national debt on trends of tax rates. Thus the national debt exerts a far more powerful and specific influence as an asset in the hands of particular individuals than as a liability of citizens in general. To shift from individual net worth to social wealth, we must accordingly eliminate government debt, although the effect of this may to some extent be offset by the inclusion of publicly owned assets.

The above considerations may have to be modified in part in the case of local debt where the overwhelming importance of the property tax as a source of local revenues with which a local debt may be serviced make the local debt a fairly closely calculable burden on the various parcels of property in the community. To some extent this burden is capable of shifting to other parcels as construction increases the tax base, and poorly designed state-aid formulas may permit some of the burden to be shifted to taxpayers in other areas, while in the larger units particularly, non-property-tax revenues may develop to the point where they take over some of the burden. But for the smaller and more stable communities, these factors are likely to be unimportant, and in strict theory one would expect market values to be depressed by the amount of the local public debt, and new construction to be retarded until the marginal productivity of taxable improvements is pushed sufficiently high (by the relatively low degree of improvement attained) to offset this overhanging burden. Actually, however, property values seem to be more affected by current tax rates than by whatever effect the local debt may be considered to have on future tax rates, and even here the relationship between tax rates and property values does not appear in practice to be at all close. For most practical purposes, we can say that an increase in government debt (produced, say, by a reduction in taxes) creates assets for individuals to hold without giving rise to any corresponding liability or impairment of the value of other assets held by individuals.

A rather subtle and difficult point in the measurement of individual and social wealth is created by the Old Age and Survivors' Insurance Program. Under this program individuals have acquired rights to future payments of benefits of varying kinds. To be sure, these rights cannot be alienated, pledged, or discounted; nevertheless, they do represent a provision for the future that provident individuals would otherwise have to make in other ways, as by increasing their savings or their insurance with private companies. Ideally, they should be considered an asset for each individual, in that their existence exerts an influence on individual behavior somewhat similar to that which the holding of a contract with a private insurance company calling for similar benefits would exert, and such a contract would have a cash value. But the valuing of these social-security rights represents a problem, since on the one hand the level of future benefits is only partly determinate, even under the assumption that the formulas will not be further changed by future legislation; they are determined in part by wages yet to be earned. On the other hand, future benefit payments will be financed in part, but only in part, by payroll taxes on the individual beneficiary and others similarly situated; a substantial share of the burden of financing the payments to beneficiaries now covered is expected to be shouldered by later generations of wage earners coming on the scene. The impossibility of converting the rights into cash and the difficulty of determining a net value for each individual have in practice been sufficient reason for making no attempt to insert this item as an asset into the balance sheet of particular individuals. It might be possible, if desired, to estimate an item to be inserted in an aggregated individual balance sheet, but since, as with government bonds, this asset would represent no net social wealth, the only purpose in doing so would be to provide a base for predicting the behavior of individuals in the aggregate; thus far this has not been done. The obverse on the government side would be the setting up of a reserve fund of a corresponding amount which would in effect be an addition to the national debt, but this would be even less useful conceptually: about the only result of such a step would be to further alarm those to whom a large national debt is a symptom of economic ill health or fiscal immorality. Similar comments of course apply to obligations toward veterans, civil servants, etc.

Another point where individual assets may not represent social wealth is where they represent a capitalization of monopoly profits. Indeed, the productivity of the economic system as a whole is ordinarily impaired rather than enhanced by the existence of monopoly rather than competition in an industry. In practice, however, there seems to be no very reliable method of eliminating from the aggregate of individual net worths the amount attributable to monopoly elements. An attempt to eliminate that part of net worth that cannot be traced to some underlying physical property is likely to go too far, in that it would also eliminate the socially valuable element of organizational momentum. Measurement of the degree of monopoly is still a difficult and controversial matter.

It may indeed be argued that if a price index is to be used to deflate a money aggregate of wealth, the presence of monopoly elements in the money aggregate will to some extent be offset in the deflation process through the inclusion of the heightened monopoly prices in the index used as a deflator. But there is no indication whatever that this correction or offset would be of the correct order of magnitude. If monopoly is concentrated in the production and sale of consumer goods and if a capital-goods price index is used as a deflator, the correction fails completely. Even if a consumption-goods index is used, there is no reason to expect the results to be even roughly correct. For example, if we consider an economy with no durable physical assets at all,

all products being highly perishable commodities, then if a company is granted a monopoly of the making and sale of, say, ice cream, shares in such a company may be sold by the grantees and thus become assets for individuals to hold. Such shares could then represent substantially the entire saleable net worth of the individuals in the community (leaving out of account the value of individuals as such and assuming that the inventories of the perishable commodities are of negligible magnitude). Even if the price of ice cream were then pushed up sufficiently to raise the entire price level by 25 per cent (which would imply an extremely inelastic demand for ice cream), this would result in decreasing the indicated deflated value of net worth by 20 per cent, whereas the proper cut would be to eliminate the monopoly value of the shares entirely, a result which even then fails to reflect the positive impairment of the productivity of the community caused by the imposition of the monopoly.

Indeed, if one were to imagine a "perishable economy" of this type burdened with several such monopolies, with each individual owning shares of roughly the same value in one or more of the monopolies, then the abolition of all the monopolies could have the paradoxical result of wiping out the net worth of every individual in the community while at the same time raising the economic welfare level of every individual.

The Structure of Liabilities

MORE SIGNIFICANT for economic analysis than even the distinction between private and social wealth is the effect that the structure of assets and liabilities may have on the net aggregate of values, if indeed the structure itself is not, for many purposes, of more importance than the aggregate. A debt owed by one individual to another, for example, does not quite cancel out in the aggregate: there is on balance a residuum reflecting the difference between the incomplete confidence felt by the creditor in the ultimate payment of the debt and the certainty the debtor feels that the debt will have to be paid. Objectively, the probability that payment will actually be made may be the same as the probability that the payment will be received, but the reaction of the two parties to the prospect is different. Concretely, this is often expressed by the creditor setting up a "reserve for bad debts" by which the face value of the "accounts receivable" is reduced to a net amount reflecting what the creditor expects, on the average, to recover. Similarly, a corporation bond may sell in the market at a substantial discount, and be included among the assets of the owner at this market price, while on the books of the corporation it must remain as a liability at full face value. The existence of debt may thus reduce the aggregate net worth of individuals as measured by balance sheets based on market prices below what it would be in the absence of debt.

The effect is not all in this direction, however. A firm that is financed by a judicious combination of common stocks and bonded indebtedness may find its securities commanding a greater aggregate market value than one that is financed wholly from common-stock equities. For example, if we ignore for the moment the discriminatory impact of the corporation income tax and similar artificial differentials, and also ignore the costs of reorganization procedures that might be required in case of default on bonds, then the holder of 10 per cent of the shares of a company *A* financed entirely by equities could provide for himself exactly the same expectation of returns of various amounts from another company *B* with similar assets and a similar business but financed partly by bonds; all that is needed is for the investor to purchase 10 per cent of the shares of *B*, plus 10 per cent of the bonds of *B*, instead of 10 per cent of the shares of *A*. Since if the market value of the securities of company *A* were greater than the total market value of the stocks and bonds of *B*, then a stockholder of *A* would be able to duplicate his income expectation at a lower price by switching from stock in *A* to proportionate shares of the bonds and stock of *B*, we could expect the price of the *A* shares to fall and the price of the *B* bonds and shares to rise until this is no longer true. The reverse does not hold, however, for if the *A* securities sell for less than the aggregate of the *B* securities, there is no way for an investor who holds only bonds or only stocks of *B* to duplicate his income expectation with securities of the *A* company. To the extent that the securities in *B* offer different investors an opportunity to invest with a degree of risk more to their liking, they may command a higher price.

Thus market conditions may well be such that a judicious use of debt instruments will enable a company to enhance the total market value of securities based on a given set of underlying real assets. There are limits to this process, of course, since when the bond issue becomes too large a proportion of the total the probability of default on the bonds becomes high enough to begin to represent a risk comparable to that of investing in equities; moreover, if a default does occur it is likely to attract superimposed costs, so that the total proceeds obtainable from firm *B* in the event of an unfavorable development may fall short of the total proceeds obtainable from firm *A* under a like development of the concrete events by reason of court fees and other similar expenses, plus the effects of the greater disruption caused to the conduct of *B*'s business.

It cannot be assumed, however, that there is any strong tendency for financial structures to be adjusted so as to maximize the market value of securities in the aggregate. The corporation income tax, for example, provides a powerful influence toward debt financing, in that interest payments on debt instruments are deductible in computing taxable income, while dividends on equity instruments are not. But a detailed consideration of these influences lies properly in the field of corporation finance or taxation rather than of economic theory. What is important here is to realize that the aggregate value ascribed to the assets of a community may vary according to the way in which the beneficial interests in these assets are arranged, aside from any change that may be induced in the physical characteristics or earning power of the assets.

Liquidity

IN A DYNAMIC situation involving uncertainty or risk, a mere statement of the net balance of assets and liabilities is insufficient as a characterization of the impact of the balance-sheet position of a firm or an individual on its plans and decisions: it is almost equally important to know the relative liquidity or solvency of the firm or individual as indicated by the relation between the immediacy of the liabilities and the liquidity of the assets. Unfortunately, we lack any simple over-all measure for this characteristic of a balance sheet. Liquidity is, indeed, to a large extent a qualitative and even a subjective variable. Moreover, it is not in general possible to consider that greater liquidity of one firm makes up in any significant sense for a lesser liquidity of another. Liquidity, however it might be measured, is, accordingly, not something that can be aggregated and treated as a global entity in the way that assets and liabilities can. Liquidity does, however, interact in a significant way with other macroeconomic variables, and ideally macroeconomic models should reflect this influence. Because of the difficulty in measuring liquidity, however, relatively few macroeconomic models make explicit use of it. Whether considered explicitly or not, great care is needed wherever liquidity is likely to play a significant role in a macroeconomic analysis.

The maintenance of an optimum amount of liquidity in its balance sheet is important for a firm or individual because on the one hand an excessive degree of liquidity ordinarily means that assets are not in the form permitting the maximum rate of return commensurate with the risk involved; on the other hand, failure to maintain adequate liquidity exposes the individual or firm to the risk that any unforeseen adversity may compel liquidation at a substantial sacrifice of assets for which it is difficult to realize full value in order to meet short-term obligations; in extreme cases, this may even result in a bankruptcy or reorganization that might have been averted had adequate liquidity been maintained. In a sense, the maintenance of adequate liquidity serves to prevent one misfortune from touching off others in a sort of chain reaction. Indeed, the taking out of insurance policies by business firms is often to be explained not so much on the basis of the declining marginal utility of income or wealth for the proprietors of the business, but rather as a means of insuring the preservation of adequate liquidity at a time of misfortune, thus making it possible to put the resources of the firm into less liquid and more productive forms.

The over-all liquidity of the economic units in an economy, however measured, is affected in a general way in the short run by four influences:

general climate of expectations, the total supply of money, the general level of prices, and the rate of interest. The climate of expectations is itself such a subjective and vague variable that no very definite relationship can be postulated beyond the vague one that optimistic expectations tend to improve liquidity in the short run, or at least to reduce the demand for liquidity relative to the supply of liquid assets, and that pessimistic expectations produce the reverse effect. The effect of changes in the total supply of money on the over-all liquidity position is likewise in a fairly obvious direction, if uncertain in magnitude, as a given addition to the total cash in circulation will obviously increase liquidity, but the effectiveness of this change will vary widely according to how strategically or otherwise the addition becomes disseminated.

Changes in the general price level also affect liquidity, but the effect is not invariably in the same direction as the price change. Moreover, the effect on liquidity can vary independently of the effect of price changes on the net worth of individuals. This can be seen most readily if we think of the assets and liabilities of an economic unit as being classified as both short term and long term, and independently according to whether they represent items fixed in terms of money, or whether they represent items defined in real or commodity terms. The effect of a general shift in the price level on net worth can be determined from the creditor or debtor position of the unit: net worth will increase by more or less than the price rise, and real net worth will, accordingly, increase or decrease, according to whether money obligations, both long term and short term, are greater or less than money assets. But the effect of the price change on liquidity will depend not on the over-all debtor or creditor position of the unit, but on the debtor or creditor position of the unit with respect to its short-term obligations.

Ordinarily, every short-term money liability of one unit is a short-term money asset of another, money itself being a short-term liability of the issuing authority, leaving short-term commodity assets and money as the short-term items in an aggregate balance sheet of all nongovernmental economic units. A fall in the price level might thus be thought to reduce liquidity on the average by reducing the value of the short-term assets (e.g., inventory of finished and nearly finished products) by more than the reduction in the value of the short-term liabilities, so that the net short-term credit balance becomes smaller relative to the gross balance sheet, which will normally contain a relatively higher proportion of money items. Conceivably, however, the reverse could be true in an economy operating with a very large stock of money and relatively few short-term real assets, i.e., assets that are normally expected to be sold in the relatively near future so as to furnish funds to meet short-term liabilities. In any case, the situation will vary from individual to individual and from firm to firm. A magazine publisher, for example, has among his liabilities a substantial item representing unexpired subscriptions, i.e., the obligation to furnish a certain commodity in the near future. If short-term assets are small, or consist mainly of cash, notes, and accounts receivable, a fall in prices improves liquidity and a rise in the price level impairs liquidity. This is true even though a price increase might improve net worth at the same time that it impairs liquidity, as might be the case if the long-term assets were chiefly physical assets while long-term liabilities included a substantial amount of money items, such as bonded indebtedness. Similarly, a fall in prices might well impair the long-run net-worth position while at the same time easing the short-term liquidity situation.

Other cases of a somewhat similar nature are those of builders or manufacturers who have contracted for the sale of their product at a fixed price in advance of purchasing the necessary factors of production; public utilities under obligation to provide the service demanded by the public at rates determined by public-utility commissions and changed only after considerable delay, and speculators short of commodity futures. These and others in like circumstances may find that their liquidity is adversely affected by a general increase in prices; here also impairment of liquidity may be accompanied by either an improvement or an impairment of real net worth. The speculator short of futures will ordinarily have both his real net worth and his liquidity impaired by a rise in prices; on the other hand, public-utility stockholders may experience an increase in real net worth, if the utility is heavily bonded, at the same time as the liquidity of the utility company decreases, provided of course that the utility company can weather the immediate difficulty without a reorganization.

If liquidity were additive and if the stock of money is low in relation to short-term real assets and the total volume of money obligations outstanding, one might be able to assume with some confidence that for an increase in the price level the increase in liquidity of those positively affected would outweigh the loss in liquidity of the others. However, it is at least conceivable that those whose liquidity is increased are already so liquid that no further effect would be produced by the improvement, whereas those whose liquidity is decreased are more susceptible to being seriously affected by the impairment. Indeed, if after a considerable period of stability in which individuals and firms have managed to adjust their liquidity to a fairly narrow margin there is a sudden and unexpected increase in prices, the over-all effect on liquidity may be predominantly the adverse effect on those losing liquidity, while a sudden unexpected fall in the price level would also have a predominantly adverse effect on over-all liquidity. Different groups would be affected in the two cases, but the aggregate effect felt would be in the same direction in the two cases rather than in opposite directions as one is at first tempted to assume.

One of the reasons that it is so difficult to analyze clearly the relations between price changes and liquidity is the fact that changes in the quantity of money have in the past been closely associated with changes in the price level; as an increase in the money supply, at least insofar as it is due to the direct expansion of currency, has the obvious effect of increasing the liquidity of the public at the expense of the irrelevant liquidity of the government, there is a natural tendency to associate rising prices with increased liquidity. But if one considers the effects of price-level changes on liquidity under circumstances in which the supply of money is kept rigorously constant, the association, as we have seen, is not nearly so uniform. Even if the possibility of an inverse effect due to the nonadditivity of positive and negative shifts is discounted, there remains the possibility of the "Pigou effect"—i.e., the effect on individual behavior of increasing the real value of the money supply and the government debt—becoming important enough to dominate. Indeed, if prices drop far enough, with a fixed quantity of money, the real value of the fixed quantity of money must eventually become large enough to dominate the picture and provide sufficient additional liquidity to outweigh all other adverse effects on liquidity.

Perhaps the most that one can conclude on this score is that under normal circumstances there may be an over-all tendency for an increase in prices to improve liquidity and for a fall in prices to impair it; that sudden changes in either direction influence liquidity adversely through maldistribution of liquidity, and extreme changes in prices affect liquidity adversely if changes in the money supply are restricted.

The fourth factor affecting liquidity in general is the rate of interest. The rate of interest is in effect the price for which those with adequate access to credit can increase their liquidity by borrowing. Lowering the rate of interest thus tends to improve the potential liquidity of good risks, if not their actual liquidity. But this recourse is available only to those whose credit is good, i.e., who are least likely to need a loan for the specific purpose of increasing liquidity. There is some truth to the wheeze that banks are institutions established to lend money to those who can prove that they don't need it.

However, lowering of the rate of interest often does mean an improvement of liquidity even for those who cannot avail themselves of it directly. Those whose credit is good may maintain a greater degree of liquidity than they otherwise would, since the cost is less, and thereby tend to pay more promptly and thus diffuse the liquidity among those with less direct access to credit. Moreover, a lowering of the interest rates often coincides with and indeed may be taken as a representative symptom of a general relaxation of the terms on which credit will be granted: lower margins on collateral loans, lower down payments and longer terms on installment purchases, and the like. Nevertheless the association of lower interest rates with increased liquidity must be thought of as a causal relation only with great caution, since in many cases the reduction in interest rates may be merely a reflection of other influences tending toward increased liquidity, such as an increase in the supply of money, rather than as a promoter of liquidity in its own right.

Under some circumstances, indeed, a reduction in the normal or standard rate of interest might lead to a reluctance to make loans except on the best security, so that pressure directly on interest rates might work in the opposite direction. From some points of view, also, it may be not the level of interest rates, or even of the short-term interest rate by itself that is controlling, but rather the differential between short- and long-term rates. If the cost of borrowing on short term is no lower, for a firm with adequate short-term liquidity, than the cost of borrowing long term, such a firm might well switch from borrowing short by taking out a line of credit at banks, to borrowing long by floating bond issues; this has the effect of converting part of the supply of short-term securities into long-term securities, and thus decreasing the liquidity of these assets. A reduction in long-term interest rates, unaccompanied by a corresponding reduction in short-term rates, might in this way actually decrease the supply of liquidity. But again care must be exercised in particular instances to avoid confusing causes with mere symptoms.

The macroeconomic theory of stocks is thus still in a moderately unsatisfactory state. Wealth and net worth can be defined but are difficult to measure in a manner that meets the more exacting requirements of the economist as contrasted with those of the accountant; liquidity is quite intractable as a macroeconomic magnitude, and it is even difficult to say with much confidence in which direction it is influenced by some of the important factors that impinge upon it. But in spite of the rather awkward questions encountered, it has still been essential to consider the nature of these stock magnitudes first, since many of the important flow magnitudes cannot be defined with accuracy and logical consistency without reference to these stocks. To the extent that the definition of the stock magnitudes has been unsatisfactory, a corresponding difficulty will be found to underlie the definitions of the flow magnitudes that relate to them. Only to the extent that errors or uucertainties may cancel out when we consider the difference between two stock magnitudes as an element in flows, or to the extent that the major part of many flow magnitudes consists of elements not dependent on stocks for their definition, will these difficulties become of less relative importance when flow magnitudes are considered.

Flow Aggregates: Consumption

THE MOST basic of the flow concepts, though one not often used directly in economic analysis, is psychic income, which consists of the sum of satisfactions derived from economic sources by an individual (or members of a household). Since this quantity is obviously not measurable directly by the means normally at our disposal, it is usual to consider instead "consumption," which is the value of the resources used directly for the production of the psychic income of the individual or household. Not only does this provide a basis for measurement, but it leaves to one side the question of interpersonal comparisons, as well as the question of whether the psychic income is experienced at the time the resource is used up or at some other time.

In principle, consumption should be measured only at the time the resource is actually used up. Thus the value of a can of soup should be included when opened and served, and not when purchased from the grocer. For durable goods, such as clothing, furniture, automobiles, housing, and so on, consumption should be measured by estimating the depreciation of the item and adding in a normal return on its (depreciated) capital value. Thus if a person owns and lives in a house worth $10,000 that has a remaining useful life estimated at 40 years, an evaluation of his consumption would in principle include something like $250 for depreciation (if figured on a straight-line basis) and $600 for imputed interest (if figured at 6 per cent) on the investment. In addition, if repairs, maintenance, and taxes amounted to another $300, the total would come to $1,150, which is comparable to what a tenant might pay outright for the rental of a similar house.

In practice, however, the data required for the measurement of consumption strictly according to this accrual theory is usually inadequate, particularly with respect to consumer inventories. Moreover, the time at which consumption has an impact on the economy at large is more nearly at the time of purchase rather than at the time of use. One can, indeed, quibble if one wants to about just what constitutes "using up" a given economic resource: is it physical destruction, as in the burning of the midnight oil, or is it the fading of the traceable consequences, as when, the examination over, the learning acquired with the midnight oil gradually fades from memory, or is it the placing of a resource in a position in which it can no longer be reintroduced into the exchange process, as when the kerosene is hauled to the student's cabin in the wilderness, assuming this to be so remote that it would never pay to haul it back, even if it were never to be used in the cabin. Even from a strictly psychic point of view, it can be maintained that much of the satisfaction derived from consumption occurs either through anticipation or reminiscence of the actual experience or activity entailing the consumption, and that, accordingly, a close attention to the exact time of physical destruction of the commodity is unwarranted. Thus the satisfaction derived from eating is in large part the avoidance of a hungry feeling for some time afterward; the satisfaction derived from a vacation trip may in considerable measure lie in the planning of it and in recalling and talking about it afterward.

Accordingly, except for a few of the larger and more durable items, consumption is usually measured by purchases of consumer goods. Purchase of a house, for example, is usually treated as an investment, and, accordingly, a calculation of the imputed services should be included in consumption. Less frequently, automobiles may be treated in a similar fashion. But where the life of the item is short, as with clothing, or the value is small, as with household tools, or where the item, though valuable and durable, is exotic, as with jewelry, ordinarily no attempt is made, for practical purposes, to differentiate between consumption and purchase, in spite of the jewelry saleman's persistence in referring to an impending sale as investment rather than spending.

Another point at which difficulties arise in the definition of consumption is the degree to which resources are consumed that are not obtained directly through purchase in the market. The most important item here is the consumption of one's own time and effort in the form of leisure, or possibly in the form of doing various jobs for oneself that might be paid for if done for one by others. The painter who takes time off from his usual job to redecorate his own home is using for his own satisfaction resources that might have been devoted to other purposes in a manner involving a market transaction. Indeed, if the painter were to remain at his job and employ another painter to do the work on his house, the real use of resources would be substantially unchanged, but in this case the consumption would be represented by a money transaction and would thus be unequivocally included in the painter's consumption. But this case shades off imperceptibly into the case where no specific work is done by the person who stays home from work, and from there to the case of the individual who chooses a job where the standard work week is shorter. If this is done voluntarily on the ground that the satisfactions derived from the leisure outweigh those to be derived from the expenditure of the additional earnings produced by more work, then the leisure is in principle clearly to be counted as a form of consumption, though in the face of tax and other deductions from the pay envelope there may be some question as to what value to place on it. More important, it is difficult to say, in any general way, to what extent such leisure is in fact voluntary and to what extent it reflects either involuntary unemployment, a collective-bargaining *démarche* designed to spread work or raise wages, or is simply the acceptance by the individual of a standard work week over which he may have little control. Because of this uncertainty, and because of the difficulty of measuring the amount of leisure and setting a value on it, particularly where hours of work are not standardized, no allowance for the value of leisure is ordinarily made in compiling estimates of aggregate consumption. If consumption figures are to be used in an appraisal of standards of living, some separate allowance must be made for any differences in the amount of leisure time consumed.

This consumption of leisure is by no means an unimportant element, as it can on occasion change quite rapidly, and substantial errors, anomalies, or distortions can result from neglecting it in some cases. There is Pigou's classic case of the man who innocently decreased aggregate nominal consumption, as computed, and with it the national income of which it is a part, by marrying his housekeeper. Conversely, nominal consumption and national income could both be increased if neighbors started to take in each other's washing for pay. More important, if in a period of national emergency there is a general movement of women away from housekeeping into remunerative employment, there is a drop in the consumption of home services that is not reflected in the usual figures on consumption, and the apparent resulting rise in the national income is to some extent fictitious. Conversely, a fall in the national income may be to some extent exaggerated if part of the fall represents merely a shift from the money economy to the self-service economy. International comparisons of standards of living are particularly subject to this type of error.

There may be less hesitancy about including items received directly in kind, such as hospitalization, meals, housing, and other fringe benefits obtained as supplementary compensation for employment; home-grown food consumed on the farm; or items taken from stock for personal use by the proprietor of a store. The difficulty here is the value to be ascribed to some of these items. Housing may range from a seaman's bunk to the White House. Other perquisites may include "professional courtesy" such as is common among doctors, free tuition for faculty children, free passes to employees of railroads and their families, special discounts to employees of a department store, and the like. There is Kleinwachter's famous Flügeladjutant, who had the privilege or duty of accompanying his general to the opera at no cost to himself, which might be a form of compensation in kind, but might also be a bore to one who did not happen to like opera. In fact, such perquisites of employment fade imperceptibly into general working conditions, and the measurement of consumption must presumably stop somewhere short of attempting to allow for all particularly pleasant or unpleasant working conditions as an adjustment to "consumption."

In practice, allowance for these items received in kind varies considerably according to the thoroughness and purpose of the investigation. Fortunately, the amount involved does not appear to be large for the economy as a whole, and is relatively stable from year to year, so that errors and omissions with respect to these items is not likely to throw any analysis seriously off, provided that the same practice is adhered to consistently.

Another difficult margin that somewhat overlaps the above is the line between personal and business expense. Here the principle of demarcation is fairly clear and simple: to the extent that an expenditure is expected to produce a financial return, it is a business expense, while to the extent that it produces a direct return in satisfaction to the individual, it is consumption. But both motives are often present, in which case an allocation may be in order; unfortunately, both motives and expectations are often difficult to determine from objective evidence, so that considerable guesswork is necessary. For example, to the extent that meals eaten on a business trip cost more than meals eaten at home, the excess may be considered a business expense and excluded from consumption; it is, however, at most only this excess that can be considered to be occasioned by the business and therefore excluded from consumption, not the whole amount. Whether part of the excess could also be considered as includable as a type of perquisite belongs in the difficult category of the Flügeladjutant at the opera, and perhaps can be dismissed as an insoluble problem.

Expenses of traveling to and from work present a substantial and knotty problem. One may consider that normally an individual has a choice between living close to his work or at a distance, and that the expense of a longer journey is a part of the price paid for more favorable living conditions. This treatment is particularly appealing in that rents are often lower for comparable accommodations as they are more remote from the center of the city or metropolis, so that in part the choice is between high rent and low travel costs or low rent and high travel costs. But in many instances it may not be possible to live close to a particular job, in which case the expense is one that is necessary if the work is to be done at all, and would, accordingly, be a business expense. In mining, the portal-to-portal-pay issue is a case in point, although here an additional argument for requiring the employer to cover this expense would be that the employer controls the conditions of transportation between portal and working station and should therefore be saddled with this cost in order to place the incentive for reducing this cost where the power to reduce it lies. But many cases are not as clear-cut as this: there may be living accommodations close to a particular job, but only of an inferior or substandard variety. A large part of the cost of the journey to work arises from the concentration of employment in the core areas of large cities; it is not at all clear to what extent this pattern of employment location is related to efficiencies resulting from the close geographical proximity of large complexes of production units, or is related to the attraction to individuals of the cultural and other facilities that tend to be available chiefly in the larger cities.

Questions of this kind are of very real importance in planning and in the making of comparisons between different times and places; for macroeconomic analysis of given economic systems at a given time and place, conundrums of this nature are fortunately of minor importance. It is not as necessary in macroeconomic analysis to make fine distinctions in individual cases as it is, for example, in defining income or consumption for tax purposes: where tax burdens hinge on the definition, matters of individual equity are at stake and if the lines are carelessly drawn substantial incentives may be created to make uneconomical shifts in the character of the operations affected. In a macroeconomic model it is usually possible to achieve an adequate degree of realism while still excluding these troublesome factors from explicit consideration in the model, while in the application of macroeconomic analysis to actual statistics, usually only changes in the macroeconomic aggregates will be of concern, and generally speaking changes in the questionable or not readily measurable items are likely to be small enough or to move closely enough in a linear relation to the measurable items so as not to affect the over-all picture too greatly. This is, of course, an assumption that cannot be taken for granted generally, however; whether it is warranted in any particular instance must, in principle at least, be examined afresh in the light of whatever information is available.

In addition to these various items of individual consumption, aggregate consumption includes, in principle, various forms of collective consumption, such as the use of public parks, highways, and the like; the enjoyment of public celebrations and such items as publicly supported radio programs; education and other services provided by philanthropic institutions. Adequate discussion of these items requires, however, that the whole role of governments in the macroeconomic structure be considered, and so with this mention we will defer a complete analysis of these items until later.

Personal Income

INCOME is the most discussed and perhaps the most important of the flow concepts, but it can be defined consistently and precisely only in terms of consumption and net worth. In principle, we shall define income for a given period as the sum of the consumption for the period, plus the increase in net worth from the beginning of the period to the end. If the net worth decreases, this decrease is of course to be subtracted from consumption to get income. The precise definition of income thus combines the difficulties of defining consumption with most of those of defining net worth. The only exception is that those items in net worth whose values can be considered the same at the end as at the beginning of the period may be left out of account.

Other definitions of income have of course been used, but this "accrued-income" definition appears to be the only one that is reasonably free from arbitrary distinctions and thus avoids capricious differences in the evaluation of income in given real circumstances that are produced with other definitions by insignificant differences in form. It is sometimes argued, for instance, that income should refer only to those receipts that belong in some sense to a continuous stream, thus excluding windfalls and other casual receipts that are not likely to be repeated. This view, indeed, was widely held in England for a long time and to some extent still stands embedded, albeit in considerably modified form, in British income-tax practice. This concept obviously gets into serious difficulty when one tries to draw a sharp line between casual and repetitive receipts, and as applied in practice has produced a number of curious and anomalous results, so that this concept has been under more or less continuous modification and adjustment without ever achieving any stable general acceptance in a specific form.

Capital Gains

ANOTHER definition frequently advanced is one that would exclude "capital gains," i.e., increases in the value of an asset or group of assets that remain physically more or less unchanged. Implicit in this concept is the idea that there is some "corpus" that can be clearly distinguished from the "fruit." This concept has its roots in the body of common law that began to take form at a time when land was one of the most important forms of property, and indeed as applied to indestructible assets such as land, the distinction between "corpus" and "fruit" is a fairly plausible and definite one. But when it is attempted to apply such a distinction with any precision to other types of assets, which change in quality through depreciation and major alterations, and even to common stocks which represent an equity in a collection of assets that may change drastically in character from time to time, the distinction between "corpus" and "fruit" becomes completely arbitrary and capricious, unless, indeed, the "fruit" is defined as that which can be detached from an asset during a given period without impairing the remaining capital value of the corpus, in which case the fruit turns out to be identical with the accrued income, inclusive of capital gains. For most assets, and particularly for securities representing a changing net balance of physical assets, other assets, and liabilities, there is no strict sense in which a "corpus" can be kept intact except in terms of its value (though there may be, as we shall see below, a choice to be made between keeping the money value intact and keeping some sort of "real" value intact).

Attempts to distinguish capital gains from other proceeds from property inevitably lead to anomalous results and differences in income depending on purely formal arrangements that will normally have little or no influence on the behavior of a rational individual. For example, we may compare several individuals as follows: *A* has 1,000 shares of corporation *X*, bought at a price of $10 for a total of $10,000, while *B*, who also bought 1,000 shares in *X*, sold them for $20,000 when the market price rose to its current level of 20, and with the proceeds has bought 2,000 shares of *Y* with a current market value of $20,000; *C* originally bought 1,000 shares in *Y* at $10, at the same time that *A* and *B* made their original purchases; in the meantime, dividends of $10 a share have been paid, with which *C* has bought additional shares of *Y* so that he now holds $20,000 worth; *D* likewise bought 1,000 shares in *Y*, but used his dividends to buy shares in *Z*; *E* bought shares in corporation *W*, which first rose in market price from $10 to $20, and then were split 2 for 1, so that *E* now has 2,000 shares worth $10 each; *F* bought 100 shares in *Y* but spent the dividends; *H* also bought 1,000 shares of *X*, but after their price had risen to 20, he posted them as collateral for a loan of $10,000 and spent the proceeds of the loan; *J* also bought 1,000 shares of *X*, but after they went up to $20, sold 500 shares outright for $10,000, spending the proceeds.

Defining income as consumption plus increase in net worth, it is clear that each of these individuals has had an income of $10,000 over the period. *A*, *B*, *C*, *D*, and *E* have spent nothing and increased their net worth by $10,000; *F*, *G*, *H*, and *J* have spent $10,000 and kept their net worth intact. *C*, *D*, and *F* have incomes of $10,000 by almost any criterion, but if capital gains are not fully included in income, the others will be considered to have smaller incomes or no income at all, depending on the precise criterion used for distinguishing the capital gains and for including them in income, in spite of the fact that their real situation is quite comparable. Assuming rational behavior, one would not predict, for example, a substantially different pattern of future consumption for *A*, *B*, and *E* than for *C* and *D*, nor for *F* than for *G*, *H*, and *J*.

But while the inclusion of capital gains in the computation of income is essential both for the comparison of different individuals and for macroeconomic purposes, some modifications may be appropriate where net worth is affected by such general influences as a change in the price level or changes in interest rates. But it should be emphasized that neither of these factors proves to justify leaving out of account altogether even those capital gains and losses that are directly associated with such changes, let alone gains and losses generally.

Price-Level Changes

OBVIOUSLY, a change in net worth that merely reflects a change in the general price level does not represent any increased command over resources as compared with the stable price-level situation that would justify its inclusion in a concept of real income. For example, suppose the price level stands at 100 at times 0 and 1, rising to 120 at time 2, and that an individual *A* has a net worth of $20,000 at time 0, $20,000 at time 1, and $24,000 at time 2, and that he spends $5,000 in the interval from 0 to 1, and $5,500 in the interval from 1 to 2. We may consider the price level to remain steady at 100 throughout period 0 to 1, and to average 110 over the period from 1 to 2. In real terms, *A*'s experience is substantially the same in the two periods, and we may say that he has an income of $5,000 in the first period, and an income of $5,500 in current dollars for the second period, which if deflated by the price index for this period of 110, would give $5,000 in base-period dollars for both periods. To add the $4,000 of increase in net worth to the income of the second period, giving a nominal income of $9,500, is to mix capital and income, and there is no general deflator which when applied directly to this $9,500 figure will make it comparable to the $5,000 income of the first period.

To take care of such cases, accordingly, the definition of income must be modified to read consumption plus the change in the *real* net worth. In the above case there was no change in real net worth, and income was equal to consumption. If instead we consider *B* who holds bonds that remain at the same nominal value of $20,000 at time 2, then *B*'s real net worth goes down from $20,000 at time 1 to $16,666 (in base-period dollars) in time 2, or a loss of $3,333 in base-period dollars which when deducted from the $5,000 of expenditure (likewise deflated to base-period dollars) gives a real net income of $1,666 in base-period dollars, or an income expressed in terms of period 1–2 prices of $1,666 × 110/100 = $1,833. Or the same result can be obtained by taking $4,000, which is the amount by which the net worth is short, at time 2, of having increased sufficiently to keep abreast of prices, multiplying this by 110/120 to express it in terms of the average price level of the period 1 to 2, and deducting the resulting $3,667 from the $5,500 of expenditure, getting again $1,833. On the other hand, if we consider *C* who invested in volatile equities which rose in value to $30,000 at time 2, this will have a purchasing power of $25,000 in base-period prices, or a real gain of $5,000, which if added to the expenditure for period 1 to 2, assumed to be the same as that of *A* and *B* gives a net real income of $10,000 altogether in base-period prices, or $11,000 in current prices.

To be sure, relatively few individuals would make such calculations if asked to determine their real income, and perhaps a considerable number would actually react substantially differently from the way that might be considered consistent with such an income figure. Indeed, for small changes in the price level, many might well ignore the price-level adjustment and treat the nominal income as the true income. But in no case would a mere noninclusion of capital gains and losses give a correct basis for predicting behavior or for evaluating the economic status of the individual, nor is there any way of abating the taxation of capital gains that is not in substantial degree arbitrary and discriminatory.

The above analysis shows further that to the extent that the selection of the norm by which we determine when the price level has remained constant is an arbitrary selection, the definition of real income and real savings is in principle likewise arbitrary. If we consider, with Marx, Keynes, and others, that labor time constitutes the standard to be taken as having a fixed price, represented by, say, the wage rate for unskilled labor, or even by some average wage rate, then the measure even of the relative incomes of *A* and *B* will differ from what it would be if, say, a consumer price index is taken as the norm to be made constant. We might for instance find that on one basis *A*'s income is higher than that of *B*, while on the other basis *B*'s income is the higher one, depending on the ratios of consumption to net worth for the two persons. By the same token, the division of individual income and of national income between earned income and property income will be similarly arbitrary. This arbitrariness is fundamental, resulting from the tendency of the real purchasing power of wages to increase over time as a consequence of economic progress, and is independent of the actual rate of inflation or deflation.

Interest-Rate Changes

IT HAS also been alleged that changes in capital values reflecting merely changes in interest rates are illusory and should not be allowed to affect computations of real current income. This contention requires somewhat more careful analysis. If we can assume for the moment that a stable general level of current consumer-goods prices is guaranteed, a drop in security prices brought about by an increase in interest rates can be taken as a reduction of the price of future goods in terms of present goods. But for the individual who has arranged his assets so that their maturity coincides with his expected future dissaving, changes in market prices of his assets that reflect only discount rates and not the certainty of eventual yields will have no "income effect" for him; if he carried out his original plans he will not be affected one way or another. To be sure, if such an individual has considerable elasticity of substitution as between present and future goods, and if the change in interest rates is sudden and substantial so that it has shifted by a considerable amount before the individual has been able to adjust, then he may be able to shift his pattern of expenditure in a direction such as to take advantage of the changed rate of exchange between present and future goods, so that his real income would increase whether the rate of interest went up or down. But the benefit to be derived in this fashion is small, and would indeed vanish if such an individual were to adjust successively to small changes in interest rates, as he would then be moving substantially along an indifference curve, rather than along a secant, to the new equilibrium position.

Interest rates will have a more definite effect where the maturity pattern of the individual's portfolio of securities differs from his planned dissaving schedule. If his assets mature later, on the average, and cannot be directly liquidated any earlier without loss, then if interest rates rise, he will be compelled to sell some of his assets sooner or later at prices lower than those he was expecting before the increase in interest rates. But this loss will occur later, and be much smaller in magnitude than the fall in the current market value of his securities, so that it would be incorrect to take the immediate loss of market value as a measure of the ultimate loss. In the opposite case where assets mature earlier than planned dissavings, so that reinvestment will be necessary, a gain will be felt, as a result of the rise in interest rates. Indeed, it is possible for an individual to be affected by a change in interest rates even though he has no assets at the moment, as he may plan later either to invest for a period or to borrow. In any case, the change in current interest rates is relevant only indirectly, as a reflection of expectations of what interest rates are likely to be in the future: it is what the interest rates will be at the time of liquidation or reinvestment that is directly relevant.

A change in interest rates will thus affect different individuals in different ways, depending not only on their asset holdings but on their plans and expectations for the future. There is obviously no adjustment in terms of recognition or nonrecognition of changes in market values that will adequately reflect these various possibilities. If we consider, however, two individuals with similar net worths and future savings plans, who differ primarily in that *A* holds primarily short-term securities while *B* holds primarily long-term securities, then including current market-value changes in their incomes, even when these reflect primarily interest-rate changes, will fairly closely reflect the difference in the way their prospects have changed, whereas if interest rates rise and *B*'s loss in market value is ignored, it would be at least awkward to attempt to preserve this differential by means of an addition to *A*'s income justified by the fact that he now can invest at higher interest rates than formerly.

If on the other hand interest-rate changes correspond to changed expectations as to future price trends, there is still no justification for eliminating the gain or loss. A given number of dollars now, whether in cash or in terms of the market value of assets, will represent the same amount of future purchasing power whether stable prices are expected with low interest rates, or inflation is expected with correspondingly higher interest rates. Any gain or loss in market value will thus be a real gain or loss.

Anticipation of Future Events

MORE FUNDAMENTALLY, the question is how far changes in future opportunities should be taken into consideration in the measurement of current income. The signing of a contract calling for higher wage rates in the future is not ordinarily considered to give rise to income at the time of the signing of the contract. If we regard interest as the incentive for postponing consumption or "waiting," an increase in interest rates represents an increase in compensation to be paid for waiting still to be performed. This is in sharp distinction from the market value of assets that is available to the individual immediately regardless of what his future performance may be.

Introduction of expectations of the future into the picture causes further difficulty in the selection of an appropriate price index by which to deflate net worth in the calculation of real income. As we noted above, in the computation of real net income, net worth has to be deflated separately; one does not get accrued real income simply by dividing accrued money income by a price index. From the point of view of the individual, net worth can be considered to have value in real terms in proportion as it enables him to purchase future consumption goods. One way of obtaining a real net worth in terms of what the individual is eventually going to use his capital for would be to deflate current market value by an index of the cost of future goods in terms of current dollars, the future goods being suitably distributed according to the pattern of dissavings of the individual. As compared with ignoring any special adjustment for interest-rate changes, this would result, for an increase in interest rates, in increasing income at the time interest rates rose, and reducing later incomes, total income over the entire period until after the liquidation of the assets being the same in the aggregate.

This procedure runs into difficulty, however, if we consider an individual who plans to make further savings in the future, for in this case there is no unique way in which the subsequent dissavings can be allocated between that future saving and the current net worth. It would be possible to adopt a "last in, first out" (LIFO) rule, but this would be essentially arbitrary and capricious in its effects in special cases. And in any case the effect of changes in interest-rate expectations on the individual who has not yet accumulated any capital will be left out of account by any process of adjusting market values.

Thus while there may be considerable uncertainty as to how the effect of changes in interest rates and other future expectations on market values and hence on net worth should be allowed for for purposes of computing real income, a reasonable case can be made for accepting market values as they stand. While other treatments may have some color of rationality, they are still not at all clear-cut or simple to carry out, and none of them are even approximately equivalent to the ignoring of the capital gain or less.

Gifts and Other Special Items

NEVERTHELESS, a certain number of exceptions are usually made to the definition of income as consumption plus change in real net worth, at least on the individual level. Changes in net worth arising from gifts and bequests are usually omitted from consideration: to deduct such gifts in computing the income of the donor would produce erratic results that would on the whole be quite at variance with the normal connotation of the term "income," while to include gifts in the income of the recipient without deduction from the income of the donor would be double counting of a sort that would make the aggregate income of a group depend on the volume of gifts exchanged among them, thus further separating the income concept from that of production.

Other deviations from the basic definition are made in varying circumstances, depending in part on the figures available and on the purposes for which the figures are to be used. For example, compensation in a lump sum for injuries or damages are ordinarily not included. In the case of damages to property, this merely means the offsetting of the indemnity against the impairment of the value of the property, with no change in net worth, and the basic definition is in effect adhered to. But in the case of personal damages, the offsetting item of impairment of earning power is not normally included in net-worth computations. Excluding the indemnity from income is an implicit recognition of changes in capitalized earning capacity in this special case.

Theory vs. Practice

THERE ARE, moreover, some purposes for which it is less important to arrive at a definition that is consistent, precise, and free from anomalies than it is to arrive at a concept that could be relied on in predicting the behavior of the individual. If we were dealing with a theoretical economic man, of course, the theoretical definition of income would serve adequately, and indeed might be considered the best parameter for the purpose. Individuals act to varying degrees in an irrational manner, however, and as a practical matter it may be possible to get better results in a macroeconomic analysis by using a concept of income that has a degree of irrationality that more or less corresponds to the behavior of the typical imperfectly rational individual. In effect, what we would be looking for would be not what the *homo oeconomicus* would regard as his income, but rather what the man on the street regards as his income. Thus as a practical matter for some purposes it might be appropriate to exclude undistributed corporate earnings from income, even though they were adequately reflected in the market value of the stock, on the ground that the average individual would not regard this as income, to the extent of being induced by such an increase in market value to increase his consumption to the same extent that a dividend of the same sum would. Concepts of this character are often difficult to define clearly, as it is not always easy to draw a sharp line between those items that will induce an increase in consumption and those that will not have this effect. Moreover, the same type of item may have such an effect for some individuals and not for others. Nevertheless, for the purposes of analyzing and predicting behavior, it is often useful to construct and use such aggregates. The Department of Commerce series on income payments to individuals is fairly close to such a concept of cash income, or "income-as-conceived-by-the-man-on-the-street."

National Income

IN A SIMPLE purely competitive economy with individuals producing and exchanging with each other at arm's length, it would be possible to obtain a measure of national income simply by adding together the individual incomes of the members of the community. Actually, however, there are various ways in which individuals deal with each other outside of the framework of pure competition, and this leads to corresponding difficulties in the aggregation process. Some individuals obtain an income not by rendering service or producing goods but by theft or fraud; others enhance their income through the exercise of monopoly power; some obtain benefits of one kind or another more or less gratuitously, as with charity, relief payments, or inheritance; and most important, governments at various levels levy taxes and distribute benefits in ways that bear no necessary relationship to each other.

The national income can be thought of in two different ways. On the one hand, the welfare concept views the national income as the combination of a flow of current satisfactions to individuals plus an accumulation of capital and other provisions for increasing the flow of such satisfactions in the future. This concept is sometimes termed, by way of distinction, "national product at market prices." On the other hand, the national income can be looked at as the sum total of the factor inputs used in the production process, measured in terms of the amounts paid to them to secure their collaboration. Profits, in this connection, are viewed as the cost of managerial services or other inputs furnished by those to whom the profits accrue. This concept of national income is referred to as "national income (or product) at factor costs."

In a simple competitive-exchange economy, these two ways of looking at national income would give the same numerical results. The amounts paid in the market for final products will be equal in the aggregate to the costs and profits involved in their production. In practice, however, when various transactions outside the framework of pure competition are taken into account, among the more important of which are the levying of taxes and the distribution of benefits by governments, these two concepts diverge and it is necessary to distinguish between them.

The Test of Deflation

ONE CRUCIAL test that can be applied to determine the proper treatment of particular noncompetitive items is to examine the results of a process of deflating the money aggregate by a price index. For many purposes, what is of ultimate interest is not the money aggregate of national income, but rather the changes through time or the differences between different economies in the physical volume of goods and services that this money aggregate measures, i.e., the "real national income." Such an aggregate is ordinarily obtained by deflating one version or another of the national income by some suitable price index. Aside from the inevitable margin of error that attends the use of any price index, there is here a considerable question of which index should be used, if indeed there is any single index that is appropriate to use with such a variegated aggregate as national income. To obtain a deflated result that is as free as possible from patent anomalies, the way the national income is defined must be appropriately correlated with the way the price index used to deflate it is constructed.

If we are interested in national income as a welfare measure, we are to a considerable extent looking at the matter from the point of view of the ultimate consumer, and thus a cost-of-living index might be considered the proper deflator, at least for that part of the national income that represents current goods and services. It is not quite so clear what should be done with that part of the national income which consists of additions to capital, even if we wish to consider such additions solely in terms of their representing increased output of consumption goods in the future. Of course, it is first necessary to be sure that the addition to capital is a real addition and not merely the result of a general rise in the price level with a concurrent rise in the prices at which items of capital are valued; let us assume that we have included in the national income not the increase in the aggregate money value of capital assets but rather the value, at current market prices, of the amount by which categories of physical capital have increased. Provided that a hypothetical current market value can be assigned to those items of capital that have disappeared from the aggregate during the interval, then this current value of the net physical increase can be given a precise conceptual meaning, however difficult the evaluation of this quantity may be in practice.

One way of looking at this increase in capital is to consider that it represents resources that in principle could have been diverted to the production of consumer goods, and to consider the national product as a measure of the total volume of consumer goods and services that could have been produced had the capital of the community been maintained at a constant level instead of having been increased, the total volume of activity being in some sense kept at the same level. If we can consider that the relative market prices of capital goods and consumer goods reflect their respective marginal cost of production, and further assume that this relationship would continue even if the resources were completely diverted to consumption goods (i.e., that the production function has perfect elasticity of substitution in this direction), then deflating the total national income by a consumers' price index gives a result reflecting this aspect of the national income.

On the other hand, one could attempt to consider directly the increase in future consumption that this capital increase makes possible. These future goods are thus part of the basket of consumer goods that constitute the national income. If future price levels are known with certainty (as could be the case if some specified price trend, not necessarily a level one, were adopted as a goal of fiscal and monetary policy and guaranteed by the assurance of a sufficiently vigorous program of control measures), if the pattern of future increments in consumption corresponding to increments in present capital is known, and if interest rates for loans of various terms are given, it would be possible to compute prices of these future goods in terms of present money and include these prices in an index. In practice, the information for doing anything of this kind is not available, of course. It is tempting to take an index of capital equipment and construction costs and deflate the value of the increase in capital with this index separately, which would in effect be assuming a constant proportionality between a physical quantity of capital and the future goods and services that could be considered to be its marginal product, or which, under competitive conditions, could be purchased for current dollars equivalent to its current value. But even under strictly competitive conditions, changes over time in the marginal productivity of capital and corresponding changes in interest rates would upset this relationship. In practice it is, on the whole, reasonably sufficient to rely on a cost-of-living index alone as a deflator; this has the very real advantage, both conceptual and practical, of avoiding the complexities that are introduced when different indexes are used for different components of the same aggregate.

Deflation of the "national income at factor prices" involves even greater difficulties. As a measure of the "total input" in the economy, this might be reduced to "real" terms by deflating by an index of the prices that the various factors of production command: wage rates, rents, and some element representing the terms on which "real capital" can be secured. This latter element might be constructed by taking the product of an index of the prices of capital goods (including inventories) and an index of rates of profit and interest. Such an index would at best be difficult to construct, and deflation of national income in just this way has hardly ever been attempted. However, it may be noted that the bulk of such an index would consist of wage rates, so that this concept corresponds roughly to Keynes's reduction of national income and other variables to "wage units." It may be noted that while in money terms national income at factor prices and national income at market prices are numerically equal, after deflation they will of course differ, even for a purely competitive economy, and indeed their ratio will become a measure of the change in the productivity of the economy from the base period to the current period.

Noncompetitive Items and the Deflation Test—Theft

MANY RATHER significant specifications as to how particular items of a noncompetitive character should be treated in the computation of the national income according to the welfare concept can be derived from considering alternative real situations and requiring that after appropriate deflation the resulting differences in "real national income" should reflect the differences in the real welfare of the community. Consider, for example, the contribution, if any, of the shoplifter to the national income. In computing the national income as a sum of factor payments, it would be logical, on the face of it, to exclude his earnings from the aggregate on the ground that his activities are not productive. Consider, however, two cases: first suppose a simple economy in which 100 tons of product are produced and sold at a price of $2 per ton, total sales being $200, and total wages and profits paid out being likewise $200; suppose in a second case that circumstances are similar except that shoplifters make away with ten tons of the product, so that to cover expenses the remaining 90 tons must be sold at a price of $2.22 to bring in the $200 to cover costs, which will also be the wage and profit incomes of the persons engaged in legitimate activity. The shoplifter may sell his ten tons to a fence for, say, $12, or $1.20 per ton, and the fence may in turn sell the ten tons at the full market price (assuming for simplicity that he has unimpaired access to the market) of for $22.22, so that total sales on the market will be $222.22. If we include in the aggregate of factor payments the income of the shoplifter and the fence, and deflate by a price index which has risen from 100 to 111.1, we get a deflated national income of $200, the same as before, reflecting properly the fact that the total amount of goods and services made available to the public is the same as before. To refuse to include the income of the lawbreaker in this instance would lead to an understatement of the national income after allowing for the change in the market prices of products.

Such a rule cannot be followed blindly, however. Consider the residential burglar: his activities will not directly result in an increase in market prices. Even if the burglar, through a fence, sells his ten tons again on the market, so that total sales are $220, this is not additional product, but merely a double counting of the same product. Even though the burglar's income must be added in to get a total market demand of $220, there has been no increase in the total product or the total amount of consumer satisfaction and the real national income must be considered to remain at $200. In the absence of any change in the price index used for deflating, this requires a money national income of $200. To be sure, in practice increased activity by burglars may result in an increase in insurance rates, but these are not ordinarily reflected in any cost-of-living index in a way that would serve to make the proper allowance; even if included, they would presumably be weighted in proportion to the amount of insurance actually taken out, and losses by uninsured households would not be represented.

Possibly such cases could be taken to indicate that index numbers should be modified to take full account of such items, rather than that such items should be excluded specifically. In any case, a reconciliation must in principle be effected between methods of computing money national income and methods of constructing price indexes. Often practical considerations will be dominant in determining whether the adjustment should be made on one side or the other. In the case of the residential burglar, reliable data on the income of burglars is fairly difficult to come by, although of course in view of the relatively small amount involved in terms of the over-all picture, a relatively large error could be tolerated; on the other hand, including an adjustment in the cost-of-living index for insurance rates, and even, in principle, in some cases for types of loss by depredation that are not readily insurable, would be both difficult to make and difficult to explain to the users of the figures. In this case, matters on the factor-payments side, can be left as they stand, although this will involve a "statistical discrepancy" between the two sides of the accounts if the sales by fences are included in an aggregate of final products at market prices. On the other hand, theft and pilferage from business firms is not ordinarily distinguished in any accounting sense from loss by breakage or other accidental destruction, so that there is no easy way to determine the amounts involved from this side, and of course even less chance of getting reliable reports from the culprits. Adjusting the cost of living downward to eliminate the effect of such theft on the price level is hardly feasible, so that to the extent that such income is not included on the factor-payments side there is again a statistical discrepancy, but this time it is the factor-payments figure that is defective and the market-values figure that is the correct measure. The amounts involved are of course trivial compared with other margins of error that necessarily occur at many points in any national-income estimates, but the consideration of such extreme cases, though trivial in themselves, serve to illustrate the theoretical principles somewhat more clearly and dramatically than is possible with more involved situations.

Gifts and "Transfer Payments"

GRATUITOUS gifts must also be treated with caution. Ordinarily it is fairly obvious that the reciprocal exchange of gifts and other amenities at Christmas and on other occasions does not constitute a net addition to the national product in itself, though the practice may be highly stimulating to economic activity. Thus if one were to treat gifts received as income from the point of view of the recipient, then it would be necessary to consider gifts made to be deductions from the income of the donor, if aggregating such incomes is not to result in double counting. Ordinarily, custom and the extreme difficulty of making such adjustments to incomes of individuals for such gifts leads to the almost universal practice of leaving them out of account. In either case, the net result on the aggregate level is that they cancel out.

Yet there are a number of occasions where what may nominally appear to be gifts should be treated somewhat differently. In particular, Christmas and other bonuses paid to employees may in form be gratuitous, but actually show up on the one hand as expenses of doing business that are deducted in computing net profit, and on the other hand are considered by employees as part of the compensation in consideration of which they have undertaken the work. Such "gifts" are obviously to be treated as compensation for services in computing individual incomes for tax purposes otherwise widespread avoidance of tax would result, and a similar treatment is appropriate for national-income purposes.

The possibility that what are nominally gratuitous transfers may in fact constitute compensation for services is somewhat more pervasive, however. In many cases, for example, a bequest may be in effect deferred compensation for services rendered. Where the bequest is to a member of the decedent's family, the services, if any, may perhaps be placed on the same basis as the domestic services of housewives, and ignored in computing the national income. On the other hand, bequests are often made to household servants, and services are often rendered in more or less definite anticipation of such bequests. The difficulties of such matters are, however, out of proportion to their magnitude.

Of greater and growing importance, both for tax purposes and for national-income accounting, are the grants, scholarships, and fellowships made available to individuals for study or research. To the extent that these grants induce study or research that would not otherwise have been done, this may be considered an addition to the national income in the form of increased individual capacity or additions to the fund of knowledge, though unlike investment in physical goods, this investment is not reflected in any marketable assets and will not normally show up in an aggregate of national wealth. The difficulty arises, from the point of view of the national income, when the grant merely facilitates study or research that would have been done, though perhaps on a reduced scale, in any case by the grantee on his own resources. The essence of the difficulty really is that study or research pursued individually without outside aid is not counted as part of the national income, and indeed as long as individual capacities are left out of account in computing both individual and national net worth, it would be difficult to fit such an element into the national-income framework in a logically consistent manner. Probably less inconsistency results from treating all such grants as outright gifts with no productive consequences: comparable research workers on industrial payrolls typically are charged to current expense, or the investment in research is amortized at a rapid rate, thus pushing the price level up to cover their earnings and showing no net addition to real national product.

An analogous item for which an adjustment is made in the national-income accounts is the cancellation of bad debts owed by individuals to business. This is, in effect, an involuntary gift by business to households, yet it is treated as a cost by business while not normally included in the incomes of individuals. It would be awkward and somewhat bizarre to adjust prices used in the construction of a price index to reflect the small but definite probability that the customer would obtain the goods without eventually paying for them; since the adjustment is not made on the index side, it must be made on the money-income side. In this case, the addition must be both to aggregate money sales and to aggregate factor payments.

The Role of Governments

THESE QUESTIONS, however interesting from a purely theoretical point of view, are quantitatively of minor importance. The most significant questions that arise in dealing with the concept of national income have to do with the activities of governments. Governments obtain funds by borrowing, by taxation, or by the sale of goods and services, and disburse funds by engaging in activity directly or by making grants to businesses or individuals, or by purchasing goods and services from businesses and individuals; the criteria by which governments make these various transactions differ from those of competitive firms and households, so that the relation of the various transactions to the national income or product is likely to differ from what it is in the case of the purely competitive economy.

As a starting point, we may consider at one extreme the cases in which government activity follows the pattern of private enterprise so that its transactions can be treated analogously. For example, some government activity can consist of the production and sale of goods and services at prices covering cost, factors being secured in a competitive market: this may be the case, for example, with municipal public-utility operations. This of course presents no problem and can be treated as merely another form of private business. Or funds can be obtained by taxes levied on individuals and spent on furnishing services directly to individuals, as when an income tax is levied to pay for schools. Here again no special adjustment is required, for the operation differs from the voluntary payment of tuition fees only in being compulsory. It is to be assumed, of course, that the decision to provide the service was wisely made so that the service is worth what it costs to the community as a whole. A third possibility is for the government to obtain funds by levying taxes on business in such a way that they appear as a cost, and to spend a corresponding amount on services to business: i.e., in activities that improve productivity rather than in activities that provide satisfaction directly to individuals. Here again, aside from the fact that the payment is compulsory and the use of the service may be free, there is little difference, from the point of view of the measurement of national income, between such a situation and the one that would prevail if instead the service were provided by a private agency charging a fee.

A fourth possibility calling for no adjustment is for the government to engage in capital construction of public improvements and to finance this by borrowing money. The result here again is comparable to what happens if a private firm invests funds that are either borrowed from the public or supplied from its own savings in the construction of capital facilities. If, further, the interest and amortization payments on the debt thus contracted are financed by taxes levied on individuals in cases where the benefits derived from the improvements take the form of direct services to individuals, and by taxes on business where the benefits take the form of services to business, the parallel between business and government operations is complete. If there is thus a complete balancing in each case of the source of payment for and the type of benefit from the various types of government activity, there would be no need to make any special adjustment in the national income accounting, and payments of wages, rent, and interest by the government will play the same role in the national income as the corresponding payments by private firms and individuals.

The contribution of the government to the national income, in such a situation, would be considered in exactly the same way as would the corresponding activity carried on by a private firm. The chief difference would be that where the activity is carried on at arm's length by a separate firm, payment and benefit are directly connected and the relationship is voluntary, insuring that the payment does not exceed the value of the benefit, whereas under government operation the making of the payment and the enjoyment of the benefit may be to varying degrees compulsory, so that the amount of the payment is not necessarily limited to the value of the benefit, and indeed the individuals making the payments may differ from the individuals deriving the benefit. But even though the individuals differ, the aggregate accounting results will be the same as in the voluntary case provided only that the individual making the payment is acting in the same capacity as the individual enjoying the benefit; i.e., either both must be acting as ultimate consumers or both must be acting as intermediate producers. And while the compulsory element in taxation introduces the possibility that the benefit conferred may be less than the cost, for the purposes of national-income analysis it is necessary to assume that government expenditures are by and large made with sufficient wisdom so that the benefits outweigh the costs, and ideally that marginal benefits equal marginal costs, so that it becomes legitimate to measure the benefits by the costs to the same degree that the benefits from the consumption of the products of private industry are measured by their costs as reflected in their prices.

Direct and Indirect Taxes—Apportionment of Receipts

UNFORTUNATELY for the simplicity of national-income analysis, governments do not in fact follow a policy of thus meticulously matching off benefits against sources of funds. Indeed, there is no reason why they should do so aside from the trivial one of making national-income computations easier. Funds, however obtained, are properly applied to various purposes in accordance with the relative importance they have for the community as a whole, ideally in such a manner as to equalize marginal benefits in all directions; the sources from which funds are to be obtained are properly determined, not alone in terms of the uses to which they are to be put, if at all, but by considering the effects of various forms of borrowing and various forms of taxes and charges. Moreover, even were it desirable to match off benefits against sources of funds, it would be extremely difficult to apply this principle in practice. While it is possible to distinguish fairly clearly between taxes on business and taxes on individuals, at least from the point of view of income analysis as distinguished from incidence theory, it is not at all easy to apportion the benefits arising from government activity between benefits going directly to individuals and benefits that are transmitted to individuals only through increased productivity and lower prices.

Taxes indeed can be distinguished fairly readily in terms of the way they are handled in the accounting procedure; the more controversial question of whether particular taxes are shifted forward to consumers or backward to producers and suppliers of factors is not relevant for income-analysis purposes. Suppose, for example, that the government sets out to provide free of charge certain services to transportation and navigation formerly performed privately by the transportation companies, thus lowering the costs borne by such companies and yielding benefits primarily in the form of lower rates and fares for transportation services, which are passed on to ultimate consumers in the form of lower prices for the commodities transported. Let us suppose this service to be financed by an excise tax on some item elastic in supply but relatively inelastic in demand: for example, clothing. In this case the price of clothing will rise by approximately the amount that transportation costs fall; an over-all consumers' price index will remain approximately unchanged; and in the accounting procedure no change in the national income should be made to show the change in the method of financing the services from the charges of the transportation companies to the excise on clothing. On the other hand, suppose that the tax is instead imposed on some item inelastic in supply but elastic in demand: for example, the rental value of building sites. Here there will be no rise in rentals to compensate for the fall in transportation costs, and thus a cost-of-living index will go down; on the other hand, the income of the landlords will be diminished, assuming the tax to be treated as a cost. Dividing the reduced cost of living by a lower price index will leave the real national income the same, to correspond with the unchanged over-all real situation. Thus whether a tax is passed forward to consumers or backward to suppliers of factors, no allowance need be made where a service to business is financed by taxes that are deducted from gross receipts, whether as costs or otherwise, in deriving the net income of the firm or individual that pays them.

Where such a service is financed by a direct tax that is not deducted before income is computed, however, the theoretically required treatment is different. If, for example, such a service to business is financed by an increased estate tax, then it will be necessary to deduct such a tax from aggregate-factor payments in computing national income, otherwise it would appear that prices fall while national income remains unchanged, producing an apparent increase in real income, whereas actually no change has taken place in the total volume of productive activity. A similar treatment must be accorded an individual income tax used for such a purpose. To be sure, in this case there would indeed be the possibility of considering in the first place only the net income after tax as the individual income to be aggregated, but this is at variance with common usage.

Similar considerations apply if current services to business are financed from borrowed funds: the amount so borrowed must be deducted in order to reduce the national income *pari passu* with the fall in the price level. This is not to say that the repercussions of such borrowing may not be such as to increase the national income, but the borrowing itself is not an actual increase in the real national product, though it may induce some change in productive activity. What such a change in the method of financing the outlay may do is to make individuals feel that their income has been increased, since ordinarily they regard government bonds as an asset no less real for their own purposes than a title to land or buildings, while at the same time few if any individuals make any close calculation as to the share of the national debt that they may at some time in the future be called upon to pay off through higher taxes. But this individual feeling of greater prosperity does not in this case correspond to any real increase in the resources available to satisfy their wants: the national product has not changed.

Similar reasoning indicates that a special adjustment is required where government outlays are of a kind to provide benefits directly to individuals in their capacity as citizen-consumers, rather than aids to production providing only indirect benefits to individuals, if these outlays are financed by indirect taxes. As we have seen, if such activities are financed by direct taxes, then if individual incomes are computed before deducting such taxes, there is no adjustment to be made and the situation can be treated as though the direct taxes were simply a specific payment for the service. But where direct taxes are used to finance such activities, the amount spent on them must be added to the incomes of individuals as otherwise computed in order that when the national income is deflated by a price index which has been increased because of the indirect taxes, the real national income will remain the same. In principle, of course, it would be possible to include an allowance in a cost-of-living index for an increase in the amount of free public service, or for the fact that what may formerly have been furnished privately for a price is now to be had at a price of zero. Actually, how‿ver, such an adjustment of price indexes would be difficult and in practice is not made, so that adjustment must perforce be made in the national-income figure, though making the adjustment in the price index would have some advantages in facilitating comparisons of living standards for individual groups.

Similarly, if additions to public investments are financed from current indirect taxes, rather than from borrowing, an addition is warranted in computing the national income. On the other hand, if additions to public investment are made from direct taxes, no adjustment need be made, since here an addition to total resources has been made that will correspond to the funds that have been taken from individuals, and the national economy is in fact as well off as if this money taken from individuals was evidenced by bonds rather than tax receipts. This remains true from the point of view of the national product even though individuals may not feel quite as well off if they are given only tax receipts rather than bonds for the funds they have supplied, or feel that they have quite so direct a stake in the improvement. And if, conversely, services to individuals are financed by borrowing, again no adjustment is needed, since even though people feel more wealthy by reason of having bonds in hand rather than the tax receipts that they would have had if the outlay had been financed by direct taxes, there are no real assets to correspond to these bonds and the increased wealth is to that extent illusory.

Accordingly, when all of these required adjustments are taken into consideration, the net adjustment to be made to the national income on account of the lack of correspondence between indirect taxes and services to business, direct taxes and services to individuals, and public borrowing and public investment, is to take the national income computed as the sum of all wages, interest, profits, and other factor payments, add the amount of indirect taxes and subtract the amount spent on services to business. The same result would be obtained by instead deducting government borrowing and direct taxes and adding government investment and outlays on benefit payments and other services to individuals.

Apportionment of Government Outlays

WE HAVE SEEN that there is not much difficulty in drawing the line between government receipts that should be considered as direct taxes and those that should be considered as indirect taxes and proceeds of borrowing, respectively. But there is a great deal of difficulty in arriving at any very satisfactory determination of what proportion of government outlays should be considered outlays on services to business that contribute only indirectly to the national product as contrasted to outlays on investment and on direct services to individuals that can be considered a part of the final output of the economy. Outlays for parks, museums, and the like are clearly direct services to individuals; outlays for education are probably also to be reckoned primarily as direct services to individuals, although when one gets to trade and vocational schools it is perhaps less clear that this is a direct service rather than a mere means to increased productivity. Even though not itself a direct service it might qualify for the direct-service treatment on the grounds of being an investment in productive capacity, but in this case the investment would have to be written off in some way over the life of the trainee. Fire protection of personal property and of owner-occupied homes is doubtless to be regarded as a direct service, particularly as the relevant insurance rates are unlikely to be fully reflected in a price index; on the other hand, fire-protection costs allocable to the cost of protecting business property and rented residential property is a service to business. Possibly it is not too difficult to make some apportionment of expenditures on highways on the basis of the proportions of business and pleasure use, though this will doubtless involve a considerable amount of somewhat arbitrary allocation, even if the marginal impact of different types of traffic on costs and congestion were fully known. Activities of the Department of Agriculture may perhaps be apportionable between those leading to greater productivity on the farm and those leading to more satisfactory living conditions for the farmer on a given income, and so forth. But it would be considerably more difficult, for example, to define the degree to which the activities of Congress contribute to welfare directly as contrasted to the degree to which they merely contribute to the productivity of the remainder of the economy.

The overwhelmingly largest item is of course military expenditure. From one point of view this is clearly not a contribution to the current standard of living of the community, and should not be included in the national income. From another point of view, however, this expenditure does represent a using up of the resources of the community that could in principle be devoted to welfare-promoting activities if fear of aggression from without or desires for dominance in international relations could be swept aside. Or from another point of view it may represent an investment in future security comparable to the construction of a fire station, albeit one with a far greater rate of obsolescence. Another difficulty peculiar to military expenditure is that when much of the manpower is conscripted, this indicates a discrepancy between the amount that is being paid by the government for the use of this manpower and what this manpower could produce in civilian life, allowance being made for differences in living conditions. Thus cost to the government in this case is no reliable measure of the resources absorbed in the activity. But where the contribution of the activity to the national product is on such a questionable basis in any case, there is little to be gained by an attempt to adjust to a hypothetical cost in free-market terms for national-income purposes, however desirable this might be for purposes of measuring the cost of military activity.

But whatever the decision that one would come to on theoretical grounds on such issues, the practical difficulties of making such an allocation of government outlays have seemed so overwhelming that in almost no case is there any serious attempt actually to make such an allocation in the calculation of national income. Many compilations of national income have made no explicit adjustment for the special roles of government in the national economy, and have, accordingly, made the tacit assumption that government services to business could be taken as equal to the indirect taxes levied upon business. Such a definition of national income is of course vulnerable in that shifts either in the orientation of government outlays or in the sources of government funds may cause the national income as computed to vary in ways not reflecting the change in the real situation. Shifts in government outlays produce inconsistencies that are less obvious, perhaps, than do shifts in sources of funds, since at best there will be a considerable difference of opinion as to the proper treatment or allocation of the activities being expanded or contracted. The ignoring of shifts in tax policy, however, leads to somewhat more glaring anomalies: if a state, for example, should decide to increase its revenues through increases in the personal income tax rather than through increased property-tax rates, national income would be reckoned under this treatment at a higher level, although neither prices nor physical output would have experienced any corresponding increase.

The expanding role of the government in the national economy has made anomalies of this sort too serious to be ignored, and the tendency has been in recent years to shift toward definitions of national income that are less susceptible to bias from such artificial shifts. Thus, for example, the more recent figures of the United States Department of Commerce include a "net national product" (at market prices) that includes, on the factor-payment side, all business taxes, and on the final-products side, all purchases by governments of goods and services. Thus in this figure all activity of government is treated as though it represented either investment or services to individuals, and this figure as a measure of output from a welfare point of view is an overstatement by almost any standard. It does have the virtue, however, of being free from obvious anomalies of the type that result when a shift is made from one form of taxation to another. And while anomalies still result when the government makes a substantial change in the amount of outlays for "services to business," such changes are by no means so well defined as are the corresponding changes in the tax sources. And of course as long as the relative magnitude of government services to business remains reasonably stable from year to year, year-to-year comparisons remain reasonably accurate. In periods when great changes are taking place in this segment of the economy, the failure of nominal national-income figures to reflect this factor must be kept in mind.

Thus while national-income or national-product figures as actually computed do not correspond as closely as might be desired to a consistent welfare concept, or even as might be actually obtainable if this were the only objective of assembling such figures, a figure more closely representing welfare would of necessity involve much subjective and debatable apportionment of government outlays between services to business and other outlays, and the possible greater significance of such a figure for welfare purposes might be outweighed by uncertainty as to its magnitude.

Gross National Product

FOR PURPOSES of studying the over-all structure of the economy there is still another aggregate-flow concept that is much used, the "gross national product," which is essentially the "net national product" (inclusive of all government services) plus the amount of depreciation allowances made by business. One can think of this as the total product coming off the national assembly line, before taking out that part that is needed to make good the wear and tear on the productive machine, and before reworking into the productive process those government services that are needed to keep the productive machine going.

In a sense the degree of "grossness" in the GNP is quite arbitrary. The production in a given plant may contribute to the exhaustion of the plant's coal pile in a manner not so very different from the way in which the productive process contributes to the wearing out of a machine; the inroads on the coal pile, whether or not made good by the purchase of new supplies, are evaluated and deducted, in principle, in computing gross national product; the inroads on the life of the machine are not, again regardless of whether the machine continues to be in running order at the end of the period or has finally had to be replaced. And there are intermediate cases where the items are so small, even though long-lived, or the life is so short and uncertain, even though the item is of substantial magnitude, that the firm tends to treat them as a current cost rather than go to the trouble of capitalizing them and subsequently writing them off through depreciation: such might be the case for a supply of hand tools, for example, or for a belt that must be renewed every two or three years. In principle, it would be possible, by increasing the amount of "grossness" or double counting in the GNP figure to arrive at a figure several times this amount, even to the point of coming to a figure approximating the aggregate sales of all business firms. Some fairly close limit would of course be placed on this process if it were agreed that in no case would double counting be permitted with respect to any factor of production of which a definite quantum is consumed in the manufacture of each unit of output. This principle would exclude any double counting of coal used for power in the production process, as well as such items as polish in a furniture factory. (A somewhat narrower criterion of "physical incorporation into the product" has sometimes been used in connection with sales taxes in order to avoid the more flagrant cases of double taxation.) Even so, a considerable degree of conceptual vagueness remains, so that GNP is essentially defined in terms of what accountants in practice do rather than in terms of any strict theoretical concept.

There is, however, a sense in which the GNP has real meaning. It is usually possible to continue production for a time without actually using up resources in replacing or making good the depreciation in existing capital equipment. One might imagine, for example, a situation where a major part of the capital equipment of an economy has been destroyed by some general disaster. The resulting relative scarcity of capital would, under competitive conditions, lead to high interest rates that would induce firms to stretch out the life of their surviving capital equipment, permitting the equipment financed by the depreciation charges to be added to capacity in lieu of the destroyed units rather than used to replace units coming to the end of what would have been their normal useful life. It is perhaps worth noting specifically that this would occur even if the supply of capital goods were completely elastic over the range of output that could be financed from depreciation charges and current savings. If on the other hand capacity for producing capital goods is limited, a similar effect would be induced jointly by increases in interest rates and in the price of capital equipment.

Similarly, in a period of emergency, it is possible to use the entire GNP either for current outlays or to increase capacity along new lines while the life of existing equipment is stretched out by patching up and making do. Such a procedure will of course result in rapidly rising costs, and if this is done for more than a very short period, the increased costs of using decrepit equipment will bring the GNP and with it the net national product down to levels below what they would otherwise have been.

Of course, it is also true that current outlays can for a time be increased by drawing down inventories and impairing stocks of resources with a much shorter life. But such a drawing on capital is limited in a different way than is the use of depreciation allowances. There is relatively little limit to the speed with which inventories can be drawn upon, inherent in the inventories themselves, though there may be sharp limits to the rate at which they can be effectively utilized or to the effective diversion of supplies that would maintain the inventories to other uses; on the other hand, the cumulative amount of draw-down of inventories is sharply limited and is not much dependent on the length of period over which it takes place. The impairment of more permanent capital, however, cannot proceed more rapidly than properly computed depreciation allowances indicate, and can often proceed only substantially less rapidly than this, since at least some replacements are likely to prove absolutely imperative as some machines reach states at which the cost of keeping them in operation becomes prohibitive. But if there is a limit on the speed, there is considerably less limit on the extent; provided that a considerable increase in operating cost can be tolerated, with a corresponding increased sacrifice of investment for the more remote future, much capital equipment, and notably many buildings and other similar structures, can continue to be used long after depreciation allowances have recovered their cost, and even long after their replacement, under more normal economic conditions, would have been profitable.

Thus GNP can be treated as a measure of the degree to which resources are available over the medium short run, if the interests of the more remote future are to be disregarded or sacrificed. At best, it is a very rough measure, however, as is indicated by the fact that the distribution of depreciation charges as between those on assets having, say, a five-year life and those having, say, a 20-year life is not specified, although such a distribution would be crucial as an indication of the extent to which depreciation could be allowed to accumulate without being made good and of the period over which this could continue. Moreover, by far the greater part of the spurt of output that is attained in a period of emergency is due not to the failure to replace old equipment but rather to more intensive use of equipment still well within its normal life span, whether through better scheduling, more overtime, double shifts, or harder driving. There is nothing in the GNP figure that reflects in any real way potential increments in production of this sort.

Thus while the excess of GNP over the net national product can be considered to be a measure of the real liquidity that the economy possesses in terms of freedom to shift resources to new uses, whether to meet temporary emergency needs or to take advantage of innovations, it does this only in a rather rough way. The more important justification for the use of the GNP figure probably lies more nearly in its being a much more solidly based figure than the net national product, even though it corresponds to a concept that is less precisely defined. For in arriving at each firm's net contribution to the national product, it is necessary to take gross sales, which is a fairly definite figure, deduct various items of current expense, which are also fairly firm figures, including purchases on current account from other firms, and then deduct the figure for depreciation, the proper estimation of which inevitably involves a good deal of judgment. In actual practice, the amounts deducted as depreciation do not even pretend to be an estimate of the amount by which the real value of the capital equipment has diminished during the year, which is what would be required if the theoretical concept of the net national product were being adhered to; rather, they represent in nearly all cases an arbitrary percentage of cost, in principle determined so as to spread the cost over the estimated lifetime of the asset, but in practice determined by arbitrary rules. This may not matter too much over the long run, when errors will tend to cancel out, particularly if, whenever equipment lasts longer than expected, depreciation allowances cease after the cost has been written off, and if, whenever equipment is scrapped before the expected term, the undepreciated value is written off as an additional depreciation allowance. But often depreciation allowances are computed for an entire group of assets, without reference to the survival or retirement of individual units, so that this long-run check fails to operate. And in any case over shorter periods, and particularly when short-term reactions are involved, the arbitrary nature of this depreciation allowance is a drawback, and gross national product is often considered to be a more reliable figure to work from than net national product. Again, strict adherence to a definite theoretical concept is sacrificed for the sake of obtaining a more objective statistic.

Gross national product, as found in current statistics, can thus be thought of as a sum total of market values of goods and services coming off the national assembly line, inclusive of the cost of all government services whether or not these confer direct benefits on individuals, after making good all inroads into short-term capital items such as inventory, but before making any allowance for the less definite impairment of more permanent items of capital that has taken place in the course of production or by reason of lapse of time.

Relationships Among Income Concepts

PROCEEDING in stages from gross national product to disposable personal income, which is in contrast perhaps the narrowest of the aggregate-income concepts, we must first simply deduct depreciation to arrive at net national product (at market prices). This depreciation figure should in principle cover all types of inroads on capital suffered in the production process, including those that may result from accident or other types of destruction. The Department of Commerce includes in this category an item of "capital outlays expensed," which in effect is a substitute for a depreciation allowance on these items. In principle, it is the depreciation on these expensed items that should be deducted, but as these items are thought to have a relatively short life, it is assumed that the amount of such items bought from year to year corresponds roughly in the aggregate to the amount of depreciation that they suffer and, accordingly, the amount charged as an expense can be used instead of the hypothetical depreciation without serious error. Inclusion of this item in GNP extends the grossness of GNP slightly as compared with usual internal accounting practices, and probably makes it more consistent, without entirely overcoming the essential arbitrariness of the distinction between capital and inventory.

We have noted before that the net national product so arrived at includes the cost of all government services, and thus overstates the national output from the point of view of consumer welfare by as much of the government output of goods and services as provides benefits only indirectly by facilitating the production of goods and services by business.

To go from national product at market prices to national income at factor prices it is necessary to deduct items that enter into costs and profits that are covered by market prices, but on the other hand do not correspond to any payment of income to any factor of production. The principal item of this kind is indirect business taxes. These enter into costs, but do not become the income of any individual, nor do they represent a payment for the use of any specific factor of production. An analogous item is the profits derived from the operation of a government enterprise: one can think of these profits as being in effect a tax which the government levies on a business that is being operated separately at cost. Conversely, losses, or subsidies paid by government to businesses, are to be added in, in that they are in effect the reverse of taxes. Similarly, "transfer payments" by business to individuals and nonprofit institutions are deducted here as they are also costs but are not payments to factors for their contribution to production. This category includes gifts from corporations to philanthropic institutions, amounts written off as bad debts owed to business by individuals, payments by business as compensation for personal injury to other than employees, cash prize awards, and losses from theft of cash and capital assets. Theft of merchandise, it would seem, involves such a loss in the economic value of the item stolen as to be more closely akin to accidental destruction than to the theft of cash, while the manpower absorbed in such activity is not considered to rank among the inputs to be evaluated and aggregated.

National income at factor prices is indeed a measure of input, but to obtain a measure of "real input" this money aggregate must of course be deflated by an appropriate price index. An index of factor prices for this purpose would cover wage rates, rentals for various types of property, and an element composed of a price index of capital goods multiplied by an average or normal rate of return on capital investments. Viewed from this angle, the classification of corporate income and profits taxes as direct taxes on the stockholder rather than as indirect business taxes appears rather dubious. Considering corporation income taxes as direct taxes, the price paid for capital supplied by the stockholder is taken to be corporation profits before rather than after these taxes. While superficially the justification for this treatment might seem to depend on whether or not the incidence of the corporation profits taxes is on the shareholder rather than on consumers or labor, from an accounting or measurement point of view this is rather irrelevant. The relevant question is whether, in computing an index of yields on investment, or an index of the cost of capital, yields would be taken more readily before or after tax. As a practical matter, it appears that a yield index would more readily be constructed from figures on earnings after taxes, or on the basis of actual dividend payments. This is particularly true since this basis would make the yields on common stocks more nearly comparable with those on preferred stocks and bonds, with which they are interchanged in the market.

This treatment is somewhat the stranger in that property taxes, normally designated a "direct" tax for legal purposes, are included in "indirect business taxes," and excluded from "payments to factors," in national-income accounting, whereas an index of property rentals is much more likely to be computed inclusive of property tax than is an index of investment yields likely to include the corporate income taxes. In effect, then, considerable care is needed if the national income at factor prices is to be used as a measure of real aggregate input into the production process.

In principle, it should be possible, by comparing real national product with real national input, each derived by deflation with its own appropriate index, to get a measure of the over-all "efficiency" of the economy. This would differ from an index of per capita income or income per man-hour in that it would make allowance for different relative amounts of capital and would thus measure technological progress through the introduction of better methods of utilizing given endowments of factors, rather than measure merely the effect of the accumulation of capital at a more rapid rate than the growth of population. On the other hand, it would differ from a mere index of real wage rates, in that it would include all incomes and not merely that of a single, albeit important, sector of the economy. However, the foregoing considerations indicate that a considerable modification of the figures presently available would be needed before such a procedure would be adequate.

If we wish to proceed from the national income to the aggregate of individual incomes, there are further adjustments to be made. On the one hand, some of the income received by corporations, trust funds, foundations, and other intermediaries is not distributed to individuals, but held for other purposes. Under this heading we can include corporate profits taxes, the undistributed earnings of corporations, and the excess of the interest, dividends, etc., received by foundations and trust funds over the amount they pay out as income to beneficiaries. Actually, however, the Department of Commerce treats trusts and foundations as individuals and makes an adjustment here only with reference to corporations, even though it would seem that the relation of an ultimate beneficiary to the undistributed income of a trust fund is much more analogous to that of the stockholder to the undistributed profits of a corporation than it is to the relation of a depositor to a savings account.

In deducting undistributed profits, the Department of Commerce makes an "inventory valuation adjustment." The effect of this adjustment is that what is deducted is not the undistributed profits as shown on the books of the corporation, but rather what this undistributed profit would have been if, instead of taking the change in inventories at book value, the change in inventories had been reckoned in terms of the value, at average prices for the year, of the physical change in the volume of the inventory. This is not the same thing as a shift to a "last in, first out" (LIFO) method of inventory accounting, since even with LIFO, inventory losses and profits will come to account every time a drawing down of inventory compels taking into costs a purchase price paid for an inventory item at a more or less remote time in the past when prices were higher or lower. The inventory-valuation adjustment excludes from net and gross national product that part of the nominal profits that has resulted from the change in the price at which the inventory is valued. This does not mean that profits due to price-level changes have been eliminated altogether, but only those that arise through the costing of inventory embodied in sales at a price differing from that required to replace the inventory at the time of sale. Profits due to the change in the value of fixed assets do in time emerge and are included in the national-income and national-product figures. These profits are just as fictitious, in relation to any measure of actual production, as are the inventory profits, but they are considerably more difficult to eliminate with any accuracy, since the time at which they emerge into the profit accounts is difficult to determine. Because nominal profits on fixed assets resulting from a rise in the price level at a given time are recognized in the accounts of firms only gradually over the remaining lifetime of the assets, year-to-year fluctuations in nominal profits caused by price-level changes tend to average out as long as the price level merely fluctuates about a constant level. But during a long period of more or less continuous inflation such profits will show up in significant amounts, and serious errors in comparing the national income of such a period with that for a period of stable or falling prices can easily result.

In principle, what is required is to use a form of replacement-cost depreciation in which the depreciation allowance computed on the basis of original cost is multiplied by a price index reflecting the increase in the general price level since the purchase of the unit. Such a treatment would give correct results in the aggregate, where intangible assets and liabilities cancel out, but it would seriously distort the picture for individual firms and sectors of the economy unless a comparable treatment is applied to all transactions and charges on capital account. Suppose, for example, that a company wishes to expand its operations temporarily by purchasing an asset for $1,000 with a life of five years. Assume the value of the asset to decline in straight-line fashion, and let us suppose that the excess of receipts over current costs resulting from the operation of the asset are just sufficient to cover depreciation plus a 10 per cent return on the depreciated value of the asset as of the beginning of the year. The situation is then as set out in lines 1 to 4 of TABLE 1, for a stable price level. If prices rise ten points each year as indicated in line 9, and replacement-value depreciation is used, we have the situation depicted in lines 10 to 15, and the deflated profits agree with those given for the stable-price-level case.

Suppose, however, that the expansion is financed with a $1,000 loan, at 6 per cent interest, with the principal repayable in five annual installments of $200. In the stable-price-level case this gives the results shown in lines 5 to 8. In the rising-price-level case, the results are shown in lines 16 to 22;

TABLE I

Inflation, Depreciation, and Real Income

I. *Stable Prices*	Year 1	Year 2	Year 3	Year 4	Year 5
1. Asset value, January 1	1,000	800	600	400	200
2. Depreciation (Δ1)	200	200	200	200	200
3. Receipts less current expenses	300	280	260	240	220
4. PROFIT (3 − 2)	100	80	60	40	20
5. Loan principal, January 1	1,000	800	600	400	200
6. Loan repayment (Δ5)	200	200	200	200	200
7. Interest (6 per cent of 5)	60	48	36	24	12
8. Net income = Cash withdrawals (3 − 2 − 7) = (3 − 6 − 7)	40	32	24	16	8
II. *Rising Prices*					
9. Price index	100	110	120	130	140
10. Asset value (1 × 9)	1,000	880	720	520	280
11. (Nominal depreciation) (Δ10)	(120)	(160)	(200)	(240)	(280)
12. Replacement-value depreciation (2 × 9)	200	220	240	260	280
13. Receipts less current expenses (3 × 9)	300	308	312	312	308
14. PROFIT (13 − 12)	100	88	72	52	28
15. DEFLATED PROFIT (14/9)	100	80	60	40	20
16. Loan principal, January 1 (= 5)	1,000	800	600	400	200
17. Loan repayment (Δ16)	200	200	200	200	200
18. Interest (6 per cent of 16)	60	48	36	24	12
19. Net income (13 − 12 − 18)	40	40	36	28	16
20. Deflated net income (19/9)	40	36.4	30	21.5	11.4
21. Cash available for withdrawal (13 − 17 − 18)	40	60	76	88	96
22. Deflated value of withdrawable cash (21/9)	40	54.5	63.3	67.7	68.6
23. "Replacement value" of loan installment (6 × 9)	200	220	240	260	280
24. Actual loan repayment (6)	200	200	200	200	200
25. Loss to lender = gain to borrower (23 − 24)	—	20	40	60	80
26. Deflated gain to borrower (25/9)	—	18.2	33.3	46.2	57.1

the deflated value of the net profit shown is no longer equivalent to that in the stable-price-level case; however, if we add the deflated value of the profit to the firm and the deflated value of the interest income of the lender, we do get back to the amounts equivalent to the corresponding totals for the stable-price-level case. Thus in an aggregate sense, replacement-cost depreciation does give correct results.

In terms of the relative real positions of the borrowing firm and the lender, however, such a treatment leaves a great deal to be desired. If we look at the amounts available to the firm for withdrawals or distribution as dividends, we find that they exceed the computed net profit by amounts reflecting the difference between the depreciation charged on the books and the amount actually needed for the repayment of the loan. As there was no advance of funds for fixed-capital purposes by the firm (we can ignore as a separate issue possible advances for short-term working capital), there is no reason to require any retention at the end of the operation: presumably if the firm was able to borrow $1,000 in year 1 it still could borrow, given like real circumstances in other respects and like prospects, $1,500 in year 6 to begin the operation over again, and so could not be said to have had its real capital position impaired. What is required, in effect, is for the replacement-value adjustment to be applied to all assets and liabilities, and if a liability is satisfied for less than this "replacement value," the difference should be recorded as a profit. Needless to say, such an adjustment would be quite unpopular with accountants and businessmen, and if made as an adjustment to the national-income accounts by sectors would be difficult to explain to the user of the figures.

On the other hand, there are, in going from national income to the aggregate of individual incomes, certain items that individuals properly regard as income for their own purposes even though there is no corresponding contribution to the productive process. These are generally designated "transfer payments" and include the transfer payments by business that were previously deducted in going from national product to national income and, in addition, transfer payments by government, which include relief and social-security benefits, veterans' bonuses, and the like. Also to be added is the interest on the public debt, since this was not included in the national product on the somewhat arbitrary assumption that government services are to be evaluated at the cost of current outlays exclusive of interest or amortization. Since interest on the national debt is rather closely associated with wartime deficits, and since there is no close relation between the size of the national debt and the amount of government capital plant and equipment employed in the production of government services, it is easy to see why there is a reluctance to include such interest in the national product, though there may be no fundamentally compelling reason for drawing the line between government expenditure deemed to be directly productive and other government expenditure at this particular point. This reason would seem to be less applicable to state- and local-debt interest, particularly that bearing a fairly close relation to public improvements, as with highway and school bonds. As a corollary to the inclusion in full of social-security benefits, employee contributions to social-security funds are deducted (employer contributions having already been deducted as a business tax). While it would be possible to regard social-security contributions as the purchase by the employee or on his behalf of a valuable right to future benefits and thus part of his income (with part or all of the benefits excluded as a return of these sums) the relation between the contribution and the benefit is neither as close nor as immutable as in the case of a private life-insurance policy, so that since a considerable degree of arbitrariness would necessarily be involved in such a treatment, the simpler cash-basis treatment is adopted, rather than the more involved and speculative accrual treatment.

The result of applying these adjustments to national income is personal income. But aside from agreeing more or less closely with what the average person tends to call his "income," this aggregate has no underlying conceptual definiteness. In particular, it somewhat arbitrarily allows for the deduction of some taxes, such as social security, corporate profits, and payroll taxes, while including amounts destined for the payment of personal income, estate, and other taxes. It should indeed make relatively little difference to an individual whether an amount withheld from his pay check is labeled social-security contribution or income-tax withholding, except to the very minor degree to which a higher contribution implies higher expectations as to later benefits. If anything, the reverse relation should hold: a social-security contribution has greater title to be deemed income used to pay an insurance premium than has the income-tax withholding, which gives no title to future benefits. Similarly, it would make relatively little difference to a shareholder whether a payment to government by a corporation is labeled "income tax on corporations" or "withholding tax on dividends." The significant variable for economic analysis, which largely avoids these arbitrary distinctions according to the precise form of the tax, is disposable income, which is income after deducting all income taxes and such other personal taxes as are not dependent on what is done with income and thus do not enter into the cost-of-living index. It is this income which is the basic parameter influencing individual decisions as to how much to spend and in what ways. Even here, as was mooted above, there is the theoretical question as to what extent increases in the value of rights to future social-security benefits should be considered as part of this income. To be sure, the impossibility of disposing of the value of these rights in advance seems to make the inclusion of such an item in "disposable" income inappropriate, but of course we are not restricted to the use of this term and could find another if this turns out to be inappropriate to the analytically useful concept. Even if these benefit rights cannot be directly turned into cash, their existence may well induce an individual to liquidate other assets under circumstances where he would be reluctant to do so if he did not have the social-security benefits in reserve. It is at least possible, for instance, that one of the major reasons for the discrepancy between prewar and postwar consumption functions is the failure of the income used as the explanatory variable to include this element of income, which of course increased greatly from the one period to the other.

Decisions on spending and saving are of course influenced by a number of factors other than the magnitude of this disposable income, even as adjusted for such items as social security. Some of these factors, notably the provision of free government services, can be assimilated to an increment in the disposable income. If, for example, school facilities for which individuals formerly had to pay tuition become a free government service, financed, say, by increased personal taxes, it is unlikely that the savings of the affected individuals would be much altered by this conversion of a tuition payment into a tax payment, or at least not by as much as would occur as a result of a reduction in salaries of a corresponding amount. Accordingly, it is often tempting to consider, as a concept of income to be used as a determinant of individual behavior, the sum of disposable income plus the value of free government services to individuals (or plus the subsidy element in these services if they are only partially supported by tax funds). Unfortunately, data that would respond to this concept are available only with great difficulty, if at all.

CHAPTER SEVEN

Macroeconomic Equilibrium

Neoclassical Interest and Monetary Theories

IT IS SOMEWHAT difficult to specify just what should be considered the typical or outstanding neoclassical or "orthodox" approach to the concept of general equilibrium. Many of the early writers indeed hardly faced the problem of over-all general equilibrium, and it was chiefly the writers who were outside and on the fringes of the main classical trend and less enamored of the classical structure who insisted that explanations were needed for periodic fluctuations and general crises in the operation of the economic system in terms other than monopoly and other interferences with the free self-regulating competitive economy. But if one can synthesize, reconstruct, and adapt the neoclassical patterns of thought in the light of the more modern attitudes toward the problem of general equilibrium, a general pattern emerges, even though in the original writings there was a great deal of heterogeneity.

Say's Law

THE PROBLEM of balance between aggregate demand and aggregate supply was for a long time dismissed rather cavalierly by the citation in one form or another of the "loi des débouchées," generally associated with J. B. Say, which says in effect that "supply creates its own demand." This concept is derived by thinking of the underlying economy as essentially a barter economy, money being thought of only as a convenience or lubricant that merely smooths and facilitates the making of the underlying transactions without changing their fundamental nature. Monetary aspects of trade were even discounted as a "veil" that had to be pierced by the analyst interested in penetrating to the essence of economic activity. Carried to its logical extreme, the "loi des débouchées" implies that there could be no limit to the amount of trade that could be carried on with a given stock of money. In effect, each trader is conceived of as coming to market with the services and commodities he is prepared to supply, and also with a certain stock of money; it is assumed that with this stock of money he can perform an unlimited amount of trading, and that each trader intends to leave the market at the end of the trading period with the same amount of money that he brought with him, regardless of what prices he finds ruling in the market. The total money demand of each trader under these circumstances, i.e., what he is prepared to spend, will be equal to the money value at the market prices of the goods he decides to sell, and thus money demand will always equal money supply: a greater supply of goods and services offered on the market implies a greater demand for them, and in direct proportion.

In this form, and on the assumption that the general price level is given, Say's law is obviously untenable, if only because the velocity of circulation of money and its aggregate supply are in fact limited, at least in terms of the orthodox monetary institutions of the nineteenth century. If Say's law is to become valid, it is necessary to assume that some adjustment takes place either in the money supply or in the general level of prices, and if the gold standard is adhered to in a form that places a limit on the expansion of the money supply, adjustment of the price level will have to be allowed for. In effect, the quantity theory of money may be regarded as a way of specifying adjustments to the price level in a way that will permit Say's law to operate. If the quantity of money is fixed, and if the velocity of circulation is constant, then MV is fixed and, accordingly, by reason of the relation $PT = MV$, PT is likewise fixed. The aggregate money demand, MV, is sufficient to take the total supply of goods T off the market only if the general price level P is properly adjusted. The classical scheme thus becomes complete if it be assumed that the general price level will automatically seek the level at which aggregate supply equals aggregate demand. But this is a long way from saying that supply automatically equals demand without the necessity for any equilibrating adjustment of the general price level.

The same concept of general equilibrium may be approached from another direction by taking the Walrasian system of equations and noting that there are a sufficient number of equations to determine all of the quantities of the various commodities bought or sold by each of the various participants in the market, and to determine relative prices, but not to determine as well the general price level. To determine the price level we can add one more equation, the quantity-theory equation, which can be expressed in the form:

$$MV = \frac{1}{2}\sum_i \sum_j |p_i q_{ij}|$$

where p_i is the price of the ith commodity and q_{ij} is the amount of the ith commodity bought (if negative, sold) by the jth person; the products $(p_i q_{ij})$ are to be summed for all possible values of i and j. In the summation process we can either make all of these product terms positive, summing without regard to sign, and take half of the result, as indicated in the above formula, or we can sum only over those terms where q_{ij} is positive, thus obtaining total purchases that must of course equal total sales. In adding this new equation, M may be taken to be given exogenously by the decision of the monetary authority, and V to be a relatively fixed quantity determined by the institutional arrangements under which trade is carried on. Thus this new equation contains no new unknown variables, and hence may be considered to contain the additional information by virtue of which the general level of prices becomes determinate.

If on the other hand we consider money stocks as being determined not by fiat of a monetary authority but rather, as under the gold standard, by the diversion of some part of the supply of the monetary commodity from direct use (as in jewelry) to monetary stocks, then the market-clearing equation for the monetary commodity must be modified as follows to take account of the shifting between monetary stocks and the production and use of the commodity as a commodity:

$$\sum_j p_m q_{mj} = -\frac{dM}{dt}$$

where the subscript m refers to the monetary commodity and the right-hand member of the equation represents the flow of the commodity into or out of monetary stocks, instead of being zero as formerly. M now becomes one of the variables to be determined, replacing p_m, which is now a constant equal to the mint par of the monetary unit, fixed by the definition of the monetary standard. The equations depict a dynamic situation: if prices are generally high in terms of the money commodity, the price of the money commodity will be relatively low, its consumption will exceed its production, and there will be a withdrawal from monetary stocks into commodity use resulting in a shortage of the circulating medium at the higher prices, a downward pressure on prices which will continue until the relative price of the money commodity has risen to a level where the demand and supply for the money commodity are in balance and no further change takes place in monetary stocks. Or if the economic system is expanding so that monetary stocks required to maintain an increasing volume of trade at stable prices is likewise expanding, a stable price state may be achieved with a price level low enough so that the purchasing power of the monetary commodity is kept high enough to stimulate production and repress demand just sufficiently so that the excess supply, flowing into the monetary stocks, is able to keep the money supply growing in line with the general expansion of activity.

Inadequacies of the Classical Approach

IN EITHER CASE, while the theory may specify adequately what a final equilibrium will have to be like, it says little about how long the process of adjustment will take. If the adjustment process is slow enough, the theory becomes inappropriate as an approximation to the real world, since with a slow adjustment new disturbances are likely to supervene before the adjustment process has had time to bring the situation anywhere near that of the specified equilibrium. Moreover, the adjustment process will not necessarily proceed in the right direction unless two other assumptions of this classical model are fulfilled: namely, that the velocity of money should remain constant, and that no creation or destruction of money should take place other than through the production of the money commodity or its disappearance into use as a commodity. In practice, both of these conditions are often violated to a degree that makes this theory completely inadequate even as a first approximation.

Indeed, observation of fairly serious crises and slumps, and on some occasions of fairly long periods of depression and unemployment, has compelled those who would adhere to the classical framework to seek some explanation for the observed phenomena. Among the explanations offered have been the rigidities in wages and prices, perverse fluctuations in the supply of money through the operations of banking systems, and speculative shifts in demand and supply where price changes are taken to indicate a likelihood of further change in the same direction. Price and wage rigidities, acting by themselves, would delay the achievement of the equilibrium, perhaps for a long time, but would not of themselves give rise to cyclical fluctuations. On the other hand, fluctuations in the money supply and speculative transactions are capable of creating movements away from the equilibrium position, and of setting up a series of movements that never reach the equilibrium position.

But the essential element that distinguishes modern approaches to general equilibrium analysis is the recognition that during the time that the classical mechanism is ponderously getting ready to bring about an equilibrium, other equilibrating forces may be at work that will strongly affect the path that the economic system takes on its way to the equilibrium point, and may even affect the nature of that equilibrium itself. Moreover, there may be more or less permanent obstacles placed in the way of the operation of the classical equilibrating mechanism, and it then becomes necessary to examine the factors that determine the "equilibrium" which the economy will approach when confronted with these obstacles. For example, there may be a floor placed under wages, whether by trade-union action, the operation of minimum-wage laws, customary standards, or the inability of the labor force to survive or work effectively unless provided with a minimum income. Or there may be institutional restrictions placed on the behavior of rates of interest. Or the responsiveness of demand and supply to prices may be perverse, although Hicks has shown that while this can conceivably occur in particular markets, it is not likely to characterize a sufficient number of the markets in an economy to constitute of itself a barrier to the reaching of equilibrium.

Many of these alternative equilibrating mechanisms seem to be most easily explained in terms of the ways in which savings and investment are brought into balance, and the more modern theories of macroeconomic equilibrium focus attention on the capital market to a much larger extent than was the case for classical analysis. Indeed, it almost seems as though in developing their general equilibrium theories classical economists were thinking primarily of models in which all that takes place is the production and exchange of current goods and services. In such an economy, whenever the aggregate of the price tags on the goods coming to market exceeds the amount of trading that can be done with a given volume of money, some of the goods will remain unsold and a downward pressure on prices will exist. If in a subsequent period we consider either that the receipts of the seller during the first period constitute the demand, or that the supply of money and its velocity of circulation remain the same, the reduction in prices will mean that a larger volume of goods will be sold. Thus if all proceeds from the sale of goods are currently spent, or at least if they are spent with a constant time lag, as when the proceeds of one period are spent in the next, then Say's law appears to hold: supply creates its own demand in the fairly short run and a surplus or glut of any one commodity persisting for any length of time necessarily implies a scarcity of some other.

Nature of the Capital-Market Equilibrium

IT IS WHEN we come to consider the capital market that the possibility of a fairly long-term disequilibrium begins to show itself. The classical approach to this segment of the market was to treat it as just another type of commodity market, with the supply of saving being equated to the demand for investment funds by the rate of interest. But a disequilibrium between the demand and supply of capital at a given rate of interest turns out to be a quite different thing from a disequilibrium between the demand and supply of a commodity at a given price, or even of all current commodities taken together.

In a commodity market, it is somewhat difficult to conceive of a situation such that there is no price that will equate supply and demand. In particular, if at some price demand falls short of supply, then it seems almost inescapable that there should be some lower price that will, in a static framework, bring equilibrium in the commodity market, for as price approaches zero, demand in terms of physical units will become indefinitely large, at least if we are thinking in terms of demand for goods in the aggregate and if goods are present in sufficient variety. At the same time, supply is likely to fall toward zero as the price falls toward zero, however perverse a slope the supply curve may have at higher prices.

The corresponding presumption regarding the possibility of having a low enough interest rate to equate savings and investment is by no means as certain. For as long as money can be easily stored and does not deteriorate in nominal value through time (and is not subject to seizure by the state or other authority) the interest rate must remain positive, or at most can be negative only to an extent that might represent a payment for safekeeping or the performing of services incidental to the safekeeping. And even at zero rates of interest, the supply of savings on the one hand may still be substantial, while on the other hand it would not always be possible to find an indefinitely large volume of current investment that would be profitable even at a zero rate of interest (as distinct from the concept that the marginal productivity of *capital* would never fall to zero no matter how large the *stock* of capital, which is itself a debatable proposition, but in any case is irrelevant here). In effect, we can regard the interest rate as reflecting the price of present money in terms of future money, and observe that this price can never fall below unity. Thus while in all other cases of exchange between current goods and services prices may be thought to be free to approach zero, if necessary, in order to equate demand and supply, in the exchange between present and future money we have a limit imposed by the storable nature of money. The type of mechanism that works satisfactorily in the market for current commodities may thus fail completely in the case of the capital market.

Failure of the interest rate to equilibrate the supply and demand in the capital market is made more likely when it is reflected that many interest rates are determined in large part by custom or by administrative decision and at times change only relatively slowly, that the supply of savings may be relatively unresponsive or even perversely responsive to changes in the rate of interest, and that investment decisions are often more determined by the credit rating of the would-be borrower and by the availability to him of capital on any conditions at all, let alone at "the" market rate of interest. This last difficulty may sometimes be dealt with for analytical purposes by considering the interest rate as representing the general state of the money market, including the extent to which capital is available to those who can offer only less than gilt-edged security, so that a lowering of the rate of interest is taken to coincide with a general willingness to lend to weak borrowers. Unfortunately, such a uniformity of movement in various segments of the capital market is not an invariable rule, and there are many instances where interest rates on gilt-edged investments fall while at the same time the security requirements for would-be borrowers are stiffening and equity capital appears to be more difficult to secure.

Since for these and other reasons equilibrium on the capital market through the adjustment of interest rates is likely to take considerable time, and may not come about at all, it becomes necessary to investigate in more detail just what does happen when the interest rate fails to bring about this adjustment, and in particular what other equilibrating mechanisms there may be that will be operating during the time when the interest adjustment is incomplete.

Ex Ante and Ex Post Variables

AT THIS POINT it is convenient to introduce a distinction between "ex ante," or anticipated, values of economic variables and "ex post," or experienced, values. Ex ante values are those that are expected or planned in advance of the event. Usually they are conceived of as single values of the variables: a definite plan to buy so much of a number of commodities at such and such expected prices, or to invest a given amount in the construction of a given plant addition. For some purposes, however, it may be desirable to think of ex ante variables as schedules: for example, an ex ante demand or supply curve expressing the amounts that an individual will attempt to buy or sell at various possible future prices, or the amount that an individual expects to save out of different amounts of income that he might receive in the next period. If we assume that each planner is internally consistent in his plans, the ex ante values that he is concerned with must form a consistent pattern for him: his planned savings plus his planned consumption must add up to his expected income. On the other hand, there is no reason to suppose that plans of different planners will necessarily fit together, and in general there will be discrepancies: sellers of a given commodity may be planning to sell more of it than buyers are planning to buy, and, most important in the present context, the total amount that individuals are planning to save may bear no relation to the total amount that firms are planning to invest.

On the other hand, ex post variables necessarily have a single definite value for a given time or a given period, and must balance in the aggregate. Sellers may plan to sell more than buyers plan to buy, or in other words ex ante supply may exceed ex ante demand, but the amount actually sold in the aggregate must equal the amount bought. In the process of bringing the two sides of the market into agreement, if ex ante values do not agree, some expectations will be disappointed. As a result of this disappointment, expectations and plans for future periods will be changed, and in general the resulting ex post values will differ from those realized in the first period. Long-run equilibrium then requires that the ex ante values become consistent so that there will be no need for ex post values to differ from the ex ante values and it will therefore be possible to avoid disappointing the expectations of individuals so that they will be able to carry out their plans without further change.

Reconciliation of Ex Post Values

IT IS NECESSARY to consider fairly carefully, however, the manner in which the immediate reconciliation of inconsistent ex ante values takes place, as alternative methods of reconciliation can, in macroeconomic terms, lead to quite different further developments and even to different ultimate equilibrium positions.

Consider, for example, a simple economy in which production is carried out entirely without fixed capital, in which all products are perishable, in which at the beginning of each market period participants fix in advance the prices at which they will begin to offer their goods, and in which participants decide in advance how much they will spend during the period. If expectations are consistent with a steady state, so that each participant expects to keep his stock of money at a stable level, each participant must expect to receive from sales an amount equal to what he expects to spend. Aggregate expected sales thus equal aggregate expected receipts. Assuming that decisions as to how much to spend can actually be carried out, and are not altered during the market period by the experience of finding relative prices different from what was anticipated when plans were made, actual spendings of each individual will equal his individual anticipated expenditure, and aggregate actual receipts will also equal aggregate expected receipts. But the corresponding equivalence between expected sales and total expected purchases need not hold for individual commodities, and, accordingly, individual sellers may find that they have sold more than they expected or have sold out at higher prices than they started selling at, and may thus wind up with more cash than they started with, while others will have sold less or will have had to cut prices toward the end of the day in order to sell out, and find their cash depleted. One may perhaps imagine the selling being done by the husband of the family, the buying being done by the wife, with no communication between them during the market period. In both cases, expectations are disappointed, and this leads to a change in plans for the subsequent market period.

There are several ways in which plans could change in response to this disappointment. Those who have sold more than they expected will revise their expectation of the demand curve for their product. They may leave their opening price unchanged for the following market period, but plan to spend an amount equal to their revised expectations of sales. They may plan to spend even a little more than this for a while, since the previous period has left them with more than the normal cash balance and they will feel it desirable to use up the excess. Similarly, we may consider that those who found the market for their product weaker than they expected may leave their opening prices unchanged but plan to spend a little less than they did in the previous period, partly because of reduced expectations as to their sales in the coming period but also partly in order to restore their cash balance to the normal level. If those who have lost cash plan to replenish their balances over the same period as those who gained cash plan to disburse their excess, and if favorable and unfavorable experience likewise affects expectations in a symmetrical fashion, then the aggregate planned expenditure for the subsequent period will be the same as for the first; aggregate expenditure will stay at the same level, and presumably variations in the receipts of individual sellers will be negligibly small if we assume that the pattern of expenditures of those who lost cash in the first period is not greatly different from the pattern of expenditures of those who gained cash in the first period. The end result is likely to be a constant level of aggregate expenditure with gradual adjustment of the distribution of this total among individuals so that each one spends an amount equal to his receipts.

Very slight modifications of the participants' reactions to surprise may yield very different results, however. One may suppose, for example, that individuals are in more of a hurry to restore a deficient level of cash than they are to dispose of an excess, and that participants plan their outlays so as to restore deficiencies of cash over a shorter period than that in which they plan to dissipate surpluses. In that event the aggregate expenditure of the second period will be somewhat less than that of the first, and there will be a downward trend in receipts and expenditure that will continue as long as some participants have more cash than normal and others have less. As long as prices remain rigid (or supply curves are perfectly elastic), and as long as the normal supply of cash is a fixed quantity independent of the amount of trade carried on, any shifting of demand that results in upsetting the expectations of the sellers, some one way and some another, will tend to produce a reduction in total sales. Conversely, if people were willing to dissipate a surplus of cash more rapidly than they attempt to replenish a deficiency, each shifting of demand would produce an expansion of expenditures and sales.

Such an expansion or contraction of expenditures and sales cannot of course go on indefinitely, and sooner or later some limiting force will come into play to stop this tendency. Here it appears likely that as the volume of expenditure in each period is diminished, the ideas of individuals as to the "normal" amount of cash needed may be revised, and the process thus brought to a halt or reversed. If we assume that the normal amount of cash is proportional to the planned level of expenditure, then we have in effect a more detailed version of the quantity theory of money with a velocity of circulation that is not absolutely constant but tends to settle toward a normal value. The level of aggregate expenditure toward which the economy tends to settle is thus determined by this normal velocity and the supply of money. As long as supply prices remain unchanged, this aggregate level may or may not indicate "full employment," however that may be defined. Indeed, if the rigidity of prices is supposed to result from a perfectly elastic supply with suppliers responding in a perfectly competitive way to the market prices, then it would appear that the utility of the participants at the given prices would be the same no matter how much or how little is actually supplied, and that thus the concept of full employment is meaningless, in that no sacrifice of utility is involved in supplying and being employed less than the maximum amount possible, within the range of variation under consideration.

To make the model more realistic and make the concept of full employment meaningful, it is necessary to consider the possibility that one reaction that suppliers will make to surprise is to change their opening prices for the subsequent period. We will assume for simplicity that there is sufficient competition among suppliers, or substitutability between their respective products, even if they be differentiated, so that each seller is faced with an elastic demand and thus a reduction in price will increase his receipts. A seller whose receipts have been disappointingly low may be expected to respond in part by lowering his price to recoup some of the loss in receipts, and in part by curtailing his expenditure, so as to bring it below his expected receipts and thus restore his cash position. Conversely, a seller whose receipts have been higher than expected may raise his price and increase his expenditure. The course the economy takes may depend to a large extent on the relative magnitudes of these two adjustments. If the bulk of the adjustment is in expenditures and little of it is in prices, there may be a fairly long period of trading on a reduced scale before the appropriate price reductions lead to a "full-employment" equilibrium. If the bulk of the adjustment is in prices, repeated experience with fairly prompt price adjustments may lead to anticipation of further price adjustments, speculation, and cyclical variations.

The fluctuations in the over-all activity in such a model, however, are the result of attempts of individuals to adjust their cash holdings. As long as it is assumed that the aggregate of cash holdings considered "normal" or "desired" by the various individuals agrees with the total amount of cash actually available, effects of disturbances on the aggregate rate of activity must depend on second-order effects, i.e., differences between the methods and speed with which persons with excess cash attempt to adjust their cash position and the methods and speed with which persons with cash deficiencies attempt to adjust theirs. When the total cash available exceeds or falls short of the aggregate of what individuals consider normal for themselves, effects of a higher order of magnitude are to be expected.

In this simplified model the capital market does not exist and there is, accordingly, no rate of interest and no investment. An individual can increase his savings, however, by simply increasing his cash holdings; similarly, he can increase his dissavings by drawing on his cash balances. But while it is possible for one individual to "enhoard" and thus to save, it is not possible for all to do this at the same time, if by enhoarding we mean an actual increase in an individual's cash balance, as distinguished from hoarding as the mere holding of a needlessly large cash balance. There is only a fixed amount of cash available in the community, and any enhoarding by some individuals implies a corresponding dishoarding by others. If the amounts of cash that individuals decide they would like to hold—either because it is needed for convenience in trading (for example, to avoid any necessity for the wife to have to come around to her husband's shop during the trading day to replenish her cash), because it is desired to have a reserve for emergencies, or because he wants to deliberately postpone consumption for some reason—exceed in the aggregate the amount of cash in existence, the result will be that in each successive period there will be a reduction in money sales, possibly accompanied by a reduction in prices, the relative amount of each depending on the reactions of sellers to a disappointing volume of sales. The theoretical possibility that each seller could expect to so expand his sales through reduction in prices that he could plan for increased purchases as well as increased cash balances may be dismissed as extremely unlikely. While each individual may plan, separately, to increase his cash holdings by planning to spend less than he expects to receive, and some indeed may succeed in this, it is impossible for all to succeed in carrying out such a plan; one can succeed only at the expense of causing others to lose cash; the attempt by individuals generally to accumulate cash merely causes a disappointment of expectations as to the money value of sales.

In effect we have an economy in which investment is zero, both ex ante and ex post, so that aggregate savings must be zero ex post. The immediate effect of a positive ex ante aggregate savings is to reduce sales. This contraction of money sales may continue until such time as the reduced turnover of money leads individuals to lower their aims as to the "normal" size of cash balance they require, or until the reduction in prices has increased the purchasing power of the money stock to the point where the desires of individuals to hoard can be satisfied. This arresting of the downward pressure by the increase in the real value of the monetary stock as prices fall is sometimes termed the "Pigou effect"; it was put forward by Pigou as one of the ways in which the classical theory could be rehabilitated. If the bulk of the reaction has been in prices rather than in planned expenditure, this equilibrium state may be achieved at a fairly high level of real activity; but if little change in prices takes place and most of the reaction to disappointment and deficient cash balances has taken the form of reduction in outlays, equilibrium will be reached only after a substantial contraction of real activity.

Classical macroeconomic models, working from a tacit assumption of perfect competition, or at least of a reasonably close approach thereto, naturally assumed that with rising supply curves a contraction in demand would lead to a reduction in prices and hence eventually to the full-employment outcome. If, however, we consider various degrees of monopoly and monopolistic competition, it is possible to conceive of a number of ways in which price reductions would be inhibited and adjustments forced to take the form of reduction in outlays. It is possible, for example, for demand to contract in such a way that the profit-maximizing price for a monopolist or quasi-monopolist remains at the same level. Even if this is not actually the case, uncertainty concerning the slope of the demand curve and its change through time may leave the seller in some uncertainty as to whether or not he would improve his profits by raising or lowering his price, and in the face of such uncertainty he may do neither. There is the kinky-demand oligopoly situation in which it may not pay to cut prices even though a considerable contraction in the demand curve occurs. There are institutional factors such as contracts, the administrative difficulties involved in price changes, and other costs of change that may drive sellers to seek to increase their cash position if necessary by contracting purchases rather than by attempting to expand sales. All of these factors lead to the strong suggestion that the more immediate reaction to any disequilibrium in the demand and supply of cash is likely to take in predominant degree the form of a change in the physical volume of activity rather than that of a change in the price level, particularly in the downward direction.

In the long run, in this model where investment has been excluded, even in the form of unsold inventories (since all products other than money are perishable), it remains likely that downward pressure on prices will continue as long as sellers are selling substantially less than they would like to sell at existing prices (making due allowance for any monopoly elements) and that assuming no contraction in the money supply, eventually some reasonable approach to full employment will be reached. Even so, "eventually" may mean only after an intolerably long delay.

The Role of the Investment Market

ADDITIONAL difficulties are placed in the way of adjustment through lowering of the price level, however, as soon as we readmit savings for the purpose of securing future consumption or of acquiring economic power (as distinct from the mere accumulation of cash balances sufficient for convenience in trading), investment in productive capital goods, and a capital market with an interest rate. In the capital-less model, the only way to plan to accumulate cash was to plan to spend less than one expected to take in from sales. Where a capital market exists, it is possible also to increase one's cash position by borrowing, or by reducing one's investments: thus an individual can now increase his cash holdings without at the same time saving, and vice versa. The rate of interest appears in a dual role: on the one hand, it appears as the cost of borrowing and the reward for saving and lending, and on the other it appears as the cost of holding cash rather than lending so as to receive interest. The higher the rate of interest, the higher will be this cost of holding cash. This is the essential link between the savings-investment market and the monetary system that was very largely ignored by the classical and neoclassical theorists.

Indeed, one can think of the neoclassical theory as considering the main macroeconomic variables to be segregated in the two distinct compartments of the theory, with savings, investment, and interest in one compartment, and money, income, employment, and prices in the other. In the one compartment interest is thought of as the variable that equates savings and investment, while in the other compartment—related only remotely if at all to the first—the price level is the variable that adjusts so as to bring the money national income at full employment into agreement with the money stock and the institutionally determined velocity of circulation.

There is nothing wrong with this, perhaps, as a method of determining a very long-run equilibrium state. Even if one consents to consider interactions between the two compartments in the form of auxiliary relationships between income and the savings and investment schedules, and between the rate of interest and the velocity of circulation, it would be possible to proceed by taking a full employment level of income as given, determining savings and investment schedules in real terms for this level of income and varying rates of interest, obtaining the equilibrium rate of interest from the intersection of these two schedules, from which rate of interest one could determine a circuit velocity of money. This circuit velocity of money multiplied by the money stock would give the money national income, and this divided by the full employment level of real income would determine the price level. Thus all the variables are determined and all the equilibrium relationships would be satisfied.

But while such a procedure may serve to determine what the equilibrium would be if it ever were reached, it fails rather drastically as a model of the steps by which such an equilibrium might be approached from some non-equilibrium state, or even of how equilibrium might be restored after a disturbance. Let us suppose, for example, that after proceeding for a while at a full-employment equilibrium, there is a falling off of opportunities for investment, causing the demand curve for investment funds as a function of the rate of interest to fall (move to the left). In the classical view, this produces an immediate drop in the rate of interest to the new intersection of the investment and savings curves; savings are again equal to investment with the stimulation of investment by the reduction in interest rates, and consumption expanding, if necessary, to take up the slack in aggregate demand left by any net reduction in investment. No further effect takes place in the "real" compartment of the analysis. To be sure, if followed through to its auxiliary impact on the monetary compartment, the lower rate of interest may lead to a lower velocity of circulation that implies a reduction in the price level if real income is to be maintained with no change in the quantity of money in circulation; but this is supposed to take place without further repercussions on the real aspects of the economy.

There are three basic assumptions involved here: first, that the excess supply of savings will cause the interest rate to fall sufficiently rapidly to restore the equilibrium between savings and investment before any other repercussions take place; second, that it is possible for the interest rate to fall sufficiently to restore this equilibrium (i.e., that equilibrium would not require a negative rate of interest, or one so low as to be incompatible with capital-market institutions); and third, either that the change in the rate of interest will have no effect on the velocity of circulation, or that the price level can fall with the velocity of circulation without repercussions on the real part of the economy.

Difficulties with the Classical Mechanism

TAKING the last of these assumptions first, a fall in the rate of interest is likely in many circumstances to lead individuals to allow their cash balances to increase; i.e., the velocity of circulation will tend to decrease. Unless the supply of money is at the same time increased, the money national income will also fall, and unless the price level is reduced at the same time, underemployment of resources will result. If prices fall, this will disappoint the expectations of investors, and if this should lead to expectations of further reductions in prices, this will still further lower the equilibrium level of the interest rate.

Thus unless there can be an expansion of the money supply every time a change in the savings-investment relationship requires a fall in the rate of interest, an extensive and substantial chain of reactions will be set off. Conversely, a rise in the equilibrium rate of interest occasioned by an opposite change in the savings-investment relationship would require contraction of the money supply if further reactions are to be avoided. Actually, monetary mechanisms do not seem adapted to the performance of such an equilibrating function. With a commodity currency, such as gold and silver coin, expansion of the money supply through increased production of monetary metals and decreased absorption into commodity use is not likely to occur until after the price level has fallen so as to increase the relative value of the monetary metals, and even then the increase is likely to be slow. A central banking system operating with a stated rediscount rate would tend to cause a contraction of the currency as market interest rates fall, since individual banks would find it less and less profitable to rediscount their paper at the fixed rate. To be effective in the desired direction, it would not be sufficient simply to lower the rediscount rate; it would have to be lowered by more than in proportion to the fall in market rates of interest. Pegging of the price and yield of government securities would have an effect similar to a fixed discount rate. Adherence by banks to the "real-bills" doctrine also tends in the same direction, as a falling off of investment would generally coincide with a contraction of the volume of appropriate paper, while a reduction in interest rates set off by an expansion of the volume of individual savings may be concomitant with a reduction in the demand of consumers for installment credit. It is possible, of course, that increased saving would increase the volume of available paper through increasing the volume of investment at the lower interest rate, but this equilibrating tendency is highly problematical. Restoration of equilibrium through an automatic or semi-automatic variation in the money supply must be considered highly unlikely: deliberate and intelligent monetary management would be required.

The second assumption, that there exists a positive rate of interest which will bring savings and investment into balance, can often be questioned during periods of substantial disturbance, or during periods when it is anticipated that prices will fall considerably further, so that even though the real rate of interest at equilibrium might be positive, allowance for the expected downward price trend turns this into a negative money rate of interest, or at least into a money rate of interest too low for the capital market to work effectively. Under such circumstances, changes in interest rates alone will be incapable of bringing about an equilibrium on the capital market, and some other mechanism must come into play.

The Mechanism of Interest Determination

THE FIRST assumption is the crucial one, however. In effect, it asserts that there exists an effective mechanism whereby a discrepancy between the demand for investment funds and the supply of savings can produce a change in rates of interest and that this mechanism will act promptly enough to forestall direct repercussions on the money-prices-income compartment. However, the more the capital market is examined the more doubtful it becomes whether any mechanism capable of performing such a function at the aggregate level is to be found.

To carry out the analysis in detail, it is necessary to specify carefully just what sort of a sequential mechanism is being substituted for the neoclassical perfect market in which reactions to changes in demand or supply take place in a negligibly short space of time. We must specify what decisions are made in advance and adhered to, so that the ex ante and ex post values are the same, and what economic variables are merely anticipated ex ante, but ex post take on values beyond the control of the individual. We must also specify, if the model is to be complete, the time span for which plans are made in advance and the information upon which the plans are based. A simple assumption, for preliminary analysis, would be that plans are made for one "period" at a time, the plan for each period being based on information as to what has happened in all preceding periods. This is of course unrealistic if taken in a strict sense, since it assumes complete knowledge of events in the past period immediately at its close, and the instantaneous formulation of plans at the moment of time between two periods. In reality, of course, plans are in a more or less continuous flux rather than being fixed at discrete intervals. But such a simplified set of assumptions gives a model sufficiently elaborate to exhibit some of the phenomena in which we are interested, without being unmanageably complex.

Taking first the supply-of-savings side of the picture, it appears that most of the macroeconomically important shifts in the income of individuals take place without the initiative of the individual concerned. To be sure, income of a given individual may increase or diminish as a result of his quitting or actively seeking a job, for example, but in most cases he will either be replacing or be being replaced by someone else. Employment as a whole rises and falls more nearly because employers decide to increase or decrease their payrolls, rather than because of fluctuations in the eagerness with which employees seek jobs. Even more so, profits of entrepreneurs rise and fall in the short run according to the state of demand for their products, while income as reflected in security and property prices reflects the operation of market forces beyond the control of the individual.

Accordingly, income can be considered a variable largely beyond the control, in the short run, of the individuals who receive it, and since income is the sum of savings and consumption, individuals may control either savings or consumption, but not both independently. Given some expectation of what income is to be for the succeeding period, there will in general be a plan that will, implicitly at least, cover both consumption and saving. If income turns out to be different than was anticipated, then there will have to be an adjustment in the planned saving or the planned consumption, or perhaps both. On the whole, if one is thinking of a fairly short time period, it seems likely that consumption will be relatively undisturbed, and that it will be the savings element in which the bulk of the adjustment takes place. This is particularly true of those surprises in income that originate in undistributed profits of corporations or in changes in market values of assets, but it is probably also true to a lesser extent of surprises in the form of bonuses, overtime pay, or layoffs. At any rate, as a first approximation it is almost certainly nearer the mark to say that consumption continues as planned and savings are adjusted to the surprise in income than to say that savings are held constant and income is adjusted. In the longer run, of course, both savings and consumption will be adjusted in varying proportions, but for the moment we are interested in adjustments that take place fairly rapidly.

On the demand side of the capital market the situation is less clear-cut. Some types of investment decisions are fairly "active" in the sense that they can be carried out fairly closely according to plan without too great dependence on what happens to the remainder of the economy. Construction of a new plant is an example of this. On the other hand, some forms of investment are a resultant of plans on the part of the investor on one side and quite independent plans on the part of others. A manufacturer or a retailer may plan to increase his investment in inventory by producing or ordering more or less than he expects to sell, but his actual increase in inventory will be more than this according to whether actual sales fall short of or exceed expectations. Such investments may be distinguished by being considered passive. Still more on the passive side are those investments that are made more or less unconsciously by the owner of a piece of property that rises in value relative to the prices of goods generally; this rise in value is income, and by the same token unless the owner actively does something to increase his consumption as a result, there will also be an increase in his savings and in his investment.

We are now ready to examine the way in which a disequilibrium between aggregate intended investment and aggregate intended savings can resolve itself. Let us suppose that a simple economy composed entirely of firms and individuals with no extra-market relationships is originally in complete equilibrium, with the amount of intended savings equal to the amount of intended investment, and both equal to actual savings and actual investment, and with money stocks distributed according to what individuals and firms desire to hold at the going rate of interest and level of income. For simplicity we may assume that it is generally expected that incomes will continue at the same level, and that on the basis of this expectation plans are made as to the consumption of the next period, which are duly carried out.

Suppose then that at the beginning of period 1 some disturbance has just been felt by individual planners which causes them to change their plans so that for period 1 planned savings, which must be equal to expected income less planned consumption, now exceed planned investment. The actual events of period 1 must be such as to make actual saving equal to actual investment, but the way in which this reconciliation comes about will depend on the way the ex ante discrepancy arises. At one extreme we may think of deciding to save more of their income and to spend less on consumer services and strictly perishable commodities, such as for haircuts, theater tickets, or travel. Leaving aside the trivial case where these services are in short supply and the place given up by one consumer is merely taken up by another, so that the planned decrease in consumption by one consumer is made up by an unplanned increase in consumption by another, the effect of this reduced patronage during period 1 is to reduce the income of the supplier of the service; since the barber, for example, will not have had time as yet to change his consumption plans, he will thus save less than he planned because of the unanticipated fall in his income. The planned increase in savings has been offset by an unplanned decrease in income and savings; savings remains in the aggregate equal to investment. The ex ante disequilibrium has been resolved ex post by a change in income; the additional funds supplied to the capital market by the individuals with planned increases in savings have been withdrawn from the capital market in the same period by the suppliers with unplanned reductions in savings; there is no unbalance in the capital market itself that would tend to drive interest rates down.

The results differ only slightly if the reduction in consumption involves goods that are not instantaneously perishable. Part of the purchase price represents the services of the retailer and to this extent the reduction in his sales is a reduction in his income, and this element can be treated in the same way as in the former case. To concentrate on the remainder, it is perhaps easiest to talk as though the retail markup were zero and the inventory value of the goods equaled their retail price. Here the failure of the consumer to buy leads to inventories being higher than they otherwise would be: this represents an unintended investment on the part of the retailer, and one may think of the added savings of the consumer as being deposited in bank accounts and lent out again to sellers to cover the additional inventory. Income in this case is for the time being the same, but actual investment has been increased from the planned level to the level of planned savings, which is also actual savings. At this stage there is again nothing that would tend to drive interest rates down.

The next step, which we may think of as occurring in period 2, is for those who have accumulated the unwanted inventory to decrease their planned investment for period 2 by decreasing orders and eventually production, resulting in layoffs and a reduction in income of primary factors. The reduction in production may be thought of as in three parts: a reduction to correspond to the lower level of anticipated sales, a further reduction to restore the inventory to the level it had before the unwanted inventory investment took place, and possibly a still further reduction to reduce the inventory to a still lower level consistent with the reduced anticipated sales. In this second stage, if planned and actual consumption remain the same as in the preceding stage, income, and with it actual savings, will be again reduced. The reduction in income may produce a further reduction in planned consumption for period 3, and the process may continue for several stages. If the reduction in planned consumption produced by a given reduction in income for the preceding period is always less than the reduction in income (i.e., if the marginal propensity to consume is less than unity), the process will converge as successive changes become smaller and smaller, and a state will again be approached where ex ante savings are equal to ex ante investment.

It is to be emphasized that until the reduction in income occurred there was no pressure brought to bear on the rate of interest. Even after income has been reduced, the pressure on the rate of interest may be a very mild one. If we assume that there is a very stable liquidity-preference function so that at the given rate of interest and a lower national income the demand for cash is diminished, and if the quantity of money has been kept constant, holdings of cash will exceed the amounts of cash wanted, and there will be a tendency for the holders of the excess cash to attempt to get rid of it by lending the excess to others, and this offer to lend cash will be the force tending to depress the rate of interest. The lending of such funds will not of course decrease their aggregate amount, and even though the amount of cash balances that individuals may attempt to get rid of in this way may be minute, actually they cannot be gotten rid of, in the aggregate; offers to lend will continue until the rate of interest has been lowered to a point where the existing cash balances are no longer deemed excessive in view of the lowered interest cost of holding them rather than interest-bearing assets. This reduction in interest rates may increase investment plans and discourage savings plans, and if this is done sufficiently to restore the equality between ex ante savings and ex ante investment, the successive downward adjustments of income may be arrested.

Thus it is only after first producing a reduction of income, and by this relatively roundabout route, that an ex ante excess of savings over investment can produce a reduction in interest rates. And even this roundabout mechanism is likely to be frustrated in any but the very long run by the lowered state of expectations about the future brought on by the reduction of income that is a necessary part of the process, or by perverse changes in the quantity of money.

If the original divergence between planned investment and planned savings is brought about by a drop in planned investment, somewhat the same results follow, but more immediately: the drop in planned investment, to the extent that it is a drop in "active" investment, becomes a drop in actual investment, which implies, if consumption remains constant in the meantime, a drop in income and hence in savings. Like the drop in the consumption of services, a drop in active investment is likely to involve to a major degree a drop in the purchases of the services of factors of production, especially labor. Here again income begins to fall off before any pressure has been brought to bear on the rate of interest.

In effect, then, no matter what the source of the ex ante disequilibrium between savings and investment, this disequilibrium does not have a chance to express itself as a net pressure on the loan market. Instead, actual saving and actual investment remain in balance in the aggregate because they are the opposite faces of the same coin, and the eventual effect on the interest rate comes about only indirectly through the effect of changing incomes on the demand and supply of money. Unlike the market for current commodities and services, where disequilibrium reflects itself in unsatisfied buyers looking for supplies to buy, sellers with unsold stocks, queues at ticket windows, or empty seats, in the balance between savings and investment there is no such thing as a surplus of uninvested savings left over from the previous trading period: any intended savings not invested in some form will be lost, in the aggregate, through a consequent reduction in income. A surplus supply of capital equipment or construction is not the same thing as a surplus of saving: if it is in the form of an inventory of capital equipment it represents unintended investment, while if it is in the form of idle construction gangs, the wages they are failing to earn are the income and savings that are being suppressed by the failure of investment demand to utilize them.

The Ultra-Keynesian Model

DEVELOPMENT of the idea that the savings-investment-interest equilibrium mechanism functions if at all only in a very roundabout way through changes in income has led to the use of a type of simplified model standing at the other extreme from the classical model. In the neoclassical model the macroeconomic variables are divided into savings, investment, and interest interacting in one compartment and money, prices, income, and employment interacting in another. The ultra-Keynesian school tends to divide the variables differently, putting savings, investment, and income (measured in real terms) in one box, together with employment, while interest and money are put in another. The general price level is left to drift without any specific mechanism for its determination, aside from the assumption that prices are sticky enough to stay put in the short run, unless expansionary forces persist after full employment is reached, in which case an increase in prices is expected, but without any precise indication of how rapidly or how far the inflation will proceed.

In the savings-investment-income compartment, planned savings and planned investment are supposed to depend on the expected level of income, which in turn is closely related, if not identified with, the income of the immediately preceding periods. Planned investment may also depend on the level of capital accumulation attained and such other exogenous influences as technological change, population growth and the like, but for purposes of short-run analysis these can be segregated as being part of the underlying data rather than being among the interacting variables. In the extreme forms of the Keynesian model, planned investment as well as consumption and savings are deemed to be little if at all affected by changes in the rate of interest.

The dependence of planned investment on expected income is assumed to be more or less direct. In some types of analysis investment plans are thought of as primarily dependent on the projected level of consumption, in that investment is considered to be investment in plant for the production of the projected flow of consumption goods. But plant must be built to produce investment goods also, and thus it seems more appropriate for most purposes to relate investment to total expected production or income. Actually, for much investment it would seem more appropriate to assume that it will vary with the *growth* of the national income, and that, accordingly, the expected change in income rather than the income itself should be the variable used. However, we can on the one hand impound past incomes among the constants of the problem, at least for fairly short-run analysis, and on the other we can note that some investment will be made simply in terms of a secular growth in the ratio of capital to income. In any case, to introduce changes in income into a relation would produce a more complicated dynamic model, and for the time being we want to stay on the simpler static level. In the extremely short run, indeed, it can be assumed that plans for a substantial fraction of total investment must be made a considerable time in advance, so that for the immediate future much of planned investment can be treated as a constant.

The Consumption Function

WHILE there is no particular reason for not considering saving as being directly a function of income, many analyses approach planned savings as the residual obtained by deducting planned consumption from expected income. Planned consumption is in turn dependent on expected income, with expected income generally taken for simplicity as equal to current income. The type of relationship usually assumed is shown in FIGURE 11, where income is plotted on the horizontal axis and consumption on the vertical axis. The curve has an upward slope of less than 45 degrees, indicating that consumption increases

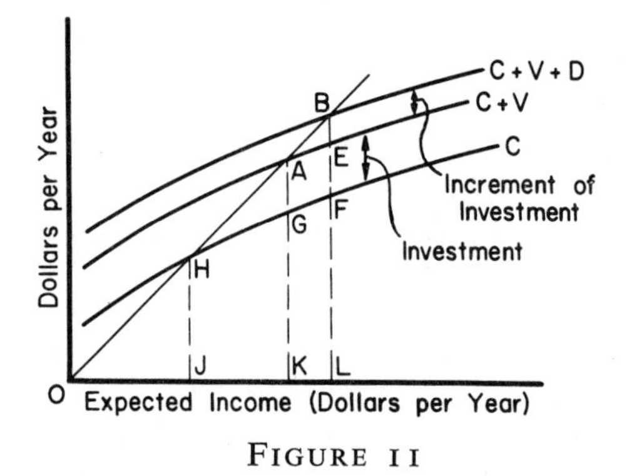

FIGURE 11

as income increases, but that the increase in consumption tends to be less than the increase in income. The slope of the curve at a given point, or the ratio of the increase in consumption produced by a small increase in income to the increase in income is termed the marginal propensity to consume. In general, the marginal propensity to consume will vary from point to point along the curve, but in spite of much research, very little is known as yet about the detailed behavior of the marginal propensity to consume, and it is often assumed for simplicity to be the same at all points, in which case the curve becomes a straight line. When the relationship is represented by a curve, it is usual to make the curve concave downward, on the a priori assumption that as income increases the marginal propensity to consume decreases, but this is by no means backed by adequate data.

The consumption curve is usually drawn to cut the 45-degree line for some low level of income, indicating that even at zero income levels some consumption will take place, being presumably financed out of dissaving. While this is actually found to be characteristic of low-income families when the curve is drawn according to cross-section data where households are grouped according to income, it is by no means certain that this would be true if the data were restricted to those with permanently low incomes, with households excluded that are fairly well off on the whole and only temporarily without substantial income. Considered as an aggregate relation, the lower end of the curve is without current relevance. It is generally believed that this consumption curve, expressed in "real" terms, is subject to a secular upward shift as individuals accumulate capital and as the living standards accepted by the community generally rise.

By subtracting the consumption curve from the 45-degree line representing income, we get a relation between income and savings. If the consumption curve is linear, the savings curve will also be linear and will have a slope equal to one minus the slope of the consumption curve (i.e., if the slope of the consumption curve is b, the slope of the savings curve is $1 - b$). If the consumption curve is concave downward, the savings curve will be concave upward. In any case, the slope of the savings curve is assumed to be positive but less than one, indicating that of any increase in income some will go to consumption and some to savings.

The simplest analysis of the interaction between income, investment, and savings occurs when it is assumed that planned investment will be determined independently of current income. The line representing investment then becomes a horizontal straight line. The point where this line intersects the savings curve indicates the income at which planned savings will be equal to planned investment and thus where the system will be in equilibrium. The same equilibrium level can be indicated by adding the constant amount of investment to the consumption curve, thus producing a new curve, "total demand" equal to the sum of planned consumption plus planned investment, similar in shape to the consumption curve but a constant distance above it. The equilibrium level of income will be indicated by the intersection of this new curve with the 45-degree line representing expected income.

If expected income is higher than this equilibrium level, planned consumption and planned investment together will fall short of the expected income. Part of this shortfall may be made up by unplanned investment in unsold inventories, but in general actual income will fall short of expected income. If there is unplanned investment in inventories, it will lead to a reduction in planned investment for the immediately succeeding period as holders of these excess stocks change their plans so as to bring them back to a normal level, while to the extent that income falls short of past expectations there is likely to be a more or less corresponding reduction of expectations of income for the subsequent period, which in turn will normally lead to a reduction in planned expenditure. Both effects will lead to a still further reduction in actual income, and this trend is likely to continue in successive periods until an equilibrium is reached where expected income is such that the expenditure planned in the light of this expectation plus planned investment together produce an actual income agreeing with the expectations so that there is no disappointment or surprise in the aggregate, and no further revision in aggregate plans. This of course does not mean that there will not be surprises and disappointments for individuals, but in a situation that is in macroeconomic equilibrium these surprises and disappointments will be in favorable directions for some and in unfavorable directions for others in roughly equal and balancing amounts, so that the aggregate plans will not be changed even though individual plans within the aggregate are changed. Conversely, if expected income falls below the equilibrium level at which planned savings and planned investment are equal, the excess of planned investment over planned savings gives rise to forces tending to raise income back toward the equilibrium level.

The Multiplier

WE NOW COME to investigate the influence on the equilibrium level of income of an addition to or subtraction from the planned investment. Such changes in investment plans can of course arise from a variety of sources, but the most

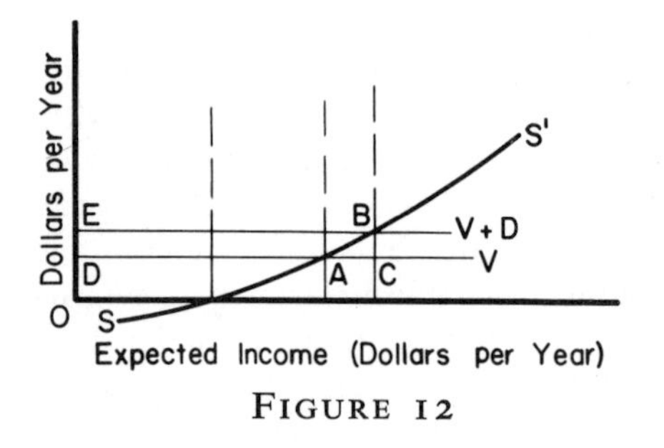

FIGURE 12

clearly independent and deliberate source of such a change is "investment" by the government. The simplest and most clear-cut case of government investment is when outlays on public works are increased and bonds are issued to finance the outlays. In FIGURE 12 we may suppose that the additional investment is *DE*, raising the total planned investment from o*D* to o*E*. As a result the equilibrium point moves from *A* to *B*. The ratio of the increase in investment, *CB*, to the increase in income it produces, *AC*, is the slope of the savings curve, or the marginal propensity to save. The "multiplier," which is the ratio of the increase in income to the increase in investment, is thus simply the reciprocal of this quantity, in this simple case. And the marginal propensity to save is in turn equal to $1 - b$, where b is the marginal propensity to consume. The multiplier k is then given by $k = 1/(1 - b)$. For example, if consumers spend 80 per cent of every increment of income, then b is equal to 0.8, and the multiplier k will be 5.0. This means that if the government increases its investment by $1 billion per year, the national income will increase by $5 billion per year. If there are idle factors available that can be brought into use without raising prices, the increase in income will be accompanied by a corresponding increase in employment.

It is important to realize, of course, that the multiplier effect is not instantaneous in its action, but may require several stages to work itself out, with these several stages involving an appreciable amount of time. Moreover, in this static form of analysis, it must be assumed that the government investment is a continuing permanent flow and is not merely a "one-shot" or "pump-priming" action.

If we assume that investment is not fixed or exogenously determined (i.e., determined entirely by forces outside and independent of the model under

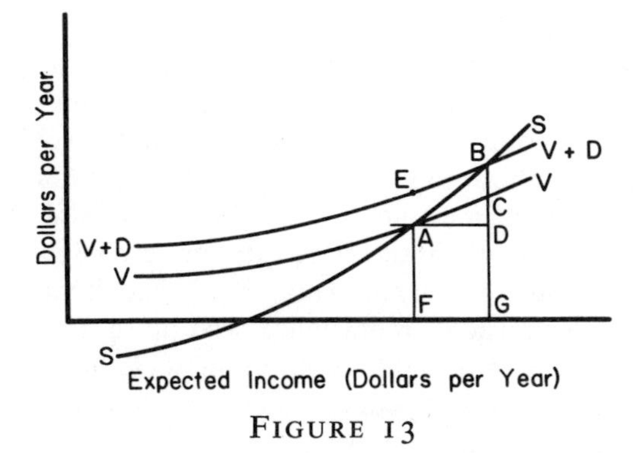

FIGURE 13

consideration), but itself responds to changes in income, then the analysis must be modified slightly. In FIGURE 13 we may have the same savings function, but the investment function now rises with rising income, although not so rapidly as savings. Equilibrium income is initially established at *A*, where the two curves intersect. If we assume that there is an exogenous addition to investment, as before, by an amount *AE*, raising the investment curve from *AC* to *EB*, the equilibrium moves from *A* to *B*. The increase in investment *CB* has produced an increase in income *AD*. From the diagram we see immediately that $BC = BD - CD$, so that, dividing by *AD*, we have $BC/AD = BD/AD - CD/AD$. Now BD/AD is the marginal propensity to save, which is equal to $1 - b$, where *b* is the marginal propensity to consume. CD/AD is the marginal propensity to invest, i.e., the number of dollars of additional investment stimulated by each additional dollar of expected income; we can call this propensity to invest *c*. Accordingly, $BC/AD = 1 - b - c$; and $AD/BC = 1/(1 - b - c)$ is the ratio of the increase in equilibrium income to the exogenous increase in investment, or multiplier. This ratio is sometimes referred to as the "supermultiplier" to distinguish it from the ratio of the increase in income to the total increase in investment that occurred as the multiplier in the preceding case. In this case if the marginal propensity to consume were .80 and the marginal propensity to invest were .10, the multiplier (supermultiplier) would be 10.0, and for every \$1 billion per year added to government investment, total income at which the equilibrium between planned saving and planned investment would be restored would go up by \$10 billion. Of course, bringing induced changes in planned investment into the picture introduces another step in the sequence, and, accordingly, it cannot be expected that this equilibrium income will be approached in as short a space of time as in the previous simpler case.

Two further cautions are necessary at this point. For the effect to be as indicated, it must be assumed that the government investment is a net addition that in no way takes the place of private investment: government investment in hydroelectric installations such as those of the Tennessee Valley Authority, for example, may well substitute for private investment in utility plants, and may in extreme cases inhibit such investment to a degree that would produce a reduction in over-all total investment; such investment would not produce as favorable results as those indicated here. In effect, the net result of the government investment of an amount *AE* would not raise the investment curve quite as high as *EB*, and in the more extreme case might even cause the total planned investment curve to fall. Another possible situation is that b and c together might under certain circumstances add up to more than unity. In this case we would have an unstable equilibrium at *A*: the investment curve would be steeper than the savings curve, and any slight increase in income or investment would make planned investment exceed planned savings, causing a further increase in income that would continue until brought to a halt by some outside restraint. Conversely, a slight reduction in income from the equilibrium level would cause savings to exceed investment and income to decline further until some underlying change in the situation brings the decline to a stop. Indeed, it is sometimes considered that this is in part what happens during the boom and collapse phases of the business cycle. However, we are here interested in a static-equilibrium model that is poorly adapted to the analysis of dynamic changes in themselves, and therefore it will be assumed for the moment that b and c have such values as will leave us with a stable system. Actual data do not seem to indicate that $b + c$ even approaches unity very closely for any but relatively brief periods.

Money, Interest, and Prices in the Keynesian Model

HAVING thus treated savings, investment, and income in one compartment, the ultra-Keynesian treatment of money and interest is to consider them to be linked within a separate compartment by means of the liquidity-preference function that we have already considered. Given a level of income, determined, say, by the balancing of savings and investment, and a supply of money given by fiat or other exogenous circumstances, the period of circulation is simply the ratio of the given money supply to the equilibrium income; given this period, we can, by reference to the liquidity-preference function such as that of FIGURE 10, find the rate of interest that will equate the supply and demand for cash balances.

The theory thus developed has relatively little to say about the general level of prices. If there is general underemployment of resources, there may, to be sure, be a general downward pressure on wages, factor prices, and eventually on all prices. However, this lowering of prices, even if it comes about, will have little effect, under the assumptions given, on the level of employment, if we continue the assumption that the savings and investment functions remain stable in real terms, and if either they are unaffected by changes in the rate of interest or the economy has already reached the horizontal portion of the liquidity-preference curve so that no further reductions in interest rates can occur. All that a fall in prices will accomplish will be to make the given real income indicated by the intersection of the savings and investment curves (which are in real terms) correspond to a lower money income, and hence, if the supply of money remains unchanged, to reduce the velocity of circulation and increase the circuit period. This in turn may or may not imply a lower rate of interest, depending on the slope of the liquidity-preference function at the relevant point. But even if interest rates are lowered, the assumption is that this would not affect the savings and investment functions, and hence would not change the equilibrium real income.

All of this abstracts from the dynamic effects of a fall in the price level, which might lead to anticipations of further price reductions, increased liquidity preference, and a reduction in investment and an increase in planned savings, all of which would tend to cause further reductions in real income and employment, so that in the short run price reductions may have the effect of making matters worse rather than better.

On the whole, however, the tacit assumption is that in the short run, at least, prices remain relatively fixed. An exception to this occurs in cases where planned investment exceeds planned saving on the basis of an expected income and price level that would imply full employment of labor and other resources. Here the real income indicated by the intersection of the savings and investment curves will be greater than can be produced with the available resources; equilibrium cannot be achieved, and the disequilibrium will express itself in a continued excess of aggregate supply over aggregate demand with a consequent tendency for an upward spiral of prices to develop. But nothing can be said on the basis of this model about the rate at which prices will rise. In practice the rate of inflation that would develop in such a case is felt to depend primarily on a number of institutional factors and psychological elements that are difficult to allow for in such a simple model.

Where interest rates are in fact down to minimum levels, there is comparatively little question that this simplified model with its denial of the influence of monetary factors on the equilibrium level of real income is of considerable relevance. Where the money supply is relatively more restricted, however, so that interest rates do change with changes in the monetary situation, there is the possibility at least that the income equilibrium will be affected through the influence of interest rates on planned savings or planned investment. Extreme Keynesians are prone to defend their simple model at this point by appeal to various considerations indicating a lack of response in practice of savings and investment to interest-rate changes. On the savings side, a fairly good case can be made in terms of classical theory for an inelastic or even a backward-sloping supply curve of savings on the ground that an increase in interest rates will be an increase in the purchasing power of current savings, and that this will have an "income effect" tending to increase current consumption at the expense of savings that may offset or even outweigh the substitution effect, as we saw on page 14.

On the investment side, however, the case is less plausible. To be sure, examples can be cited where investments are subject to such a high rate of obsolescence or depreciation that gross rates of return of 20 to 30 per cent are required before they will receive favorable consideration: changes in interest rates of 1 or 2 per cent would be of minor influence on such investment decisions. But there are also long-term investments, such as office and residential buildings, utility improvements, and the like, that have a relatively long useful physical life and are relatively little subject to the risk of obsolescence through technological advance or shifts in demand, where interest rates would be a more significant part of the total annual capital charge. Even here, however, appeal is made to the rigidity of technological coefficients, so that the ratio of capital invested to the amount of output cannot be altered much, at least in the short run, without unfavorable effects on costs: a production function between, say, capital and labor would be characterized by a fairly sharp curvature of the iso-product contours in the neighborhood of the current point of operation, and even, perhaps, by a relatively narrow margin altogether between this current operation point and the line along which the marginal product of capital is zero; under such circumstances, and if, as is often the case, the ratio of interest or profit to the total cost of the product is small, or if the demand for products is considered to be inelastic, the interest elasticity of investment may indeed be quite small. If in addition we consider that the savings curve may be backward-sloping, possibilities exist for the perverse elasticity of savings to offset any normal elasticity there may be in the investment curve, so that these curves run more or less parallel. Thus at a given level of income there may be no intersection of the savings and investment curves for any realizable rate of interest, or they may coincide for a considerable distance so that no change in the rate of interest will induce a disparity between planned savings and planned investment at the level of income for which this coincidence takes place, or the disparities may be so small as to produce no major pressure on incomes in the context of a system containing a substantial amount of friction and uncertainty. In such circumstances the simple Keynesian model is a useful first approximation.

Integration of the Keynesian and the Classical Models

BUT WHILE the simple Keynesian model may be sufficiently realistic in particular circumstances, in general there will be cases where the particular assumptions necessary for it to be a useful approximation may not hold, and it is desirable to have a more comprehensive model in which both the classical and the Keynesian modes of reaction will be allowed for. That is, we want to allow on the one hand for the effect of the rate of interest on the Keynesian consumption, savings, and investment functions, and to allow on the other hand for the effect of changing income on the classical supply and demand curves for capital.

The influence of changes in income on the supply of savings and on the demand for investment as function of the rate of interest is shown in FIGURE 14b, which is simply an elaboration of the classical demand and supply curves for capital. For example, if income were to remain at 200 (in units of, say, one billion dollars per year), savings and investment would be given by the curves S_{200} and V_{200} in FIGURE 14b, with an equilibrium at *b*, indicating a rate of interest of about 1 per cent. Similarly, if income falls to 150, savings and investment will both shrink and the curves will shift to the left; it is assumed that the savings curve will shift by more than does the investment curve, measuring the shifts horizontally (this assumption is necessary, as we saw on page 192, if we are to have a stable equilibrium), and as a result the intersection at *a* will be at a higher level of interest, in this case 3 per cent, and a lower level of savings and investment. A further cut in income to 100 produces the curves V_{100} and S_{100} intersecting at *c*, indicating an equilibrium rate of interest of 5 per cent. These various intersections can be joined by a line of equilibrium *DD* showing the various savings and investment levels that will constitute the equilibrium levels for different rates of interest, it being assumed that income is adjusted to bring savings and investment into equality at the given rate of interest.

The same relationships may be shown by an elaboration of the Keynesian diagram, consisting of a series of curves giving planned savings and planned investment as a function of expected income, a separate pair of curves being drawn for each rate of interest to be considered. Such a diagram is given in FIGURE 14a; as compared with FIGURE 13, we have interchanged the axes in order to permit the savings-investment axis to be aligned with the savings-investment axis of FIGURE 14b, and have expanded the savings-investment scale relative to the income scale so as to make it agree with that of FIGURE

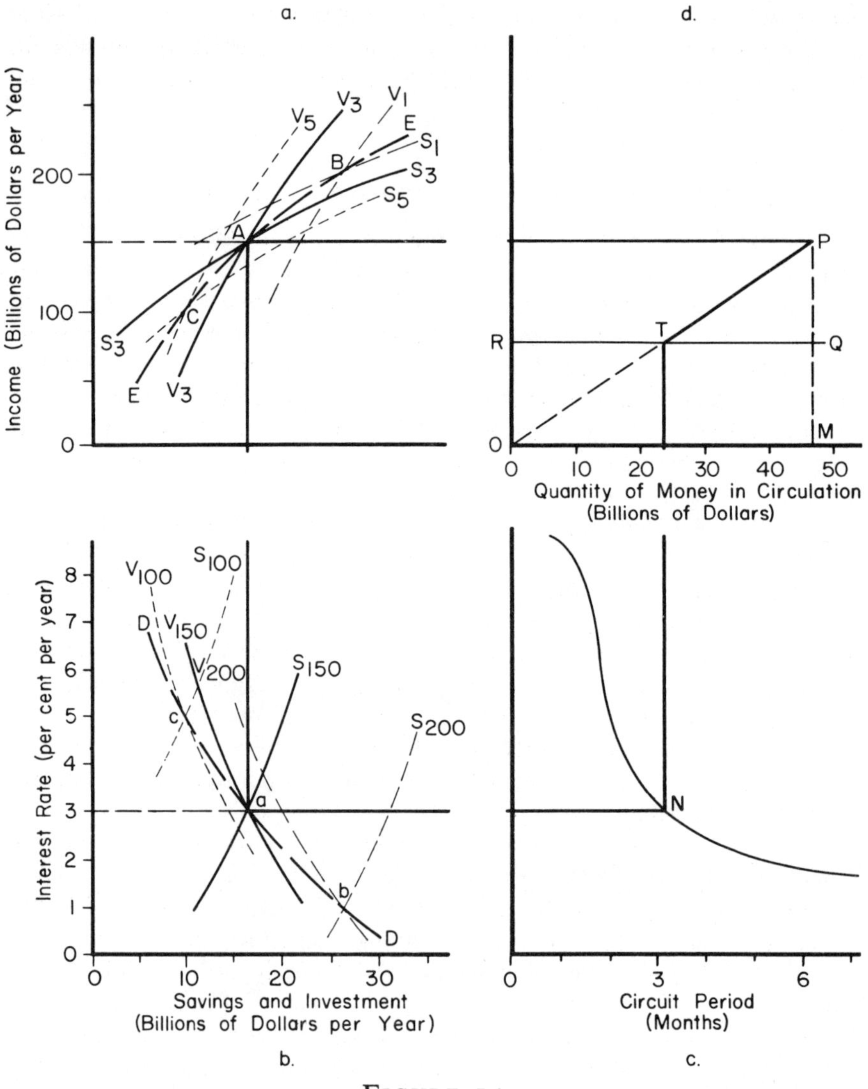

FIGURE 14

14b and permit more detail to be shown, while keeping the income scale to dimensions that avoid running off the page. Thus the horizontal and vertical scales of FIGURE 14a now differ, so that a 45-degree line no longer has any special significance. Curves S_1 and V_1 in FIGURE 14a are identical in content with the savings and investment curves of FIGURE 13, except that where in FIGURE 13 they were assumed to represent the savings and investment functions that would be valid for all rates of interest, here these curves are considered to hold only for a specific rate of interest, taken in this case to be 1 per cent. The equilibrium for this rate of interest is at *B*, indicating an equilibrium income of 200. This agrees with the income required in FIGURE 14b to produce an equilibrium at an interest rate of 1 per cent as shown at *b*.

If the rate of interest is raised to, say, 3 per cent, investment will be reduced and the investment curve will be shifted to the left to the position shown by curve V_3; at the same time savings may be increased so that the savings curve moves to the right to S_3. As a result the equilibrium moves from *B* to *A*, corresponding to an income of 150. Again, this agrees with what is shown in FIGURE 14b, in that there it takes an income of 150 to produce curves that intersect at an interest rate of 3 per cent. The shift in the savings curve may be smaller than that of the investment curve, and may not occur at all if income effects are sufficiently strong to produce a vertical supply curve of savings in relation to interest rates. A backward-sloping supply curve for savings would even call for the *S* curve in FIGURE 14a to shift to the left, but as long as this shift is by less than that of the investment curve, the analysis still holds. Similarly, corresponding to an interest rate of 5 per cent, we can draw a pair of curves V_5 and S_5, intersecting at *C*, at an income of 100, which again corresponds to the income required to produce an intersection in FIGURE 14b at a 5 per cent level of interest as indicated at *c*. These various intersections can also be joined by a line of equilibrium *EE*; this line will indicate the various amounts of savings and investment that will be required if an equilibrium is to be maintained at any given level of income, assuming the rate of interest to be adjusted so as to make the equilibrium at this level of income possible.

It remains to link up this dependence of savings and investment on income and interest to the liquidity-preference function. As we already have an interest axis in FIGURE 14b, we can line up the liquidity-preference diagram with this axis as in FIGURE 14c. To show the relation between income and the stock of money, we construct FIGURE 14d, in which the vertical axis is income and agrees with the vertical axis of FIGURE 14a, while the horizontal axis measures the stock of money. A point *P* on this diagram will represent a combination of a rate of income flow and a stock of money, and the slope of the line o*P* drawn from the origin to this point will be the ratio of income to money, or the circuit velocity.

We now need a device to relate FIGURE 14d, with a horizontal axis measuring money stock, to FIGURE 14c, with a horizontal axis measuring the circuit period. If we lay off some convenient vertical distance o*R* along the income axis of FIGURE 14d (in this case arbitrarily taken at an income of 80), and draw a horizontal line *RQ*, the intersection of this line and the line o*P* at *T* will indicate the amount of money that would be necessary, at the velocity of circulation indicated by o*P*, to sustain an income o*R*. The circuit period is the ratio of money to income, or $RT/\text{o}R = \text{o}M/MP$, and *RT* can be thought of as the amount of money equal to the income flow at the annual rate o*R* for a

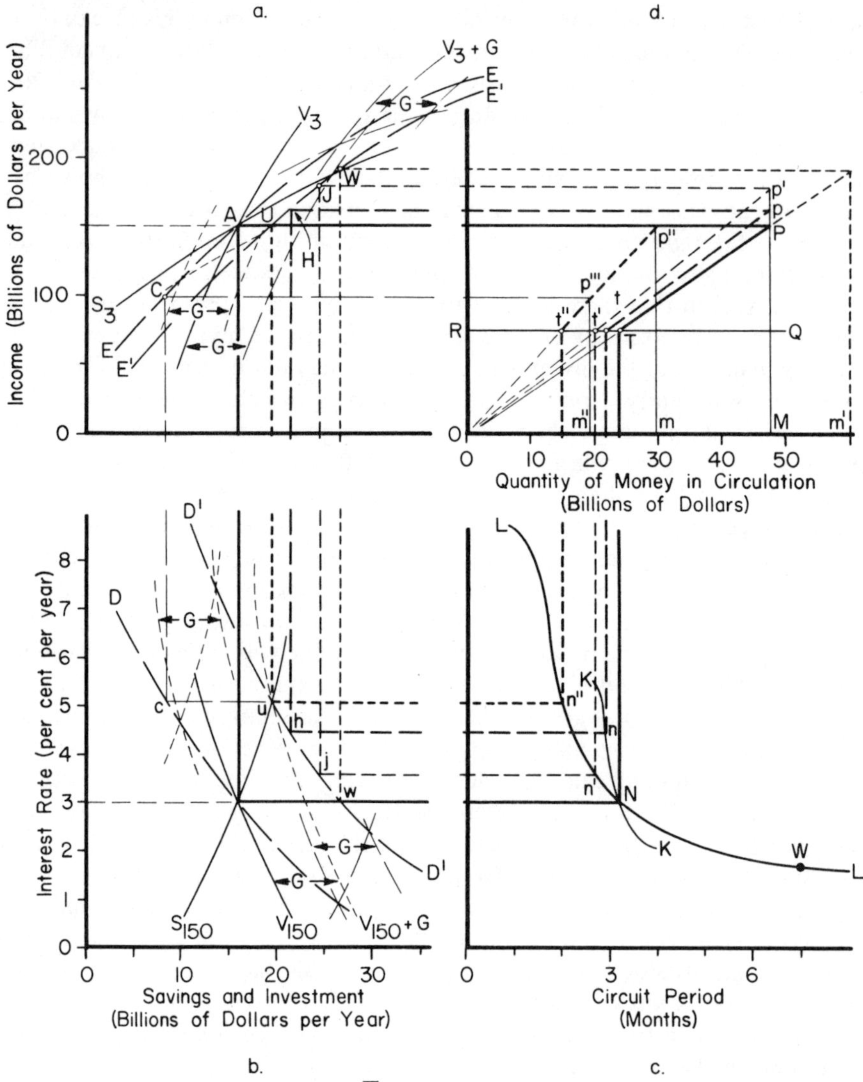

FIGURE 15

period equal to the circuit period, corresponding to the velocity of circulation indicated by the line 0*P*. By a suitable choice of scale, we can take *RT* as a measure of the circuit period, since 0*R* is a constant, and use this as a basis for determining the scale of FIGURE 14c.

A complete equilibrium exists, with this model, when we can trace around the circuit and come back to the same point. For example, if interest is set at 3 per cent, curve *DD* shows the level of savings and investment that will correspond, in this case as shown by point *a*; the corresponding point *A* on curve *EE* shows the income that will be necessary if this is to be an equilibrium situation, and together with a given money supply o*M* this income determines the point *P* in FIGURE 14d; the point *T* on this line determines the circuit period measured by the distance *RT*. This circuit period must agree with that indicated by the liquidity-preference function in FIGURE 14c as corresponding with the assumed 3 per cent rate of interest, as indicated by the point *N*. If this agreement is not found, some adjustment will take place.

In general, there will be only one level of income, savings, investment, and interest, for a given money supply, for which this agreement will be found and an equilibrium therefore exist. This can be shown by adding to FIGURE 14c a curve *FF* showing the various intersections produced by starting at various points on the curve *EE* and proceeding in both directions around the circuit. This is shown in FIGURE 15. As the starting point on *EE* is moved downward to the left in the direction of lower incomes, the corresponding interest rate indicated by curve *DD* rises, while the corresponding circuit period increases as *P* falls and *T* moves to the right. Accordingly, the curve *FF* must be rising upward to the right, and since the liquidity-preference curve is falling to the right, there can be but one intersection.

Effects of Monetary Changes

ONE WAY in which the operation of this model may be studied is by tracing out the effects of a change in the money supply. To keep from complicating the picture by introducing exogenous changes in investment, we will assume that this change in the money supply is accomplished by a purely monetary operation, i.e., by having the monetary authority print additional money and with it buy up some of the national debt. In this way there is merely a change in the form of the liabilities of the government and the authority; there need be no change in government expenditures or in the aggregate of tax revenues. To be sure, there may be a delayed second-order effect resulting from the fact that the interest payable on the national debt will be slightly reduced for the future, but even this may be assumed away by supposing that some other factor purchase is increased, or some other income distribution made so that incomes remain unchanged. The essential matter is that the total governmental debt remains the same, since the money supply can be regarded as a non-interest-bearing demand note.

Putting the additional money into circulation by buying up bonds tends immediately to increase the price of the bonds and thus lower the rate of interest. This may be illustrated in FIGURE 15, which is similar to FIGURE 14, by shifting *M* to the right to *M'*. Initially, if income remains unchanged, *P* moves to the right to *P'*, and the slope of the line o*TP* is reduced to indicate a lower-circuit velocity. The corresponding shift of *T* to *T'* is a measure of this reduction in velocity converted to terms of the circuit period, and the movement of the corresponding point on the liquidity-preference curve from *N* to *N′* indicates the reduction in interest rates that will immediately result from the purchase of the bonds. At this level of interest and with an income remaining for the time at 150, the curves S_{150} and V_{150} indicate a reduction in planned saving and an increase in planned investment; the resulting discrepancy between planned investment and planned savings will tend to produce an upward shift in income.

At this point it simplifies the diagram considerably to suppose that there is a supplementary increase in the money supply, proportional to the rise in income, so that the reduced velocity of circulation can be maintained as indicated by the line o*P′*; the total supply of money will then finally increase to o*M″* so that the corresponding point *P″* lies along o*P′*. In this case equilibrium is now established at the levels of the various variables indicated by the circuit *P″T′N′a′A′*: interest is lower, savings investment, and income are higher, and the velocity of circulation is reduced as a result of the shift in the supply of money from *M* to *M″*. If there is no second dose of monetary expansion, the increase in income will imply a reduction in the circuit period, increase in interest rates, further disequilibria between savings and investment and so on in a succession of adjustments that will ordinarily converge to an equilibrium somewhere between the circuit *P″T′N′a′A′* and the original circuit *PTNaA*, its position relative to the other two circuits corresponding roughly to the position of *M′* relative to *M* and *M″*.

It is of course theoretically possible that a sufficiently sudden increase in the money supply might, if the *DD* curve were sufficiently flat and the *EE* curve sufficiently steep, result in an increase in income more than in proportion to the money supply, which would then result on the second round in an increase in velocity of circulation to a velocity greater than the one in the original equilibrium state, producing on the second round a rate of interest higher than the original one, thus giving rise to a sequence of diverging oscillations rather than an approach to an equilibrium. However, the various reactions postulated by this model are likely to take place sufficiently gradually and with a sufficient degree of overlap so that a development of this kind would be unlikely; in any event, a discussion of such possibilities involves dynamic considerations that we prefer to exclude at this point.

It is worth noting that the sequence of causation in this analysis is a one-way clockwise circuit of the diagrams. Classical monetary theory postulated a more or less direct relation between the money supply and money income, but here we see that the effect operates only via the change in the rate of interest and the savings-investment balance. On the other hand, for the ultra-Keynesians, an increase in the quantity of money exerts its influence as far as FIGURE 14c, but never reaches the income quadrant, either because the nexus between 14c and 14b is ignored entirely, or because the liquidity-preference curve is horizontal at the relevant point, or because the *DD* curve is in effect assumed to be vertical.

Effects of Investment Changes

ANOTHER way in which a disturbance to the equilibrium of the system may occur is through a shift in the investment curves, as, for example, through an increase in government investment. The most straightforward disturbance of this sort to analyze is that produced when a government sells bonds and uses the proceeds for added outlays on public works, meanwhile keeping the money supply constant. If we suppose such an increment of government investment amounting to $10 billion per year, this can be shown by shifting all the investment curves of FIGURE 14a and FIGURE 14b to the right by this amount which we will designate *G*, as shown in FIGURE 16. This results in shifting the equilibrium lines *DD* and *EE* to *D′D′* and *E′E′*, respectively; the horizontal shift of the *DD* curve will generally be greater than *G*, that of the *EE* curve less than *G*. If the government investment is in no way complementary to or a substitute for other investment, it can be assumed as a first approximation that the investment curves shift without changing their shape; even if this is so, however, the *DD* and *EE* curves may and probably will change shape as they shift.

We may think of the government-investment outlay as initially constituting in itself an addition to income: if income was formerly at 150, it will then rise immediately to 160, which will determine the point *H* on curve *E′E′*, and with the given money supply *M*, the velocity of circulation will be determined by the slope of the line *op*, and the circuit velocity will be indicated by *Rt*. The rate of interest for which total planned savings will balance total planned investment, including the new government investment, at this level of income is shown by point *h* on the *D′D′* curve immediately below *H*. If the liquidity-preference curve should be such that this interest rate corresponds to this circuit period, as would be the case if the liquidity-preference curve were *KK*, as shown by the point *n*, then the equilibrium would be complete and there would be no further change in income. If, however, the liquidity-preference curve is more elastic than this, as illustrated by the curve *LL*, then the pressure of the income *H* on the transactions capacity of the money supply will not be sufficient to push interest rates up to the level of *h*, and a further increase in income will take place as a consequence of the resulting excess of planned investment over planned saving; equilibrium will occur at the still higher income and lower interest rate level indicated by the circuit *Jp′t′n′j*. On the other hand, if the liquidity-preference curve had been steeper than *KK*, equilibrium would have involved an income of less than 160, so that the increase in income would have been less than the increase in government investment.

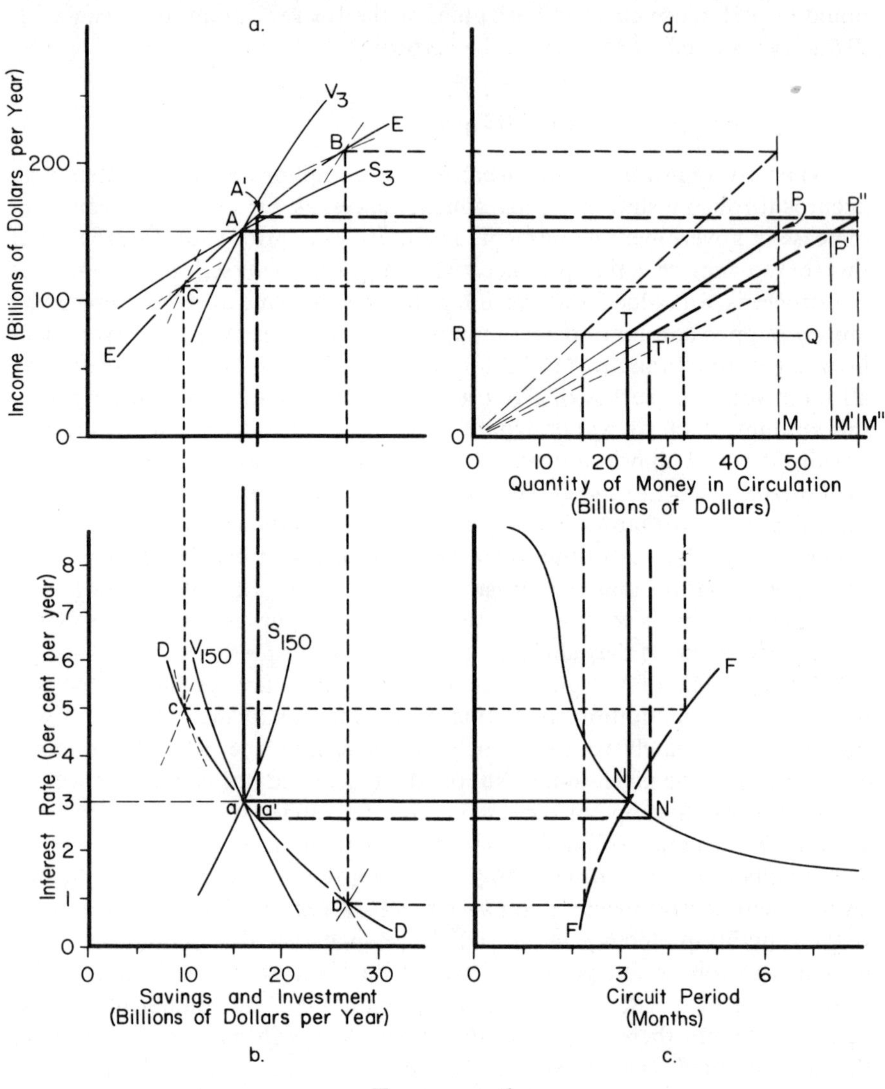

FIGURE 16

Combined Changes of Money and Investment

IF A GOVERNMENT were to wish to undertake additional investment involving a transfer of resources from private investment and consumption to public investment without inflation of the national income, this analysis shows that it is not sufficient merely to borrow the funds while keeping the stock of money constant. Since the *DD* curve shifts to the right by more than does the EE, the point U on $E'E'$ corresponding to unchanged income will correspond to a point u on $D'D'$ calling for a higher rate of interest, which in turn, according to the liquidity-preference curve, requires a shorter circuit period (unless curve LL is vertical) and an increase in the velocity of circulation; this can only be reconciled in equilibrium with a constant money income if the money supply is curtailed, in this case from M to m, in FIGURE 16, as indicated by the equilibrium circuit $Up''t''n''u$. Thus an actual contraction in the money supply must accompany the expansion of government investment activity if inflation of money incomes is to be avoided, at least as long as the investment is to be financed by borrowing rather than by additional taxation.

Another interesting case arises if, as the government investment is increased, a monetary policy is followed of issuing as much money as is demanded at the initially prevailing interest rate, a policy that is approximated either by the offer to rediscount at a fixed rate or by the offering to buy specified issues of government bonds or other securities that are outstanding in sufficient volume, in unlimited quantities at a specified price or "peg." The rate of interest being thus fixed, in this case at 3 per cent, the point N will determine the circuit velocity RT, so that income-money combinations will have to lie along oP. Investment and savings will be in equilibrium with this interest rate at the level indicated by w, which in turn implies an income at the level indicated by W on $E'E'$, and this in turn calls for an increase in the money supply from M to m'. In other words, since at a constant interest rate the circuit period tends to remain constant, the money called for by the public through rediscounting operations or through the sale of securities at the peg price will raise the total supply proportionally to the increase in the national income. On the other hand, since interest rates are not allowed in fact to influence the savings and investment functions, the analysis of FIGURE 13 remains valid and the Keynesian relationship between the increase in investment and the increase in income would hold. In such circumstances both Keynesians and quantity theorists could point to the results as a vindication of their theory, yet both would in a sense be wrong, since it is only the contribution of the monetary expansion that makes the multiplier analysis give the correct results, while it is the fact that the stock of money is being adjusted passively so as to keep interest rates constant that makes the quantity-theory assumptions hold.

The Keynesian and the Classical Modes of Reaction

WHEN THE IMPACT of monetary changes and investment changes are examined separately, the slope of the liquidity-preference function is often crucial in determining the character of the reaction the economy will make. Where the liquidity function is very steep, the behavior of the model approximates that assumed by classical writers, though the mechanism may be a little more roundabout than the one they contemplated. On the other hand, where the liquidity-preference function is very flat, the model follows the Keynesian pattern of reaction fairly closely.

Suppose, for example, that the rate of interest is 5 per cent, so that the economy is at n'' on the liquidity-preference curve in FIGURE 16. The corresponding levels of savings, investment, and income are given by c and C, and in order to have equilibrium at this level of income we must have a money supply that will give a circuit period of Rt'' as indicated by the point p'', which indicates an amount of money m''. Now if we suppose an increase in government borrowing and investment, while the money supply remains fixed, then instead of income rising, which would require an increase in the velocity of circulation of the fixed amount of money, the initial attempt of income to increase pushes the rate of interest up sufficiently, by reason of the difficulty people have in increasing the velocity of circulation of money as indicated by the steepness of the liquidity-preference function, so that private investment is diminished, and possibly savings are increased, sufficiently to close the gap between planned saving and planned investment (including in this latter the government borrowing) and eliminate the upward pressure on income. The resources for government investment will be obtained in part possibly by the reduction of consumption corresponding to the increased saving induced by the higher interest rates, and for the remainder by the elimination of such private investment as is made unprofitable by the increase in interest rates. Here we have substantially the classical result.

A monetary expansion, starting from the same position, however, would tend to increase income. As we have seen putting the new money in circulation (by buying securities with it) will of itself drive the rate of interest down, causing planned investment to exceed planned savings, and causing income to expand. Because of the steepness of the liquidity-preference curve, a very small monetary expansion will be sufficient, initially, to drive interest rates down quite substantially, so that the secondary dose of monetary expansion needed to keep pace with the income expansion will be the dominant element in the total increase in the money supply, and the increase in income will be very nearly proportional to the increase in the money supply. This is likewise substantially the classical result with the added feature that the increase in income is accompanied by a decrease in interest rates, and indeed is only brought about through the effects of the decrease in interest rates on investment plans rather than through a supposed inherent tendency of money to circulate at a given velocity. Velocity of circulation is to be sure relatively constant in this case, but only because interest rates remain in the range where the liquidity-preference function is relatively inelastic.

On the other hand, if we start from a position such as w on the liquidity-preference curve, and increase the supply of money, this increased money supply will be absorbed at the given level of income with very little if any change in interest rates; the circuit velocity will drop, the period of circulation will rise, and there will be no substantial change in income, savings, or investment. Under such circumstances, monetary action taken by itself has little or no effect on the real parameters of the economy.

Increasing investment, however, under these circumstances, will have the effects postulated under the simplest Keynesian theory. Even though national income may change, and with it the circuit velocity of money, this change can be accommodated with little or no change in interest rates, since the liquidity function here is horizontal or nearly so. With interest rates again held constant, it makes no difference whether savings and investment are in fact unresponsive to interest-rate changes, or merely find no change in interest rates to respond to; the analysis presented in FIGURE 13 holds, and income will increase by k times the amount of the investment increase, where $k = 1/(1 - b - c)$ is the multiplier and b and c are the marginal propensities to consume and to invest, respectively.

Forms of Fiscal Policy

IN THE EXAMPLES above, deficit financing was given the form of an actual investment by the government, involving the expenditure for factors of production of the funds borrowed; this form of deficit financing was chosen in order to keep the operation as closely parallel as possible to private investment, making the fiscal-policy operation in effect a supplement to private investment. Similar results obtain for other forms of deficit financing, though the analysis must be slightly modified if the details are to be kept accurate. If, for example, expenditure is for current services rather than for capital outlay, then the results are essentially the same except for the relatively minor difference that total capital formation will be that much lower and the rate of economic growth correspondingly slowed.

A more important qualification is in order if we consider fiscal policy in its "pure" form in which the deficit is brought about without allowing either a change in the money supply or a change in government outlays. If, for instance, we consider the results of borrowing \$1 billion and distributing the proceeds as a pension or bonus, the nominal results, at least, are likely to be quite similar, measured in terms of the aggregate of what individuals take to be their income and savings, respectively. But in real terms the national income will be \$1 billion smaller than it would have been had the deficit financing taken the form of actual construction of capital improvements, corresponding to the fact that in the bonus case the bonds issued to finance the operation represent wealth to their owners, but correspond to no increment of physical assets, in contrast to the case where the bonds finance actual capital construction. If, for example, the multiplier is $k = 1/(1 - b - c) = 10$, income payments to individuals would increase by $10 billion as the result of the deficit-financing operation, but whereas with an actual investment program this would all represent an actual increase in the national product, and would correspond to increased employment of manpower and other resources, in the bonus-pension case only $9 billion of this would represent actual increased national product and employment, and the remaining $1 billion would represent illusory income.

This may perhaps be most clearly seen if we think of the fiscal policy consisting of borrowing $1 billion and simultaneously cutting taxes by the same amount. In effect, the same amount of money is transferred from individuals to the government, whether by borrowing or by taxation, but in the one case the individuals receive bonds in exchange, while in the other case they merely receive valueless tax receipts. The stimulating effect of the borrowing plus tax relief depends primarily on the fact that individuals will tend to spend a larger amount on consumption when they are given bonds in return for their contributions to the government than when they are given tax receipts. To be sure, if each individual were to draw up a balance sheet in which his share of the national debt was entered as a liability, so that it would offset, in the aggregate, the government bonds held as assets, then the aggregate of individual incomes would stand at the same figure in either case. If there was a correspondence between the taxes remitted now and the discounted value of the taxes to be paid in the future to service the bonds, the distribution of income would remain unchanged, in addition. If under such circumstances individuals were to give full weight to this eventual liability for paying off the bonds, there would be no change in consumption outlays and no stimulating effect on the economy. Fortunately for the effectiveness of this most flexible form of fiscal policy, few if any individuals take very seriously any remote prospective liability for paying off a share of the national debt, except as the current service of the national debt is reflected in tax rates. Moreover, to the extent that fiscal policy is effective, it will generate the income from which the taxes can be derived with which the increased debt can be serviced, so that at this level of sophistication it would actually be irrational for even the most farsighted consumer to save the entire amount of the tax reduction.

Thus the government, by simply giving taxpayers certificates that represent no real assets and that the taxpayers themselves will eventually have the burden of repaying, brings into being real assets (and additional corresponding titles) greater in volume than the face value of the unbacked certificates, and thus provides the resources for repayment without an additional net aggregate burden on taxpayers. Even if individuals were inclined to take these future liabilities into full consideration, consumption would be quite likely to operate to shift some of this burden from spenders to savers, so that even in this case there would be some stimulating effect, though of course it would be of substantially smaller magnitude and would not be analyzable along the foregoing lines.

Even a genuine investment on the part of governments in public improvements may involve somewhat the same difficulty, except in the case where the project is expected to become self-liquidating through charges on users, since in the absence of such charges, the debt incurred to finance the improvement is still an eventual charge on taxpayers. In some cases, individuals might be willing to regard future tax payments to service the debt as being offset by the services they may obtain at that time directly or otherwise from the project. But such considerations would be tenuous at best, For most practical purposes it will be sufficiently close to the facts to assume that the behavior of taxpayers is not significantly affected by any considerations of their possible future tax liabilities for taxes that might be levied to service the national debt, at least insofar as these future levies are not reflected in any taxes currently in force. This appears to hold even when the form in which the tax will eventually be levied appears to be moderately certain, as is the case with most local indebtedness which is likely to be serviced almost entirely from property-tax revenues.

Where fiscal policy involves changes in taxes or in government transfer payments, some additional caution must be observed in interpreting FIGURE 16. In order to avoid turning an already complicated diagram into an impossible one, it is necessary to consider income at any one time as a single magnitude, and to regard investment, savings, and the demand for money as all related to this same income magnitude. Actually, of course, savings and consumption are related more closely to disposable income—i.e., income after taxes—whereas the income to which the demand for money and investment are most closely related is more nearly the net national income produced, or possibly the gross national product. So long as these various versions of aggregate income move more or less in unison, no trouble arises from using a single version of this variable to represent all of them. Changes in fiscal policy involving taxes or transfer payments, however, specifically change the relation of disposable income to the other income measures, and a careful analysis must take this fact into consideration.

If taxes are reduced, for example, disposable income rises in relation to income produced, so that if we consider the income axes of FIGURE 16 to be defined in terms of income produced, we must be prepared to see a shift in the savings curves to the right in the two left-hand panels, to reflect the fact that more will be saved out of a given level of income produced if a larger part of that income produced is allowed to appear as disposable income. A similar effect would result from an increase in transfer payments, such as unemployment benefits. This will mean, in turn, that the *DD* and *EE* curves will not move quite so far to the right as for the case of a like increase in government expenditure, so that the corrected $D'D'$ and $E'E'$ curves will be somewhat to the left of the positions shown, by an amount sufficient to reflect the difference between the disposable-income multiplier and the income-produced multiplier (10 and 9, respectively, in the example of page 192. In a quantitative analysis this difference might become important, though the degree of success that has thus far been achieved with quantitative macroeconomic analysis is extremely disappointing, so that other errors and uncertainties are likely to mask this particular detail. For over-all qualitative purposes the picture presented in FIGURE 16 can be considered to be an adequate first approximation.

Monetary and Fiscal Policy Compared

THE RESULTS of this analysis can be summarized by saying that according to this model monetary policy is chiefly effective in controlling the level of money income and with it the volume of employment or the degree of inflation when interest rates are high and the demand for cash balances is inelastic, while under these circumstances fiscal policy used alone without monetary corollaries will have little effect on aggregate income or employment. On the other hand, at low levels of interest where the demand for cash balances tends to be very elastic, monetary policy loses nearly all effectiveness and fiscal policy becomes the effective means of control. Another way of putting it is that monetary policy can be relied on for purposes of checking the rise of income and inhibiting inflation, but may not be able to produce an expansion of income from a low level; fiscal policy will nearly always be able to stimulate a depressed economy, but even heroic fiscal measures may be insufficient to halt an inflationary boom in the absence of an adequate restraint on the volume of money.

To be sure, the distinction between the effects of monetary policy and fiscal policy is often blurred by the fact that many actual policies contain elements of both of these pure policies. If, for example, it is proposed to finance public works by printing money, or by borrowing from banks in such a manner as to expand their deposits, or by borrowing while maintaining a fixed rediscount rate in such a way as to prevent any increase in interest rates, then there is in effect a combination of monetary expansion and deficit financing. Such a combination will have a stimulating influence at all points along the liquidity-preference curve, but the effects will differ from one point to another and it will be different aspects of the policy that will be producing the effects at different stages or under different circumstances. It is necessary to keep these various elements and their effects separate if confusion is to be avoided in their analysis.

Interest-Rate Control as a Form of Monetary Policy

A FEW SPECIAL comments are perhaps needed here concerning that special variant of monetary policy which consists of controlling one or more leading or basic interest rates, rather than controlling the quantity of money in circulation directly. The setting of a central-bank rediscount rate, to be held constant until deliberately changed as an act of policy, and the pegging of the yields of one or more classes of securities, the level of the peg being changed only at intervals, if at all, are both examples of such policy. On the whole such a policy tends to operate in the long run in much the same way and with much the same effect as a direct control over the quantity of money. In the short run, however, control via the establishment of a stated or implied interest rate is much more likely to allow an incipient disequilibrium to gain substantial momentum before corrective measures are applied, and to involve successive overshooting of the mark when corrective measures are applied, than is control defined in terms of the aggregate money supply without direct reference to interest rates. For example, in the case of an incipient recession, if the development of pessimistic expectations has produced a tendency for planned savings to exceed planned investment and for the equilibrium rate of interest to sag, either as a result of an actual reduction of income or in anticipation of such developments, a fixed interest-rate policy tends to cause a contraction in the money supply and to accentuate the decline until such time as the stated policy is changed and a new interest rate or peg price established. Likewise a policy of pegged security prices at a time when inflationary pressure is developing tends, until the peg is either moved or taken out, to feed more money into the economy at a time when, if anything, the reverse should be done. Moreover, if the procedures and long-run aims of the monetary authority are established and generally known, speculation against the peg is likely to develop in a manner that may accentuate the short-run destabilizing aspects of the policy. If monetary control is to be exercised, it can be done much more safely and with a greater degree of automaticity and freedom from "hunting" characteristics through a control in terms of the quantity of money in circulation than through a control in terms of interest rates.

Fiscal Policy, Monetary Policy, and Capital Formation

IT MIGHT appear from the above analysis that we have merely two alternative methods of macroeconomic control which can be used alternatively, or in varying combinations, to secure full-employment levels of national income. But it is not a matter of indifference which of these two methods of control is used. It may prove possible, for example, to maintain full employment without inflationary pressure either with a large deficit, low taxes, a tight money supply, and high rates of interest, or with no deficit or even a surplus, high taxes, an easy money supply, and low interest rates. Assuming that government-capital formation is the same in the two cases, and that there has been merely a substitution of borrowing for taxation in the government finances, private-capital formation will presumably be higher in the low interest case, with a lower proportion of the national product being devoted to current consumption and a larger proportion being devoted to provision for the future, implying, presumably, a higher rate of economic growth. Within limits, then, even in the framework of a predominantly private-enterprise economy, it is possible to modify, through the appropriate selection of over-all economic controls such as fiscal and monetary policy, the degree to which resources are allocated between current consumption and provision for the future.

On the spendthrift side, indeed, the limits to what is possible without explicit expansion of the sphere of government activity are very wide. Conceivably, by sufficiently lowering taxes and increasing the deficit, while at the same time restricting the money supply and raising interest rates, net private-capital formation could be completely choked off, and even made negative through inadequate replacement, with the result that the entire net national product, other than that required for government activity, would be devoted to current consumption. Individual savings would go into government bonds and thus finance current government outlays, while the high level of consumer outlays would be maintained through the effect of acquisition of these bonds on the propensity to consume; nominal consumer income could conceivably exceed the entire net national product. In such a case the national debt would indeed be the counterpart of a real burden thrown on future generations in the form of a reduced heritage of capital goods.

On the accumulation side, within the limits of a stable price level and the preservation of the relative importance of the free-enterprise sector of the economy, the limits are somewhat more constraining. Interest rates cannot be pushed below the level indicated by the lower tail of the liquidity-preference function, so that capital formation is limited to at most that volume that can be made to yield a marginal net return of this minimum amount. Perhaps occasions are unlikely to arise where it would be considered desirable to stint the present in favor of the future to an extent where the future goods made available were hardly greater or perhaps even less in quantity than the present goods sacrificed, yet such occasions are at least conceivable as curiosa, and might even be elevated to a normal state of affairs if sufficient external economies are held to be characteristic of investment generally; it is one of the awkward asymmetries of our economic institutions that they fail to provide a mechanism whereby such an exchange, should the occasion arise, could be carried out.

Price-Level Changes

As we mentioned above, it is one of the deficiencies of the Keynesian analysis that it fails to provide any mechansim for the determination of the price level, and this deficiency carries over into this synthesis of Keynesian and classical analyses. While a model of the determination of the price level lies outside the scope of the present discussion, and indeed such models of this sort as exist are still in a very inadequate state, it is worth indicating at this point some of the ways in which price-level changes may impinge on this model.

It should be noted first of all that the left-hand side of the diagram is to be thought of in real terms, whereas the right-hand side is more nearly in money terms. Specifically, the interest rate that determines the demand and supply for savings and investment is a real rate of interest: savers are interested in the real rate of exchange between the present and the future, and investors are prepared to pay a return based on the real product to be expected in the future. The interest rate of the liquidity-preference function, however, is a money rate of interest, for since the zero rate of return earned on cash balances is a zero money rate of return, the sacrifice entailed in holding cash balances rather than interest-earning assets is measured by the money rate of interest. If there develops a general expectation that the price level is going to decline, the savings-investment-interest diagram will be thrown out of line with the liquidity-preference diagram; this can be thought of as a vertical shift of one diagram relative to the other.

Again, if income on the left-hand side is considered to be measured in real terms, to obtain a consistent value for the circuit period the quantity of money must be measured in terms of its real purchasing power. Thus if the quantity of money remains fixed over a period when prices are rising, then this must be represented by a leftward shift of the corresponding point M to indicate the reduced purchasing power of this fixed money stock. To carry out the analysis along these lines is fairly difficult, however, and for the moment we must leave the matter here.

An Alternative Representation of the Model

IT MUST be admitted that the representation of this comparatively simple macroeconomic model by the techniques used in FIGURES 14–16 suffers considerably from the necessity of shifting back and forth from one panel of the diagram to another, and the complexity of the diagram in general, especially when used to depict the consequences of fiscal policy, as in FIGURE 16. Unfortunately, any reasonably complete economic model involves relating saving and investment to both interest rates and income, and the influence of each of these factors in either case cannot be simply ignored without slurring over some potentially crucial elements in the situation. The above treatment has the advantage of starting with representations of the savings and investment functions that are direct extensions of the already familiar classical and ultra-Keynesian treatments, respectively. It is, however, also possible to represent the model graphically in a quite different way, which even though not really simpler, at least provides an alternative way of looking at the model which may help in understanding its operation.

In FIGURE 14b we first drew a twn-dimensional relation between savings and the rate of interest, and then showed the shifts in this relationship that occur with changing income. In FIGURE 14a we did the reverse by showing first the relation between savings and income, and then the shifts caused by interest-rate changes. A third possible representation, which we will now use, is to take interest and income as our axes, as in FIGURE 17, and draw a series of contours indicating the combinations of interest rates and income that will give rise to various given levels of savings (ex ante), each contour being identified with a particular amount of saving, and, accordingly, labeled S_{10}, S_{20}, S_{30}, etc. Similarly, we can draw on the same diagram a series of investment contours, labeled V_{20}, V_{30}, etc., showing the combinations of interest rates and income that will induce investors to plan the indicated amounts of investment. Where S_{30} intersects V_{30} is a combination of income and interest that will give rise to equality between planned savings and planned investment, and that will thus be an equilibrium point if the budget is balanced. Another zero-deficit equilibrium point is given by the intersection of S_{40} and V_{40}. By picking out from the diagram all of the points where it is thus indicated that savings and investment are equal ex ante, we can determine a locus of points of balanced-budget equilibrium, and can show this locus as the line D_0.

Further, if we assume that instead of a balanced budget we have a deficit of, say, 10 (or if there is any other exogenous addition of 10 to investment, not included in the endogenous investment represented by the investment contours), we can find a second series of equilibrium points such as the intersection of S_{40} with V_{30}, the intersection of S_{50} with V_{40}, etc., at each of which the excess of savings over investment is just absorbed by the deficit. In this way we can obtain a second line of equilibrium positions D_{10}, and similarly for the line D_{20}, and also lines such as D_{-10} where a negative deficit, or surplus, of 10 will produce equilibrium.

It is important to note that the D curves slope downward to the right: this is a necessary consequence of the fact that we assume changes in income to cause greater changes in savings than in investment, so that it takes more of an increase in income to increase investment by 10 units than to increase savings by the same amount; thus the horizontal distance between the investment contours is greater than the horizontal distance between the corresponding savings contours (at the same level of interest). If this condition were not realized, at least in the medium long run, an explosively unstable situation would exist, as we noted on page 192. Accordingly, for a given deficit, the lower the rate of interest the higher the equilibrium level of income.

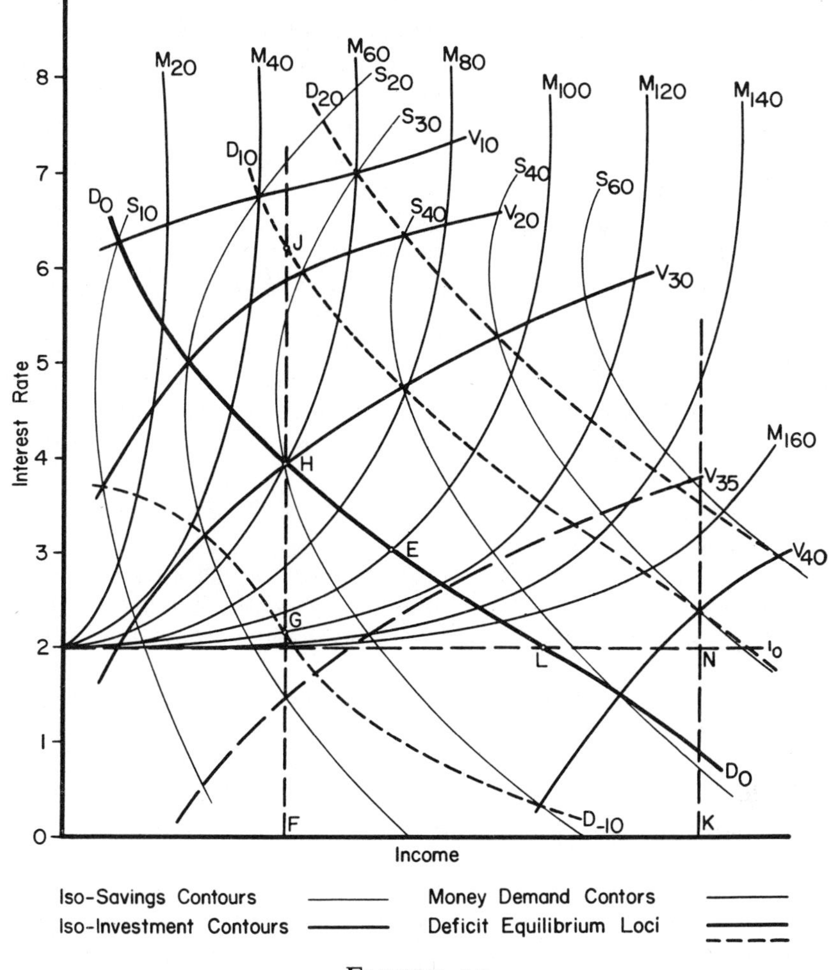

FIGURE 17

Usually, however, we consider that it is not the rate of interest directly, but the money supply that is subject to control, and to complete the picture in terms of a controlled money supply we need another set of curves, the money contours. For a given supply of money, say 100, there will be various combinations of income and interest rates such that the demand for money will be equal to the specified supply. The locus of these combinations can be shown as M_{100}. Toward the bottom-left-hand part of the curve, the velocity of circulation is so low that considerable changes in income can take place without much affecting the equilibrium rate of interest which remains close to its lowest technically possible value. This region is the Keynesian "liquidity trap." At the upper-right-hand end of the curve, the velocity of circulation is close to the maximum technically possible, only minor further increases in income are possible and then only with sharply increased rates produced by the increased relative shortage of the money supply, this supply being assumed held rigidly fixed at 100. The equilibrium produced by holding the money supply at 100 and the deficit at zero is readily determined on this diagram by the intersection of D_0 and M_{100} at E.

To show the effects of varying the money supply we need to add money contours for other levels of the money supply. If we adhere to the assumption that at a given interest rate the demand for money is directly proportional to income, these additional contours can be obtained from M_{100} by merely stretching or contracting the curve proportionally in the horizontal direction. This completes the basic construction of FIGURE 17. With the aid of this diagram it is possible to determine immediately the equilibrium that will be produced by any given combination of monetary supply and deficit or surplus.

Though FIGURE 17 does indicate the final equilibrium produced by a given combination of fiscal and monetary policy somewhat more directly than does FIGURE 16, it does this at the expense of losing track of the detail of the process by which this final equilibrium is brought about. Nevertheless, by recalling what has been learned from other representations, some indications of the equilibrating process can be read into FIGURE 17. For example, if the point H, representing the current interest rate and income combination, lies on the zero-deficit locus but above the money-demand contour corresponding to the current money supply of, say, 100, then if the budget is actually balanced this indicates a money supply that is high relative to current demand, producing a tendency for interest rates to be reduced and the representative point to move downward. As it does so it falls below the zero-deficit locus onto a surplus or negative-deficit locus, indicating an excess of ex ante investment over ex ante saving which it would require a surplus to offset. If there is no such surplus, but the assumed balanced budget continues, then the excess of ex ante investment induces an expansion of income moving the representative point to the right. A sequence of such moves would eventually bring the representative point to the equilibrium point at E. A similar picture of the equilibrating process can be presented for other types of deviation from equilibrium.

No assumptions have been made in constructing this diagram as to the location of the various curves relative to the full employment level of income, and indeed there is no a priori reason why the full-employment income level should fall at any particular point on the diagram. We could, for example, have a situation where the point F on the income axis represents full employment. The diagram will then immediately indicate that there are a number of alternative combinations of fiscal and monetary policy that would produce an equilibrium at this full-employment level of income. The point *G*, for example, would indicate a surplus of 10, a money supply of 120, an interest rate of 2.2 per cent, investment of 33, and savings of 23; *H* indicates a balanced budget, an interest rate of 3.9 per cent, a money supply of 60, and savings and investment equal at 30; *J* indicates a deficit of 10, a money supply of 44, an interest rate of 6.2 per cent, savings of 28, and investment of 17.

It should be obvious that while *G*, *H*, and *J* can each represent a full-employment equilibrium, these three points are by no means equivalent in their implications for the structure of the economy and its rate of growth. Even assuming that government expenditure is the same in all three cases (i.e., the change in fiscal balance represents a change in taxes, not in government expenditures), there will be a significant real difference in that *G* represents a higher level of private capital formation and a lower level of consumption than *J*. The differences between *G* and *J* represent the range of choice that is possible, through the appropriate balancing of fiscal and monetary policy, between the alternatives of a higher immediate standard of living and a higher rate of economic growth, all in conformity to the same requirement as to the level of aggregate employment.

On the other hand, it is quite possible that the full-employment level of income should stand at *K*, relative to the curves shown. In this case, there is still a range of full-employment combinations of monetary and fiscal policy, but the range does not include the balanced budget. Indeed, a deficit of at least 8 is now needed to bring about full employment, even when combined with the most extreme easy-money policy as indicated at *N*. There is still a range of choice, but it is a choice between larger and smaller deficits, and not a choice among a deficit, a balanced budget, and a surplus. Nor should it be thought that *K* is an abnormal situation occurring only in periods when there is a cyclical tendency toward depression. There may indeed be a cyclical tendency for the relative positions of the curves and the full-employment income to shift back and forth; such a "cycle" could even persist in the face of a successful policy of maintaining full employment by monetary and fiscal measures. But there is no inherent reason why the point *L* should on balance lie to the right of the full-employment point even at the "top" of these cyclical swings. What the relative positions of *L* and the full-employment income will be at any given time will be a resultant of the strength of the propensity to consume, time preference, and the historical development of technology and capital accumulation. In terms of conventional assumptions as to the determinants of investment demand in the long run, indeed, the faster the rate of growth has been in the past the smaller is likely to be the demand for further new investment and the more likely it is that full-employment income will be to the right of *L*. On the other hand, one should not place too much reliance on a concept of the long-term demand for capital that is based on static and sort-run considerations, or is a mere aggregation of microeconomic relationships. It is at least conceivable that the dynamics of capital formation are such that either through widespread external economies or through the impact of capital formation on technological advance, the satisfaction of one demand for capital merely creates new demands that more than replace the old. The fruit of capitalism that the Marxist takes to be the seeds of capitalism's own destruction through the exhaustion of investment opportunities may in fact be merely the seeds of further development.

Even if the full-employment level of income lies to the left of L at a point such as F, there is still a limit to the rate at which the national debt can be paid off without precipitating unemployment, and even this rate cannot be maintained consistently with full employment unless the monetary policy is appropriately expansionary. But within the available limits, it is worth noting that the full-employment policies contemplating a larger surplus are also the policies inducing a greater rate of economic growth. There is thus a sense in which deficit spending in excess of the amount needed to maintain full employment, or a surplus of less than the maximum amount that is compatible with full employment, is a burden on future generations. There is thus considerable justification, within the appropriate limitations, for the classical attitude toward the national debt. The correspondence, however, need not be one to one: a reduction of \$1 billion in the national debt coupled with the appropriate expansionary change in monetary policy, even if it succeeds in maintaining full employment, will in general produce an increase in capital formation by something less than \$1 billion. And of course if the debt retirement is excessive (or the deficit inadequate, in the case of K), the consequences will be not an increased capital heritage for the future, but unemployment and reduced production of both capital and consumer goods.

Another important differential between alternative full-employment policies is their influence on the distribution of income. In static terms, low interest rates imply, in the long run, low rates of profit and low rentals for reproducible capital goods. Rentals on land and other nonreproducible capital, to the extent that it is substitutable for rather than complimentary with reproducible capital, may also be reduced, though increased rentals could occur if the complimentarity relation predominated. A low-interest, low-consumption, rapid-growth program is likely to result in a smaller relative share of the total national product going to property than would be the case in a high-consumption, low-growth-rate, high-interest policy. This tendency may be reinforced by the impact of the higher taxes called for by the low-interest-rate policy if these are progressive in their incidence.

On the other hand, it is important to note that this distributional effect is a long-run effect that can be expected to develop if a policy is adhered to consistently over a considerable period. In the short run a reduction of interest rates brought about by fiscal and monetary policy could result in substantial capital gains through the revaluation of existing assets as their expected future income yield is discounted at the reduced interest rates. Such gains would be particularly likely to occur with assets having a moderately short life, since in such cases much of the anticipated yield that is to be discounted would occur in the period before the competition of the new additions to capital induced by the lower interest rates could develop sufficiently to drive the anticipated rentals and quasi-rents down. This short-run effect may even be so strong as to mask the long-term effect; nor is it possible always to distinguish clearly between income that is strictly a current yield and income that derives indirectly from partial liquidation of a capital value enhanced by the reduction in interest rates. The long-run effect may thus take considerable time to make itself evident, and even be preceded by a short-term effect of opposite sign. It is also possible that the reduced rate of return on capital would be offset by the larger total amount of capital on which this return is earned, but this effect would be likely to take a very long time indeed to show up, and even in longest-run terms this would require an improbably high elasticity of demand for capital.

Marxist and Socialist Macroeconomics

IT IS OF SOME interest to see how Marxist and other socialist theories of macroeconomic development can be illustrated in terms of this model. Marx, for example, like the ultra-Keynesians, paid no attention to interest as an equilibrating link between saving and investment. The Marxian equivalent of the consumption function shows consumption as being largely dependent on the distribution of income between the wages of the proletariat and the surplus value extracted by the capitalists. Wages, in line with Ricardo's "iron law," reinforced by the continued maintenance of the reserve army of the unemployed, remain continually at a subsistence level, in spite of the nonrevolutionary activites of labor unions and the ineffectual meddling of reformist legislation, and hence allow for little or no savings; capitalists, on the other hand, whether driven by competition, the urge to accumulate, or the sheer inability to squander, have a relatively high propensity to save. The savings ratio of the community is thus linked to the distribution of income, which in turn becomes more and more unequal as the productivity per capita rises and a larger and larger proportion of the total product consists of a margin in excess of the subsistence required by the workers, which margin is the surplus value appropriated by capital. On the investment side, opportunities are subject to temporary expansion through technological innovation and imperialistic expansion into foreign markets, but in the long run these investment opportunities are limited by the low level of proletarian consumption. Intended savings by capitalists thus eventually overtake investment, leading to capitalist crisis, overproduction, unemployment, and eventually to revolution.

In the dictatorship of the proletariat that is to succeed the revolution, overproduction will of course be prevented through centralized planning, or, in more modern terminology, savings and investment will be brought into line at a full-employment level of income, although the details of how this is to be done are rather obscure in the pre-Soviet literature. Still more mysterious is the mechanism whereby this is to be accomplished in the anarchic communism of the classless society that is to succeed the proletarian dictatorship with the withering away of the state.

Actual Soviet practice is difficult to relate to any theoretical macroeconomic scheme. The broad outlines of investment are of course centrally planned, though there remain a large number of more or less detailed technical decisions that are necessarily made in a fairly decentralized manner at the local level. Here those who would articulate a rational basis for such decisions find great difficulty in doing so within the requirements of Marxist dogma: since labor is the only source of value, and capital can be considered to contribute only to the extent that it is the embodiment of previous labor—i.e., to the extent to which its own "labor value" is used up in terms of depreciation, without any allowance assimilable to interest—and since marginalism is taboo as a bourgeois approach, the usual result is either the setting up of rather arbitrary rules of thumb resting on fairly flimsy foundations and tending to produce absurd results in extreme cases, or the *sub rosa* introduction of an equivalent to interest under devious and tortuous semantic disguises. But even where occasionally interest has thus been introduced under a disguise by the back door, it has been used more as a criterion for detailed minor decisions rather than as a factor affecting very greatly the aggregate volume of investment. The disguise, moreover, has usually been penetrated sooner or later, with the condemnation of the device in consequence as a form of bourgeois deviationism. More recently, however, there have been indications that planners in Soviet-type economics are being driven by the inherent logic of the problem of rational choice to accept interest as a legitimate element in costs and prices.

More moderate socialists have in some cases agreed with so much of Marx's thesis as lays unemployment at the door of inadequate demand resulting from the relatively high proportion of saving out of an unduly high share of the national income going to the wealthier classes, without accepting revolution as the only way out. Proposed remedies for this situation have included equalization of the distribution of income through progressive taxation, the raising of wages, the abolition of profits and interest, the distribution of a social dividend, and the planning of investment outlays by the state through public-works programs and investment in publicly owned enterprises on a large scale. Most of these proposals had other objectives, of course, besides the mere reconciliation of savings and investment. For income redistribution, in particular, as more data has become available on savings propensities and distributions of income it has become apparent that the quantitative effects on aggregate savings are likely to be considerably smaller than would be necessary to make this an important factor in maintaining full employment.

The advent of the Keynesian analysis has to a considerable extent taken the wind out of the sails of those socialists who were prone to make much of the claim that only through extensive socialization and centralized planning could unemployment and recurrent business cycles be averted. While of course there are still some who cling to this thesis, on the whole the impact of Keynes has been to remove very largely the issue of over-all control of business cycles and the elimination of general unemployment from debates over socialism, and to cause this debate to become more and more concentrated on such issues as the control of monopoly, the use of centralized planning versus the market mechanism as methods of coordinating various elements of the economy, public vs. private forms of operation of natural monopolies and large-scale enterprise, and the like. The susceptibility of a private-enterprise economy to recurrent cycle-like crises is no longer the focal point of the socialist attack.

PART III

The Dynamics of Changing Expectations

CHAPTER EIGHT

Expectations and Change

WE NOW COME to the discussion of what can be thought of as the crucial aspect of economic theory for short-range analysis: how the economic process works itself out in terms of the constantly changing expectations of the participants in the economic process. In pure statics, there is no room for changes in the state of individual expectations, except possibly in the relatively unimportant sense of random and offsetting variations in the expectations of individuals. Even when risk is introduced in the static picture, there is variation, but no essentially dynamic element to the process, in that while a particular venture may be uncertain of success, and in the event may succeed or fail, this success or failure is considered to have no bearing on the chances of success of a further venture, much as to a sophisticated observer of the fall of a balanced coin, the happening of a long sequence of heads will not lead to his appraisal of the probability of another head as other than 1/2. Metastatics is an essentially artificial concept introduced as an aid in analysis: the institutionally important fact that a particular commodity, money, becomes the predominant medium for the expression of future obligations and the predominant intermediary in terms of which intertemporal exchange is conducted, and that this money is a readily storable commodity, leads to phenomena which the metastatic model cannot adequately reflect. The macroeconomic analysis of the preceding section considers the implications of these institutional facts for general equilibrium; i.e., given the way in which individuals behave with respect to money, what are the possibilities that exist for the economy to remain in an equilibrium state in which there are no unbalanced forces tending to produce a movement away from this equilibrium, or at least from a progressive equilibrium trend consonant with the potentialities of the economy for growth and progress? To be sure the macroeconomic analysis had to concern itself with at least the minimum amount of dynamic analysis necessary to show the existence of forces tending to convert a disequilibrium into an equilibrium. The exact time sequence of the stages in the progress towards equilibrium, however was ignored, as was indeed the question of, whether the mere presence of forces tending in the general direction of equilibrium could ensure that the equilibrium target would in fact be reached rather than overshot or circled.

The short-run dynamics that we will now consider attempts to delineate more specifically the successive stages that an economy or some of its elements may go through as a result of an equilibrium being disturbed, or as a result of having previously reached a state of disequilibrium. In this context, the term "equilibrium" may have to be interpreted fairly broadly: an economy may be considered to be in "dynamic" equilibrium under almost any circumstances, if the concept is interpreted to include a balance between the forces impinging on the economy and the response that the economy is making to these forces. More usefully, equilibrium may be considered a state in which an economy, though not static, is moving in such a way that expectations are on the average fulfilled. It would of course be too much to ask that the expectations of each individual be fulfilled, since individuals may entertain conflicting expectations; it seems sufficient to consider as an equilibrium a situation in which the unfavorable surprises balance the favorable ones.

In the absence of a complete futures market such as was envisaged in the metastatic analysis, or of a master plan developed by some over-all planning agency, individuals and firms will have to make their individual plans in the light of such guesses as they are able to make concerning the future course of the economic variables that are likely to affect their plans. These guesses or expectations can arise from several sources, but the basic sources that are of interest for analytical purposes are the recent course of economic events, insofar as the information is available at the time of planning, and the announced plans or proposed policies of other economic units, notably those of large business firms and governments. Particular importance of course attaches to the announced policies of governments in relation to such matters as monetary and fiscal policy. Many dynamic models, however, ignore this announcement effect and consider expectations to be derived from experience only.

Given such a set of expectations for all firms and individuals, it will generally be possible by the application of some profit or utility-maximization criterion to derive a set of plans of action for the firms and individuals severally. But of course even if the expectations of the various parties agreed, which they need not, the resulting plans may be and usually will be inconsistent in one or more particulars: for example, buyers and sellers of a given commodity may all expect a price of P_e for a given future period, but on the basis of this expected price buyers in the aggregate may plan to buy more or less than sellers in the aggregate plan to sell. In the face of such inconsistency, some plans at least are not carried out in their original form and expectations are not realized. It is of course possible, if expectations are sufficiently vague, that experience, though differing in some way from what was thought to be most likely, or what was the mean or model expectation on which plans were based, is still not so unexpected as to make individuals and firms feel that their original expectations were proved "wrong" in some sense, and thus no revision of these expectations for future periods is called for. In this case the dynamic movement can be thought of as a steadily progressing equilibrium rather than as fluctuation of the type in which we are more particularly interested in short-run dynamic analysis. More generally, experience will be such as to change expectations, or at least to make them more definite and narrow their range as regards any given future date. In the light of these changed expectations, plans will be adjusted, and the adjusted plans may again interact to produce variations in experience that will further change the course of events, leading to new experience, new expectations, new plans, and so on. This sequence of experience giving rise to expectations, expectations providing the basis for plans, plans implying action to carry them into effect, and these actions interacting to produce consequences that are observed as a new or added experience, after which the sequence can repeat itself indefinitely, is the basic underlying concept of dynamics proper.

Converting this underlying concept of the structure into a workable dynamic model is, however, a difficult process unless a great deal is done to simplify matters. To begin with, those who are interested in confronting their models with empirical data have to face the fact that while the data that constitute the experience of firms and individuals can be observed, their plans and expectations are much more difficult to "observe." Indeed, in most cases it is not the actual plans or expectations that are observed but what the individuals concerned can be induced to say about them, which is a different matter. Economists have traditionally been more reluctant to treat verbal expressions as data than have sociologists and psychologists, preferring to restrict themselves to such objective data as prices and quantities. On occasion, to be sure, even prices and quantities have taken on a nominal character when accountants' valuations rather than market transactions are concerned. Economists are, however, gradually learning to accept statements concerning plans and expectations as data worthy of serious attention. But while much has been done in recent years to obtain data on expectations and plans by interview and questionnaire methods, or by examining the internal communications of firms, such data is relatively scanty and often not cast in a form that would be required if it is to be directly interpreted in terms of the concepts of the models. Many models therefore jump directly from experience to action, leaving the intervening expectations and plans without explicit formulation.

A more significant difficulty is that the lapse of time between the occurrence of a set of events and the occurrence of further events which the first set will have influenced (through the earlier events being observed or experienced, used as a basis for the projection of expectations and plans leading to action producing the further events), will vary greatly from one situation to another. At one extreme, speculators may observe a change in the price of some stock, develop expectations concerning the future price as a result, place orders for purchase or sale, which orders will change the market price, all within hours or even minutes. At the other, a fruit grower may, on the basis of present relative fruit prices develop expectations as to future prices and plant one variety rather than another, but this action may not be reflected in price changes that could be used as a basis for further expectations and actions for several years.

Of course, this cycle of information-expectation-plan-action-results-information may not always require that time enough elapse for an entire production process to take place and for goods to come to market. If information is available on the number and age of fruit trees already planted, fruit growers may be guided in part by this information rather than go ahead blindly on the basis of current crop prices. The mere announcement of plans by large firms or by governments may be sufficient to produce a substantial revision of expectations on the part of others. All of the vast economic reporting that goes on may indeed be regarded as an attempt to shorten the reaction period for various types of activity. The futures economy itself may be regarded as an economy in which all reaction periods have been reduced to zero by a system of universal interchange of tentative plans.

To steer a middle course between the complexities of many different reaction periods and simplifying the dynamic problem out of existence by reducing reaction periods to zero, it is usual to assume that the reaction period is the same for all information cycles under consideration. Some more complex models have been constructed with more than one length of information cycle, but even here it is usual to keep to a very small number of cycles, usually taken to be small multiples of a common base period.

The Cobweb Model

PERHAPS the simplest of the dynamic models is the "cobweb" model, so called from the appearance of the diagram used to depict it. In this model suppliers plan their output for the succeeding period on the basis of the currently ruling price, and then sell this output on a competitive market for what it will bring. For annual crops, to which this model is often applied, the reaction period is naturally a year. In FIGURE 18 *SS* is the "supply" curve, indicating the amount that producers will plan to produce for the succeeding period as a function of the price they expect to rule at the time of sale, and *DD* is the demand curve, indicating the price which a given output will bring when marketed. Suppose that the price ruling for the season 1 crop is P_1, and that producers' expectations of the price for the succeeding season are equal to the price experienced for the season just ended. The production planned for season 2 will then be Q_2, and if, abstracting from weather and other variations, this planned production actually comes to market, the price will be P_2 rather than P_1 as expected. If producers plan production for

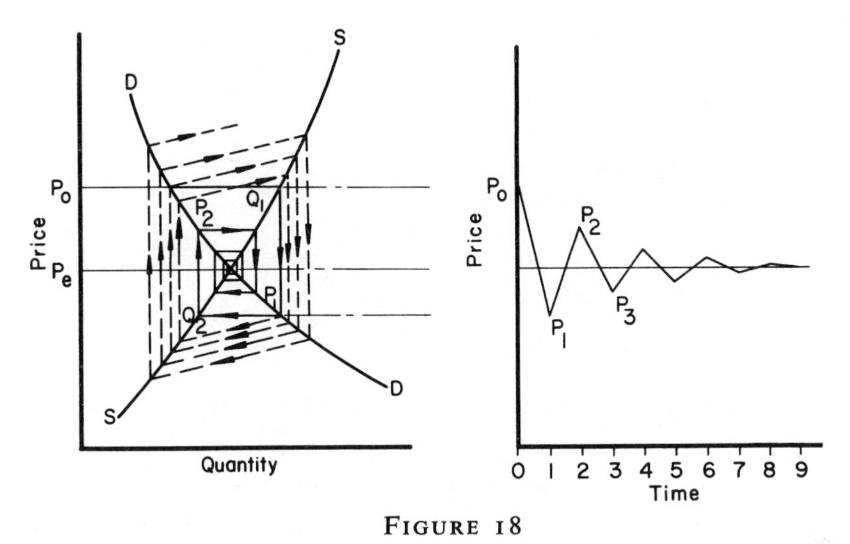

FIGURE 18

season 3 on the basis of P_2, the resulting output is Q_3, and the sequence can be extended indefinitely on this basis for any given demand and supply curves.

In FIGURE 18 it happens that the supply curve is steeper than the demand curve, and in this case it is seen that price and quantity approach the equilibrium point indicated by the intersection of the supply and demand curves, being in alternate years greater and less than the equilibrium values, as shown in FIGURE 18b. However, with differing relations between demand and supply, the picture may be considerably different. For example, with the demand curve steeper than the supply curve, as in FIGURE 19, the process diverges and the alternate swings of price and output become more and more violent, there being no tendency to approach the equilibrium. An intermediate case, shown in FIGURE 20, is where the supply and demand curves

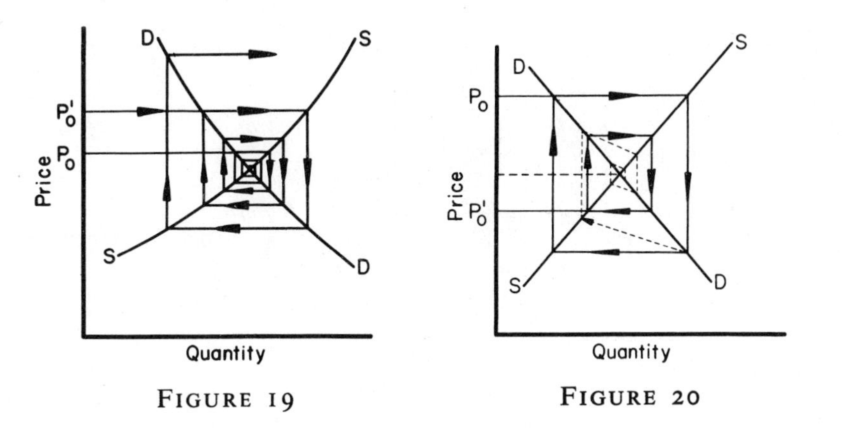

FIGURE 19

FIGURE 20

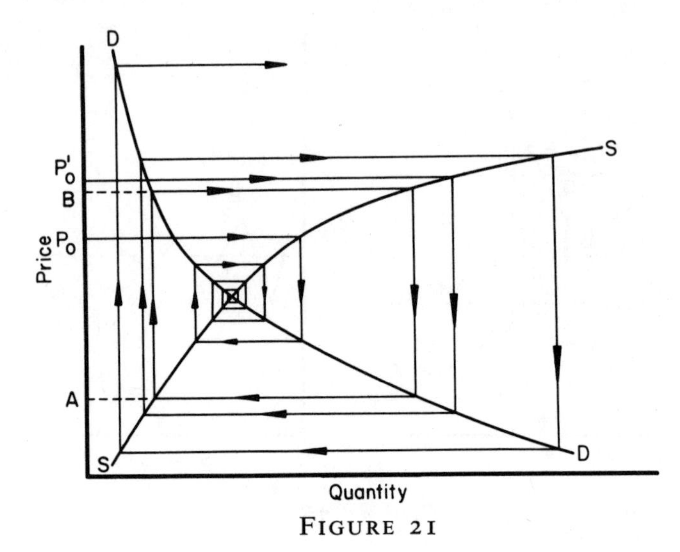

FIGURE 21

have equal slopes, prices and quantities alternate in a more or less steady fashion, with neither convergence nor divergence. Where the demand and supply curves are curved, further possibilities arise: FIGURE 21 shows a case where as long as the price remains close to the equilibrium, there is a tendency to converge to the equilibrium; but if price once gets outside of a certain range (in the case depicted, $A - B$), an explosive oscillation results. On the other hand, in FIGURE 22 is a case in which the process converges to a steady oscillation of a magnitude determined by the shape of the supply

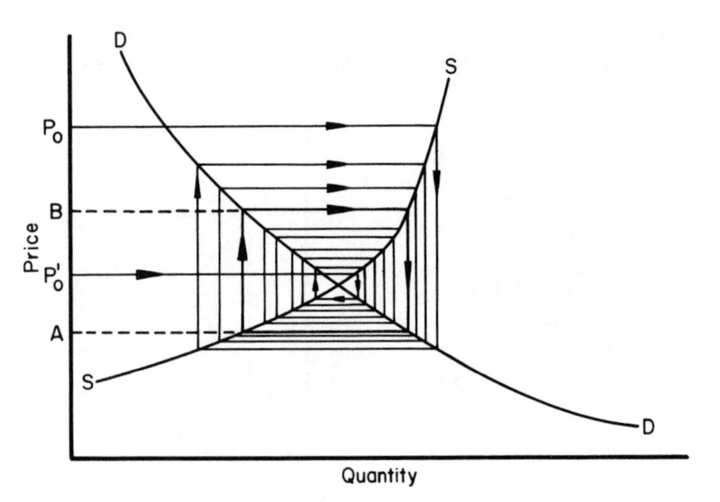

FIGURE 22

and demand curves, whether the original deviation of price from the equilibrium value is greater or less than this. And of course various combinations are possible if the demand and supply curves are irregular.

Aside from assumptions as to the stability of the demand and supply curves, and to the effect that production plans once decided upon are carried through to completion and produce the anticipated output, the assumption that gives this model its peculiar character is the one that the expected price for the coming season is always equal to the price most recently experienced. This in effect assumes that producers have a very short memory, and that no recollection of repeated disappointments and surprises in the past clouds their confidence that the most recent price is the one that will prevail in the future. To be sure, the practical working of a cobweb cycle is always considerably obscured by demand shifts, weather variations, and the like; yet it is hard to maintain that producers would go through very many swings of the cobweb cycle without revising their "forecasting formula" so as to take into account more than the most recently experienced price in developing an expectation as to future prices.

One simple way of doing this is to suppose that producers take as their expected future price some average of the current price and the price for the preceding year. The effect of this is generally to increase the stability of the system, as can be seen, for example, in FIGURE 20, where the dotted path is the convergent sequence resulting from the assumption that the future price will be a simple average of the current and the past year's prices. The shift in method of constructing expectations thus converts a divergent to a convergent sequence.

While the effect of thus introducing previous price experience into the formation of price expectations can be stabilizing, it can also have the opposite effect. For example, it is possible to put too much weight on the preceding year's price and to little on the current price in setting up price expectations; indeed, if the preceding year is given all the weight, the effect is simply to make the reaction period two years rather than one, so that if the sequence converges, it converges just half as rapidly as it does when current price takes all the weight.

A more violently destabilizing situation arises when a change in price from the previously experienced level is taken as an indication of a trend in the price so that further change in the same direction is expected. Such an allowance for a supposed trend can turn a convergent situation into a divergent one, as is indicated by the dotted lines on FIGURE 18.

All of the above cobweb models are characterized by alternations in the prices and quantities concerned from one period to the next, rather than true wave-like cyclical movements. The "period" of the cycle is always two reaction periods long, and does not vary with shifts in the other elements in the model. Moreover, the models relate essentially to a single market and are in effect a form of partial equilibrium analysis rather than of general equilibrium. The results of such models are thus of relatively limited interest and serve primarily as an introduction to the notion of a cyclical reaction sequence, though, to be sure, examples of what appear to be cobweb-type cycles have actually been observed in certain agricultural markets.

Inventory Cycles

TO GENERATE true wave-like cycles, a cumulative element is needed such as is supplied by having in the model both stock and flow quantities, interacting by virtue of the feedback properties of general equilibrium systems. One

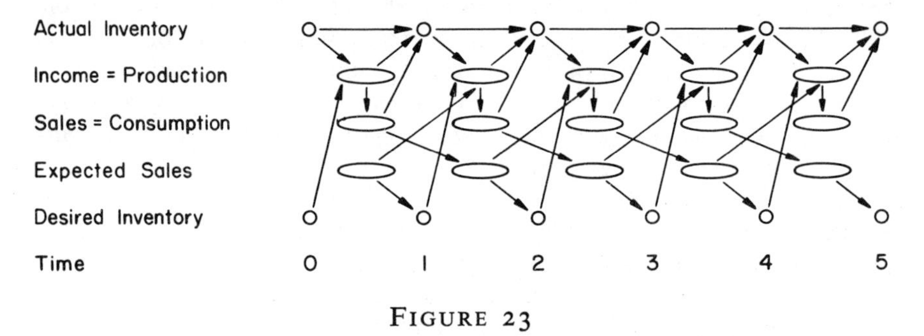

FIGURE 23

simple type of such a model is the inventory cycle. The essential elements of such a cycle are the determination of production plans from expectations as to sales, corresponding desired levels of inventory to be attained, and existing inventories; expected sales are derived from experience as to past sales; production gives rise to income; income in turn determines consumption, which expresses itself as sales, which when subtracted from the sum of production and the previous inventory determines the new inventory, and the process repeats itself. This may be represented on an "influence-sequence diagram" as shown in FIGURE 23.

In the simplest case, expected sales are merely equal to the sales of the period just closed, and there is a fixed inventory norm, with production being planned to exceed or fall short of expected sales by just enough to bring inventory from its current level to this norm. Income that arises from production is spent in accordance with a consumption function with a constant marginal propensity to consume. Suppose, for example, that the consumption function is $C = 20 + .8Y$, and that the normal inventory is 50. If we start with a period in which production, and hence income, is 100, consumption as given by the consumption function is likewise 100, and the inventory at the end of the period is 40, the development for the successive periods can be determined step by step as in TABLE 2.

TABLE 2

PERIOD	PRODUCTION (= INCOME)	CONSUMPTION (= SALES)	INVENTORY AT END OF PERIOD
0	100	100	40
1	110	108	42
2	116	113	45
3	118	114	49
4	115	112	52
5	110	109	54
6	104	103	55
7	98	98	55
8	93	94	54
9	90	92	52
10	90	92	50
11	92	94	48
12	96	97	47
13	100	100	47
14	103	103	47
15	106	105	48
16	107	106	49
17	107	106	50
18	106	105	51
19	104	103	52
20	101	101	52
21	99	99	52
22	97	98	51
23	97	98	50
24	98	99	49
25	100	100	49

For period 1, expected sales are 100, equal to the actual sales for period 0; inventory at the beginning of the period is 10 short of normal, so planned production is 110, of which 100 is intended for sale and 10 for inventory; this production however generates an income of 110, which gives rise to consumption and sales of 108, leaving the inventory at the end of the year at only 42 instead of the planned 50, and the process is repeated the following period. The economy goes through damped oscillations about the equilibrium level of income and consumption of 100, with inventory at 50.

In a more complete model, income would be generated not only by the production directly under consideration, but by production destined for exogenous investment (by "exogenous," it will be recalled, we mean a variable whose magnitude is determined by forces outside the model and determined independently of the action of the model mechanism). Here for simplicity we have left this out, with the consequence that as there is no provision for the absorption of permanent savings in fixed capital, equilibrium requires that the income be at a level where savings are zero. Lowering the marginal propensity to consume will have the result of increasing the frequency of the oscillations and also of increasing the rate at which they are damped out through time.

Increasing the marginal propensity to consume will of course have the opposite effect. But as long as it is less than one, the oscillations will be damped and a stable equilibrium will be approached through time. Other slightly more complicated models are possible, however, in which the oscillations become explosive and there is no approach to any equilibrium; though an equilibrium exists, it is unstable. For example, if in the above model we merely assume that instead of aiming at a fixed inventory, the producers aim at inventories equal to half of the expected sales for the following period, the oscillations do not die out but become larger and larger, as follows:

TABLE 3

PERIOD	PRODUCTION (= INCOME)	CONSUMPTION (= SALES)	INVENTORY AT END OF PERIOD	DESIRED INVENTORY
0	100	100	40	50
1	110	108	42	54
2	120	116	46	58
3	128	122	52	61
4	131	125	58	62
5	129	123	64	61
6	120	116	68	58
7	106	105	69	53
8	89	91	67	46
9	70	76	61	38
10	53	62	52	31
11	41	53	40	27
12	40	52	28	26
13	54	63	19	32
14	76	81	14	41
15	108	106	16	53
16	145	136	25	68
17				

On the next cycle, if productive capacity is not exceeded during the boom, inventory will fall to zero during the recovery from the slump and the expansion of consumption will be impeded so that the model can no longer be followed exactly. Something of this sort is, indeed, the inherent fate of all explosive models.

A wide variety of models of this general character can be constructed, in varying degrees of complexity and of realism. Consumption may be made to depend not only on the current income, but on income of previous periods, or upon accumulated savings; producers may determine their sales expectations by extrapolating a trend of previous sales, by taking into account consumers' assets, or other means. Perhaps one of the most significant elements that can be introduced is to provide for investment in fixed productive capital, as well as in relatively liquid inventory, such investment being determined by a number of factors such as the anticipated level of output, capacity limitations of the capital-goods industries, the age and composition of existing plant, rates of innovation, and the like.

Linear and Nonlinear Reactions

IN SOME respects the role that investment plays in a model of this kind is much the same whether the investment be in liquid form as in inventory or in fixed form as in plant and equipment. There is, however, one very important difference: liquidation of inventory merely requires that production be cut back below sales, and there is a certain symmetry between the accumulation of inventory that takes place at one phase of the cycle and the liquidation of inventory that takes place at the opposite phase. Liquidation of fixed capital, however, is often not possible without the writing off of much of its value as a loss, and even when liquidation is possible with little or no loss, the period of time required may stretch over a much longer period, or there may be a relatively low limit to the rate at which fixed assets of a given type may be liquidated. Construction of new fixed capital, on the other hand, can often proceed at a fairly rapid pace, limited only by the capacity of the capital-goods industries. These characteristics of investment and disinvestment in fixed capital often express themselves in dynamic models by a certain lack of symmetry in the way the model behaves in upward phases and in downward phases. Such asymmetry is produced whenever the relation between a variable and the factors which determine its behavior is nonlinear.

Three important types of nonlinearity can be distinguished, though they can occur in various combinations. In the curvilinear case the relationship is single-valued and reversible, but not linear; a simple example would be if the marginal propensity to consume is not constant, but tends to decline, for example, as income reaches higher levels. Another example is where capacity limitations prevent the other causal factors from having their full effect at the upper end of the scale, but produce no corresponding damping influence at the lower end of the scale. Or limitations may occur at both ends of the scale, but be of a different character: it is impossible to reduce inventory below zero, and goods not in existence cannot be delivered to customers; excessive inventory may run into a shortage of warehouse or storage space, but this restraint is not quite so strict in its force.

Another factor in nonlinearity is the tendency of many economic variables to remain fixed in the face of moderate forces tending to displace them, and to move only after a substantial pressure on them has been built up. Consumption habits may tend to remain much the same in the face of minor changes in income, in prices, or in the variety of goods available. This has sometimes been given effect by using a consumption function in which current consumption depends not only on current and recent income, but on consumption levels previously attained. Administered prices often behave in this way, it being not worthwhile to undergo the expense and disturbance involved in promulgating a new set of prices if the change is to be only slight. It is probably not very important, in terms of the macro-variables of an aggregative model, whether the adjustment when it does come is made to the frictionless equilibrium level, on the principle that it costs no more to make a large change than a small one, or whether, by analogy to physical models involving friction, the adjustment is always somewhat smaller than would be made in the absence of friction. By analogy to electromagnetism, this phenomenon is sometimes referred to as "hysteresis."

A more marked departure from linearity often occurs when at some critical stage in the development of the economic process a change takes place in the way the various variables are related, so that in effect a new regime is entered upon which may have only a slight resemblance to the preceding one. In the more dramatic cases this may take the form of a collapse of confidence, or a chain reaction wave of insolvencies and bankruptcies such as may occur at the end of a boom or at critical points in a downturn. Or there may be merely a transition from one method of determining a variable to another, as when production becomes limited by capacity constraints rather than varying freely in accordance with anticipated demand. It is perhaps a matter of degree whether such shifts in regime are considered as complete breaks or are merely the result of a change in emphasis by reason of the curvilinearity of the relations: approximately the same results can be achieved in both types of model. Generally speaking, however, a model will be more clear-cut and less difficult to handle if a shift, for example, from anticipated demand to capacity as the dominant determinant of production is handled as a change in regime rather than as a movement to flatter or steeper parts of the relevant relationships. On the other hand, the curvilinear treatment of such cases may often be more realistic, if more difficult to handle. When the treatment emphasizes the idea of a change in regime rather than a mere shift in the coefficients, the model can be termed a "relaxation" model, by analogy to certain physical oscillatory systems where a "trigger action" plays an important role.

Linear models, while capable of reproducing a variety of phenomena, are still fairly restricted in their realism. The cyclical behavior that they give rise to tends generally to be fairly smooth and symmetrical with respect to behavior on the upswing and on the downswing; they are also typically either damped or explosive. While it is possible to have a linear model that produces an oscillation of constant magnitude, or that produces an asymmetrical behavior, this will in general be true only for very special values of the various constants that enter into the equations and relationships, values that would occur only by a very unlikely coincidence. The nonlinear models are at the same time more interesting and more realistic. And while curvilinear elements and hysteretic elements do undoubtedly exist in the real economies that are being studied, it is the relaxation elements, with the implied changes of regime, that appear to give the most insight into the interaction of real economic forces.

The "Hicksian" Cycle

FOR SOME TIME now investment and the factors influencing it have held the center of the stage in the explanation of cyclical fluctuations; this has been particularly true since Keynes's general theory and the various elaborations and reinterpretations that followed it have shown the crucial role that investment does play in the determination of the level of economic acitivity, particularly for the case of underemployment equilibrium. The manner in which investment is determined is likely to be quite different for different types of investment and at different phases of the cycle. The role of price change in the generation of the cycle, as distinguished from price changes as consequences of and modifications to a cycle finding its fundamental source elsewhere, has at the same time been minimized, so that we find in many cases that price is left out of the picture almost entirely. This is seen, for example, in the above inventory cycles in which price does not appear explicitly. While many attempts have been made to deal with business fluctuations in terms of the relative prices of investment goods and consumption goods, as well as with prices in general, the combination of real and price elements in a single model is not at all easy, and it simplifies matters greatly if at least as a first approximation we consider only the real aspects of the situation. This amounts to an assumption that interest rates and prices are relatively rigid, or that demand patterns are so inflexible that price changes have relatively little influence.

Setting up of a set of relations by which investment is to be determined requires a closer examination of the relation between production and the use of capital. One of the elements that exerts a strong influence on the character of a dynamic model is the short-run substitutability between capital and labor. Particularly in the short run, there is a strong tendency to regard the substitutability in this direction as strictly limited: there is very little that can be accomplished with extra labor to increase the output of electricity, for example, if generator capacity or reservoir pondage is short. To some extent, even here labor can be used to minimize shutdowns for overhaul, and the like, but numerous cases can be found where it is a fairly close approximation to the truth to say that for a given output, a minimum number of capital units of a given type are indispensable, while an excess will not materially reduce the labor requirements.

Unfortunately, in the construction of dynamic models an assumption of no short-run substitutability between capital and labor means that at any moment production is strictly limited to that volume for which the requisite capital has been provided by investment decisions made in the past. If investors provide the capital only for that volume of production which they expect, this means that in an expansionary phase, in the absence of excess capital equipment left over from a previous boom, production can never be greater than what was expected by investors so that there can in the aggregate only be unfavorable surprises with respect to the volume of production, though favorable surprises can occur with respect to price. To surmount this difficulty, it is necessary either to bring prices into the model, or to assume some form of queuing or rationing, or to assume that investors are sufficiently uncertain as to their predictions of future demand so that they plan a capital investment with a capacity somewhat in excess of the mean of their expectations. Even this requires a price structure sufficiently profitable to make it an attractive proposition to make an investment in capital equipment even though the chances are better than even that it will be superfluous.

The construction of dynamic models is considerably simplified, however, if we make the opposite assumption that over a moderate range, at least, there is a fairly high degree of substitutability between capital and labor, even in the short run. Even though there may be a fairly well-defined optimum relation between capital and labor, at given interest rates, in terms of that combination that produces a given output at minimum cost, output is capable of being expanded, even in the short run, with given fixed capital, beyond this point without producing too sharp a rise in average costs. Such an assumption becomes more plausible when we consider that for the great bulk of industry overtime or multiple-shift operation is a possibility if capital facilities are inadequate, and that in other cases there is nearly always available a certain amount of quasi-obsolete or decrepit equipment that can be pressed into use, the low opportunity cost, or rental, or capital charges for the use of this equipment making up, at least in part, for its higher operating cost.

With such an assumption, it becomes possible to set up a model in which output at any given moment is physically constrained only by the over-all capacity of the economy in terms of manpower and capital together, and not by the capacity of physical plant alone. That is, capacity output is equal to the marginal product of labor times the labor force plus the marginal product of capital times the stock of capital, rather than to the product of the stock of capital and a fixed output-capital ratio. Within this limit, producers are able to expand their production as they wish, in conformity to their expectations concerning future sales and their desired inventory position. Over a somewhat longer time span, producers can adjust their capital equipment so as to produce the expected output at a minimum cost. The crucial fact here is that the adjustment can take place much more rapidly in the upward direction than in the downward. Typically it will take several times as long to liquidate a piece of capital equipment through use as it did to construct and install it. Accordingly, it is convenient to distinguish as separate regimes, subject to different laws of behavior, situations where the actual capital-output ratio is below that which is considered to give a minimum cost from those where the actual capital-output ratio is greater than the optimum. In addition, of course, situations where aggregate output is at capacity in terms of full use of both capital and labor must be distinguished from those where output is below capacity.

We are now in a position to be able to set up a simple relaxation model incorporating three regimes. In the expansion regime, total output is less than capacity, capital equipment is below that deemed optimal for the anticipated output, and producers therefore invest at a rate sufficient to bring the stock of capital up to the optimum level corresponding to the anticipated output over some suitable period of time. Just how this suitable period of time is arrived at we leave undetermined for the moment; while there is no particular reason for supposing that it does not vary considerably according to circumstances, we will assume, for the sake of simplicity that this period is fairly constant. Of course, it cannot be shorter than the length of time required to construct and install the capital equipment, but this will vary according to the type of capital involved and even according to the degree of completeness in which stocks of the components are kept. In the capacity regime, total output is limited by the capital and manpower available; it will be here assumed, again for the sake of simplicity, that consumers have priority and that investment is therefore limited to the productive capacity that is left after supplying consumer demand. While this assumption may be rather arbitrary, it does have the effect of minimizing the severity of the cyclical fluctuations as compared with alternative assumptions that would allow a larger volume of investment during the capacity phase. In the contraction regime, existing capital is in excess of that deemed optimal for the anticipated output, and, accordingly, no investment takes place, but the existing stock of capital is allowed to depreciate. This rate of depreciation, however, bears no direct relation to the degree to which the stock of capital is excessive (except perhaps when the excessiveness is slight), but is primarily a function of output and of lapse of time.

One further stipulation that must be made if the model is to be fully specified is in the manner in which capital equipment wears out. The simplest assumption to work with, albeit a somewhat unrealistic one, is that equipment is destroyed only through casualty, the probability of which depends only on the use made of the equipment and not on its age. Examples of this are glassware used in restaurants, electric fuses and similar items. Such items, as long as they are usable at all, are just as efficient and have just as long an expectation of further service life as new items. They suffer no depreciation in value, even though they have a limited expected service life, and it is unnecessary to distinguish between the quantity of capital measured in terms of its gross productivity and the quantity of capital measured in terms of value, at least in the case of finished equipment as distinguished from equipment in process of construction.

We can now proceed to the details of the model. Some increase in realism results if we consider that consumption lags behind income. The simplest relationship would be to assume a lag of one period; however, a lag of exactly one period, without any smoothing, is likely, in conjunction with inventory adjustments, to set up cobweb-type cycles or alternations that may obscure the more significant characteristics of the model. It is both more realistic and less confusing to use a "distributed lag" such as occurs in the following relationship:

$$\text{Consumption} = .2\,(\text{income of current period}) + .5\,(\text{income of preceding period}) + 30$$

It is readily seen that if income remains steady at 100, consumption will also be steady at 100; that if income jumps from 100 to 110 and then remains at 110, consumption will go to 102 the first year, and 107 in the second year and subsequent years after the change; the marginal propensity to consume can thus be said to be 0.7 for purposes of medium-run or long-run analysis.

Somewhat arbitrarily, we can think of the "period" of our model as having a duration of about six months. Some reactions of course take much longer than this in practice, while others are much more rapid; six months is a not unreasonable average, and has the advantage of avoiding the temptation to consider a period of one year as the only reasonable one.

The optimum ratio of fixed capital to output we shall put at five periods, corresponding to two and a half years. This is near the lower end of the range of values observed in modern industrial countries; higher values would in general tend to intensify the fluctuations that we shall observe in our model. Adjustment of fixed capital to the desired level, however, may be expected to require more than one period. Upward adjustments require the planning and construction of new plant and equipment; while the time required for this may vary according to the type of investment, for the purposes of the model we will assume that decisions to invest or not are made at the end of each period on the basis of the income of the immediately preceding period and the investment projects currently under way; that the outlays in conjunction with a given project will be evenly spread over the four subsequent periods, and that the project will begin its contribution to production with the fifth period following the decision to invest. In determining the amount to be invested, we will assume that investors expect the rate of income and sales of the immediately preceding period is to continue and that projects already started will be completed; new projects will then be started in such amounts that, if these expectations are borne out, upon the completion of the new projects four periods hence the total fixed capital will be equal to five times the assumed income for one period.

Unlike the inventory model previously considered, the speed with which an excess of capital can be liquidated is much smaller than that with which a deficiency can be made good. In this case it will be assumed that retirements of fixed capital in each period are equal to 25 per cent of the net income produced during that period, and this sets the upper limit at which an excess of fixed capital can be economically reduced. That is, when the amount of fixed capital in sight for a time four periods hence exceeds the desired level as determined from the income of the period just ended, no new investment will be undertaken, but on the other hand no deliberate destruction of fixed capital takes place other than through the normal wearing out in the course of production.

This difference between the rate of wearing out and the rate of new construction is one of the elements that produces the essential characteristics of the model. The ratio between the change in the rate of investment (or disinvestment) produced by a change in income and the change in income itself is termed the "accelerator." In this model, the fixed capital accelerator is the ratio between the number of periods of income that is equal to the optimal level of fixed capital, and the number of periods required to adjust fixed capital to a given level. The upward accelerator is thus $5/4 = 1.25$; it is of special significance that this accelerator is greater than unity. In the downward direction the fixed-investment accelerator is much smaller, becoming zero or even negative under circumstances where a reduction in income reduces the rate at which capital equipment is retired and thus may actually decrease rather than increase the rate at which total fixed capital is being reduced. This makes the downward phase of an adjustment essentially different from the upward phase.

The desired inventory level we will again take as half of the sales of the most recent period; however, to reduce the "inventory accelerator" to a level where it will not obscure the other characteristics of the model, we will assume that production plans contemplate making only half of the adjustment from the actual to the desired level of inventory in the immediately ensuing period; in effect, the duration of the inventory-adjustment process is taken as two periods rather than as one period as in the previous model. For simplicity we will assume that inventories consist solely of consumption goods: i.e., that all fixed capital is produced to order; actually, of course, some consumption goods are produced to order and some capital goods are produced for stock.

Finally, we will assume that the labor force by itself has a productive capacity of 150, to which is to be added the productive capacity of the fixed capital at the rate of one unit for each entire 20 units of fixed capital completed and ready for use (i.e., excluding partially constructed capital assets). We will initially assume that where capacity is inadequate to meet total demand, that priority is given to the production of consumer goods, capital projects then being worked on to the extent of the remaining capacity in the order in which the projects were started. This assumption is somewhat unrealistically one-sided, but it avoids the rather difficult problem of how to handle repressed consumer demand. These assumed relationships can be summarized in the equations given at the bottom of TABLE 4 (page 245, below).

The results of all of these assumptions can be illustrated by TABLE 4. We begin in period 0 with a stationary equilibrium situation: income and consumption are at the no-savings level of 100, completed fixed capital is at the desired level of 500, and inventory is at the desired level of 50. In each period there is a production of 100 units of consumer goods, all for sale, there being no adjustment in inventory to allow for; production is started on 25 units of capital goods, and a like 25 units of capital goods started in a previous period are completed. Outlay on capital-goods production is spread over projects started during four different periods, the input for the period being one-fourth of the total cost of the project, so the total input for the period is likewise 25, which added to the consumption-goods output gives a gross national product of 125. Retirements (i.e., depreciation) bring the net national product or national income to 100; this can be computed as either 25 per cent of net income or 20 per cent of GNP. In addition to the fixed capital in usable condition of 500, there will be at the end of each period unfinished capital projects with a value on completion of 75, bringing the total capital "in sight" to 575. If the income of 100 continues for the next four periods, there will be retirements of 25 in each period, or a total of 100 of retirements, which when added to the desired capital level of 500 that corresponds to this income, gives 600 units as the desired level for capital in sight, and substracting from this the capital already in sight of 575 leads to the starting of capital projects amounting to 25 units in the immediately following period. All of this is well within the capacity limit of 175.

This equilibrium, however, is unstable. To see this, we suppose that some disturbance takes place: for example, suppose that some disaster destroys 4 units of capital, reducing completed capital and capital in sight to 496 and 571, respectively. If nothing in the disaster changes expectations as to future income, the desired capital in sight level remains at 600, and 29 units of construction rather than 25 are started in the immediately following period, inaugurating an expansion regime. This increased construction involves an increase in outlays in the initial period (period 2) of 1, leading to an increase of income to 101. This in turn raises the level of desired capital in sight, so that although the increased investment has restored the actual capital in sight to the normal level of 575, investment projects of 30 are put under way in period 3, with a further resulting increase in the amount of construction in progress to 27, producing an increase in gross income to 127 and in net income to 102. The impact of this increment and of the increase in the previous year on consumption raises consumption to 101, involving a drawing down of inventories to 49, while desired inventories rise simultaneously to half of 101, or 50.5, which has been rounded in the table to 51. (This rounding, where called for, has been done in such a way as to make $H - J$ an even number, so as to obviate further rounding in the computation of column T.) In period 4 the increased consumer demand of the previous period leads to expected sales of 101, and in addition one unit is produced for addition to inventory, the intent being to make up half of the deficiency of $51 - 49 = 2$ during the year. This gives a production of consumer goods of 102; a further 30 of capital goods starts brings capital goods production to 29, raising gross income to 131, and the expansion process continues in this way at an accelerating pace until capacity is reached in period 8. Here the difference between capital desired and capital in sight as of the end of period 7 would have indicated a volume of capital goods starts of 109, which in conjunction with construction already started in previous years would require a current input to capital construction of 69, which added to consumer goods production of 120 would require total inputs of 189, whereas capacity is only 174. Assuming that consumer goods take priority, production goods starts have to be cut back to 48, and we enter the capacity regime.

From period 8 to period 22, income grows at a slower pace, and somewhat more irregularly. The curtailment of construction starts in period 8, and the even sharper curtailment in period 9 leads to an "echo effect" when this curtailment is reflected in period 12 in a failure of capital-goods completions to make good the retirements, so that a reduction in capacity occurs. By period 17 this echo effect has become so strong that capacity available after meeting consumer demand is insufficient to carry on capital projects already under way, and 7 units of construction have to lay over a period without any progress being made on them for lack of manpower or supplies; priority being given to projects already under way, no new projects can be started. Finally, by period 20 it is for the first time again possible to undertake all of the new capital-goods projects that are indicated by prospective output as called for in columns L and M; production falls slightly below capacity, but hits capacity again for the next two periods. The final downturn takes place in period 23, when after the completion of 132 units of capital goods in the preceding period, the starts that are warranted by the relation of current income to capital in sight amount to only 98, and this in turn involves a substantial drop in current income from 180 (gross) to 171, inaugurating the contraction regime. Completion of capital projects already undertaken

TABLE 4

Detailed Model of a Hicksian Cycle

		PRODUCTION						DISPOSITION OF OUTPUT				END OF PERIOD POSITION				
		CONSUMER GOODS			CAPITAL GOODS							INVENTORY		FIXED CAPITAL		
PERIOD	CAPACITY	For Sale	For Inventory	Total	Begun	Completed	Gross Value Added	Gross National Product	Retirements	Income	Consumption	Actual	Desired	Complete	Already in Sight	Desired
t	Z	S	T	U	B	E	D	G	R	Y	C	H	J	K	L	M
0	175	100	0	100	25	25	25	125	25	100	100	50	50	500	575	600
1	175	100	0	100	25	25	25	125	25	100	100	50	50	496	571	600
2	174	100	0	100	29	25	26	126	25	101	100	50	50	496	575	605
3	174	100	0	100	30	25	27	127	25	102	101	49	50	496	580	610
4	174	101	1	102	30	25	29	131	26	105	102	49	51	495	584	629
5	174	102	1	103	45	29	33	136	27	109	104	48	52	497	602	653
6	174	104	2	106	51	30	39	145	29	116	108	46	54	498	624	696
7	174	108	4	112	72	30	49	161	32	129	114	44	57	496	664	773
8	174	114	6	120	48	45	54	174	35	139	122	42	61	506	677	835
9	175	122	9	131	5	51	44	175	35	140	128	45	64	522	647	840
10	176	128	9	137	31	72	39	176	35	141	128	54	64	559	643	845
11	177	128	5	133	92	48	44	177	35	142	129	58	64	572	700	850
12	178	129	3	132	56	5	46	178	36	142	129	61	65	541	720	854
13	177	129	2	131	5	31	46	177	35	142	129	63	65	537	690	850
14	175	129	1	130	27	92	45	175	35	140	129	64	64	594	682	840
15	179	129	0	129	112	56	50	179	36	143	129	64	64	614	758	859
16	180	129	0	129	60	5	51	180	36	144	130	63	65	583	782	864
17	179	130	1	131	(D7)	27	48	179	36	143	131	63	65	574	748	859
18	178	131	1	132	12	112	46	178	36	142	130	65	65	650	722	854
19	182	130	0	130	132	53	51	181	36	145	130	65	65	667	818	869
20	183	130	0	130	51	7	51	181	36	145	132	63	66	638	833	869
21	181	132	2	134	(D7)	12	47	181	36	145	132	65	66	614	797	869
22	180	132	1	133	5	132	47	180	36	144	132	66	66	710	766	864
23	185	132	0	132	98	44	39	171	34	137	130	68	65	720	830	821
24	186	130	−2	128	0	7	28	156	31	125	124	72	62	696	799	749
25	184	125	−5	120	0	5	26	146	29	117	116	76	58	672	770	701
26	183	116	−9	107	0	98	24	131	26	105	110	73	55	744	744	629
27	187	110	−9	101	0	0	0	101	20	81	99	76	49	719	719	480
28	186	99	−13	86	0	0	0	86	17	69	84	77	42	702	702	413
29	185	84	−18	66	0	0	0	66	13	53	75	68	38	689	689	317
30	184	75	−15	60	0	0	0	60	12	48	66	62	31	677	677	288
31	183	66	−16	50	0	0	0	50	10	40	62	50	31	667	677	240

TABLE 4 [continued]

		PRODUCTION						DISPOSITION OF OUTPUT				END OF PERIOD POSITION				
		CONSUMER GOODS			CAPITAL GOODS							INVENTORY		FIXED CAPITAL		
PERIOD	CAPACITY	For Sale	For Inventory	Total	Begun	Completed	Gross Value Added	Gross National Product	Retirements	Income	Consumption	Actual	Desired	Complete	Already in Sight	Desired
t	Z	S	T	U	B	E	D	G	R	Y	C	H	J	K	L	M
32	183	62	−10	52	0	0	0	52	10	42	58	44	29	657	657	250
33	182	58	−8	50	0	0	0	50	10	40	59	35	29	647	647	240
34	182	59	−3	56	0	0	0	56	11	45	59	32	30	636	636	269
35	181	59	−1	58	0	0	0	58	12	46	62	28	31	624	624	278
36	181	62	2	64	0	0	0	64	13	51	63	29	31	611	611	307
37	180	63	1	64	0	0	0	64	13	51	66	27	33	598	598	307
38	179	66	3	69	0	0	0	69	14	55	66	30	33	584	584	331
39	179	66	2	68	0	0	0	68	14	54	68	30	34	570	570	326
40	178	68	2	70	0	0	0	70	14	56	68	32	34	556	556	336
41	177	68	1	69	0	0	0	69	14	55	69	32	34	542	542	331
42	177	69	1	70	0	0	0	70	14	56	69	33	35	528	528	336
43	176	69	1	70	0	0	0	70	14	56	69	34	34	514	514	336
44	175	69	0	69	0	0	0	69	14	55	69	34	34	500	500	331
45	175	69	0	69	0	0	0	69	14	55	68	35	34	486	486	331
46	174	68	−1	67	0	0	0	67	13	54	68	34	34	473	473	322
47	173	68	0	68	0	0	0	68	14	54	68	34	34	459	459	326
48	172	68	0	68	0	0	0	68	14	54	68	34	34	445	445	326
...																
56	167	68	0	68	0	0	0	68	14	54	68	34	34	333	333	326
57	166	68	0	68	0	0	0	68	14	54	68	34	34	319	319	326
58	165	68	0	68	7	0	2	70	14	56	68	34	34	305	312	336
59	165	68	0	68	24	0	8	76	15	61	70	32	35	290	321	365
60	164	70	2	72	44	0	19	91	18	73	75	29	37	272	347	437
61	163	75	4	79	90	7	41	120	24	96	86	22	43	255	413	576
62	162	86	10	96	106	24	66	162	32	130	104	14	52	247	487	778
63	162	104	19	123	(D84)	44	39	162	32	130	121	16	60	259	455	778
64	162	121	22	143	(D120)	76	19	162	32	130	121	38	60	303	423	778
65	165	121	11	132	12	14	33	165	33	132	121	49	61	284	402	792
66	164	121	6	127	30	22	37	164	33	131	122	54	61	273	399	788
67	163	122	4	126	22	84	37	163	33	130	122	58	61	324	388	783
68	166	122	2	124	104	12	42	166	33	133	122	60	61	303	459	797
69	165	122	1	123	12	30	42	165	33	132	123	60	62	300	438	792
70	165	123	1	124	26	22	41	165	33	132	122	62	61	289	431	792
71	164	122	−1	121	30	104	43	164	33	131	122	61	61	360	428	788
72	168	122	0	122	116	12	46	168	34	134	122	61	61	338	510	806
73	166	122	0	122	4	26	44	166	33	133	124	59	62	331	481	797
74	166	124	2	126	10	30	40	166	33	133	123	62	62	328	458	797

TABLE 4 [continued]

		PRODUCTION						DISPOSITION OF OUTPUT				END OF PERIOD POSITION				
		CONSUMER GOODS			CAPITAL GOODS							INVENTORY		FIXED CAPITAL		
PERIOD	CAPACITY	For Sale	For Inventory	Total	Begun	Completed	Gross Value Added	Gross National Product	Retirements	Income	Consumption	Actual	Desired	Complete	Already in Sight	Desired
t	Z	S	T	U	B	E	D	G	R	Y	C	H	J	K	L	M
75	166	123	0	123	42	116	43	166	33	133	123	62	62	411	467	797
76	170	123	0	123	132	4	47	170	34	136	124	61	62	381	565	816
77	169	124	1	125	(D8)	10	44	169	34	135	125	61	63	357	531	811
78	167	125	1	126	(D10)	42	41	167	33	134	124	63	62	366	498	802
79	168	124	−1	123	48	122	45	168	34	134	124	62	62	454	512	806
80	172	124	0	124	134	2	48	172	34	138	125	61	63	422	612	826
81	171	125	1	126	(D10)	8	45	171	34	137	126	61	63	396	578	821
82	169	126	1	127	(D14)	48	42	169	34	135	126	62	63	410	544	811
83	170	126	1	127	38	120	43	170	34	136	125	64	62	496	548	816
84	174	125	−1	124	148	4	50	174	35	139	126	62	63	465	661	835
85	173	126	1	127	(D12)	10	46	173	35	138	127	62	64	440	626	830
86	172	127	1	128	(D10)	38	44	172	34	138	127	63	63	444	592	820
87	172	127	0	127	32	136	45	172	34	138	127	63	63	546	590	826
88	177	127	0	127	156	2	50	177	35	142	127	63	63	513	711	850
89	175	127	0	127	(D6)	10	48	175	35	140	129	61	65	488	676	840
90	174	129	2	131	(D16)	32	43	174	35	139	128	64	64	485	641	835
91	174	128	0	128	28	140	46	174	35	139	127	65	63	590	634	835
92	179	127	−1	126	168	10	53	179	36	143	128	63	64	564	766	859
93	178	128	1	129	(D6)	6	49	178	36	142	130	62	65	534	730	854
94	176	130	1	131	(D16)	28	45	176	35	141	129	64	64	527	695	845
95	176	129	0	129	20	152	47	176	35	141	129	64	64	644	680	845
96	182	129	0	129	165	10	50	179	36	143	129	64	64	618	809	859
97	180	129	0	129	13	6	51	180	36	144	130	63	65	588	786	864
98	179	130	1	131	(D6)	20	48	179	36	143	131	64	66	572	750	859
99	178	131	1	132	6	165	46	178	36	142	130	66	65	701	720	854
100	185	130	−1	129	134	7	38	167	33	134	128	67	64	675	821	802
101	183	128	−2	126	0	6	37	163	33	130	123	70	62	648	788	782
102	182	123	−4	119	0	6	35	154	31	123	120	69	60	623	757	739
103	181	120	−5	115	0	134	33	148	30	118	115	69	57	727	727	710
104	186	116	−6	110	0	0	0	110	22	89	107	72	54	705	705	528
105	185	107	−9	98	0	0	0	98	20	78	90	80	45	685	685	470
106	184	80	−18	72	0	0	0	72	14	58	81	71	41	671	671	346
107	183	81	−15	66	0	0	0	66	13	53	70	67	35	658	658	317
108	182	70	−16	54	0	0	0	54	11	43	65	56	32	647	647	259
109	182	65	−12	53	0	0	0	53	11	42	60	49	30	636	636	254
110	181	60	−10	50	0	0	0	50	10	40	59	40	30	626	626	240
111	181	59	−5	54	0	0	0	54	11	43	59	35	29	615	615	259

TABLE 4 [continued]

		PRODUCTION						DISPOSITION OF OUTPUT				END OF PERIOD POSITION				
		CONSUMER GOODS			CAPITAL GOODS							INVENTORY		FIXED CAPITAL		
PERIOD	CAPACITY	For Sale	For Inventory	Total	Begun	Completed	Gross Value Added	Gross National Product	Retirements	Income	Consumption	Actual	Desired	Complete	Already in Sight	Desired
t	Z	S	T	U	B	E	D	G	R	Y	C	H	J	K	L	M
112	180	59	−3	56	0	0	0	56	11	45	62	29	31	604	604	269
113	180	62	1	63	0	0	0	63	13	50	62	30	31	591	591	302
114	179	62	1	63	0	0	0	63	13	50	65	28	32	578	578	302
115	178	65	2	67	0	0	0	67	13	54	66	29	33	565	565	322
116	178	66	2	68	0	0	0	68	14	54	68	29	34	551	551	326
117	177	68	3	71	0	0	0	71	14	57	68	32	34	537	537	336
118	176	68	1	69	0	0	0	69	14	55	69	32	34	523	523	331
119	176	69	1	70	0	0	0	70	14	56	69	33	35	509	509	336
120	175	69	1	70	0	0	0	70	14	56	69	34	34	485	485	336
121	174	69	0	69	0	0	0	69	14	55	69	34	34	471	471	331
122	173	69	0	69	0	0	0	69	14	55	68	35	34	457	457	331
123	172	68	−1	67	0	0	0	67	13	54	68	34	34	444	444	322
124	172	68	0	68	0	0	0	68	14	54	68	34	34	430	430	326
125	171	68	0	68	0	0	0	68	14	54	68	34	34	416	416	326
...																
131	167	68	0	68	0	0	0	68	14	54	68	34	34	332	332	326

At which point the situation is substantially the same as in period 56, with the exception of a one-unit difference in the capital stock; the cycle will repeat itself from this point with only minor and insignificant differences.

$Z = 150 + \text{Int}\left(\frac{K_{-1}}{20}\right)$, where Int (x) means the largest integer not greater than x.

$S = C_{-1}$ $\qquad T = \text{Int}\left(\frac{J_{-1} - H_{-1}}{2}\right)$ $\qquad U = S + T$

$B = M_{-1} - L_{-1}$ or $Z - U - \frac{1}{4}(B_{-1} + B_{-2} + B_{-3})$, if smaller. If $B < 0$, a delay occurs.

$E = B_{-4}$ [but is adjusted for delay if capacity limit becomes effective].

$D = \frac{1}{4}(B + B_{-1} + B_{-2} + B_{-3})$, or $Z - U$, if smaller, in which case a delay occurs, as explained in the text.

$G = D + U$ $\qquad C = .2Y - .5Y_{-1} + 30$ $\qquad K = K_{-1} - R + E$

$R = \frac{1}{5}G$ $\qquad H = H_{-1} + U - C$ $\qquad L = K + B - B_{-1} + B_{-2}$

$Y = G - R$ $\qquad J = \frac{1}{2}C$ $\qquad M = 5Y + 4R = 4G + Y = 5G - R$

at first keeps income from dropping too rapidly, but after this has run off (and of course in a more realistic but more complicated model some of this investment in progress might be simply abandoned or indefinitely postponed as a result of the reduced current income) income drops sharply to a low of 50 (gross) then following a series of damped oscillations which gradually die out, a no-gross-investment equilibrium at a GNP of 68 is reached. This low-level equilibrium lasts from periods 48 to 58, during which period more fixed capital is retired without replacement until the fixed capital in service is down to a level corresponding to the low income level. Further retirements then require replacement, inaugurating a new expansion regime during which there is an increase in income and a rapid expansion to capacity output in period 62. Thereafter there is a slow growth under the capacity regime as capital is gradually added to the extent that there is capacity left over from the provision for consumer goods, modified by a four-period cycle corresponding to the time required to bring new capacity into active production. This slow growth with capacity output lasts until period 100, when fixed capital catches up with the desired level based on the current income, after which a contraction regime is established in which investment is cut off and income declines rapidly at first, and then goes into damped oscillations that converge to the same low-level equilibrium as in the preceding cycle, after which the process can repeat itself indefinitely with only minor variations.

Even in such a simple model the patterns generated are fairly complex. In addition to the major trade cycle with a duration of about 75 periods, there is an inventory cycle that develops during the downswing, about 7 periods long, but which is so rapidly damped that it is just barely discernible. There is the rather pronounced construction echo cycle, four periods long, that shows up in construction starts and to a lesser extent in the remainder of the economy, and a mild cobweb cycle, two periods long, that arises from the delayed reaction of consumers to income, just barely discernible at various points along the sequence. The echo cycle and the cobweb cycle are, to a greater extent than the other two cycles, artifacts resulting from the oversimplified and rigid manner in which the model is generated: in practice, projects will vary in the period that elapses between their initiation and the time when they are contributing to output and constitute an effective addition to capacity. Construction costs will not be spread evenly over the period of construction, and many projects will not be fully utilizable immediately upon completion, so that in practice there is not likely to be any pronounced cycle corresponding to the four-period echo cycle shown here, at least not a cycle pervading the whole economy as contrasted with a cycle related to a particular industry. Similarly, reactions of consumers will vary in the length of the lag between the receipt of income and the consequent consumption, which will tend to eliminate the cobweb cycle.

Schumpeter has given currency to a scheme containing three distinguishable types of cycles: the long, or Kondratieff, cycle with a length of the order of 50 to 60 years; the medium, or Juglar, cycle of about 8 to 10 years' duration; and the short, or Kitchin, cycle of 40 months or so. The Kitchin cycle can, without too much stretching, be identified with the inventory cycle of the model, and the Juglar with the major or trade cycle. There is nothing in the model to correspond to the Kondratieff, unless indeed the "period" of the model is made implausibly long; this would be in any case to be expected, since this model excludes secular progress and the Kondratieff cycle is rationalized, if at all, in terms of waves of innovation which are thus specifically excluded from this model. Actually there is considerable doubt as to whether the long waves of the Kondratieff cycle should be regarded as a cycle of economic origin, possibly based on the slow response of demographic factors to changing conditions, or should be considered merely an adventitious historical pattern touched off by key historical events such as wars, basic technological innovations and the like, of exogenous origin and which do not, themselves, have any well-defined endogenous basis for their occurrence.

The two most obviously unrealistic characteristics of the above model are the absence of secular growth and the assumption that consumer-goods production has an absolute priority over capital-goods production in the event of shortage of capacity. This latter assumption is admittedly extreme, but was dictated by a desire to preserve simplicity. The opposite assumption, that producer goods get absolute priority, is considerably more difficult to handle. It could lead to absurdly low levels of consumption if the acceleration factor were strong enough. Even without this, there is the problem of what to do with the unsatisfied demand: to the extent that consumer durables are temporarily unavailable, demand for them may be transferred to later periods; at the same time the accumulation of savings enforced by the nonavailability of goods will tend to raise demand in subsequent periods beyond what it would have been on the basis of income alone. Such a model would thus tend to require additional variables and a more complicated consumption function. In general, the effect of giving consumer goods the priority is to lengthen the period of "dwell" at the top of the cycle, the duration of which is determined by the length of time it takes for the capacity left over for the production of capital goods, which corresponds to the savings that consumers will make out of the capacity level of income, to bring the stock of capital up to the desired level in relation to current income. This period of capacity output will also of course depend on the capital deficiency existing at the time capacity output is first reached. This capital deficiency, in turn, depends on the rate of growth of income immediately preceding the attainment of capacity, and on the lag between the production of income and the effective beginning of actual construction of the capital induced by the income, in this model one period. Thus in this model the harder the capacity ceiling is hit, the longer the dwell at the ceiling level; this is contrary to widely held views to the effect that the greater the boom, the greater the bust. In Hicks' own version of the model, the dwell at capacity is made rather short by reason of the determination of investment entirely in terms of the income history of the immediately preceding periods, without explicit reference to the level of capital accumulation, There is thus no backlog effect, and if, as is normally assumed in his model, investment at levels dictated only by replacement and improvement considerations is insufficient to maintain total demand at the capacity level, the downswing gets under way as soon as investors give effect to their realization that the upswing is over. Hicks' own model can be thought of as one in which investment takes priority when capacity is limited, while there is no carry-over of unsatisfied consumer demand, as would be the case, for example, if the excess demand were absorbed by price increases that produce inventory profits that increase the incomes of groups with a zero marginal propensity to consume.

The absence of secular growth is perhaps a more conspicuous differentiating feature of the present model as contrasted with most other dynamic models. Introduction of secular growth, in the form of a growing population, a shifting propensity to consume, or perhaps merely technological advance, would considerably complicate the relations between the variables, but as long as these relationships show only a steady secular shift, the main characteristics of the model are relatively little affected. The amplitude of the cycle might possibly be narrowed if, as a result either of technological progress or of random shifts in demand, there is a certain amount of capital-goods production even at the bottom of the cycle. A similar result follows if we take account of the heterogeneity of capital so that some capital that is retired must be replaced immediately, even though other types of capital goods are available in excess of the amounts called for by current production rates.

Another very restrictive feature of the above model is the absence of any explicit reference to prices or interest rates. In conformity with this absence, the relations assumed in the models were relatively rigid: for example, we assumed an unvarying desired capital to net output ratio of 5 periods. It is possible, actually, to insert an interest rate into the model without changing its major features, if it can be assumed that there is some well-defined lower bound to the interest rate. Then the desired capital-output ratio of the model is identified with the profit-maximizing capital-output ratio when the interest rate is at this lower bound, and the assumption is made that the interest rate is kept at this lower bound whenever output is below capacity, and is raised above this lower bound whenever total demand exceeds capacity in such a way as to depress the demand for capital goods to the level corresponding to the resources available after satisfying the demand for consumer goods. It might indeed be felt appropriate to allow interest rates to affect the desired inventory level as well as the fixed capital, and to this extent the model would be materially altered; the general pattern, however, would remain much the same.

It is difficult to conceive of such a model operating in complete independence of a monetary medium, however. In a barter economy, where all commodities have equal standing as media of exchange and as denominators of loans, it is somewhat difficult to conceive of a situation where there is both a lower bound to interest rates and a finite demand for capital at this lower-bound interest rate. In the absence of one or the other of such bounds, it would be possible, at least, for the economy to be kept at capacity operation through appropriate fluctuation of interest rates. In a monetary economy, if it be required that some kind of a price index be kept fairly constant, then zero is almost inevitably an effective lower bound to the real rate of interest in terms of the selected index, and it is possible to imagine a technology under which the amount of capital equipment that could earn enough to cover its maintenance and depreciation cost would be limited, while at the same time the population, possibly because of looking forward to a long period of retirement, would want to accumulate savings in excess of this, out of a capacity level of income. Cycles of this sort then become a distinct possibility.

But while a monetary environment thus appears to be a prerequisite for the development of Hicksian cycles, analysis of the Hicksian cycle appears also to indicate that it may be extremely difficult or impossible to eradicate this type of cycle by monetary measures alone. The crucial question is whether, for capacity levels of income, there exists a monetarily feasible rate of interest that would induce a volume of investment sufficiently great to absorb the savings which individuals tend to make out of their capacity-level incomes. If there is, then it would be possible to have a monetary policy which would keep interest rates at a minimal level during the below-capacity stage of development, raise interest rates drastically as capacity production is approached, and subsequently lower interest rates gradually so as to keep investment at a level sufficient to absorb all otherwise unutilized capacity. If no interest rate sufficiently low to do this is monetarily feasible, then monetary policy may defer the eventual slump, but cannot by itself avert it permanently. Actually, the period of dwell at the top of the cycle may at best be so short that the sharp rise in monetary restraint and in interest rates, especially short run, that occurs at the moment capacity is reached, and which is partly responsible for the capacity dwell being as long as it is, may appear to be responsible for the subsequent collapse, when actually no monetary manipulation could have averted the collapse. Of course, if at any time during the dwell period interest rates are pushed up to such an extent that investment is curtailed below the level of available capacity, this may result in income falling below capacity, and if this in turn leads to lowered expectations on the part of investors and lowered investment at the going rates of interest, the collapse may be precipitated immediately. It is possible, at this point, that an immediate lowering of interest rates to the minimum level might cause investment to take up the slack once again; however, the sluggishness of interest rates generally and the various lags that intervene between action designed to change interest rates and the carrying out of investment decisions to the point of generating income together with the limited degree to which in many situations it is possible to effectively lower interest rates makes it extremely likely that a downturn could in a very brief space of time gather sufficient momentum to place it beyond the reach of monetary remedies.

Interest-Rate Structure and the Effectiveness of Monetary Policy

IT IS, OF COURSE, the "real" interest rate that is in the long run the interest rate to be considered as a determinant of investment, and the prospects of preventing a Hicksian cycle from developing by monetary controls depend on the level of the lower bound on real interest rates imposed by the mechanics of the money market and the nature of expectations of investors concerning the trend of prices. If investors generally expect the prices at which they will sell the product produced by their investments to average out at about the same level as the prices at which they expect to make their investment, then for them the real and money rates of interest will be the same. An investment will appear profitable if its real rate of return exceeds the market rate of interest, and not otherwise. Prima facie, it would appear that the interest rate that would be relevant for the determination of the level of investment under conditions of stable price expectations would be a rate for a loan having a term of the same order of magnitude as the investment being considered. Thus inventory, being a relatively short-term investment, would be increased or decreased, *ceteris paribus*, according to whether short-term interest rates are high or low, whereas investment in plant and equipment would be responsive to longer-term rates of interest. Actually, however, to the extent that interest rates play a role in the matter, short-term rates appear to have a more widespread influence than this would indicate, even apart from the tendency of the short- and long-term rates to move in the same direction.

Much investment in a modern economy is quasi-oligopolistic in character, in the sense that it is not possible to assume that if a given item of investment is not undertaken by one firm, it will be undertaken by another, which would be the case under perfect competition. Rather there are many types of investment that are closely attached to the operations of a particular firm, and if they are not undertaken by that firm they cannot in any closely equivalent sense be undertaken by any other firm, even in the sense of some substitute alternative. As a result, in many cases the choice facing the investor-entrepreneur is often not that of investing now or else seeing the opportunity either pass completely away or become pre-empted by a competitor, but is rather in many, if not most, cases a choice between making an investment now and making a similar investment, say, a year from now. For such investments to take place, it is then not sufficient that a comparison of the expected return from the investment and the cost of obtaining funds for the duration of the investment, by a long-term loan or otherwise, show a positive margin; it is also necessary that the comparison between the immediate investment and the comparable deferred investment show up favorably in relation to the short-term rate of interest: a high short-term rate of interest might make it more profitable to borrow at long term immediately, but instead of making the immediate investment, lend at short term and plan to make the investment later on, getting the benefit of a comparable investment return plus the high return on the short-term loan. The alternatives may not always show up as directly as this: for example, the high short-term interest rate may be taken as an indication that long-term rates will decline and that long-term financing a year hence will be easier to arrange or available on more favorable terms than it would be immediately. The short-term rate of interest may thus have an important influence on the volume of investment currently being undertaken through its influence on the deferment or immediate inception of long-term as well as of short-term projects.

Interest Rates in Relation to Price Expectations

IN AN ACTUAL situation one must look to the expectations of investors concerning prices and interest rates as well as concerning sales volumes. To be sure, some types of investment are more sensitive to price–interest-rate relationships, and others to sales volume, and it is often useful to make distinctions between the "widening" of capital through additions to capital that expand capacity as distinguished from the "deepening" of capital through capital installations designed primarily to lower over-all costs. Thus for a railroad the purchase of additional freight cars would be considered widening, while the installation of an automatic hump yard would be considered deepening. Capital-deepening investments tend generally to be more price sensitive while capital-widening investments tend to be volume sensitive and little affected by prices and interest rates. Keynesian analysis tends to be formulated in terms that would imply the dominance of the widening type of investment, while classical analysis placed more emphasis on the deepening aspects.

The pursuit of a theory that will account adequately for fluctuations in the deepening types of investment drives us sooner or later to ask how the price expectations themselves develop, since these are one of the elements that enter into the making of decisions as to these investments. And to investigate the development of price expectations, we need also to know something about the way the actual course of the general price level is determined, in the short run as well as in the long run. In this area it must be stated at the outset that economic theory is in a very unsatisfactory state indeed, and all that can be done here is to indicate some of the lines of approach that have been used in attacking the problem, without reaching any very clear-cut conclusions.

In the classical theory, prices in the long run were supposed to gravitate to a level that would reconcile the exogenously determined money supply with a full-employment level of real income at a velocity of circulation that was either institutionally fixed, in the older quantity theory of money, or was a function of the money rate of interest, in the Cambridge development. The money interest rate was in turn equated, under a tacit assumption of a price level moving so slowly that its rate of change could be ignored, to a real interest rate determined so as to equilibrate the supply of savings and the demand for investment at the full-employment level. Even though this theory has relatively little to say directly about short-run fluctuations in the general price level, the existence of a determinate long-run equilibrium price level as a norm about which the short-run fluctuations were expected to center had a certain stabilizing influence over the short-run situation, as we shall see in more detail later.

But even this long-run theory has a certain indeterminacy to it if we drop the somewhat gratuitous assumption that only an equilibrium involving a steady price level is legitimate. The following illustration may be a bit artificial but it will serve to point up the difficulty. Suppose that we have a long-run constant-price Cambridge-classical equilibrium with real full-employment output equal to 100, money national income 100, price level 100, real interest rate 4 per cent per year, the money interest rate likewise 4 per cent, and firm expectations by all concerned that the price level will continue its constant level. For simplicity we will assume in addition that there is no progress and that all of these variables remain constant through time. The trouble is that this equilibrium is not unique: even keeping the same real variables and the same supply of money, it is at least formally correct to say that other equilibrium paths through time exist. They may not enjoy the distinction of having a stable price level, but they will be equilibrium paths in the sense that if the pattern is known and correctly anticipated, there will be no incentive for any individual to take action that will cause a deviation from the pattern.

For example, we can assume that we start with a price level of 110, and that this price level is initially rising at a rate of 0.4 per cent per year, so that the money rate of interest corresponding to a real interest rate of 4 per cent becomes 4.4 per cent; if now the velocity of circulation rises in proportion to the money interest rate, the same money supply would be sufficient to maintain the same real income at this higher level of prices. To maintain this situation on the basis of a constant stock of money would require that as the price level rises the money rate of interest should also rise because of the required greater velocity of circulation, which in turn requires that the rate of increase of the price level would itself be increasing. If as we implied above the demand for money is assumed to have unit elasticity, equilibrium with a constant money supply would require an accelerating inflation: starting in year 1 with a price level of 110 and the price level rising at the rate of 0.4 per cent per year, it will take 20 years for the price level to rise to 125, at which time the rate of increase will be 1 per cent per year and the money interest rate 5 per cent. The acceleration of inflation that is required to maintain this equilibrium becomes more and more severe, however, so that after 34 years the price level has reached 150, in 43 years it reaches 200, with money interest rates at 8 per cent and the rate of inflation 4 per cent per year; in 50 years the price index reaches 300, and after about 60 years the model blows up completely.

On the other hand, a downward price trend could produce equilibrium for a time also: if we were to start with a price level of 90, a money rate of interest of 3.6 as compared with the real rate of interest of 4.0 would correspond to the needed drop in the velocity of circulation of money, which would imply a price level falling initially at the rate of 0.4 per cent per year. Twenty-eight years later the price level would have fallen to 75, the money interest rate to 3 per cent, with the price level now falling at 1.0 per cent per year. If we could assume that there is no lower bound on money interest rates, and if the demand for money keeps its unit elasticity, there would be no sudden collapse in this direction: the rate of decline of prices would approach 4 per cent per year as the money rate of interest approaches zero. This could perhaps be considered the path of approach to the ultimate stationary state that some classical writers have alluded to. Or this model could also be taken to indicate the kind of economy implied by Schumpeter's dictum that "neither capitalism nor the social institutions associated with it, democracy among them, can work efficiently with comparative smoothness except on a falling trend in prices."[1]

Of course neither of these models, even under very restrictive assumptions, can be taken as what would actually develop, but rather as what would have to be made to happen in order that all disequilibrating forces be counterbalanced, while still maintaining unchanged the money supply and the underlying real parameters of the model. And in a sense the inflationary

1. Joseph Schumpeter, *Business Cycles* (New York: McGraw-Hill, 1939), Vol. II, p. 465.

model hardly qualifies as an equilibrium alternative, inasmuch as it eventually ends in an explosive inflation and the anticipation of such an event would interfere with the holding of expectations over the earlier periods that would make the model work as it is supposed to. The deflationary model is in better shape: even if we deny the possibility of the money rate of interest approaching zero, and substitute, for example, a liquidity-preference function in which the elasticity of demand for money becomes large as the money interest rate approaches some limiting value of, say, 1.5 per cent, it is still possible to have an equilibrium model in which the rate of price decline approaches 2.5 per cent per year while the money rate of interest approaches 1.5 per cent: the equilibrium may become highly unstable, but it is still formally at least an equilibrium, and we have no indication that the instability that develops is anything more than an exaggerated case of the basic instability that may perhaps already infect the stable-price-level model.

Further variations can of course be produced by allowing the money supply to be varied through time. For example, in the inflationary model, it would be possible to modify the money supply so as to produce an equilibrium price trend that rises at a steady exponential rate indefinitely, without any sudden explosion; all that is required is to increase the money supply at a constant proportional rate of 0.4 per cent per year, in which case the equilibrium inflation rate would likewise be 0.4 per cent per year and the money rate of interest would remain constant at 4.4 per cent, giving a constant velocity of circulation so that money and money income grow together at the same rate. The apparent paradox that increasing the money supply results in a lower equilibrium path for the price level can be resolved by remembering that this equilibrium does not purport to be an equilibrium necessarily or even probably generated by the system, but rather the path that must be expected and followed if the system is not to be driven away from the expected path. It is of course one thing to answer the question, "What is the future course of the price level that, if it is universally expected, can eventuate as expected?" It is another to tell, in a given situation, what price individuals will actually expect; what the actual course of prices will be will of course depend in part on these expectations and may not agree with them. Indeed, while imparting an upward trend to the money supply would require that any price trend that is to be both expected and realized be made less steep, in practice the effect of an increase in the money supply would almost inevitably be to steepen both expectations and the actual course of the price level, *ceteris paribus*. If one thoroughly understands the meaning of this seeming paradox, one will be less likely to get confused by the frequent cases where the causal relation between two variables is in the opposite direction from their historical co-variation, as when high interest rates are historically associated with high incomes, but raising interest rates has the effect of lowering income.

The Cyclical Role of Expectations

THE CRUCIAL role of expectations shows up particularly strongly in the interplay of forces that influence the duration of the capacity phase of the Hicksian cycle. If we examine in somewhat more detail the period of capacity growth at the top of the cycle, it is not at all clear just what mechanism can be relied upon to keep investment at a level just sufficient to absorb all of the capacity output not pre-empted by consumption. To be sure, appropriate adjustment of the interest rate could in principle perform this task, but there is no obvious automatic mechanism, as we have seen, whereby this adjustment of the interest rate is assured in a manner that will not in itself precipitate the slump, the means of avoiding which we seek to discover.

Assume that as we first reach capacity the rate of interest is at the technically feasible minimum, and that there is no deliberate control of the money supply, the stock of money remaining fixed. As capacity limitations make themselves felt, a perfectly competitive market would result in a tendency for prices to rise; with a fixed money supply this eventually requires a higher velocity of circulation that induces an increase in interest rates. This increase in interest rates, if sharp enough, would have a tendency to reduce investment demand, provided that the price increases have not set off expectations of further price increases that would counterbalance the effect of the higher interest rates on investment demand. Under favorable circumstances the interest-rate increase might bring about an equilibrium, for a short time, in which full capacity is maintained, and if the interest rate can thereafter be reduced gradually as the backlog of investment deferred by the high interest rates is run off, the dwell at capacity may be prolonged. The mechanism that would bring about this salutary and neatly timed lowering of the interest rates is again a precarious one, involving a reduction in prices as demand subsides, and a reduced velocity of circulation. Not only does the recession in demand have to be taken up by price reductions rather than cutbacks in production, but the experience of these price reductions must not give rise to unfavorable expectations on the part of investors.

The Elasticity of Expectations

AUTOMATIC adjustment via the interest rate thus necessarily involves some form of price variation which may have repercussions that upset the adjustment process. Everything depends, at this point, on what effect the experience of a price change in the immediate past has on the expectations of investors and others regarding possible further price changes in the immediate and more distant future. At this point recourse is often had to the concept of "elasticity of expectations," which is usually defined as the ratio of the relative rate of change in an expected future price to the relative change in the current price that induces the changed expectations. It is somewhat anomalous, however, to speak of the change in the current price, since in a sense an actual price at a given time is a datum not subject to change, and since on the other hand it is not the actual change in price from one moment of time to another that is significant, since if this change in price was correctly anticipated, there is no reason to suppose that expectations as to the future course of prices would be altered by the occurrence of an event that was fully anticipated and discounted in advance.

The intent of the elasticity-of-expectations concept would seem to be rather to measure the influence on expectations of *surprises* in price or in other related developments. To help clarify the issues, we will introduce a simple notation for price expectations: we will write P_{tes} for the value of the price at time t that is expected at some earlier time s; P_{tet} is then of course the actual price at time t, which we can also write simply P_t. It is already straining at reality to say that P_{tes} has a well-defined single value, since in practice expectations are more or less uncertain; we will, nevertheless, perpetrate the certainty-equivalent fallacy here by assuming that P_{tes} is in some sense a certainty-equivalent price, i.e., a price such that if it were expected with certainty it would be rationally consistent with the behavior actually induced by the less well-defined distribution or range of expectations held at time s with respect to the price that is to rule at time t. We will further strain reality by considering only prices at discretely spaced moments of time. While we can still space these moments as close together as we wish, our model would tend to lose its clarity if we distinguish price quotations at too short intervals.

Suppose now that we start at time $t = 0$, and are given an initial set of price expectations for the future, $P_{1e0}, P_{2e0}, P_{3e0}, \ldots P_{te0}, \ldots$ held at this time 0. We now proceed to time $t = 1$, and find that $P_1 = P_{1e1}$ may or may not be equal to P_{1e0}. If $P_1 = P_{1e0}$, then it would be reasonable to suppose that price expectations for later periods would remain unchanged, so that we would have $P_{2e1} = P_{2e0}$, $P_{3e1} = P_{3e0}, \ldots P_{te1} = P_{te0}$, etc., even though P_1 may be quite different from P_0. To be sure, price expectations may change for other reasons than the observation of P_1, but this is not relevant, and in any case the change is equally likely to be in either direction.

If on the other hand P_1 is greater than P_{1e0}, this experience of finding the price P_1 to be higher than had been expected earlier is likely to give rise to a change in the expectations held as to later prices. We define for this case the elasticity of price expectations as

$$e_{1t} = \frac{\dfrac{P_{te1} - P_{te0}}{P_{te0}}}{\dfrac{P_1 - P_{1e0}}{P_{1e0}}}$$

in approximate form for small changes in prices and price expectations, or more precisely in the case of large changes

$$e_{1t} = \frac{\log P_{te1} - \log P_{te0}}{\log P_1 - \log P_{1e0}}$$

An elasticity of zero would mean that the price observed at time 1 is regarded as a purely temporary aberration having no influence on expectation for later dates. Elasticity of one indicates that the price surprise experienced at time 1 is regarded as being in some way representative of the future as a whole, and that the ratio of the price at time t to the price at time 1, which is now expected, is the same as the ratio previously expected for the prices at these two times. Unit elasticity of price expectations is thus in a sense neutral in that while an unexpected price increase or decrease may result in a windfall gain or loss, with unit elasticity of expectations it does not affect the anticipated profitability or otherwise of further investments to be made after the price surprise, though the windfall gain or loss may, of course, affect investment decisions through its effect in changing the wealth or liquidity of the investor.

Price elasticities greater than one reflect the belief that the surprise experienced is the harbinger of further trends or deviations in the same direction; price elasticities of less than one in general indicate a belief that the current aberration from previous expectations reflects forces that are likely to subside in the future, with a corresponding diminution in the deviation of prices from the previously expected course. Negative elasticities are in principle possible, but would represent something of an anomaly: the widespread belief that the higher the boom the deeper the subsequent recession would perhaps be an example of the type of thinking that would be involved.

As is indicated by the notation e_{1t}, there may exist at one time several elasticities of expectations relative to different future periods, and they may differ significantly. For example, an unexpected announcement of an increased price for steel may be expected to involve a short-run elasticity of price expectations of close to 1, on the ground that given such a price change, prices are not likely to be changed again in the immediate future; elasticities for the more remote future may be greater than 1 if the price increase is taken as an indication of a long-term policy of raising prices as often as the market will stand for it. On the other hand, if a price change of this nature had previously been expected, it being merely the date of the change that was uncertain, the elasticity of expectations for the immediate future may still be nearly unity, tapering down to zero for expectations referring to the latest date to which the price change could have been deferred.

The significance of the notion of price-expectations elasticity stems from the fact already noted that if price expectations exceed unity, then the experience of a price higher than anticipated tends to make investment or anticipatory purchase seem more attractive, while the experience of prices lower than anticipated tend to induce deferment of purchases and curtailment of immediate investment. High elasticities of expectations tend to have a destabilizing influence, while low elasticities of expectations result in responses to price surprises more in line with what the purely static theory would indicate.

To push matters further and inquire what factors make for high or low elasticities of expectations is to get into difficult territory. For longer run expectations, experience over a fairly long past history must probably be taken into account, though subject to strong reservations to the effect that history never repeats itself exactly and that there is usually some new element in a situation that can be appealed to as an excuse for refusing to be bound by past precedents in developing one's expectations. Increasingly important is the view that the individual concerned has of the nature of the technological, institutional, and governmental forces that determine or influence such factors in the situation as the money supply, aggregate demand, and the impact of technological innovations. In a classical world in which money stocks are constrained in the long run by a fairly constant set of monetary institutions and a constant gold-production technology, one might reasonably assume that long-run elasticities of expectations would be smaller than unity. One of the more valid arguments for the retention of a rigid gold standard was that it was the only sure way of preserving a low long-run elasticity of price expectations with its stabilizing influence, though of course the argument was seldom expressed in these terms. Actually, there never has been a time when investors could be justified in assuming that over a period comparable to the duration of their commitment the money supply would not be drastically altered, either by the debasing of the coinage, the development of new and plentiful sources of monetary metals, expansion or contraction of the bank-credit mechanism, issuance of fiduciary or fiat currency, devaluation, or currency conversion. Thus a great deal of uncertainty surrounds any prediction of the long-term trend of prices, and current events can cause substantial changes in long-term expectations. It is not possible, therefore, to rely on the stabilizing effect of a low elasticity of long-run price expectations.

In any case, the stabilizing influence of price changes acting through a low long-run elasticity of expectations is likely to be fairly restricted. A long-run elasticity of expectations would be comparitively irrelevant for investment in inventory, for example; the short-term variability of inventory makes it a more important factor in the stability of the economy than the absolute value of inventories at any given time would tend to indicate. Moreover, the volume of long-run investment going on at any particular time is in large part a result of past decisions and commitments that cannot be altered or reversed without considerable loss, so that all but the most catastrophic changes in long-run expectations would be likely to have but little stabilizing influence through this channel. Even investment decisions that are flexible are, as we have seen, often a matter of investing immediately rather than at some later time, and are heavily influenced by short-run expectations as to prices and as to long-term interest rates, and particularly as to the prices of investment goods. Thus the immediate stability of the system is likely to hinge very strongly on the elasticity of short-run expectations, and the existence of short-run instability may prevent the potential long-run stability induced by long-run expectations from ever being realized. Because of this greater importance of the short-run expectations, when the term "elasticity of expectations" is used without further specification, it is likely to be the short-run expectations that are referred to.

Relative Prices of Investment Goods

IN SIMPLE models it is convenient to treat all prices as though they moved more or less uniformly, and to neglect divergences of individual prices from this general movement as being merely of microeconomic significance and as not substantially affecting the aggregate equilibrium of the macroeconomic model. Realistically, however, it is often necessary to take some account of divergences in the price trends of different categories of commodities. This is, particularly true of the possible divergence between the prices of capital goods and the prices of consumer goods. For if we consider the factors affecting the making of a capital investment, the cost or price of the capital goods involved relative to the prices at which the output is expected to be sold is an important element. In the long run, of course, barring some kind of technological bias in the development of innovations, or perhaps some form of differential taxation, the costs of producing capital goods should move more or less parallel to the costs of producing consumer goods, so that the relative costs of "capital" and "labor" are reflected in the real rate of interest. Thus in the long run it is the interest rate rather than the relative prices of consumer goods and capital goods that must be relied upon for adjustments in the amount of investment. In the short run, however, when there is specialization in the resources needed for the production of many types of capital goods, prices can get substantially out of line with long-run costs as a result of excess capacity or shortages at various strategic points. For short-run analysis, therefore, it may be necessary to take into account specific expectations and trends as to capital-goods prices as contrasted to product prices generally.

Indeed, at this point there arises the possibility of a much-needed stabilizing factor in the economy. If long-run price elasticities are generally low, the influence of price expectations on investment is likely to be dominated by the influence of short-run expectations as to capital-goods prices. These expectations will of course be determined in part by the behavior of capital-goods prices in the immediate past, and also in part by the behavior of the general price level in the immediate past. It would be possible to build some stability into a model by assuming that during a boom investment goods prices rise by more than do consumer goods prices, but that this nevertheless gives rise to a sufficiently small expectation of further increases so that on the one hand the attractiveness of the investment already planned for the current period diminishes, while on the other hand this damping effect is not offset through the acceleration of investment planned for later dates in anticipation of further capital-goods price increases. A corresponding stabilizing effect is possible on the downward side.

Possibilities thus exist that price adjustments may produce a short-run equilibrating mechanism that would permit the dwell at the top of the cycle to continue until the stimulating force provided by the backlog of unsatisfied investment demand subsides with the working off of the backlog. Under favorable circumstances this phase might last for a considerable time. At best, however, in the absence of deliberate macroeconomic policy the delicate balance that this would require is easily upset. In any case, once the attempt is made to combine price dynamics with aggregative macroeconomic analysis in a well-defined model, the complexities multiply to the point where they tax even the most skillful analysts, and we will have to leave the matter with these introductory remarks.

EXERCISES

1. Work out a version of the model of TABLE 4 on the assumption that when demand exceeds capacity, capital construction obtains absolute priority and consumers are rationed. Assume that demand is perishable, i.e., that neither the unsatisfied wants of an earlier period nor the additional accumulation of forced savings induces any higher consumption in later periods than would be indicated by the income of the current and immediately preceding periods.

2. Assume instead that half of any demand that is unsatisfied by reason of shortage of capacity and rationing consists of postponable items that become a backlog of additional demand to be satisfied at the first opportunity, in addition to the demand related to current income.

3. In the absence of price controls and rationing, would allowing for a price increase permit the model to be worked out? If so, what additional assumptions would be required? Is it possible to work this out without a money illusion, i.e., on the assumption that the price increase is generally anticipated? In such a case does the consumption function given at the top of page 238 make better sense if interpreted in real terms or in money terms?

4. Suppose that consumer goods are completely perishable, so that no inventory can be carried over from one period to the next. What effect does this have on the model, assuming that producers plan their production of consumer goods for each period on the basis of the demand, satisfied or otherwise, of the preceding period, rather than on

actual sales and consumption. What would be implied if this change in the determination of production were not made?

5. Beginning with period 8, find a pattern of transfer payments that when added to or subtracted from the income Y would give a disposable income such as to result in keeping output at capacity. What is the resulting long-term trend in total output? In the national debt?

6. Suppose the model of TABLE 4 to involve a fixed money interest rate of 5 per cent. Instead of investment being independent of the interest rate, suppose the desired level of capital in sight to be given by $M = 4R + 5Y(1/20i)$ where i is the rate of interest. What does a monetary authority with complete control over the rate of interest have to do to keep total output at capacity, beginning in period 8? Assume that capital starts are completely determined by the interest rate ruling at the end of the preceding period, and that once started such projects are carried through by depleting consumer-goods inventories if necessary.

7. Assume that instead of a monetary authority ensuring capacity output there is a fixed money supply and a liquidity-preference function such that at the end of each period the interest rate is $.0004\,G$, G being given its value for the immediately preceding period, i.e., for $G = 125$, the interest rate is 5 per cent. Prices are fixed, and output is rationed first to the completion of previously started capital projects, then to building up of inventory to desired levels, then to new capital construction. The current interest rate at the end of each period is assumed to depend on the GNP of the period just completed, and to govern the starts made in the period immediately succeeding.

8. Indicate how the model might be modified to accommodate (a) a steady increase in the labor force, (b) a steady improvement in productivity.

CHAPTER NINE

Growth Models

The Harrod-Domar Dynamics

ENOUGH has been said in the preceding section to show that even when dynamic models are set up in terms of a relatively simple long-run steady state environment, the difficulties are fairly formidable. Before attempting to transpose these models into a framework allowing for long-term economic growth, it is desirable to look at the bare essentials of what is involved in long-term growth. For this purpose a body of literature has grown up that achieves simplicity by making heroic assumptions as to the underlying constancy of certain ratios. While in important respects this analysis is a caricature of reality, increasingly so as the importance of deliberate government intervention grows, it does serve as a basic framework that will be of considerable help in the elaboration of a more realistic analysis.

Growth models of the type we are about to consider focus their attention on two coefficients: a savings coefficient s and a capital coefficient k. Various interpretations are given to these two coefficients, and depending on the meanings assigned, different types of model emerge. Perhaps the simplest, though perhaps not the most realistic meaning to assign to the savings coefficient, is that of the ex post ratio of savings to income. Whatever the precise meaning assigned, the ratio is thought of as exhibiting a high degree of stability; it is thus implied that the marginal propensity to save and the average propensity to save are constant and equal, and are not subject to influence by such factors as the distribution of income, tax policy, interest rates, the standard of living, or the rate of change of income. Considering the ex post ratio to be constant can be thought of as tantamount to an assumption that the effect of income on consumption and savings decisions is instantaneous and that there is no unintended saving or dissaving, so that ex ante saving and ex post saving remain identical. At least, differences of this kind are considered to be insignificant in the context of the time scale under consideration. Whatever the detailed interpretation, s is a pure magnitude, being the ratio between two flow magnitudes.

The capital coefficient k is most simply taken to be a capital-output ratio. It may be thought of either as the amount of capital technologically necessary to produce a unit of output per unit time period in a world of rigidly fixed proportions, or as the amount of capital investors will feel justified in adding to the preexisting stock in order to take care of a given expected increase in income and hence in aggregate demand. In either case, this coefficient is supposed to exhibit considerable stability through time, and be insignificantly affected by changes in such factors as interest rates or price expectations. The coefficient k has the dimension "time," since it is the ratio of a stock magnitude to a flow magnitude; it is equal to the number of years of income that would be required to equal the amount of capital forming the other factor in the ratio. Magnitudes are often stated for k without specifying the unit of measurement, but this unit of measurement is almost always one year.

From these two coefficients, Harrod derives what is called, not too happily, the "warranted rate of growth," $G_w = s/k$. For example, if total capital is valued at four years' flow of income, so that if we assume constant returns to scale we can put $k =$ four years, and $s = .20$, then $G_w = .20/4 = 5$ per cent per year. If in particular we start in year 1 with income flowing at the rate of 100 per year and capital stock of 400, then if during that year savings of 20 are invested and added to the capital stock, bringing capital at the beginning of year 2 to 420, this amount of capital will now support an income flow of 105. If k is interpreted as the investor's norm, then the warranted rate of growth is that rate of growth which if expected by investors will cause them to plan voluntarily an investment equal to savings that would be voluntarily made out of the projected income according to the fixed savings ratio s. Thus if the warranted rate of growth is both expected and realized, investment will be carried out as planned with no involuntary investment or disinvestment in the aggregate, and investors will feel ex post that the investment they made was "warranted" by the rate of growth actually experienced. Thus in a sense it is not the growth rate itself that is warranted, but the investment associated with it.

However, there is no assurance that the warranted rate of growth would actually occur merely because investors expect it to. The warranted rate of growth is thus not necessarily an equilibrium rate of growth in the sense of equilibrium as "that which, if expected, will happen." To be sure, in the Keynesian short-run sense, expectation by investors of growth at the warranted rate tends to produce an equilibrium in the short run between planned investment and planned savings, but while there is thus no "gap," there is no mechanism assuring growth at the warranted rate. It might be thought that if the actual rate of growth falls below the warranted rate, this would cause savings to turn out to be smaller than planned investment, so that some of the planned investment fails to take place, and the attempt of investors to recoup this deficiency would produce an expansionary force that would tend to bring income back up toward the warranted-growth-trend line. However, this effect is likely to be outweighed by the disappointment of the expectations of investors with respect to sales, which lowers the sights of investors concerning the level of capital that it is desirable to achieve. Thus in the above example, if instead of growth from an income rate of 100 at the beginning of the first year to 105 at the end, income had grown only to 104, making the average income over the year 102 instead of 102.5, then savings for the year would be 19.9 instead of 20.0, so that at the end of the year capital would stand at 419.9 instead of 420. But whereas most Keynesian models at this point have the investors striving to make up for the 0.1 deficiency in investment and planning a higher level of investment for the future because of their failure to carry out their plans in the past, the Harrod model now has them figuring that the capital level appropriate to an income of 104 is only 416, so that a cutback of investment is in order and a downward spiral is begun.

If on the other hand investors expect a rate of growth less than the warranted rate, then if we start from a situation where the actual capital-output ratio is equal to k, investors will plan to invest an amount that is less than the savings that would be made out of a future income growing at the warranted rate. Under these circumstances, if income did start to grow at the warranted rate in spite of the more pessimistic expectations of the investors, the Keynesian mechanism would immediately produce a downward deviation. Thus whether the warranted rate of growth is expected but fails to materialize, or whether it actually occurs but is not expected, there will be a tendency to diverge further and further from the path indicated by the warranted rate. Thus while an economy advancing at the warranted rate can be said to be in equilibrium in the sense that it is possible for expectations to be borne out on the average, this equilibrium is unstable, in the absence of some mechanism not inherent in the model which will restore growth to the warranted rate upon the occurrence of random deviations.

Such a restoring force might exist, for example, if investors were to believe firmly enough that income in the long run would fluctuate about a trend line that rises steadily at the warranted rate of growth, regarding any deviations from this trend as mere temporary aberrations, so that they in effect have an elasticity of income expectations of zero. At the moment such an attitude on the part of investors seems highly unlikely. Other more or less automatic stabilizing mechanisms can be postulated, such as an inelastic money supply coupled with flexible interest rates, a very inelastic demand for money (as in the older quantity theory) and a high interest elasticity of investment. Some of these mechanisms have been examined in more detail elsewhere; in general, it appears unlikely that any such automatic stabilizing mechanism or at least any that could be expected to develop spontaneously without deliberate public action, could maintain the stability of a model in which the level of capital which investors seek to attain is so rigidly related to income flows.

At this point one is tempted to ask what the use of a model is that is so inherently unstable. One answer of course is to claim that the instability of the model reflects a corresponding instability in real economic systems and that the study of such a model will serve to put us on our guard against underestimating the difficulty of stabilizing a real system. A more pertinent answer would be that growth models indicate some of the boundary conditions that must be satisfied over the long run if an economic system is to behave in a desirable manner, even though they may have relatively little to contribute to the problem of how to insure the meeting of these boundary conditions.

A major objective of economic policy in the long run is of course the maintenance of some standard of full employment. Thus far our growth models have said nothing about labor; indeed, all that has been said about the production function is that the capital coefficient is a constant. Labor is of course also involved in production and it is natural to ask what rate of increase in employment is required to sustain a warranted rate of growth. For simplicity we can start with the case where the production coefficients are both fixed and constant over time. Or as a concession to realism we may suppose that while as a result of the limited availability of natural resources we cannot have strictly constant returns to scale in the static sense, nevertheless technological advance is such as to just counterbalance the increasing relative scarcity of natural resources and maintain the constancy of the labor-output ratio as well as the capital-output ratio (where we include in capital both natural and man-made resources and beg the question of what is meant by a unit of capital where the capital category thus includes both the endowment of nature and the artificial additions).

In this case of effectively constant technology, maintenance of the warranted rate of growth would imply a corresponding rate of growth in employment. If the warranted rate of growth is greater than the rate of increase in the labor force, eventually warranted growth would culminate in a state of full employment, after which growth would necessarily fall short of the warranted rate, leading to an excess of planned savings over planned investment and a consequent downward cumulative tendency for income. Even if as full employment is reached full employment could for a time be maintained with a growth rate equal to the rate of population increase by investors anticipating, in spite of indications to the contrary that the growth at the warranted rate or at even a higher rate would continue, this would result in the accumulation of capital beyond the amount deemed appropriate for any level of income that could possibly be expected by the investors, and the system would collapse.

If on the other hand the warranted rate of growth is smaller than the rate of increase in the labor force, growth at the warranted rate implies a gradual increase in the proportion of unemployed. In this case what happens if there are deviations from the warranted rate of growth will depend on the specific assumptions of the model. If we assume rigidly fixed production coefficients, the warranted rate of growth is also a maximum possible equilibrium rate of growth, since on the one hand if production is capital-limited, production can grow only at the rate at which capital is expanded, which in an equilibrium situation cannot exceed the limit imposed by savings, which gives the warranted rate of growth. If on the other hand production is labor-limited, this condition can continue only if there is an excess of capital, as capital is growing more slowly than labor. But where there is an excess of capital, investors may fail to carry out any investment at all, pending a time when more capital will actually be needed; failure to carry out investment in the face of an excess of capital leads to a Keynesian failure of aggregate demand and a downward trend of income, The only alternative possibility is that investors should expect a growth rate greater than the warranted rate, which of course creates an inflationary situation. If the savings ratio then remains fixed in spite of the inflation, investment will be limited to the amount that will permit the warranted rate of growth to be maintained, with growing unemployment. If, however, the operation of inflation is such as to lower the amount that consumers succeed in saving in real terms, or if in any other way investors are able to pre-empt a larger share of the national product for investment than would normally be made available to them by savings at the ratio s, the rate of growth can be stepped up, possibly even sufficiently to match the growth of population and permit the maintenance of full employment. In these relationships we see reflected some of the elements of the stagnationist argument to the effect that a relatively low rate of population growth may be a factor leading to depression, while a high rate of population growth produces a tendency toward inflation.

Progress in Growth Models

IN THIS CONSTANT coefficient model, long-run "growth without progress" would be possible if the warranted rate of growth and the rate of growth of the population were the same; in this case we would have a constant output per capita, and growth would consist merely of maintaining a steadily growing population at the same standard of living.

To allow more specifically for "progress" in the sense of an increased output per head, it is necessary to admit of some significant secular change in the production function that will allow this, or at least of some change in the production coefficients. In classical economics, progress was at least possible under a fixed set of technological production possibilities through the accumulation of capital at a more rapid rate than the increase in the labor force, resulting in the substitution of capital for labor and an increase in the average product per unit of labor. This form of progress, however, specifically requires a change in the value of k, which growth economics characteristically regards as fixed, at least over the spans of time with which the theory is concerned. A form of production function more readily reconcilable with the literature of economic-growth models is one that specifically allows for improvement in the set of potentially available technologies, but with respect to each given point of time keeps to the assumption of fixed coefficients and constant returns to scale. Thus at a given time t we will have a pair of fixed coefficients $w(t)$ and $k(t)$ describing the amounts of labor and capital, respectively, required at that time per unit of output. The total productive capacity of the economy is then given by either $L(t)/w(t)$ or $K(t)/k(t)$, whichever is smaller, where $L(t)$ stands for the size of the labor force at time t and $K(t)$ stands for the amount of capital in existence at time t. If these ratios are unequal, any excess of one factor or the other is assumed to be entirely unusable by reason of the relative dearth of the complimentary factor.

A model including this type of production function gives rise to the possibility of two clearly distinguishable types of general underemployment of labor: demand deficiency of Keynesian unemployment, resulting from actual output being below capacity because of inadequate effective demand, and underdevelopment unemployment, resulting from a deficiency of capital equipment with which to employ the labor. While in such models the marginal productivity of excess labor is taken to be zero, in practice it is hard to imagine a situation where there is not at least some flexibility in the factor proportions in some productive processes so as to produce a positive marginal productivity for labor. Cases may arise, however, where the marginal productivity of labor becomes so low that under imperfectly competitive institutional arrangements, and in particular in the face of inhibitions of one kind or another against offering less than what is considered a living wage, it becomes impossible in practice to employ the excess labor.

While in principle L, w, k, and K may all develop through time as a function of current and past experience, for the sake of simplicity it is worthwhile to operate with some rather special assumptions. The effects of economic factors on population growth are still so little understood that for this purpose it is best to consider L as exogenously given, possibly as having a steady rate of growth. K of course grows at a rate that is simply the flow of investment. In addition it is convenient to assume initially that k is constant over time and that the improvement in productive techniques makes itself felt entirely through the reduction in w. This is not unreasonable: desirable innovations can occur that either increase or decrease the amount of capital required per unit of product; if the labor requirement is sufficiently reduced, an innovation will constitute progress even though the capital requirement is increased. The opposite assumption that w remains constant and progress is embodied in reductions in k would be only a very limited sort of progress, since output per head would not be increased (unless, that is, we started with a deficiency of capital and underdevelopment unemployment); an increase in consumption would be made possible, but only by reducing the amount of the fixed national product required for investment purposes.

With k constant, the formulation $G_w = s/k$ retains its significance. The growth of K through investment is given by

$$K(t + 1) = K(t) + V(t) = K(t) + sY(t)$$

L for present purposes we may take as a constant proportion of the population, assumed to be growing at a constant exogenously determined rate. The rate of growth of $L(t)/w(t)$ is then called the "natural rate of growth" G_n, and is the rate at which the total productive capacity of the labor force is increasing. If the capital supply is sufficient, G_n is the effective rate of growth of the productive capacity of the economy. We can write $G_n = n + \lambda$ where n is the relative rate of growth of population and λ is the relative rate of improvement in the average productivity of labor.

Here again, as in the stationary case, if the warranted rate of growth exceeds the natural rate, then if income grows at the warranted rate it will eventually hit a full employment ceiling which will set off a downward Keynesian spiral; if the warranted rate is less than the natural rate, growth at the warranted rate leads to increasing unemployment, while growth at more than the warranted rate is possible only in a context of inflationary pressure and involuntary saving.

Thus even when specific allowance is made for technological progress, models of this type tend to exhibit some kind of eventual breakdown unless very specific relationships can be maintained, in this case the equality between the warranted and the natural rates of growth. More details could be added to obtain a more elaborate or a more realistic model, but as long as the basic foundation of fixed or exogenously determined savings and capital-output ratios is retained, the general conclusions remain the same. And while models of this type are incomplete in that they do not specify precisely what happens when the actual rate of growth deviates from the warranted rate of growth, they do serve to point out that unless the warranted and natural rates of growth coincide, trouble results sooner or later.

Equilibrating Variation in the Coefficients

THE REASON that other theoretical models were able to achieve some sort of stable equilibrium is that they permitted s and k to be influenced by the other variables. In the classical theory it was the interest rate that reconciled the warranted and natural rates of growth through its influence on s and k; in the Keynesian theory it was the variation of income that produced changes in s and k, since the marginal propensity to save was assumed to be greater than the average propensity and since the responsiveness of investment to changes in income in the short run was heavily discounted. But if s and k are held to be substantially immune to influence through interest-rate changes, the classical mechanism breaks down; the Keynesian mechanism may operate only at an unsatisfactory equilibrium level of employment, and even then may break down if the influence of income changes on s and k is either lacking or fails to bring them into proper relationship. Indeed, recent investigations seem to indicate that while empirically s does vary with income in the short run, over longer-run periods it has shown remarkable stability, which may mean that for long-run purposes the Harrod model is more pertinent than the Keynesian.

But while the automatic mechanisms available for reconciling the natural and warranted rates of growth may be inoperative or too weak to do the job, this does not mean that the reconciliation cannot be accomplished by deliberate policy measures. To be sure, the factors entering into the determination of the natural rate of growth may be determined fairly completely by exogenous forces, at least in the short run, and not amenable to deliberate manipulation; trends of population and of the labor force may be influenced in the long run by various social-welfare programs and other pertinent policies, but this is a long way from a control that would contribute significantly to the stability of the economy even were it desirable to pervert policy in these areas from pursuing the more directly relevant objectives. Similarly, the rate of growth of labor productivity may depend to a considerable extent on education, research, and on capital growth itself, but again this factor is not easily controlled in the medium short run, and to the extent that it is controllable, it is something that it is desirable to maximize, subject of course to limitations on the costs incurred in the process, rather than to restrict productivity to a given value or rate of progress merely for the sake of preserving stability. Thus even if the natural rate of growth could be influenced for the sake of achieving stability, it would be desirable to seek other measures first and leave this as a last resort.

The warranted rate of growth is, however, subject to more or less precise adjustment in the short run through fiscal and monetary policy, both in terms of s and in terms of k. We may take s to be the ratio of private savings to the net national product, and out of a given net national product more or less will be saved as more or less is left to individuals after taxes as disposable income. Fiscal policy in the form of changes in tax rates thus has a direct impact on s.

Influences of public action on k are somewhat more complex. A stringent monetary policy may tend to lower k if carried sufficiently far, by lowering liquidity and raising interest rates, provided that the demand for capital is at least slightly interest elastic. Also the entrance by the government into fields of investment competitive with private investment may lower k, if k is taken to refer only to the private sector. Or the government may carry out investment on its own or encourage private investment by subvention or otherwise. Thus the instability revealed by these models is not hopelessly beyond remedy.

CHAPTER TEN

Macroeconomic Cybernetics

THE DYNAMIC models thus far discussed have all been concerned primarily with the behavior of economic systems in the absence of deliberate monetary or fiscal intervention, and only secondarily and in a much more qualitative way with the possible effects of such intervention. Even from the point of view of disinterested description, however, it has become increasingly necessary to pay much more attention both to the genesis and to the consequences of such intervention, as we have reached a stage of economic sophistication where it is unlikely that a drastic slump of the type contemplated by the Hicksian model, for example, would ever be allowed to work out its full effects. These models are thus more than ever hypothetical models not to be used without proper regard for the important forces and adjustments arising from public policies that they have deliberately slighted in the interest of simplicity.

More important is the fact that economics can be normative as well as descriptive, and we may wish to determine by our analysis what specific forms of macroeconomic control or intervention are desirable in terms of such goals as economic stability and growth. Our analysis has indicated that there exist, in principle, fiscal and monetary policies that if followed with sufficient vigor would significantly moderate the major swings of the business cycle. But it is one thing to say that such a set of measures exist, or even to point out their salient qualitative features; it is quite another to show how one can determine from the available data just what the appropriate policy is in quantitative terms at a specific point in time. Moreover, we may not be content with merely moderating the major swings; we may wish at least to investigate the possibility of damping out even the minor undesirable fluctuations.

Announcement Effects and Public Forecasting

ONE OF THE BASIC difficulties in making quantitative predictions of the effects of public-policy changes on the course of economic events is the uncertainty concerning the impact of the inauguration of a new program on the expectations of individuals. Under some circumstances, for example, it is even conceivable that a sufficiently authoritative and credible announcement that steps will be taken to stabilize the economy may so change expectations that stabilization is achieved without any concrete steps actually having to be taken. Attempts by various governments to meet economic crisis by putting up a bold front and issuing assurances that "the economy is fundamentally sound" or that "prosperity is just around the corner" were not inherently absurd, though the particular circumstances were in many cases such as to make failure almost certain. Under more favorable conditions such tactics might succeed, and indeed may have done so without attracting much attention, for it is unlikely that success in such cases will be of a spectacular nature. A possible example of such success is the relative ease with which the transition from a war economy to a peace economy was accomplished in 1945–48, which is ascribed by many in considerable measure to the activities of such organizations as the Committee for Economic Development in persuading business men that the transition would not be as difficult as many had been expecting on the basis of the experience of 1919–22, in spite of the fact that no promise of remedial measures was involved. A firm statement of policy by a governmental body having the power and presumably the intention, if need arises, to take measures acknowledged to be effective would be likely to have an even greater effect on expectations.

The problem of predicting the effects of a given public policy is somewhat analogous to what is sometimes referred to as the problem of public prediction. A private prediction or forecast, announced only to persons who play no substantial active role in the realization or otherwise of the prediction, is no different from the usual scientific prediction that purports to subject a theory to test by seeing how far a prediction based on a given theory is realized. What actually happens is not dependent on the prediction made, and presumably if a theory is sufficiently valid the prediction based on it will be verified. Where the prediction itself can influence the event, however, there is a possibility that there exists no "public prediction" such that if it is made it will be realized; there is also the possibility that there may be several distinct public predictions which if made will be realized.

For example, an economist in the Department of Agriculture might predict privately that the price of wheat one year later would be $1.50 per bushel, and if this prediction is not made public he might prove to be correct. But if the Secretary of Agriculture were to promulgate this figure as an official estimate, this might well increase the cultivation of wheat to an extent that would actually bring the price down to $1. In a case such as this there would normally be some intermediate prediction that would, if announced, prove correct (though how to find out what it is is another problem). Nevertheless, there is at least a theoretical possibility that there might be several large "commuting farmers" in Kansas, all of whom would go into production if the announced price were $1.20 or higher but who will stay home and let their land lie fallow if the announced price is lower than this. If their production is large enough so that with their land in production the actual price that eventuates is $1.15, while without their production the price would be $1.25, then there is no price that the Secretary can announce publicly that will prove correct.

In this case the trouble is caused by the discontinuous nature of the response to the prediction. Fortunately, it can be shown, by applying a fundamental topological theorem known as Brouwer's fixed-point theorem, that if the prediction is capable of being varied continuously and in a "simply connected manner,"[1] if the outcome depends on the prediction in a bounded and smooth manner without any jumps or explosions to infinity, and if the possible predictions include all the possible outcomes, then there is at least one prediction that coincides with the outcome it induces. This will be true even of complicated situations and predictions involving many parameters. The theorem fails, however, if one of the parameters describing the outcome can take on discrete values separated by a gap of inadmissible values.

For most practical situations the parameters describing the possible outcomes can vary in a reasonably continuous fashion, so that we need not worry very much about the theoretical possibility that no correct public prediction exists. There are analogous problems, however, in the determination of public policy, where the answer is not quite so simple.

The Problems of Open Public Policy

WE MAY BEGIN by thinking of a policy goal as the selection of a certain subset from among all of the possible future states that are considered to be capable of emerging. We assume in effect that in some sense the goal selected is a possible one. Even so, the very real possibility does arise that although the goal state is one that is capable of emerging, there is no publicly announced policy that is capable of reaching it. That is, the goal can be reached only by inadvertence or by pursuing a policy that is not publicly announced. In a game situation, for example, the selected goal may be one of winning by the use of a particular type of strategy, but if this goal is announced, it may give the opponent information enabling him to prevent this goal from being reached. An example of this in the field of macroeconomic controls would arise if the selected goal were one of securing full employment with a price level declining at, say, 5 per cent per year for some short period. It is conceivable that this result could emerge in an economy where prices are highly flexible and investors incurably optimistic; but if the optimism of investors as to prices is dampened by the announcement of this goal, the emergence of the selected result may become virtually impossible.

1. A simply connected set is one in which every loop in the set can be contracted continuously to a point without breaking out of the set; roughly speaking, the set must have no holes through it. A dumbbell is simply connected, a doughnut is not.

There are thus economic goals that are attainable only by accident or by obfuscation and concealment of policy. The concealment or even deliberate misrepresentation necessary to assure reaching such goals implies procedures that are inherently inequitable in that they involve the disappointment of legitimately formed expectations. In a completely authoritarian state such measures might be acceptable and feasible, but in a democracy public affairs are normally or at least ideally carried on in full public knowledge of the goals that are at least nominally being sought. To this extent a democracy is inherently limited in the scope of the economic ends that it can achieve consistently with its underlying principles.

This may not, however, be such a severe limitation as might at first appear. It can be argued that most of the more important goals that are likely to be selected in a democratic society from among those attainable by all forms of policy, secret as well as open, are likely to be goals that can be attained almost as well if not better by open-policy methods than by secret-policy methods. But while one may accept this proposition in general and for the more important elements of policy, it is not at all difficult to point out instances where a little deliberate vagueness as to the policy actually being pursued may have results that many will consider salutary. This may be illustrated by the contrast between the philosophy of the tax law in the United States and that in the United Kingdom. In the United States there is a strong tradition of strict interpretation of tax laws, tracing back, some will say, to the Boston Tea Party; the letter of the tax law is laid down in great detail by statute and by the accumulation of published administrative rulings and court decisions, relatively little discretion being left to the administrators of the law. In the United Kingdom, on the other hand, there is much more of a tendency to legislate in terms of laying down broad principles, leaving the details to administrative decision; there is even some tendency to make something of a state secret of the details of administrative policy. The result is that while many consider that the loopholes that exist in the British law as in fact administered are almost as wide if not wider than those that exist more explicitly in the United States law, actual tax avoidance through the use of these loopholes seems to many relatively less intense in the United Kingdom than in the United States, in part because the uncertainty surrounding the situation in the mind of the British taxpayer and the fear that if he pursues his avoidance scheme too blatantly or too far he may get caught by an unexpectedly unfavorable administrative ruling. This is not to say that the comparable situation does not exist in the United States, but only that it seems to exist to a lesser degree. Thus vagueness of policy, whether deliberate or otherwise, may prove beneficial in smoothing off, ex ante, the many necessarily arbitrary distinctions between the taxable and the exempt, even though in the event the sharp dichotomy remains ex post. And even though it could be maintained that many if not most of these arbitrary distinctions are the result of basic remediable inconsistencies in the concepts of taxation being applied, and that placing the tax structure on a sounder theoretical basis and following this basis consistently would eliminate much of the difficulty, there would remain even in the most highly perfected tax structure a need for drawing arbitrary lines that will produce wasteful reactions on the part of taxpayers; the sharpness of the discrimination and the amount of waste induced may often be mitigated by a little appropriate uncertainty.

Another area where adherence to a precisely defined and publicly declared policy may have undesirable consequences is in certain forms of monetary and foreign-exchange control. If an attempt is being made to control a given exchange rate, or if a specific rediscount rate is being used as an instrument of control, and if the conditions under which a change in the official rate is to occur are fairly well defined, then if circumstances become such as to make it fairly apparent that the conditions requiring such a change will shortly be fulfilled, speculation against the change may take place that will in general increase the amount of disturbance induced by the change, advance the time when the change is called for, and perhaps even force the change when in the absence of such speculative opportunities there might have been no need for the change, either because there would have been time to bring other remedies to bear or because there would have been no opportunity for the self-justifying speculative expectations of a change to have developed. It is of course possible to argue that controls of this type are not the best way of handling the problem, or that the changes should be made frequently and in small amounts so that transaction costs would largely eat up any possible profits from purely speculative transactions. It is not always possible to do this, however, where the possibility exists that fairly rapid and drastic action may become appropriate.

On the other hand, excessive uncertainty has its drawbacks, even from the broadest point of view, in that, wholly aside from the objections on grounds of equity, it makes planning difficult and subjects many to needless risk. Of course, if the uncertainty is only over a relatively small range the undesirable consequences may be correspondingly small, and this consideration might well be thought to point to a system of controls where major patterns are public and predetermined while minor elements are discretionary and confidential. This economic requirement would then agree rather well with administrative and political requirements for public-policy determination.

Preset Controls and Hunting

IT IS TEMPTING to think of macroeconomic controls in terms of a more or less rigid rule under which the appropriate administrative officials are required, upon the occurrence of some specified event, such as a price index rising by a given amount or unemployment exceeding a certain figure, to take some specified corresponding corrective action, such as the raising or lowering of the discount rate by such and such a step or raising or lowering tax rates in such and such a manner. Indeed, a dynamic model that contemplates governmental action cannot be completely specified without setting up some rule according to which controls are assumed to be applied, whether this rule is embodied in administrative prescriptions or is merely a means of describing within the model the behavioral pattern according to which the administrator applies his discretionary powers. Some rule, either express or implied, must exist if anything definite is to be said about the way the economy will develop. However, wholly aside from the possibility that if the rule is rigid and public there may arise considerable disturbing speculation, even if the rule is implicit or private there is the difficulty of establishing a rule that is reasonably sure to work well. Knowledge of the quantitative dynamics of the economy has not yet reached the stage where it is possible to predict with any great accuracy the effects of any given measure; and, accordingly, rather than attempting to develop a comprehensive theory concerning the effects of all possible rules, it will suffice to investigate the most likely rules and see if we can find some good ones. A search for the best rules may come later when more has been learned.

One possible approach at this point is to proceed on the assumption that if the measures to be taken are made sufficiently drastic one can be reasonably sure of overcoming any divergence from the desired equilibrium, provided this is at all possible with any feasible policy measures whatever. In effect, if reduction of taxes by $2 billion would be a desirable step to take as soon as unemployment rises above a specified tolerable level, would not a deficit of $5 billion be even better, particularly if the tax cut can be restored as soon as matters improve? The obvious *reductio ad absurdum* response to this proposition is that any policy carried to extremes will have undesirable side effects which are to be avoided if it is possible to achieve the desired degree of control with less drastic measures. There may still be a fairly wide range of action between the degree of action that just might be sufficient if all goes well and the degree of action that begins to have serious side effects, however, and the above approach might be interpreted as an injunction that when in doubt one should not stop with minimal measures but should carry action immediately to the point where the side effects become serious.

A more sophisticated objection, though maybe not a fatal one, to this position is that very often control systems that are too sensitive, i.e., that produce too drastic a reaction in response to deviations from the desired norm, often give rise to a type of cyclical oscillation known as "hunting." Hunting oscillations are particularly likely to be troublesome if the control operates with a considerable time lag, as is particularly the case, for example, if fiscal policy takes the form of enlarging or contracting the program of public works. If an excessively large public-works program is started at the onset of a slump, and the program continues to be augmented as long as the symptoms of the slump persist, then at the end of the slump the public works then in process may give a substantial inflationary boost to the economy before their construction can be efficiently terminated or even curtailed. In an extreme case the result might well be oscillations just as violent as those the scheme was set up to control. This is aside from the consideration that the timing of these public works induced by their use for cyclical-control purposes may be inefficient from the point of view of their productive role in the economy.

If the instrument of control consists of changes in tax rates, the lag may not be so long, but the same problem recurs. Even if the legislative lag is overcome by the delegation of the authority to change tax rates to some executive authority, there are still several unavoidable lags between the time the deviation from the norm occurs and the time the deviation is detected in the aggregate statistics, between the time the decision is taken and the time it goes into effect, and between the time the change takes place in the tax collections and the beginning of the resulting change in consumer behavior. And of course too frequent or too drastic changes in tax rates, unless they are buffered by some kind of averaging device, are very likely to lead to undesirable inequities and discriminations between those who happen to get caught in the high-rate period and those who happen to have more income or transact more business in the low-rate period.

In the case of monetary policy, the lag between administrative decision and the effective carrying out of, say, a change in the rediscount rate is likely to be relatively short. But even here there will be a substantial lag between the change in rediscount rate and the change in investment plans and outlays of all those this measure is intended to influence, and too high a control coefficient (by which is meant the ratio of the amount of change in the controlled parameter to the change in the index that is the basis for the control) can easily result in hunting oscillations even here.

On the other hand, in the case of controls over interest rates, both direct and indirect, the speculative possibilities inherent in the highly organized money market create difficulties for the case where the control coefficient is too low. If, in response to indications of a slump, monetary measures are taken that are inadequate to produce an immediate halt to the decline, expectations of further measures, involving further reductions in interest rates, would in general induce potential borrowers to hold off, with the result that these expectations might rob the initial measures of most of the effectiveness that they might have had. Only when the measures have reached a cumulative level where further steps are not generally anticipated will the measures begin to take hold with full effect.

The danger of "too little too late" if the control coefficient is set too low is not merely that the impact of the corrective measure may be undesirably small or that it may only take effect after considerable delay: there may well be a critical level of the control coefficient below which there is no effect at all. For example, much of the effect of the rediscount-rate reductions made in the fall of 1957 was lost because of the general anticipation that further reductions in interest rates were still to come. In a severe downturn, it is even possible that with a low control coefficient business expectations may have dropped so low by the time interest rates have been reduced to the point where no further reductions are anticipated by borrowers that the reduced interest rates are almost completely ineffective in stimulating investment, whereas with a higher control coefficient interest rates may reach their minimum level in time to have some stimulating effect. Fiscal policy does not seem to be subject to this speculative danger to anywhere near the same degree, and while too low a control coefficient in this case may still lead to inadequate corrective action, the effectiveness of such corrective action as is taken is likely still to be roughly in proportion to its magnitude.

The danger of provoking hunting oscillations by too high a control coefficient does not seem as great in real economic systems as might be inferred from analogies with mechanical control systems or from the examination of rigidly specified economic models. While most models, in order to avoid unmanageable complexity, deal with specific control coefficients and sharply defined lags, in reality the lags in the response to control measures seem to be fairly widely dispersed over time so that the response is not sharply concentrated at a point in time and the possibilities for serious hunting conditions to develop are greatly reduced. Moreover, to the extent that hunting phenomena do develop, the resulting cycles would tend to be of short duration and sharply defined. The reaction of individuals to cycles of this sort, clearly associated with changes in control measures, would seem more likely to be similar to reactions to generally anticipated seasonal fluctuations than to the reactions to the uncertain alternations of the business cycle, so that many of the undesirable effects of the fluctuations might be ironed out. For example, if a policy is adopted involving drastic tax cuts at the first sign of a slump, and drastic tax increases at the first sign of overexpansion or inflation, then even if drastic fluctuations in tax rates did occur in response to minor fluctuations in economic activity, it is doubtful that these alternations in tax rates would give rise to any serious hunting phenomena, since individual expenditure would tend to be based on the current asset position resulting from past tax variations rather than on any expectation that the current tax rates would continue for any extended period of time. This appraisal applies with particular force to the present situation where tax changes can be given fairly prompt effect through collection at the source. It might not apply quite so decidedly to the situation that existed in the 1920's where tax was collected in the year following the receipt of the income on which the tax was based and where there was considerable hesitancy in raising tax rates by legislation enacted very far into the income year. Nor would this argument apply necessarily to a situation where control was being exercised primarily through changes in long-term public-works programs. The problem posed by the possibility of hunting should the control measures be too drastic is thus not a spurious one, but it is not on the other hand a conclusive argument by itself for keeping control measures and control coefficients down to the lowest levels that are expected to be sufficiently effective.

Suggestive as it may be to construct models in which the discretion of a control authority is exercised according to some rigidly specified rule, in actual practice it seems unlikely that any administration would tie itself down to any foreordained formula. One of the crucial problems of practical political economy is that of trying to determine from the available data just what the timing and extent of macroeconomic-control measures should be at a given juncture to produce the best results. At this point the practicing economist will have to overlay his neat theoretical models with a mass of fuzzy detail, psychological insights and hunches, impressionistic adjustments of incomplete and tardy data, and especially with some allowance for the inevitable modification of his recommendations in the course of their execution, all the while keeping a weather eye out concerning the possibilities for later corrective measures should his expectations prove faulty in one direction or another. At this point economic theory is still far short of fully meeting the need, and economic policy is still an art rather than an exact science.

If we can draw any lessons from our experience to date with macroeconomic controls, it seems to be that the danger of undue hesitation, delay, and temporizing with homeopathic doses is still much closer than that of producing excessive disturbances to the economy with unduly precipitate and drastic action. Error in the latter direction would at least produce the experience and data from which more accurate judgments could be made in the future, whereas the effects of timid action are likely to be so obscured by fluctuations arising from other sources that relatively little can be learned.

Inflationary Depression

THERE is one major unsolved macroeconomic problem that persists even in theory. We have been accustomed to thinking in terms of models where deviations from the desired norm can take the form either of underutilization of resources due to lack of effective demand, or of undesired price inflation, but not both simultaneously. In most models in which price changes are considered at all, price competition is assumed to be strong enough to produce a fairly reliable tendency for prices to fall in the presence of inadequate demand, or at least not to rise, and for prices to rise only in response to demand in excess of supply. Price rigidities or reaction lags were appealed to to keep prices from collapsing completely in the presence of a shortage in aggregate demand, and these same rigidities were assumed to suffice to keep prices from rising unless pushed upward by an excess in aggregate demand. And until relatively recently economists in the United States in particular were inclined to assume that comparable conditions would necessarily prevail in the real world, even though contrary indications were abundantly available in the annals of other economies. Recent experience has rudely disturbed this complacency.

There is, indeed, no fundamental reason why inflation cannot be accompanied by generalized unemployment, confronting the framer of economic policy with the dilemma that stimulative measures are called for by the presence of excessive unemployment while at the same time sedative and restrictive measures are called for to halt the inflation; in large measure the two types of action are either incompatible or mutually frustrating. To this there is no easy answer. The sources of the difficulty presumably lie in some form of rigidity or resistance in the real economy to the forces that are supposed to be at work in the model economy to prevent such an occurrence. In an underdeveloped economy this may take the form of rigidities in factor proportions coupled with a shortage of the capital necessary to provide all of the labor available with the complementary capital required under the established modes of production. In more highly developed countries the difficulty may perhaps be traced to the lack of effective competitive forces acting on large industrial employers on the one hand and strongly entrenched labor unions on the other in major sectors of the economy.

In neither case is the remedy easy. The theoretically indicated solution in the latter case, of breaking up the large industrial and labor units sufficiently to restore competitive pressures on prices and wages, may not be feasible either for technological or for political reasons; public ownership or public-utility-type regulation of such industries may be an equally unattractive solution. In the capital-poor countries the theoretically indicated attempt to push factor rewards to the level of the respective marginal products of labor and capital is likely to involve an intolerable redistribution of income in favor of capital and against labor which the redistributive facilities of the economy are insufficiently well developed to offset to the point where the net result would be politically and socially tolerable. It is quite possible that the introduction of modern techniques under competitive conditions at the capital-labor ratios prevailing in underdeveloped and overpopulated areas has been labor-spurning to the extent that the competitive solution is unworkable. While the free-trade–free-competition model of world economics would have this difficulty being resolved by massive flows of capital from the capital-rich to the capital-poor countries, induced by the higher marginal productivity of capital in the capital-poor countries, this has not happened and is not likely to happen in the volume required by such a model, whether because of normal frictions associated with such capital movements, inhibitions due to political uncertainties, national antagonisms, or more fundamentally because of the operation of the external economies of investment within the various countries.

There appears to be no dearth of problems requiring new and more effective tools of economic analysis for their solution.

READINGS AND REFERENCES

PERIODICALS CITED

Accounting Review	*Acctg R*
American Economic Review	*AER*
———, Supplement (Papers and Proceedings, American Economic Association, Annual Meetings)	*AER/S*
American Journal of Economics and Sociology	*AJES*
American Journal of Sociology	*AJS*
American Sociological Review	*ASR*
American Statistician	*AmStat*
Annals of the Hitotsubashi Academy	*AnHit*
Applied Statistics (Royal Statistical Society)	*AppStat*
Cahiers du Séminaire d'Économetrie	*CSE*
Canadian Journal of Economic and Political Science	*CJEPS*
Comparative Psychology Monographs	*CPM*
The Controller	*Controller*
Current Economic Comment (Urbana, Illinois)	*CEC*
Dun's Review	*Dun's*
Econometrica	*Ecomet*
Economia Internazionale	*EcInt*
Economic Journal (Royal Economic Society)	*EcJ*
Economic Record (Australia)	*EcR*
———, Supplement	*EcR/S*
Economica, New Series	*Eca*
Économie Appliquée	*EA*
De Economist	*Economist*
Federal Reserve Bulletin	*FRBull*
Finanzarchiv	*Finanz*
Giornale degli Economisti e Annali di Economia	*GdE*
Harvard Business Review	*HBR*
Indian Journal of Economics	*IJE*
L'Industria	*L'Industria*
International Economic Papers	*IEP*
International Social Science Journal (Bulletin International des Sciences Sociales)	*ISSB*
Investigación Económica	*IE*
International Labour Review	*ILR*
Jahrbücher für Nationalökonomie und Statistik	*JNOS*
Journal of the American Statistical Association	*JASA*
Journal of Applied Psychology	*JAP*
Journal of Business (of the University of Chicago)	*JBUC*

Journal of Conflict Resolution	*JCR*
Journal of Farm Economics	*JFE*
Journal of Finance	*JFin*
Journal of Law and Economics	*JLE*
Journal of Marketing	*JM*
Journal of Political Economy	*JPE*
Journal of the Royal Statistical Society (Series A)	*JRSS* (A)
Kyklos	*Kyklos*
Land Economics (formerly Journal of Land and Public Utility Economics)	*LEc*
Lloyds Bank Review	*LBR*
Manchester School of Economic and Social Studies	*MSchl*
Metroeconomica	*Met*
Metron	*Metron*
Michigan Business Review	*MBusR*
Michigan Law Review	*MLawR*
Monthly Labor Review	*MLR*
National Association of Cost Accountants Bulletin	*NACA Bull*
Nationalökonomisk Tidsskrift	*NT*
Osaka Economic Papers	*OEP*
Oxford Economic Papers	*OxEP*
Oxford University Institute of Statistics Bulletin	*BOUIS*
Political Science Quarterly	*PSQ*
Psychometrika	*Psychomet*
Public Finance (Finances Publiques)	*PF*
Quarterly Journal of Economics	*QJE*
Review of Economic Studies	*RES*
Review of Economics and Statistics	*REStat*
Revista de Economia Politica	*Revista*
Revue d'Économie Politique	*REP*
Revue Économique	*REc*
Revue de Sciences et Legislation Financière	*RSLF*
Rivista di Politica Economica	*RPE*
Sankhya: Indian Journal of Statistics	*Sankhya*
Schmollers Jahrbuch	*SJ*
Schweizerische Zeitschrift für Volkswirtschaft und Statistik	*SZVS*
Science and Society	*S & S*
Scottish Journal of Political Economy	*SJPE*
Social Psychology	*SP*
Social Research	*SocRes*
South African Journal of Economics	*SAJE*
Southern Economic Journal	*SEJ*
El Trimestre Económico	*Trim*
Weltwirtschaftliches Archiv	*WA*
Yale Law Journal	*YLJ*
Zeitschrift für die Gesamte Staatswissenschaft	*ZGS*
Zeitschrift für Nationalökonomie	*ZNO*

CHAPTER ONE

The Metastatic Model

The insistence here in developing the metastatic model to its full extent as an analytic device is somewhat of a departure from the more usual course, and appropriate references are scanty. The following may serve:

1.1. J. R. HICKS, *Value and Capital* (Oxford: Clarendon Press, 1946, 1953), Chs. 9–11, pp. 115–52.

1.2. F. H. KNIGHT, *Risk, Uncertainty and Profit* (Boston: Houghton Mifflin, 1921), Chs. 5 and 6, pp. 141–94.

The Supply and Demand for Capital

1.3. IRVING FISHER, *The Theory of Interest* (New York: Macmillan, 1930; Kelley and Millman, 1954), xxvii, 566 pp.

1.4. THEODORE MORGAN, "Interest, Time Preference, and the Yield of Capital," *AER*, 35 (March 1945), 81–98.

1.5. D. H. ROBERTSON, "Some Notes on the Theory of Interest," in *Money, Trade, and Economic Growth: Essays in Honor of J. H. Williams* (New York: Macmillan, 1951), pp. 193–209; rep. in *Utility and All That* (New York: Macmillan, 1952), pp. 97–115.

1.6. M. J. BAILEY, "Saving and the Rate of Interest," *JPE*, 65 (August 1957), 279–305.

1.7. ROMNEY ROBINSON, "The Rate of Interest, Fisher's Rate of Return over Cost, and Keynes' Internal Rate of Return: Comment," *AER*, 46 (December 1956), 972–73.

1.8. W. C. HOOD, "Some Aspects of the Treatment of Time in Economic Theory," *CJEPS*, 14 (November 1948), 453–68.

CHAPTER TWO

Capital Accumulation and Growth

2.1. R. F. HARROD, *Towards a Dynamic Economics* (New York: St. Martin's, 1948), 169 pp.

2.2. JOAN ROBINSON, *The Accumulation of Capital* (Homewood, Ill.: Irwin, 1956), 440 pp.

2.3. EUGEN VON BÖHM BAWERK, *Capital and Interest* and *The Positive Theory of Capital*, W. Smart, tr. (London, 1890, 1891).

2.4. A. C. PIGOU, "Economic Progress in a Stable Environment," *Eca*, 14 (August 1947), 180–88.

2.5. ADOLPH LOWE, "The Classical Theory of Economic Growth," *SocRes*, 21 (Summer 1954), 127–58.

2.6. F. H. KNIGHT, "The Quantity of Capital and the Rate of Interest," *JPE*, 44 (August, October 1936), 433–63, 612–42.

2.7. PIERRE DIETERLEN, *L'investissement* (Paris: Marcel Rivière, 1957), 362 pp.

Innovations

2.8. W. M. BROWN, "Labor Saving and Capital Saving Innovations," *SEJ*, 13 (October 1946), 101–14.

2.9. H. J. BRUTON, "Innovations and Equilibrium Growth," *EcJ*, 66 (September 1956), 455–66.

2.10. NATHAN BELFER, "Implications of Capital Saving Innovations," *SocRes*, 16 (September 1949), 353–65.

2.11. J. J. SPENGLER and O. D. DUNCAN, eds., *Population Theory and Policy—Selected Readings* (Glencoe, Ill.: Free Press, 1956), 622 pp.

Population

2.12. GUNNAR MYRDAL, *Population: A Problem for Democracy* (Cambridge: Harvard University Press, 1940), xiii, 237 pp.

2.13. D. V. GLASS, ed., *Introduction to Malthus* (New York: Wiley, 1953), 205 pp.

2.14. T. R. MALTHUS, *Essay on the Principles of Population* (London: Ward, Lock, 1890, 1926), 619 pp.

2.15. HARVEY LEIBENSTEIN, *A Theory of Economic-Demographic Development* (Princeton: Princeton University Press, 1954), 204 pp.

2.16. IAN BOWEN, *Population* (London: Nisbet, 1954), 256 pp.

2.17. MANUEL GOTTLIEB, "The Theory of Optimum Population for a Closed Economy," *JPE*, 53 (December 1945), 289–315.

2.18. J. J. SPENGLER, "Some Economic Aspects of the Subsidization of the State and the Formation of Human Capital," *Kyklos*, 4 (1950), 316–43.

2.19. COLIN CLARK, "Population Growth and Living Standards," *ILR*, 68 (August 1953), 99–117.

2.20. SIMON KUZNETS, "Population, Income and Capital," *ISSB*, 6 (1951: 2), 165–70.

2.21. EMMA S. & W. S. WOYTINSKY, *World Population and Production, Trends and Outlook* (New York: Twentieth Century Fund, 1953), 1268 pp.

2.22. FRANK LORIMER, *Culture and Human Fertility* (Paris: UNESCO, 1954), 514 pp.

2.23. KINGSLEY DAVIS and OTHERS, "The Population Specter: Rapidly Declining Death Rate in Densely Populated Countries," *AER/S*, 46 (May 1956), 305–51.

2.24. LÉON BUQUET, *L'optimum de population* (Paris: Presses Universitaires, 1956), 312 pp.

2.25. J. J. SPENGLER and O. D. DUNCAN, eds., *Demographic Analysis—Selected Readings* (Glencoe, Ill.: Free Press, 1957), 219 pp.

CHAPTER THREE

3.1. J. M. CLARK, "Business Acceleration and the Law of Demand," *JPE*, 25 (March 1917), 217–35.

3.2. HANS NEISSER, "Critical Notes on the Acceleration Principle," *QJE*, 68 (May 1954), 253–74.

3.3. POUL WINDING, *Some Aspects of the Acceleration Principle* (Amsterdam: North Holland, 1957), 254 pp.

3.4. ADOLPH LOWE, "A Structural Model of Production," *SocRes*, 19 (June 1952), 135–76.

3.5. R. S. ECKAUS, "The Acceleration Principle Reconsidered," *QJE*, 67 (May 1953), 209–30.

3.6. W. J. BAUMOL, "Acceleration Without Magnification," *AER*, 46 (June 1956), 409–11.

3.7. HOLBROOK WORKING, "The Theory of Price of Storage," *AER*, 39 (December 1949), 1254-62.

3.8. M. J. BRENNAN, "The Supply of Storage," *AER*, 48 (March 1958), 50–72.

CHAPTER FOUR

4.1. R. D. LUCE and HOWARD RAIFFA, *Games and Decisions* (New York: Wiley, 1957), Chs. 2, 13, and Appendix 1: pp. 12–38, 275–326, and 371–84.

4.2. WILLIAM VICKREY, "Measurement of Marginal Utility by Reactions to Risk," *Ecomet*, 13 (October 1945), 319–33.

4.3. A. G. HART, *Anticipations, Uncertainty, and Dynamic Planning* (New York: Kelley, 1940, 1951), especially pp. 33–98.

4.4. S. A. OZGA, "Measurable Utility and Probability: A Simplified Rendering," *EcJ*, 66 (September 1956), 419–30.

4.5. DANIEL ELLSBERG, "Classical and Current Notions of Measurable Utility," *EcJ*, 64 (September 1954), 528–56.

4.6. A. A. ALCHIAN, "The Meaning of Utility Measurement," *AER*, 43 (March 1953), 26–50.

4.7. DANIEL BERNOUILLI, "Specimen Theoriae Novae de Mensura Sortis," *Commentarii Academiae Scientiarum Imperialis Petropolitanae* 5 (1738), 175-92; Louise Sommer, tr., "Exposition of a New Theory on the Measurement of Risk," *Ecomet*, 22 (January 1954), 23–36.

4.8. I. N. HARSTEIN and JOHN MILNOR, "An Axiomatic Approach to Measurable Utility," *Ecomet*, 21 (April 1953), 291–97.

4.9. P. A. SAMUELSON, "Probability, Utility, and the Independence Axiom," *Ecomet*, 20 (October 1952), 670–78.

4.10. EDMOND MALINVAUD, "Note on von Neumann-Morgenstern's Strong Independence Axiom," *Ecomet*, 20 (October 1952), 679.

4.11. MILTON FRIEDMAN and L. J. SAVAGE, "The Utility Analysis of Choices Involving Risk," *JPE*, 56 (August 1948), 279–304; rep with a correction, in G. J. Stigler and Kenneth E. Boulding, eds., *Readings in Price Theory* (Homewood, Ill.: Irwin, 1952), pp. 57–96.

4.12. MILTON FRIEDMAN, "Choice, Chance, and the Personal Distribution of Income," *JPE*, 61 (August 1953), 277–90.

4.13. MAURICE ALLAIS, "Le comportement de l'homme rationnel devant le risque: critique des postulats et axiomes de l'école américaine," *Ecomet*, 21 (October 1953), 503–46.

4.14. J. C. HARSANYI, "Cardinal Utility in Welfare Economics and in the Theory of Risk Taking," *JPE* 61 (October 1953), 434–35.

4.15. JAKOB MARSCHAK, *Three Lectures on Probability in the Social Sciences* (New Haven: Cowles Commission, 1954), 55 pp.

4.16. R. M. THRALL, C. H. COOMBS, and R. L. DAVIS, eds., *Decision Processes* (New York: Wiley, 1954), 332 pp. Note especially W. K. Estes, "Individual Behavior in Uncertain Situations," pp. 127–37.

4.17. E. H. HILGARD, *Theories of Learning* (New York: Appleton-Century-Crofts, 1956), 2nd ed., especially pp. 368–406.

4.18. L. J. SAVAGE, *Foundations of Statistics* (New York: Wiley, 1954), especially pp. 1–104.

4.19. R. D. LUCE, "Semi-orders and a Theory of Utility Discrimination," *Ecomet*, 24 (April 1956), 178–91.

4.20. HERMAN WOLD, "Ordinal Preferences or Cardinal Utility?" with additional notes by L. J. Savage, G. L. S. Shackle, and H. Wold, *Ecomet*, 20 (October 1952), 661–64.

4.21. G. L. S. SHACKLE, *Expectation in Economics* (Cambridge: Cambridge University Press, 1949), 146 pp.

4.22. ———, *Uncertainty in Economics and Other Reflections* (Cambridge: University Press, 1955), 267 pp.

4.23. C. F. CARTER, G. P. MEREDITH, and G. L. S. SHACKLE, eds., *Uncertainty and Business Decisions: A Symposium* (Liverpool: Liverpool University Press, 1954), 104 pp.

4.24. G. L. S. SHACKLE, "On the Meaning and Measure of Uncertainty," *Met*, 4 (December 1952), 87–104; *Met*, 5 (December 1953), 97–115.

4.25. ———, "The Logic of Surprise," *Eca*, 20 (May 1953), 112–17.

4.26. R. S. WECKSTEIN, "On the Use of the Theory of Probability in Economics," *REStud*, 20 (1952–53), 191–98.

4.27. A. D. ROY, "On Choosing between Probability Distributions," *REStud*, 22 (1954–55), 194–202.

4.28. ———, "Risk and Rank; or Safety First Generalized," *Eca*, 23 (August 1956), 214–28.

4.29. K. J. ARROW, "Alternative Approaches to the Theory of Choice in Risk-Taking Situations," *Ecomet*, 19 (October 1951), 404–37.

4.30. GERALD GOULD and G. L. S. SHACKLE, "Odds, Possibility, and Plausibility in Shackle's Theory of Decision: A Discussion," *EcJ*, 67 (December 1957), 659-64.

4.31. M. B. NICHOLSON, "Note on Mr. Gould's Discussion of Potential Surprise," *EcJ*, 68 (December 1958), 830–33.

4.32. R. D. LUCE, "A Probabilistic Theory of Utility," *Ecomet*, 26 (April 1958), 193-224.

4.33. J. H. DRÈZE, "Individual Decision Making Under Partially Controllable Uncertainty," doctoral thesis, Columbia University, 1958.

CHAPTER FIVE

5.1. A. G. Hart, *Money, Debt and Economic Activity* (Englewood Cliffs, N.J.: Prentice-Hall, 1961), 513 pp.

5.2. G. N. Halm, *The Economics of Money and Banking* (Homewood, Ill.: Irwin, 1956, 1961), 551 pp.

5.3. James Tobin, "Liquidity Preference and Monetary Policy," *REStat*, 29 (May 1947), 124–31.

5.4. William Fellner, "Monetary Policy and the Elasticity of Liquidity Functions," *REStat*, 30 (February 1948), 42–44.

5.5. Clark Warburton, "Monetary Velocity and Monetary Policy"; James Tobin, "A Rejoinder," *REStat*, 30 (November 1948), 304–17.

5.6. James Tobin, "The Interest-Elasticity of Transactions Demand for Cash," *REStat*, 38 (August 1956), 241–47.

5.7. W. J. Baumol, "The Transactions Demand for Cash: An Inventory Theoretic Approach," *QJE*, 66 (November 1952), 545–56.

5.8. William Vickrey, "Stability Through Inflation," in Kenneth Kurihara, ed., *Post-Keynesian Economics* (New Brunswick: Rutgers University Press, 1954), especially pp. 107–10.

5.9. W. L. Miller, "The Multiplier Time Period and the Income Velocity of Active Money," *SEJ*, 23 (July 1956), 74–79.

5.10. Kenneth E. Boulding, *Economic Analysis* (New York: Harper, 1955), Chs. 16 and 17, pp. 308–58.

5.11. A. W. Stonier and D. C. Hague, *Textbook of Economic Theory* (London: Longmans, Green, 1957, 1960), Ch. 18, pp. 361–79.

5.12. John F. Due, *Intermediate Economic Analysis* (Homewood, Ill.: Irwin, 1956), pp. 267–87.

5.13. R. V. Roosa, *Federal Reserve Operations in the Money and Government Securities Markets* (New York: Federal Reserve Bank, July 1956), 108 pp.

5.14. H. C. Simons, "Debt Policy and Banking Policy," *REStat*, 28 (May 1946), 85–89.

5.15. L. V. Chandler, "Federal Reserve Policy and the Federal Debt," *AER*, 39 (March 1949), 405–29.

5.16. P. A. Samuelson, "The Effect of Interest Rate Increases on the Banking System," *AER*, 35 (March 1945), 16–27.

5.17. P. G. Fousek, *Foreign Central Banking: The Instruments of Monetary Policy* (New York: Federal Reserve Bank, 1957), 116 pp.

5.18. Paul Einzig, *How Money Is Managed: The Ends and Means of Monetary Policy* (Harmondsworth, Middlesex: Penguin Books, 1954), 368 pp.

5.19. Irving Fisher, *100 Percent Money* (New York: Adelphi, 1935), xxiv, 257 pp.

5.20. R. A. Radford, "The Price System in Microcosm: A P.O.W. Camp," *Eca*, 48 (November 1945), 189–201; rep. in A D. Gayer, C. L. Harriss, and M. H. Spencer, *Basic Economics* (New York: Prentice-Hall, 1951), pp. 77–90.

CHAPTER SIX

National Income Analysis Generally

6.1. KENNETH E. BOULDING, *Economic Analysis*, 3rd ed. (New York: Harper, 1955), Chs. 13 and 14, pp. 237–86.

6.2. RICHARD RUGGLES and NANCY RUGGLES, *National Income Accounts and Income Analysis* (New York: McGraw-Hill, 1949, 1956), 452 pp.

6.3. C. S. SHOUP, *Principles of National Income Analysis* (Boston: Houghton Mifflin, 1947).

Aggregation

6.4. HENRI THEIL, *Linear Aggregation of Economic Relations* (Amsterdam: North Holland, 1954), 205 pp.

6.5. M. J. FARRELL, "Some Aggregation Problems in Demand Analysis," *REStud*, 21 (1953–54), 193–203.

National Income Concepts

6.6. U. S. DEPARTMENT OF COMMERCE, National Income Division, *National Income, Supplement to the Survey of Current Business* (1947, 1951, 1954).

6.7. T. C. SCHELLING, "National Income, 1954 Edition," *REStat*, 38 (November 1955), 321–35.

6.8. SIMON KUZNETS and OTHERS, "Discussion of the Department of Commerce Income Series," *REStat*, 30 (August 1948), 151–97.

6.9. GEORGE JASZI, "National Income," *JASA*, 47 (September 1951), 345–57.

6.10. MILTON GILBERT and GEORGE JASZI, "The 1945 White Paper on National Income and Expenditure," *EcJ*, 55 (December 1945), 444–53.

6.11. JOSEPH MAYER, "Deficiencies in the Gross National Product Concept as a National Measure," *JPE*, 53 (December 1945), 357–63.

6.12. D. C. MACGREGOR, "Recent Studies on National Income," *CJEPS*, 11 (February 1945), 270–80.

6.13. J. R. HICKS, "The Valuation of the Social Income," *Eca*, 7 (May 1940), 105–24.

6.14. SIMON KUZNETS, "On the Valuation of the Social Income: Reflections on Professor Hicks' Article," *Eca*, 15 (February, May 1948), 1–16, 116–31.

6.15. J. R. HICKS, "The Valuation of the Social Income. A Comment on Professor Kuznets' Reflections," *Eca*, 15 (August 1948), 163–72.

6.16. I. M. D. LITTLE, "The Valuation of the Social Income," *Eca*, 16 (February 1949), 11–26.

6.17. JAN SANDEE, "Independent Applications of National Accounts," *Eca*, 16 (August 1949), 249–54.

6.18. S. H. FRANKEL, "Psychic and Accounting Concepts of Income and Welfare," *OxEP*, 4 (February 1952), 1–17.

6.19. JOSEPH MAYER, "Proposals for Improving Income and Product Concepts," *REStat*, 36 (May 1954), 191–204.

6.20. J. W. KUHN, "The Usefulness of the Factor Cost Concept in National Income Accounting," *REStat*, 36 (February 1954), 93–99.

6.21. R. M. BIGGS, "Income at Product and Factor Prices," *JFin*, 8 (March 1953), 47–55.

6.22. J. L. NICHOLSON, "National Income at Factor Cost or at Market Prices?" *EcJ*, 65 (June 1955), 216–24.

Diagrammatic Presentations of National Income

6.23. A. O. DAHLBERG, *National Income Visualized* (New York: Columbia University Press, 1956), 117 pp.

6.24. D. K. BURDET, "Social Accounting in Relation to Economic Theory," *EcJ*, 64 (December 1954), 679–97.

6.25. E. C. TRESS, "The Diagrammatic Representation of National Income Flows," *Eca*, 15 (November 1948), 276–88.

Government Activity and National Income

6.26. *L'adaptation de la comptabilité publique aux principes de la comptabilité nationale* (Paris: Institut International de Finances Publiques, Travaux, 1955.)

6.27. MAX FRANK, "L'adaptation de la comptabilité publique dans le revenu national," *Finanz*, 16 (1956), 461–71.

6.28. BERNARD DUCROS, "Les intérêts de la dette publique dans le revenu national," *RSLF*, 46 (April–June 1954), 323–51.

6.29. R. T. BOWMAN and R. A. EASTERLIN, "An Interpretation of the Kuznets and the Department of Commerce Income Concepts," *REStat*, 35 (February 1953), 41–50.

Foreign National Income Problems

6.30. NATIONAL BUREAU OF ECONOMIC RESEARCH, *Problems in the International Comparison of Economic Accounts: Studies in Income and Wealth*, Vol. XX (Princeton: Princeton University Press, 1957), x, 404 pp.

6.31. HARRY OSHIMA, "The Price System and National Income and Product," *REStat*, 33 (August 1951), 248–54.

6.32. J. B. D. DERKSEN, "Comparing National Incomes: Problems, Progress and Facts," *Dun's* (June 1948), p. 14.

6.33. W. W. COOPER and J. M. CRAWFORD, "The Status of Social Accounting and National Income Statistics in Countries Other Than the U. S.," *Acctg R*, 28 (April 1953), 221–38.

Accounts and Estimates

6.34. UNITED NATIONS, STATISTICAL OFFICE, *Methods of National Income Estimation*, Studies in Methods, Series F, No. 8 (New York, 1955), 58 pp.

6.35. GREAT BRITAIN, CENTRAL STATISTICAL OFFICE, *National Income Statistics, Sources and Methods* (London: H.M. Stationery Office, 1956), 387 pp.

6.36. *A Critique of the U.S. Income and Product Accounts: Studies in Income and Wealth*, Vol. XXII (Princeton: Princeton University Press, 1958), 589 pp.
6.37. C. L. Nelson, "Use of Accounting Data in National Income Estimation," *Acctg R*, 28 (April 1953), 186–90.
6.38. Paul Kircher, "Accounting Entries and National Accounts," *Acctg R*, 28 (April 1953), 191–99.
6.39. P. D. Henderson, Dudley Seers, and P. F. D. Wallis, "Notes on Estimating National Income Components," *BOUIS*, 11 (February–March 1949), 59–70.
6.40. H. P. Brown, "Some Aspects of Social Accounting: Interest and Banks," *EcR*, 25 (August 1949), 73–92.

Marxist Approaches

6.41. A. Nove, "The U.S. National Income à la Russe," *Eca*, 23 (August 1956), 244–52.
6.42. Shigeto Tsuru, "On the Soviet Concept of National Income," *AnHit*, 5 (October 1954), 37–49.
6.43. Dudley Seers, "A Note on Current Marxist Definitions of the National Income," *OxEP*, 1 (June 1949), 260–68.

Multi-sector Models

6.44. National Bureau of Economic Research, *Input-Output Analysis: An Appraisal* (Princeton: Princeton University Press, 1955), 371 pp.; Supplement (New York: National Bureau of Economic Research, 1954), 510 pp.
6.45. M. A. Copeland, *A Study of Moneyflows in the U.S.* (Princeton: Princeton University Press, 1952), 338 and 235 pp.
6.46. Almarin Phillips, "The Tableau Économique as a Simple Leontieff Model," *QJE*, 69 (February 1955), 137–44.
6.47. Nicholas Georgescu-Roegen, "Leontieff's System in the Light of Recent Results," *REStat*, 32 (August 1950), 214–22.
6.48. Wassily Leontieff, "The Economics of Industrial Interdependence," *Dun's* (February 1946), 22.
6.49. Richard Stone, "Simple Transaction Models, Information and Computing," *REStud*, 19 (1951–52), 67–84.

Miscellaneous

6.50. International Association for Research in Income and Wealth, *International Bibliography on Income and Wealth*, Vol. I (1937–47), Daniel Creamer, ed.; II (1948–49), III (1950), IV (1951), V (1952), VI (1953–54), VII (1955–56), Phyllis Deane, ed. (London: Bowes and Bowes, 1952–60).
6.51. ———, *Income and Wealth*, Vol. I (1949) through Vol. IX (1959) (London: Bowes and Bowes, 1951–61).

6.52. BERNARD DUCROS, "Les problèmes de la comptabilité nationale dans les pays sous-developpés, *REc* (September 1954), 725–45.

CHAPTER SEVEN

Difficulties with General Equilibrium Along Classical Lines

7.1. W. J. FELLNER, "The Robertsonian Evolution," *AER*, 42 (June 1952), 265–82.
7.2. H. M. SOMERS, "A Theory of Income Determination," *JPE*, 58 (December 1950), 523–41.
7.3. J. R. HICKS, *Value and Capital* (Oxford: Clarendon Press, 1939), Chs. 20–22, pp. 245–82.
7.4. DON PATINKIN, *Money, Interest, and Prices* (Evanston: Row Peterson, 1956), 510 pp.
7.5. KARL BRUNNER, "Inconsistency and Indeterminacy in Classical Economics," *Ecomet*, 19 (April 1951), 152–73.
7.6. OSKAR MORGENSTERN, "Professor Hicks on Value and Capital," *JPE*, 49 (June 1941), 361–93.
7.7. DON PATINKIN, "Dichotomies of the Pricing Process in Economic Theory," *Eca*, 21 (May 1954), 113–28.
7.8. C. A. HALL, JR., and JAMES TOBIN, "Stability Conditions for a General Neoclassical Model," *EcInt*, 8 (August, November 1955), 522–38, 742–58; 9 (February 1956), 1–7.
7.9. SIDNEY WEINTRAUB, "The Theory of the Consumer Price Level," *CJEPS*, 18 (May 1952), 163–72.
7.10. J. K. MEHTA, "Equilibrium in Macroeconomics," *IJE*, 1 (July 1953), 20–30.
7.11. C. G. PHIPPS, "Money in the Utility Function," *Met*, 4 (August 1952), 44–65.
7.12. J. K. MEHTA, "Income and Employment in a Crusoe Economy," *EcInt*, 9 (February 1956), 9–33.

Price Flexibility and the Pigou Effect

7.13. J. R. HICKS, "Recent Contributions to General Equilibrium Economics," *Eca*, 12 (November 1945), 235–42.
7.14. MILTON FRIEDMAN, "Lange on Price Flexibility and Unemployment," *AER*, 36 (September 1946), 613–31.
7.15. A. C. PIGOU, *Lapses from Full Employment* (London: Macmillan, 1945), 75 pp.
7.16. OSKAR LANGE, *Price Flexibility and Employment* (Bloomington, Ind.: Principia Press, 1945), 114 pp.
7.17. DON PATINKIN, "Price Flexibility and Full Employment," *AER*, 38 (September 1948) 543–64.

7.18. G. C. ARCHIBALD and R. G. LIPSEY, "Monetary and Value Theory: A Critique of Lange and Patinkin," *REStud*, 26 (October 1958), 1–22.

7.19. R. J. RANDALL, "The Pigou Effect and Other Aspects of Asset Holdings on Consumption," *SAJE*, 21 (June 1953), 31–40.

7.20. D. G. FRANSZEN, "Methodological Issues in the Theory of Price Flexibility," *SAJE*, 15 (June 1947), 87–115.

Keynesian Analysis

7.21. I. O. SCOTT, JR., "An Exposition of the Keynesian System," *REStud*, 19 (1950–51), 12–18.

7.22. T. C. SCHELLING, "Income Determination: A Graphic Solution," *REStat*, 30 (August 1948), 227–29.

7.23. WILLIAM FELLNER, "Keynesian Economics after 20 Years," *AER*, 47 (May 1957), 67–76.

7.24. J. R. SCHLESINGER, "After 20 Years: The General Theory," *QJE*, 70 (November 1956), 581–602.

7.25. J. R. HICKS, "Mr. Keynes and the 'Classics': A Suggested Interpretation," *Ecomet*, 5 (April 1937), 147–59.

7.26. ———, "A Rehabilitation of Classical Economics," *EcJ*, 67 (June 1957), 278–89.

7.27. J. W. ANGELL, "Keynes and Economic Policy Today," *REStat*, 30 (November 1948), 259–64.

7.28. H. S. ELLIS, "The State of the New Economics," *AER*, 39 (March 1949), 465–77.

7.29. S. E. HARRIS, ed., *The New Economics: Keynes' Influence on Theory and Public Policy* (New York: Knopf, 1947), especially Chs. 11, 42, 43, and 44.

7.30. L. R. KLEIN, *The Keynesian Revolution* (New York: Macmillan, 1947), 218 pp.

7.31. A. H. HANSEN, *A Guide to Keynes* (New York: McGraw-Hill, 1953), 237 pp.

7.32. D. DILLARD, *The Economics of J. M. Keynes* (New York: Prentice-Hall, 1948), 328 pp.

7.33. J. M. KEYNES, *The General Theory of Employment, Interest and Money* (London: Macmillan, 1936), xii, 403 pp.

7.34. W. L. SMITH, "A Graphical Exposition of the Complete Keynesian System," *SEJ*, 23 (October 1956), 115–25.

7.35. J. R. HICKS, "Mr. Keynes' General Theory and the Theory of Employment," *EcJ*, 46 (June 1936), 238–53.

7.36. JAMES TOBIN, "The Fallacies of Lord Keynes' General Theory, Comment"; reply by J. Rueff, *QJE*, 62 (November 1948), 763–70, 771–82.

7.37. M. F. TIMLIN, *Keynesian Economics* (Toronto: University of Toronto Press, 1942), ix, 198 pp.

7.38. A. C. PIGOU, *Keynes' General Theory* (London: Macmillan, 1950), 69 pp.

7.39. ERIK LINDAHL, "On Keynes' Economic System," *EcR*, 30 (May, November 1954), 19–32, 159–71.

7.40. M. E. POLAKOFF, "Some Critical Observations on the Major Keynesian Building Blocks," *SEJ*, 21 (October 1954), 141–51.

7.41. C. B. HOOVER, "Keynes and the Economic System," *JPE*, 56 (October 1948), 392–402.

7.42. NICHOLAS KALDOR, "L'evoluzione capitalista alla luce dell' economia Keynesiana," *RPE*, 48 (February 1958), 113–23.

The Consumption Function: Analytical Approaches

7.43. W. W. HELLER, E. M. BODDY, and CARL NELSON, eds., *Savings in the Modern Economy* (Minneapolis: University of Minnesota Press, 1953), 370 pp.

7.44. J. S. DUESENBERRY, *Income, Saving and the Theory of Consumer Behavior* (Cambridge: Harvard University Press, 1949), 128 pp.

7.45. A. C. PIGOU, "Professor Duesenberry on Income and Savings," *EcJ*, 61 (December 1951), 883–85.

7.46. R. W. CLOWER, "Professor Duesenberry and the Traditional Theory," *REStud*, 19 (1952–53), 165–78.

7.47. MILTON FRIEDMAN, *A Theory of the Consumption Function* (Princeton: Princeton University Press, 1957), 243 pp.

7.48. H. S. HOUTHAKKER, "The Permanent Income Hypothesis," *AER*, 48 (June 1958), 396–404.

7.49. GEORGE KATONA, "Effects of Income Changes on the Rate of Saving," *REStat*, 31 (May 1949), 95–103.

7.50. W. S. WOYTINSKY and NATHAN KOFFSKY, "Two More Contributions on the Consumption Function," *REStat*, 30 (February 1948), 45–56.

7.51. IRWIN FRIEND and I. B. KRAVIS, "Consumption Patterns and Permanent Income," *AER/S*, 47 (May 1957), 536–55.

7.52. FRANCO MODIGLIANI and R. E. BRUMBERG, "Utility Analysis and the Consumption Function. An Interpretation of Cross-Section Data," in *Post-Keynesian Economics*, Kenneth Kurihara, ed. (New Brunswick: Rutgers University Press, 1954), pp. 388–436.

7.53. FRANCO MODIGLIANI, "Fluctuations in the Saving Ratio: A Problem in Economic Forecasting," *SocRes*, 14 (December 1947), 413–20.

7.54. GEORGE KATONA and OTHERS, "Five Views on the Consumption Function," *REStat*, 28 (November 1946), 197–224.

7.55. JAMES DUESENBERRY, "Innovation and Growth," *AER/S*, 46 (May 1956), 134–41.

7.56. R. C. O. MATTHEWS, The Saving Function and the Problem of Trend and Cycle," *REStud*, 22 (1954–55), 75–95.

7.57. GEORGE GARVY, "The Effect of Private Pension Plans on Personal Saving," *REStat*, 32 (August 1950), 223–26.

7.58. J. N. MORGAN, "The Structure of Aggregate Personal Saving," *JPE* (December 1951), 528–34.

7.59. KARL BORCH, "Effects on Demand of Changes in the Distribution of Income," *Ecomet*, 21 (April 1953), 325–31.

7.60. E. F. DENISON, "A Note on Private Saving," *REStat*, 40 (August 1958), 261–67.

7.61. THOMAS BALOGH, "The Limitations of the Short-run Consumption Function," *BOUIS*, 16 (May–June 1954), 190–96.

7.62. W. S. WOYTINSKY, "Relationship between Consumers' Expenditures, Savings, and Disposable Income," *REStat*, 28 (February 1946), 1–12.

7.63. P. R. KERSCHBAUM, "Income Reverses and Family Expenditures," *MLR*, 79 (March 1956), 298–99.

7.64. R. P. MACK, "The Direction of Change in Income and the Consumption Function," *REStat*, 30 (November 1948), 239–58.

7.65. A. H. HANSEN, "Note on the Secular Consumption Function," *AER*, 41 (September 1951), 662–64.

7.66. MORRIS COHEN, "Liquid Assets and the Consumption Function," *REStat*, 36 (May 1954), 202–11.

7.67. P. J. LAWLER, "The Consumption Function," *EcR/S*, 25 (August 1949), 93–122.

7.68. H. R. BOWEN, "Technological Change and Aggregate Demand," *AER*, 45 (December 1954), 917–21.

7.69. WILLIAM HAMBURGER, "The Determinants of Aggregate Consumption," *REStud*, 22 (1954–55), 23–44.

7.70. MARC NERLOVE, *Distributed Lags and Demand Analysis for Agricultural and Other Commodities*, Department of Agriculture Handbook, No. 141 (Washington: Superintendent of Documents, 1958), 121 pp.

7.71. N. X. OANH, "Patterns of Consumption and Economic Development," *EcInt*, 10 (February 1957), 30–46.

7.72. I. F. PEARCE, "Demand Analysis and the Savings Function," *EcR*, 34 (April 1958), 52–66.

7.73. LEO FISHMAN, "Consumer Expectations and the Consumption Function," *SEJ*, 20 (January 1954), 243–51.

7.74. C. L. BARBER, "The Concept of Disposable Income," *CJEPS*, 15 (May 1949), 227–29.

7.75. J. C. HUBBARD, "The Marginal and Average Propensities to Consume," *QJE*, 68 (February 1954), 83–96.

The Consumption Function: Empirical Approaches

7.76. ROBERT FERBER, *A Study of Aggregate Consumption Functions* (New York: National Bureau of Economic Research, 1953), 72 pp.

7.77. R. D. WILLIAMS, "Fiscal Policy and the Propensity to Consume," *EcJ*, 55 (December 1945), 390–97.

7.78. R. C. CAVE, "Prewar-Postwar Relationships between Disposable Income and Consumption Expenditures," *REStat*, 32 (May 1950), 172–76.

7.79. J. A. FISHER, "Postwar Changes in Income and Savings among Different Age Groups," *Ecomet*, 20 (January 1952), 47–70.

7.80. WILLIAM HAMBURGER, "The Relation of Consumption to Wealth and the Wage Rate," *Ecomet*, 23 (January 1955), 1–17.

7.81. GEORGE KATONA, "Analysis of Dissaving," *AER*, 39 (June 1949), 673–89.

7.82. GEORGE GARVY, "The Role of Dissaving in Economic Analysis," *JPE*, 56 (October 1948), 416–27.

7.83. FRANCO MODIGLIANI and OTHERS, "Savings Behavior: A Symposium," *BOUIS*, 19 (May 1957), 99–199.

7.84. L. R. KLEIN, "The British Propensity to Save," *JRSS* (A), 121, (1958), 60–96.

7.85. T. M. BROWN, "Habit, Persistence, and Lags in Consumer Behavior," *Ecomet*, 20 (July 1952), 355–71.

7.86. L. R. KLEIN, G. H. STRAW, and PETER VANDOME, "Savings and Finances of the Upper Income Classes," *BOUIS*, 18 (November 1956), 293–320.

7.87. ARNOLD ZELLNER, "The Short Run Consumption Function," *Ecomet*, 25 (October 1957), 552–67.

7.88. RICHARD STONE and D. A. ROWE, "Aggregate Consumption and Investment Functions for the Household Sector Considered in the Light of British Experience," *NT*, 94 (1956), 1–32.

7.89. G. D. N. WORSWICK, R. F. HARROD, and E. F. JACKSON, "The Fall in Consumption," "Comment," "Note," "Rejoinder," "Reply," *BOUIS*, 10 (June–September 1948), 195–208, 235–44, and 284–93.

7.90. L. R. KLEIN, "Estimating Patterns of Savings Behavior from Sample Survey Data," *Ecomet*, 19 (October 1951), 438–54.

7.91. T. E. DAVIS, "The Consumption Function as a Tool for Prediction," *REStat*, 34 (August 1952), 270–77.

7.92. GEORGE KATONA, "Federal Reserve Board Committee Reports on Consumer Expectation and Savings Statistics," *REStat*, 39 (February 1957), 40–45.

7.93. IRWIN FRIEND and I. B. KRAVIS, "Entrepreneurial Income, Savings, and Investment," *AER*, 47 (June 1957), 269–301.

7.94. ROBERT FERBER, "The Accuracy of Aggregate Savings Functions in the Post-War Years," *REStat*, 37 (May 1955), 134–48.

7.95. L. R. KLEIN and H. W. MOONEY, "Negro-White Savings Differentials and the Consumption Function Problem," *Ecomet*, 21 (July 1953), 425–56.

7.96. ARNOLD ZELLNER, "Consumption and the Consumption Function in the U.S. 1948–49 Recession," *REStat*, 39 (August 1957), 303–11.

7.97. R. V. ROOSA, "Use of the Consumption Function in Short Run Forecasting," *REStat*, 30 (May 1948), 91–105.

7.98. V. L. BASSIE, "Woytinsky on Consumption and Savings," *REStat*, 30 (November 1948), 298–300.

7.99. IRWIN FRIEND, "Consumption-Saving Function, Comment," *REStat*, 30 (November 1948), 301–03.

Aggregate Supply

7.100. DON PATINKIN, "Involuntary Unemployment and the Keynesian Supply Function," *EcJ*, 59 (September 1949), 360–84.

7.101. F. J. DEJONG, "Supply Functions in Keynesian Economics," *EcJ*, 64 (March 1954), 3–24.

7.102. R. G. HAWTREY, "Keynes and the Supply Function"; Rejoinder by F. J. DeJong, *EcJ*, 64 (December 1954), 834–42.

7.103. G. B. RICHARDSON, "Demand and Supply Reconsidered," *OxEP*, 8 (June 1956), 113–26.

7.104. J. R. SARGENT, "The Supply Factor in Professor Hicks' Theory of the Cycle," *EcJ*, 66 (December 1956), 635–61.

7.105. C. S. SOPER, "The Supply Curve in Keynesian Economics," *SAJE*, 24 (March 1956), 1–8.

Marxist, Keynesian, and Classical Macroeconomics

7.106. P. A. SAMUELSON, "Wages and Interest: A Modern Dissection of Marxian Economic Models," *AER*, 47 (December 1957), 884–912.

7.107. FRANCIS SETON, "The Transformation Problem," *REStat*, 24 (June 1957), 149–60.

7.108. MICHIO MORISHIMA, "An Analysis of the Capitalist Process of Reproduction," *Met*, 8 (December 1956), 171–85.

7.109. JACQUES LECAILLON, "Marx et Keynes devant la pensée économique contemporaine," *REc*, 1 (May–July 1950), 72–87 and 203–20.

7.110. L. R. KLEIN, "Theories of Effective Demand and Employment," *JPE*, 55 (April 1947), 108–31.

Monetary and Fiscal Policies

7.111. L. W. MINTS and OTHERS, "Symposium on Fiscal and Monetary Policy," *REStat*, 28 (May 1946), 60–84.

7.112. E. C. SIMMONS, "The Uses and Limitations of Monetary-Fiscal Policy in Economic Stabilization," *SEJ*, 18 (April 1952), 510–15.

7.113. WILLIAM VICKREY, "Limitations of Keynesian Economics," *SocRes*, 15 (December 1948), 403–16.

7.114. W. L. SMITH, "Monetary–Fiscal Policy and Economic Growth," *QJE*, 71 (February 1957), 36–55.

7.115. G. L. BACH, "Monetary–Fiscal Policy Reconsidered," *JPE*, 57 (October 1949), 383–94.

7.116. D. A. WORCESTER, JR., "Monetary versus Fiscal Policy at Full Employment," *JFin*, 12 (March 1957), 1–15.

7.117. J. C. HUBBARD, *Creation of Income by Taxation* (Cambridge: Harvard University Press, 1950), 239 pp.

7.118. J. M. BUCHANAN, *Public Principles of Public Debt* (Homewood, Ill.: Irwin, 1958), 223 pp.

7.119. J. E. MEADE, "Is the National Debt a Burden?" *OxEP*, 10 (June 1958), 163–83.

7.120. HERBERT STEIN, "Managing the Public Debt," *JLE*, 1 (October 1958), 97–104.

7.121. FRANZ GEHRELS, "Inflationary Effects of a Balanced Budget under Full Employment," *AER*, 39 (December 1949), 1276–78.

7.122. CLARK WARBURTON, "Hansen and Fellner on Full Employment Policies," *AER*, 38 (March 1948), 128–34.

CHAPTER EIGHT

8.1. H. S. Ellis, ed., *Readings in Business Cycle Theory* (Philadelphia: Blakiston, 1944), 487 pp. (Contains an extensive classified bibliography to that date.)

Cobweb Models

8.2. Mordecai Ezekiel, "The Cobweb Theorem," *QJE*, 52 (February 1938), 255–80; rep. in 8.1.

8.3. Marc Nerlove, "Adaptive Expectations and Cobweb Phenomena," *QJE*, 73 (May 1958), 227–40.

8.4. A. C. Enthoven and K. J. Arrow, "A Theorem on Expectations and the Stability of Equilibrium," *Ecomet*, 24 (July 1956), 288–93.

8.5. Gustav Åkerman, "The Cobweb Theorem: A Reconsideration," *QJE*, 71 (February 1957), 151–60.

Simple Accelerator Models

8.6. P. A. Samuelson, "Interactions between the Acceleration Principle and the Multiplier," *REStat*, 21 (May 1939), 75–78.

8.7. P. A. Samuelson, "A Synthesis of the Principle of Acceleration and the Multiplier," *JPE*, 47 (December 1939), 786–97.

8.8. L. A. Metzler, "The Nature and Stability of Inventory Cycles," *REStat*, 32 (August 1941), 113–29.

8.9. ——, "Factors Governing the Length of Inventory Cycles," *REStat*, 29 (February 1947), 1–15.

8.10. R. S. Eckaus, "The Stability of Dynamic Models," *REStat*, 39 (May 1957), 172–82.

8.11. S. S. Alexander, "The Accelerator as a Generator of Steady Growth," *QJE*, 63 (May 1949), 174–97.

8.12. M. H. Peston, "Acceleration and Magnification," *AER*, 47 (December 1957), 1000–28.

8.13. H. B. Chenery, "Overcapacity and the Acceleration Principle," *Ecomet*, 20 (January 1952), 1–28.

8.14. J. K. Mehta, "A New Approach to the Phenomena of Disequilibrium and the Acceleration of Derived Demand," *ZGS*, 111 (1955), 519–28.

Hicksian and More Elaborate Models

8.15. J. R. Hicks, *A Contribution to the Theory of the Trade Cycle* (Oxford: Clarendon Press, 1950), 201 pp.

8.16. W. W. Rostow, "Some Notes on Mr. Hicks and History," *AER*, 41 (June 1951), 316–41.

8.17. E. D. Domar, "Depreciation, Replacement and Growth and Fluctuations," *EcJ*, 67 (December 1957), 655–58.

8.18. H. P. MINSKY, "Monetary Systems and Accelerator Models," *AER*, 47 (December 1957), 859–83.
8.19. TRYGVE HAAVELMO, "A Note on the Theory of Investment," *REStud*, 16 (1949–50), 78–81.
8.20. A. L. WRIGHT, "The Rate of Investment in a Dynamic Model," *QJE*, 72 (August 1958), 327–50.
8.21. JAN TINBERGEN and J. J. POLAK, *The Dynamics of Business Cycles* (Chicago: University of Chicago Press, 1950), 366 pp.
8.22. FRANZ GEHRELS, "Factor Substitution, Consumer Wealth, and Growth Stability," *AER*, 47 (September 1957), 625–33.
8.23. H. R. HUDSON, "A Model of the Trade Cycle," *EcR*, 33 (December 1957), 378–89.
8.24. HANS BREMS, "Constancy of the Proportionate Equilibrium Rate of Growth: Result or Assumption?" *REStud*, 24 (February 1957), 131–39.
8.25. P. A. SAMUELSON and R. M. SOLOW, "A Complete Capital Model Involving Heterogeneous Capital Goods," *QJE*, 70 (November 1956), 537–62.

Expectational Models

8.26. DIRAN BODENHORN, "The Stability of Growth Models," *AER*, 46 (September 1956), 607–31.
8.27. M. D. BROCKIE, "Expectations and Economic Stability," *WA*, 70 (1953:1), 95–109.
8.28. WILLIAM VICKREY, "Stability Through Inflation," in Kenneth Kurihara, ed., *Post-Keynesian Economics* (New Brunswick: Rutgers University Press, 1954), pp. 89–122.

CHAPTER NINE

Growth Models

9.1. E. D. DOMAR, "Expansion and Employment," *AER*, 37 (March 1947), 34–55.
9.2. R. F. HARROD, *Towards a Dynamic Economics* (London: Macmillan, 1949), ix, 169 pp.; see especially pp. 63–100.
9.3. E. D. DOMAR, *Essays in the Theory of Economic Growth* (New York: Oxford University Press, 1957), 272 pp.
9.4. W. J. BAUMOL, "Notes on Some Dynamic Models," *EcJ*, 58 (December 1948), 506–21.
9.5. F. M. BATOR, "On Capital Productivity, Input Allocation, and Growth," *QJE*, 71 (February 1957), 86–106
9.6. JOAN ROBINSON, "Mr. Harrod's Dynamics," *EcJ*, 59 (March 1949), 68–85.
9.7. ———, "The Model of an Expanding Economy," *EcJ*, 62 (March 1952), 42–53.
9.8. D. M. WRIGHT, "Mr. Harrod and Growth Economics," *REStat*, 31 (November 1949), 322–28.

9.9. H. D. DICKINSON, "A Note on Dynamic Economics," *REStud*, 22 (1954–55), 169–80.
9.10. H. G. JOHNSON, "A Further Note on Dynamic Economics," *REStud*, 23 (1955–56), 245–46.
9.11. D. G. CHAMPERNOWNE, "Capital Accumulation and the Maintenance of Full Employment," *EcJ*, 68 (June 1958), 211–44.
9.12. KENJIRO ARA, "Capital Theory and Economic Growth," *EcJ*, 68 (September 1958), 511–27.
9.13. L. B. YEAGER, "Some Questions about Growth Economics," *AER*, 44 (March 1954), 53–63.
9.14. G. M. MEIER, "Some Questions About Growth Economics"; Reply by L. B. Yeager, *AER*, 45 (December 1954), 931–27.
9.15. NICHOLAS KALDOR, "A Model of Economic Growth," *EcJ*, 67 (December 1957), 591–624.
9.16. R. M. SOLOW and P. A. SAMUELSON, "Balanced Growth Under Constant Returns to Scale," *Ecomet*, 21 (July 1953), 412–24.
9.17. R. M. SOLOW, "A Note on the Price Level and Interest Rate in a Growth Model," *REStud*, 21 (1953–54), 74–79.
9.18. WASSILY LEONTIEFF, "Theoretical Note on Time Preference, Productivity of Capital, Stagnation, and Economic Growth," *AER*, 48 (March 1958), 105–10.
9.19. KLAUS ROSE, "Der Erkenntniswert der Wachstumsmodelle," *JNOS*, 168 (February 1957), 321–36.
9.20. TRYGVE HAAVELMO, *A Study in the Theory of Economic Evolution* (Amsterdam: North Holland, 1954), 114 pp.

Economic Development and Growth in General

9.21. W. A. LEWIS, *The Theory of Economic Growth* (Homewood, Ill.: Irwin, 1955), 453 pp.
9.22. ———, "Economic Development with Unlimited Supplies of Labor," *MSchl*, 22 (May 1954), 138–91.
9.23. ———, "Unlimited Labor: Further Note," *MSchl*, 26 (January 1958), 1–32.
9.24. J. H. POWER, "The Economic Framework of a Theory of Growth," *EcJ*, 68 (March 1958), 34–50.
9.25. H. S. ELLIS, "Big Push Theories of Economic Development," *L'Industria* (April–June 1957), 384–93.
9.26. GERHARD COLM, "Long Range Economic Projections: Tools of Economic Analysis and Decision-Making," *AER/S*, 48 (May 1958), 178–87.
9.27. KENNETH KURIHARA, "The Fiscal Role of Governments in Economic Development," *IJE*, 37 (July 1956), 39–47.
9.28. ———, "Distribution, Employment, and Secular Growth," in *Post-Keynesian Economics* (New Brunswick: Rutgers University Press, 1954), pp. 251–76.
9.29. WILLEM BRAND, *The Struggle for a Higher Standard of Living: The Problem of the Underdeveloped Countries* (Glencoe, Ill.: Free Press, 1953), 438 pp.
9.30. ALEXANDER MAHR, "Einige Grundprobleme der Theorie der wachsenden Wirtschaft," *ZNO*, 16 (1956:3), 301–23.

9.31. ERNST HEMSTÄDTER, "Produktionsstruktur und Wachstum," *JNOS*, 169 (March 1958), 173, 427.

9.32. ALBERT MASNATA, "Structures sociales et croissance économique sous les régimes socialistes et collectivistes," *REP*, 68 (March–April 1958), 405–32.

9.33. CHARLES BETTELHEIM, "Le problème de la maximation de la croissance économique," *REc* (January 1957), 3–39.

CHAPTER TEN

Conjuncture Cycles

10.1. GOTTFRIED HABERLER, *Prosperity and Depression—Theoretical Analysis of Cyclical Movement*, rev. ed. (London: Allen & Unwin, 1958), xviii, 520 pp.

10.2. G. MALECOT, "Sur les oscillations aléatoires des systèmes économiques," *EA*, 10 (January–March 1957), 161–69.

10.3. R. P. MACK, "Notes on Subcycles in Theory and Practice," *AER*, 47 (May 1957), 151–74.

Cycles and Growth

10.4. W. J. FELLNER, *Trends and Cycles in Economic Activity: An Introduction to Problems of Economic Growth* (New York: Holt, 1956), 411 pp.

10.5. A. H. HANSEN, "Trends and Cycles in Economic Activity," *REStat*, 39 (May 1957), 105–15.

10.6. MICHAEL KALECKI, *Theory of Economic Dynamics—An Essay on Cyclical and Long Run Changes in a Capitalist Economy* (New York: Rinehart, 1954), 178 pp.

10.7. J. S. DUESENBERRY, *Business Cycles and Economic Growth*, (New York: McGraw-Hill, 1958), 341 pp.

10.8. ARTHUR SMITHIES, "Economic Fluctuations and Growth," *Ecomet*, 25 (January 1957), 1–52.

10.9. DANIEL HAMBERG, *Economic Growth and Instability—A Study in the Problem of Capital Accumulation, Employment and the Business Cycle* (New York: Norton, 1956), 340 pp.

Macroeconomic Stabilization and Control

10.10. E. R. WALKER, and OTHERS, *National and International Measures for Full Employment* (New York: United Nations Secretariat, Department of Economic Affairs, 1949), vi, 104 pp.

10.11. W. W. ROSTOW, "The United Nations Report on Full Employment," *EcJ*, 60 (June 1950), 323–50.

10.12. M. BOUNATIAN, "Le problème du plein emploi et les experts des Nations Unies," *REP*, 60 (November–December 1950), 573–600.

10.13. M. DODRETSBERGER, "A Critical Review of the Discussions on Full Employment," *Kyklos*, 1 (1947: 1), 19–25.

10.14. W. W. COOPER, "Some Implications of a Program for Full Employment and Economic Stability," *PSQ*, 63 (June 1948), 230–56.

10.15. D. McC. WRIGHT, *The Creation of Purchasing Power* (Cambridge: Harvard University Press, 1942), xvi, 251 pp.

10.16. LYLE FITCH and HAROLD TAYLOR, eds., *Planning for Jobs* (Philadelphia: Blakiston, 1946), 463 pp.

10.17. E. G. NOURSE, "Ideal and Working Concepts of the Employment Acts," *MLR*, 80 (February 1957), 161–64.

10.18. E. B. GEORGE, "Should Full Employment Be Guaranteed?" *Dun's* (October 1947), pp. 17ff, (November 1947), pp. 20 ff., (December 1947), pp. 18 ff.

10.19. ROY HAROOD, "Measures to Prevent a Slump," *Foreign Affairs*, 27 (July 1949), 630–39.

10.20. FRANCOIS PERROUX, "Das Streben nach Stabilität: die realen Faktoren," *ZNO*, 18 (1958: 1, 2), 102–24.

10.21. OTTO NATHAN, "Private Enterprise and Full Employment," *S & S*, 15 (Summer 1951), 232–61.

10.22. P. T. BAUER, "Lord Beveridge on Full Employment," *Kyklos*, 1 (1947), 166–76.

10.23. FRANCOIS PERROUX, "Sur la politique du plein emploi," *EA*, 8 (January–June 1955), 285–306.

10.24. F. D. GRAHAM and A. P. LERNER, eds., *Planning and Paying for Full Employment* (Princeton: Princeton University Press, 1946), 222 pp.

10.25. A. W. PHILLIPS, "Stabilization Policy and the Time Form of Lagged Responses," *EcJ*, 67 (June 1957), 265–77.

10.26. J. K. GALBRAITH, "Market Structure and Stabilization Policy," *REStat*, 39 (May 1957), 124–33.

10.27. J. H. G. PIERSON, *Full Employment* (New Haven: Yale University Press, 1941), 297 pp.

10.28. ———, *Full Employment and Free Enterprise* (Washington: Public Affairs Press, 1947), vii, 183 pp.

10.29. ———, "The Underwriting Approach to Full Employment: A Further Explanation," *REStat*, 31 (August 1949), 182–92.

10.30. ———, "The Underwriting of Aggregate Consumer Spending as a Pillar of Full-employment Policy," *AER*, 34 (March 1944), 21–55.

10.31. A. D. MYERS, "Some Implications of Full-employment Policy," *JPE*, 54 (June 1946), 258–65.

10.32. A. H. HANSEN, "Cost Functions and Full Employment," *AER*, 47 (September 1947), 552–65.

10.33. O. H. BROWNLEE, "On the Theory of Employment and Stabilization Policy," *JPE*, 58 (October 1950), 412–24.

10.34. A. E. HOLMANS, "The Eisenhower Administration and the Recession, 1953–55," *OxEP*, 10 (February 1958), 34–54.

10.35. A. F. BURNS, "The Current Business Recession," *JBUC*, 31 (April 1958), 145–53.

Built-in Stabilizers

10.36. MILTON FRIEDMAN, "A Monetary and Fiscal Framework for Economic Stability," *AER*, 38 (June 1948), 245–64.

10.37. PHILIP NEFF, "Professor Friedman's Proposal: Comment"; rejoinder by Milton Friedman, *AER*, 39 (September 1949), 946–56.

10.38. W. W. HELLER, "The C.E.D.'s Stabilizing Budget Policy after 10 Years," *AER*, 47 (September 1957), 634–51.

10.39. N. F. KEISER, "The Development of the Concept of Automatic Stabilizers," *JFin*, 11 (December 1956), 122–41.

10.40. K. E. POOLE, "The Impact of the Erosion of the Personal Income Tax on Economic Stability," *Finanz*, 18 (1957: 1), 44–51.

10.41. P. B. TRESCOTT, "The Idea of Built-in Flexibility, 1837–1860," *PF*, 11 (1956: 4), 366–70.

Forecasting

10.42. HENRI THEIL, *Economic Forecasts and Policy* (Amsterdam: North Holland, 1958), 562 pp.

10.43. H. J. LEVIN, "Public Prediction in Theory and Fact," *SEJ*, 24 (January 1958), 338–52.

10.44. EMILE GRUNBERG and FRANCO MODIGLIANI, "The Predictability of Social Events," *JPE*, 62 (December 1954), 465–78.

10.45. S. S. ALEXANDER, "Rate of Change Approaches to Forecasting: Diffusion Indexes and First Differences," *EcJ*, 68 (June 1958), 288–301.

10.46. B. G. HICKMAN, "An Experiment with Weighted Indexes of Cyclical Diffusion," *JASA*, 53 (March 1958), 39–53.

10.47. STEFAN VALAVANIS, "Must the Diffusion Index Lead?" reply by G. Moore, *AmStat*, 11–4 (October 1957), 12–17.

10.48. FRANCO MODIGLIANI and H. M. WEINGARTNER, "Forecasting Uses of Anticipatory Data on Investment and Sales," *QJE*, 72 (February 1958), 23–54.

10.49. NATIONAL BUREAU OF ECONOMIC RESEARCH, *Short Term Forecasting: Studies in Income and Wealth*, Vol. 17 (Princeton: Princeton University Press, 1955), 506 pp.

10.50. ———, *Long Range Economic Projection: Studies in Income and Wealth*, Vol. 16 (Princeton: Princeton University Press, 1954), 476 pp.

Monetary Policy

10.51. THOMAS MAYER, "The Inflexibility of Monetary Policy," *REStat*, 40 (November 1958), 358–74.

10.52. RENDIGS FELS, "Warburton vs. Hansen and Keynes," *AER*, 39 (September 1949), 923–29.

10.53. R. V. ROOSA, *Federal Reserve Operations in the Money and Government Securities Markets* (New York: Federal Reserve Bank, 1956), 107 pp.

10.54. L. V. CHANDLER, "Federal Reserve Policy and the Federal Debt," *AER*, 39 (March 1949), 405–29.

10.55. W. W. RIEFFLER, "Open Market Operations in Long-Term Securities," *FRBull*, 44 (November 1958), 1260–74.
10.56. THOMAS WILSON, "The Rate of Interest and Monetary Policy," *OxEP*, 9 (October 1957), 235–60.
10.57. C. R. WHITTLESEY, "Monetary Policy and Economic Change," *REStat*, 39 (February 1957), 31–39.
10.58. E. C. SIMMONS, "A Note on the Revival of Federal Reserve Discount Policy," *JFin*, 11 (December 1956), 413–21.
10.59. C. E. WALKER, "Discount Policy in the Light of Recent Experience," *JFin*, 12 (May 1957), 223–37.
10.60. PHILLIP CAGAN, "Why Do We Use Money in Open Market Operations?" *JPE*, 66 (February 1958), 34–46.
10.61. H. C. BOS, *A Discussion on Methods of Monetary Analysis and Norms for Monetary Policy*, Netherlands Economic Institute (Schiedam: H. A. M. Roelants, 1956), vii, 52 pp.
10.62. W. J. SEDWITZ, "Inflexible Interest Rates and Economic Policy in the Case of Norway," *PSQ*, 71 (December 1956), 569–96.
10.63. E. A. GOLDENWEISER, *Monetary Management* (New York: McGraw-Hill, 1949), 175 pp.

Monetary Panaceas

10.64. MARTIN BRONFENBRENNER, "A Loan Ratio for Inflation Control," *JPE*, 59 (October 1951), 120–33.
10.65. L. M. VALENTINE, "A Proposal for the Automatic Neutralization of Currency Flows," *AER*, 48 (March 1958), 11–18.
10.66. *The Townsend Crusade*, Twentieth Century Fund, Committee on Old Age Security (New York: Twentieth Century Fund, 1936), p. 13.
10.67. RICHARD HAZELETT, "Public Management of Private Employment"; comment by A. G. Hart, *AER*, 47 (March 1957), 148–52.
10.68. P. D. LAGOMARCINO, "The Impact of the 12 Percent Reserve Income Tax Provision upon the Banking Structure," *MLawR*, 56 (January 1958), 401–14.

Inflation

10.69. S. H. SLICHTER, "Thinking Ahead: On the Side of Inflation," *HBR*, 35–5 (September-October 1957), 15 ff.
10.70. A. SMITHIES, "The Control of Inflation," *REStat*, 39 (August 1957), 272–83.
10.71. THOMAS BALOGH, "Productivity and Inflation," *OxEP*, 10 (June 1958), 220–45.
10.72. P. L. BERNSTEIN, "Is Long Term Inflation Inevitable?" *HBR*, 35 (July–August 1957), 51–57.
10.73. F. A. LUTZ, "Inflationsgefahr und Konjunkturpolitik," *ZVWS*, 93 (June 1957), 195–205.

10.74. F. K. Mann, "Die Bekämpfung der Inflationen: Amerikanische Methode und Erfahrungen," *SJ*, 77 (1957), 75–92.

10.75. A. D. Campbell, "Reflections on Inflation," *SJPE*, 3 (October 1956), 221–33.

10.76. Henri Mercillon, "L'inflation importée: l'inflation à facteurs externes dominants et son développement," *REc* (May 1958), 461–81.

10.77. J. Noyola Vasquez, "El desarrollo económico y la inflación en México y otros países latinoamericanos," *IE*, 16 (1956: 4), 603–48.

10.78. S. Inaba, "A Note on the So-called Secular Inflation," *U Osaka Prefecture Bull*, 2 (1958: 2), 21–33.

10.79. C. R. Ross, "Price Stability in the U.K.," *BOUIS*, 20 (August 1958), 265–84.

Inflationary Underemployment

10.80. H. W. Singer, "Wage Policy and Full Employment," *EcJ*, 57 (December 1947), 438–55.

10.81. R. E. Mooney and E. L. Dale, eds., *Inflation and Recession?* (New York: Doubleday, 1958), 96 pp.

10.82. J. R. Schlesinger, "Market Structure, Union Power, and Inflation," *SEJ*, 24 (January 1958), 296–312.

10.83. J. C. R. Dow, "Analysis of the Generation of Price Inflation: A Study of Cost and Price Changes in the U.K.," *OxEP*, 8 (October 1956), 252–301.

10.84. Émile James, "La inflación por el alza de los costos," *Trim*, 25 (January–March 1958), 27–44.

10.85. A. F. Burns, *Prosperity Without Inflation* (Garden City: Doubleday, Economica Books, 1958), viii, 88 pp.

10.86. A. R. Oxenfeldt and Ernest van den Haag, "Unemployment in Planned and Capitalist Economies," *QJE*, 68 (February 1954), 43–60.

Measurement of Underemployment

10.87. T. K. Hitch, "The Meaning and Measurement of Full or Maximum Employment," *REStat*, 33 (February 1951), 1–11.

10.88. Jan Tinbergen, "The Analysis of Unemployment Figures and the Alleged Correspondence between Causes and Cures," *Met*, 5 (August 1953), 43–49.

10.89. F. F. Stephan and others, "Symposium on Unemployment Statistics," *AmStat*, 9–1 (February 1955), 8–17.

10.90. B. F. Bierra and A. J. Jaffe, "The Concept and Measurement of Underemployment," *MLR*, 78 (March 1955), 283–87.

10.91. L. J. Ducoff and M. J. Hagood, *Labor Force Definition and Measurement* (New York: Social Science Research Council, 1947), 134 pp.

INDEX

D

G

H

I

J

K

L

M

T

U

V

W

Y

Z

A 4
B 5
C 6
D 7
E 8
F 9
G 0
H 1
I 2
J 3